Branding Post-Communist Nations

Routledge Research in Cultural and Media Studies

1 Video, War and the Diasporic
Imagination
Dona Kolar-Panov

2 Reporting the Israeli-Arab
Conflict
How Hegemony Works
Tamar Liebes

3 Karaoke Around the World
Global Technology, Local Singing
*Edited by Toru Mitsui and
Shuhei Hosokawa*

4 News of the World
World Cultures Look at Television
News
Edited by Klaus Bruhn Jensen

5 From Satellite to Single Market
New Communication Technology
and European Public Service
Television
Richard Collins

6 The Nationwide Television
Studies
*David Morley and
Charlotte Bronsdon*

7 The New Communications
Landscape
Demystifying Media Globalization
*Edited by Georgette Wang, Jan
Servaes, and Anura Goonasekera*

8 Media and Migration
Constructions of Mobility and
Difference
*Edited by Russel King and
Nancy Wood*

9 Media Reform
Democratizing the Media,
Democratizing the State
*Edited by Monroe E. Price, Beata
Rozumilowicz, and Stefaan G.
Verhulst*

10 Political Communication
in a New Era
*Edited by Gadi Wolfsfeld and
Philippe Maarek*

11 Writers' Houses and the
Making of Memory
Edited by Harald Hendrix

12 Autism and Representation
Edited by Mark Osteen

13 American Icons
The Genesis of a National
Visual Language
Benedikt Feldges

14 The Practice of Public Art
*Edited by Cameron Cartiere and
Shelly Willis*

15 Film and Television After DVD
*Edited by James Bennett and
Tom Brown*

16 The Places and Spaces of
Fashion, 1800–2007
Edited by John Potvin

17 Communicating in the
Third Space
*Edited by Karin Ikas and
Gerhard Wagner*

18 **Deconstruction After 9/11**
Martin McQuillan

19 **The Contemporary Comic Book Superhero**
Edited by Angela Ndalianis

20 **Mobile Technologies**
From Telecommunications to Media
Edited by Gerard Goggin and Larissa Hjorth

21 **Dynamics and Performativity of Imagination**
The Image between the Visible and the Invisible
Edited by Bernd Huppauf and Christoph Wulf

22 **Cities, Citizens, and Technologies**
Urban Life and Postmodernity
Paula Geyh

23 **Trauma and Media**
Theories, Histories, and Images
Allen Meek

24 **Letters, Postcards, Email**
Technologies of Presence
Esther Milne

25 **International Journalism and Democracy**
Civic Engagement Models from Around the World
Edited by Angela Romano

26 **Aesthetic Practices and Politics in Media, Music, and Art**
Performing Migration
Edited by Rocio G. Davis, Dorothea Fischer-Hornung, and Johanna C. Kardux

27 **Violence, Visual Culture, and the Black Male Body**
Cassandra Jackson

28 **Cognitive Poetics and Cultural Memory**
Russian Literary Mnemonics
Mikhail Gronas

29 **Landscapes of Holocaust Postmemory**
Brett Ashley Kaplan

30 **Emotion, Genre, and Justice in Film and Television**
E. Deidre Pribram

31 **Audiobooks, Literature, and Sound Studies**
Matthew Rubery

32 **The Adaptation Industry**
The Cultural Economy of Literary Adaptation
Simone Murray

33 **Branding Post-Communist Nations**
Marketizing National Identities in the "New" Europe
Edited by Nadia Kaneva

Branding Post-Communist Nations

Marketizing National Identities in the "New" Europe

Edited by Nadia Kaneva

First published 2012
by Routledge
711 Third Avenue, New York, NY 10017

Simultaneously published in the UK
by Routledge
2 Park Square, Milton Park, Abingdon, Oxon OX14 4RN

*Routledge is an imprint of the Taylor & Francis Group,
an informa business*

Typeset in Sabon by IBT Global.
Printed and bound in the United States of America on acid-free paper by
IBT Global.

Library of Congress Cataloging-in-Publication Data

Branding post-communist nations : marketizing national identities in the
    "new" Europe / edited by Nadia Kaneva.
        p. cm. — (Routledge research in cultural and media studies ; 33)
    Includes bibliographical references and index.
    1. Political culture—Europe, Eastern.   2. Nationalism—Europe, Eastern.
3. Europe, Eastern—Politics and government—1989–   I. Kaneva, Nadia.
    JN96.A58B73 2011
    306.20947—dc22
    2011004553

ISBN13: 978-0-415-88275-0 (hbk)
ISBN13: 978-0-203-80681-4 (ebk)

Contents

List of Figures   ix
Preface   xi

PART I
Promises and Problems of Post-Communist Nation Branding

1   Nation Branding in Post-Communist Europe:
    Identities, Markets, and Democracy   3
    NADIA KANEVA

2   Systemic Propaganda and State Branding in Post-Soviet
    Eastern Europe   23
    GERALD SUSSMAN

3   Brand Interrupted: The Impact of Alternative Narrators on
    Nation Branding in the Former Second World   49
    ROBERT A. SAUNDERS

PART II
Agents, Institutions, Practices

4   Redesigning a Nation: Welcome to E-stonia, 2001–2018   79
    SUE CURRY JANSEN

5   Who Can Play This Game? The Rise of Nation Branding in
    Bulgaria, 2001–2005   99
    NADIA KANEVA

6   Toward Corpo-Nationalism: Poland as a Brand   124
     PAWEŁ SUROWIEC

PART III
Representations, Mediations, Narrations

7   Branding *Slov*enia: "You Can't Spell Slovenia Without Love . . ."   147
     ZALA VOLČIČ

8   Vampire Branding: Romania's Dark Destinations   168
     ALICE BARDAN AND ANIKÓ IMRE

9   One Nation, One Brand? Nation Branding and Identity
     Reconstruction in Post-Communist Hungary   193
     LÁSZLÓ KULCSÁR AND YOUNG-OK YUM

10   The Musical (Re)branding of Serbia: *Srbija Sounds Global,*
     Guča, and EXIT   213
     BRANISLAVA (BRANA) MIJATOVIĆ

     Contributors   237
     Index   241

List of Figures

2.1   Logo of the *Otpor* movement in Serbia.   38
2.2   Logo of the *Kmara* movement in Georgia.   38
3.1   The homepage of UK tour operator Pissup Tours.   57
3.2   Sacha Baron Cohen as Borat.   60
3.3   Map of the fictional country Molvanîa.   67
3.4   Coat of arms on Molvanîa's fictional flag.   67
4.1   "Welcome to Estonia" logo.   86
5.1   Bulgaria's national logo.   109
7.1   "I feel *Slove*nia" logo.   154
8.1   Romania's tourism logo.   183

Preface

The chapters in this volume bring into focus the encounters of nation branding with post-communist Europe and document how the branded imagination has intervened in the national identity struggles of countries in the region. These investigations are intended as a contribution to the ongoing inquiry into the post-communist condition, as it is experienced through the mediations of nationhood and globalization.

My own interest in nation branding and post-communism stems from my personal experiences of growing up in a former communist country and working in the promotional industries before adopting my current role as a scholar and student of media, culture, and society. In many ways, this volume came about as a result of my enduring fascination with the rise of consumerism in the post-communist world and the changes in the fabric of social relations that it engenders. Many of the contributors to the volume also have personal biographies that connect them to Central and Eastern Europe; others are thoughtful external observers. All of them, however, share a critical interest in the region's transformations in the aftermath of Soviet communism.

The volume is structured in three parts, with Part I outlining a broad framework for critical investigations into the phenomenon of nation branding, and Parts II and III including seven country-specific studies. Chapter 1 is intended as a general introduction to the volume and lays out some of the overarching themes that emerge from the analyses in the other nine chapters.

In approaching the topic of nation branding, this collection aims to offer an alternative viewpoint to the one presented in writings by marketing and branding practitioners and academics. This volume sets out to outline the beginnings of a critique that relates nation branding to the rise of a neoliberal hegemony and a global promotional culture. Such critical work depends on the thoughtful engagement of scholars across disciplines and, for this reason, the volume includes a number of different approaches. Nevertheless, the following chapters offer partial accounts of a relatively new phenomenon and leave many questions unanswered. It is my hope that the volume will stimulate greater critical interest and invite future conversations on this topic.

This book has benefited from the support and contributions of many individuals and organizations. Above all, I wish to thank the volume's contributors, whose intellectual curiosity, hard work, and collegiality made the editing of this collection an enlightening and personally enriching experience. I have come to regard many of them as friends, as well as colleagues, and I look forward to future collaborations and conversations. I also wish to thank the Department of Media, Film & Journalism Studies at the University of Denver for institutional and financial support during the completion of this project. Among my colleagues there, I want to mention especially Renée Botta, Margie Thompson, Lynn Schofield Clark, and Diane Waldman, whose encouragement has meant a lot. Special thanks are also due to my graduate research assistants at the University of Denver, Jen Cupp and Lynn Sywyj, for their hard work on the copyediting of these chapters.

Many other colleagues and friends also lent advice, thoughtful comments, and critical feedback, including Stewart Hoover at the University of Colorado at Boulder, Ed Lenert at the University of San Francisco, Lisa Peñaloza at EDHEC Business School in France, Elza Ibroscheva at Southern Illinois University at Carbondale, and Sabina Pavlovska-Hilaiel at the University of Denver. My wonderful editor at Routledge, Erica Wetter, saw the project to its completion with kindness and professionalism. My warmest personal thanks go to Steven Mayer.

Part I

Promises and Problems of Post-Communist Nation Branding

1 Nation Branding in Post-Communist Europe
Identities, Markets, and Democracy

Nadia Kaneva

ENCOUNTERS WITH NATION BRANDING

During a recent trip to a European capital, I found myself in a hotel room, flipping through television channels. I landed on CNN's weather report and paused to listen. As the forecast ended, a colorful logo popped up on screen and an off-camera announcer declared: "The weather, brought to you by Croatia." This matter-of-fact promotional tag is but one example of a global phenomenon that has come to be known as nation branding. Yet, the seemingly trivial plug for Croatia on CNN would have been unthinkable only 20 years ago. To begin with, Croatia was not an independent nation-state then, but a member of the Yugoslav federation. At the time, CNN did not receive advertising revenues from Eastern Bloc countries, whose economies and media were largely closed off to the rest of the world. Most importantly, the very idea that a nation could be thought of as a brand—comparable to the commercial brands that typically underwrite television programs—had not entered popular discourse. A lot has changed in the past two decades.

Today, nation branding is widely recognized in many corners of the world and its advocates have succeeded in channeling significant funds from state budgets into various communication campaigns and, not coincidentally, into the revenue streams of media corporations and marketing consultancies. At any major international airport you are likely to come across a variety of billboards promoting countries through colorful logos and catchy slogans. Turn on CNN, Euronews, Eurosport, or any other commercial transnational television network and you will encounter slickly produced advertising spots for countries, some of which were not in existence as sovereign states 20 years ago. Leaf through the pages of international publications like *The Economist*, the *Financial Times*, or the *International Herald Tribune*, or open any major airline's in-flight magazine and you'll find yet more advertisements for nations—touting them as tourist destinations, investment havens, cultural treasures, or simply as "likeable." You will read that Greece is "A Masterpiece You Can Afford," Egypt is the place "Where It All Began," and Malaysia is "Truly Asia." The outward manifestations of nation branding also extend to major sporting events, like the World Cup or the Olympics, to branded national stands at international trade expos, and the list goes on.

It is easy to dismiss this as "just advertising," an extension of marketing for the purposes of promoting national assets; but nation branding has greater aspirations. Its advocates argue that brand management must become "*a component of national policy*" and inform "the way a country is run," rather than be "put into a silo of 'communication' or public affairs" (Anholt, 2008, p. 23, emphasis in original). A "brand-led approach to public affairs" is presented as "inherently democratic" because it, allegedly, ensures "a fair contest between the public and private bodies of the state and the domestic and foreign publics (with the media and other commentators helping out)" (Anholt, 2007, p. 40). Furthermore, it is argued that, in the contemporary world of global markets and global media, nation branding is a necessary response to the changing rules of international relations, which are increasingly shaped by "a shift in political paradigms, a move from the modern world of geopolitics and power to the postmodern world of images and influence" (van Ham, 2001, p. 4). Clearly, in its most expansive articulations, nation branding refers to much more than slogans, logos, and colorful advertisements. Rather, it seeks to reconstitute nationhood at the levels of both *ideology* and *praxis*, whereby the meaning and experiential reality of national belonging and national governance are transformed in unprecedented ways.

The explosion of nation branding practices since the mid-1990s has coincided with an explosion of publications—churned out by academics and branding practitioners alike—which attempt to theorize, codify, and legitimize these practices. The majority of scholarly work on nation branding to date has been produced within the field of marketing and tends to focus on instrumentalist concerns, related to advancing branding applications.[1] Nation branding has also attracted the attention of public relations scholars (Dinnie, 2008) and is further discussed in reference to international relations (Gilboa, 2008; van Ham, 2002) and public diplomacy (Szondi, 2008; Wang, 2006, 2008).

More recently, critical scholars from a number of disciplines—including media studies, sociology, and cultural anthropology—have begun to focus on nation branding as well. The main distinction between critical and marketing-driven approaches is that critical studies focus on the ideological underpinnings of nation branding. A number of critical studies look specifically at Central and Eastern Europe (CEE), where nation branding has proliferated particularly fast, and examine the challenges of national re-definition through branding in the post-communist context (Aronczyk, 2007; Baker, 2008; Dzenovska, 2005; Jansen, 2008; Kaneva, 2007; Volčič, 2008; Widler, 2007).[2]

Despite the expanding literature on the topic, the very meaning of the term "nation branding" remains hotly contested within and across disciplinary boundaries (see Fan, 2005; Szondi, 2008). This should give us occasion to recognize that nation branding is, in an important sense, an ideological construction of its practitioners and scholars. This, in turn, carries methodological implications for studies that draw on critical social theories—as do the ones included in this volume—because the uncritical and facile use of concepts like nation branding as neutral descriptors of events and processes, rather than as constitutive discursive devices, works to reproduce particular ideological structures. In the case of marketing and branding, academics are no less implicated in the advancement and perpetuation of marketing ideology than marketers themselves (O'Reilly, 2006).

Although most of the chapters in this volume propose working definitions of nation branding, they do not attempt a "general theory of branding." At the same time, they share a broad view of nation branding (in its local and global manifestations) as a set of discourses and practices located at the intersection of the economy, culture, and politics. Furthermore, the perspectives presented in this volume are concerned with nation branding's aspirations to exercise symbolic power in defining the meaning of nationhood. This collection is not interested in addressing instrumentalist questions about the "effectiveness" of nation branding in terms of strategic or tactical marketing outcomes. Nor does it intend to make recommendations for more "efficient" branding applications. Rather, the following chapters seek to uncover the ways in which nation branding operates as a new site upon which national identities and globalization come into contact and are reconfigured in the post-communist environment. By examining these reconfigurations, the chapters reveal particular interests, both locally and globally, that nation branding serves, and the ways in which it does so. In sum, this collection continues the tradition of critical inquiry into nation branding with a particular focus on the specificities of its encounters with post-communist Europe.

The focus on the post-communist experience is motivated by a broader goal of contributing to the study of changes in the structures and relations of power, identification, and mediation that were enabled by the end of communism. A widely acknowledged characteristic of the post-communist condition was the rapid and often dramatic "reawakening" of nationalisms in the region (Rupnik, 1996). Jacques Rupnik outlines three primary causes for the return of nationalism to post-communist Europe, which include "the end of the Cold War and the transformation of the international system; the ideological vacuum after communism; the economy, caught between globalism and the decomposition/recomposition of systems" (1996, p. 44). Because nation branding implicates ideas about nationhood, marketization, and globalization within a common promotional framework, its critical analysis can render insights into the ways countries in the CEE region have contended with these challenges. At the same time, a fuller understanding of the historical processes shaping the region before, during, and after the communist period is needed to better explain the appeal of nation branding in post-communist Europe, as well as the problems it encounters there.

"TRANSITION" REVISITED

Nation branding's ability to intertwine nationalism with globalization resonated in the post-communist social and political space because of a set of challenges often designated by the metaphor of "transition." In its most simplistic articulations, the transition was understood as a period during which CEE countries were supposed to undergo a linear transformation from state command economies to free market ones, and from authoritarian one-party systems to liberal democracies. The transition designation has been contested on various grounds by scholars across disciplines. However, despite its many problematic implications, it continues to have significance in popular and academic discourse by providing a set of frames that inflect the processes of social change in post-communist Europe with particular meanings. Burawoy and Verdery (1999) identify two such frames in (Western) theorizations of transition, which they see as connected to two opposing views of the project of modernity:

> At one extreme we find partisans of modernity who claim that the disintegration of communism is the final victory of modernity's great achievements, market economy and liberal democracy . . . At the other extreme are those who view the end of communism as the twilight of modernity. The collapse of the administered society marks the exhaustion of the enlightenment project to direct and regulate the world we inhabit. (p. 1)

Burawoy and Verdery recognize that there are more nuanced perspectives between these two poles but argue that, overall, much of the theorization of transition has suffered from the ideological effects of these two "grand narratives." From this vantage point, any study of the post-communist transition(s) is, by necessity, a study of the struggle of ideologies for the power to describe the meaning of the past and determine the direction of the future.

In more immediate terms, this struggle has to be played out within the particular historical contexts of specific national experiences of post-communism. Scholars from the region focus on the experiential and political realities of transition and point out that the term has come to signify a period of indeterminacy between the communist past and the post-communist future. Its meaning is particularly unstable because neither the meaning of the "communist past" nor that of the "post-communist future" is agreed upon within the local contexts, opening up multiple sites for social contestation. Znepolski (1997) argues that the transition is experienced as "a state of inadequacy," which manifests itself "on a psychological plane or on the plane of political decisions" (p. 9). This inadequacy is the result of destabilization of social structures after the collapse of the totalitarian order and a pervasive sense of social and individual uncertainty. Thus, the idea of transition is linked to post-communist identity politics, rather than being a neutral descriptor of a historical period. In short, transition is an ideological construct.

This has given the idea of transition the power of "an incantation" that serves as a "fundamental legitimizing resource for political elites" (Ditchev, 2000, pp. 92–93) in the region as they promise to take their nations through this intermediary period and into a better future. This is also how the ideology of transition relates to the ideological project of post-communist national identity construction, which could be summarized as "the transition between a shameful and a desired identity" (Ditchev, 2000, p. 93). All of this is experienced as an acute "crisis of representations" (Spassov, 2000, p. 37), which is also connected to larger processes of a postmodern decentering of identities.

The accession of 10 former communist countries to the European Union (EU) has been hailed by some commentators as the end of the post-communist transition. However, nation branding arrived to CEE in the thick of transition and is, therefore, inevitably intertwined with post-communist identity struggles. What kinds of identities were marked as "shameful" or as "desired" became a central area of contestation in nation branding initiatives. Indeed, one of the promises of nation branding was to resolve the crisis of representations by offering a different "discursive technology" (to paraphrase Norman Fairclough) for the construction of identity narratives. In that regard, nation branding throughout the region is marked by ontological aspirations, related to re-inventing national identities, which go beyond commercial motives.

THE EAST/WEST HERMENEUTIC

The crisis of representations in CEE is also related to broader discursive and ideological oppositions; specifically, the opposition of East and West dates back to the beginning of modern nationalisms in the region after the decline of the Ottoman, Russian, and Austro-Hungarian Empires. Many scholars have written about the role of the "Western gaze" in "inventing" the East in a variety of forms: as Eastern Europe (Wolff, 1994), as Balkans (Bjelić & Savić, 2002; Todorova, 1997), or more broadly as Orient (Said, 1978). Some have suggested that the opposition between East and West holds a generative status in East European discourses of national identity.[3] The processes through which Eastern European nations internalize and reproduce the East/West binary as legitimate have been theorized as "self-colonization" (Kiossev, 2002) or "self-exoticization" (Volčič, 2005). Such trends are seen as particularly relevant to the national identity narratives of Balkan nations, but can be detected throughout the entire CEE region, which has a complicated history of imperial colonization.

In many ways the competition between the Soviet Bloc and the West during the Cold War reproduced the East/West hermeneutic, at the same time that it sought to transcend it. The rapid, centrally imposed industrialization of communist countries after World War II represented an effort to get out from a "subordinated position" in the East/West relationship and become "the second core of the industrial civilization and eventually the leader in the technological and economic development" (Genov, 2002, p. 13). The collapse of communist economies in the 1980s dashed such aspirations.

During the harsh economic crises that followed the 1989 velvet revolutions, the West was reinstated as the locus of superior knowledge, technology, and ideals. Western consultants—dispatched by organizations like the International Monetary Fund (IMF), the World Bank, the U.S. Agency for International Development (USAID), and others—crisscrossed the region, dispensing recommendations that were intended to "cure" the ailing post-communist economies and kick-start democratic reforms. The policies they recommended became known as "shock therapy"; they called for rapid privatization of state-owned enterprises, price liberalization paired with wage reductions, slashing of social services, and the opening up of trade and the financial system. Beyond having an economic impact, these reforms were presented by consultants as the only path towards democracy in CEE. In the words of American economist Jeffrey Sachs, a key architect of shock therapy, the ultimate goal was "a recovery of human freedom and a democratically based rise in living standards" (cited in Gowan, 1995, p. 5).[4]

The East/West hermeneutic implicates nation branding as well and provides a rationale for its historical necessity for post-communist nations. This rationale is consistent with a "modernization by imitation" (Ditchev, 2000) thesis, where the West is posited as the model Other to be emulated. Some of the chapters in this volume (Bardan & Imre; Jansen; Kaneva; Surowiec) document how nation branding reproduces the East/West dichotomy within the national imaginaries of specific countries and gains part of its legitimacy from this reproduction. The gospel of nation branding was also "imported" from the West, with the main branding consultants operating in the CEE region hailing from the United Kingdom and the United States. Following the lead of Western branding gurus, a new group of local "image experts" from the emerging marketing, advertising, and public relations industries in the region also became active in negotiations over national identity within the framework of nation branding.

Nevertheless, the ability of these "cultural intermediaries" (Bourdieu, 1984)—both local and international—to advance the nation branding agenda depended heavily on their ability to gain the support of state bureaucracies and local political elites who controlled access to the economic capital necessary for branding campaigns. Hence, although nation branding initiatives in the region have often paraded as technocratic (i.e., "post-ideological"), they were very much entangled with the political palace struggles of the post-communist period. Several of the chapters in this volume (Kulcsár & Yum; Mijatović; Surowiec; Volčič) address this theme in the particular contexts of individual CEE countries. The types of relationships between branding experts and government functionaries vary from country to country; however, in each case, these relationships provide important clues about shifting networks of power in the post-communist environment.

The national identity struggles of post-communism were also significantly impacted by a widely held desire to "return to Europe," which led former communist countries to seek formal accession into the structures of the EU. The conflicting discourses of national self-identification and of European integration coexist in the post-Soviet environment and are continually renegotiated in political, economic, and cultural terms. In this context, nation branding provided one opportune site for such negotiations, and a discourse of identity construction that could, at least superficially, accommodate the conflicting pressures of differentiation and integration. In the context of EU accession aspirations, nation branding offered the illusion of a mutual engagement with the West by providing a mechanism for CEE nations to "tell their stories" to international audiences through mediated communication campaigns. None of this would have been possible without the privatization and liberalization of media systems in the region and the existence of transnational distribution networks, which made possible the transmission of branded media messages to audiences throughout Europe and beyond.

GLOBALIZATION AND THE BRANDED IMAGINATION

Beyond its profound implications for the CEE region, the end of the Cold War allowed for the acceleration of a set of processes, commonly referred to by the term "globalization," which have led to greater interdependence among nations worldwide in both economic and cultural terms. As *The Economist* wrote on the 20th anniversary of the fall of the Berlin Wall:

> Globalization would have meant much less if half of Europe had been bricked in; many instinctively statist giants of the emerging world, such as Brazil, India or even China, would have been far slower to open up their economies if a semi-credible alternative had still existed. ("So Much Gained," 2009, p. 11)

Indeed, 20 years after the end of communism, the world is more "global" than ever. Capital, people, and ideas flow more easily across borders, leading to new forms of social affiliation as well as the emergence of new sites for social conflict. The advances of global, neoliberal capitalism have resulted in profound economic restructuring. Financial capital has been freed from many of the constraints imposed by territorial, political, or cultural boundaries. Moreover, the new hegemony has been accompanied by the rise of a global promotional culture, fueled also by the liberalization of media industries and by new communication technologies that fail to respect national borders. Promotional culture, as Wernick (1991) theorized, has become "virtually co-extensive with our produced symbolic world" (p. 182). In other words, promotional culture interpellates us as consuming subjects first, rather than as citizens, and transforms all social relations into relations of value exchange. Ultimately, this means that the lines between production and consumption, between economy and culture, between the material and the symbolic, between the Marxist base and superstructure have been profoundly blurred and subsumed within the structures of information capitalism, where the metaphors of "free markets" and "consumer choice" serve as the new utopias.

It is within this context that the ideology of branding has come to prominence on a global scale. Branding is a neoliberal tool that creates value through the commodification of affective attachments. Through the magic of branding, individual and collective loyalties enter into market circulation as symbolic capital and work to generate economic capital. This allows for the extraction of economic profit from all realms of life (Lury & Moor, 2010; Thrift, 2005), including areas of experience that were relatively independent from the market in the era of industrial capitalism. Branding is now applied to such diverse realms of social practice as religion (Einstein, 2008), politics (Cosgrove, 2007; Sussman, 2010), education (Hearn, 2010; Twitchell, 2004), social activism (Bennett & Lagos, 2007; Knight, 2010), personal relationships (Hearn, 2008), and—yes—nationhood (Anholt, 2007; Dinnie, 2008). Under the regime of promotional culture, where the economic and the ideological are no longer separable, branding acquires a constitutive role in the production of social meaning. As O'Reilly (2006) puts it, "Branding is the principal symbolic practice of the marketing imagination" (p. 268). This is precisely why it has become a central mode of address, which, in turn, calls for the particular skills of branding and marketing consultants as the new storytellers of promotionalism (Aronczyk, 2008; Moor, 2008).

NATION RE-IMAGINED

One of the most insightful scholars of post-communism, anthropologist Katherine Verdery, points out that nation is "an aspect of the political and symbolic/ideological order and also of the world of social interaction and feeling" and, as such, "it has been an important element of systems of social classification for many centuries" (1993, p. 37). Starting with this recognition, any account of nationhood today would be naive to ignore the parallels between the abilities of national and brand identities to mobilize affective attachments, as well as to classify and control social subjects. It should come as no surprise, then, that the branded imagination seeks to infiltrate and subsume the symbolic order of nationhood. However, the outcomes of this intervention should not be taken for granted or viewed with resignation as the inevitable result of "natural" forces.

Critical scholarship needs to ask: What happens to notions of national sovereignty, citizenship, and democratic governance under a regime of branding? In other words, what are the consequences of re-imagining nation as brand? These are questions that we need to raise if we are to take seriously the claims that the end of communism was about more than satisfying the consumer desires of Eastern Europeans, but also about replacing an oppressive system of governance with a more equitable one. The moral superiority of capitalism and democracy were closely linked in the Western version of the just causes for the Cold War. Nation branding purports to be one outcome of this linkage and, therefore, merits further investigation.

Simon Anholt, one of the most celebrated and influential proponents of nation branding, argues that the growing interest in "competitive identity" (his latest euphemism for nation branding) is, in fact, "the consequence of a realization that public opinion is an essential component of achieving a political end. It is, one might say, a necessary consequence of democracy and the globalization of media" (2007, p. 39). Another advocate of nation branding, political scientist Peter van Ham (2001), argues that "branded states depend on trust and customer satisfaction" and claims that this is "a positive development, since state branding is gradually supplanting nationalism" (p. 3).

Such claims represent a form of free market utopianism, which imagines the market as "a comprehensive, unbiased, efficient, and just solution to all allocative decisions" (Bernhard, 2010, p. 120). Moreover, it implies that public opinion is equivalent to consumer choice and that market-based transactions may be the best mechanism for exercising political agency as well. The validity of such claims can only be tested through grounded examinations of the realities of globalization and its articulations with nationhood, as these emerge in the particular sociohistorical experiences of countries and their peoples. The recent wave of financial crises around the world has illustrated the downsides of global interconnectedness and cast a shadow on the market utopia. In addition, ongoing controversies generated by the activities of WikiLeaks and its virtual network of supporters have served as a powerful reminder of the complex implications that global media technologies can have for national and transnational politics. Such developments further reinforce the need for a critical investigation into nation branding and the truth claims of its advocates.

IN SEARCH OF A CRITIQUE

The mutations of post-industrial capitalism and the advent of promotional culture present a challenge for critical scholarship in that they necessitate a revision of the theoretical and methodological tools for inquiry and critique. In many ways, this is not a new challenge for thinkers in the Marxist tradition, who have long debated the relationship between "economy" and "culture." These discussions have often revolved around the question of determination between "base" and "superstructure." The infamous sparring matches between the Political Economy and Cultural Studies schools of thought (Gandy, 1995) are one well-known example of how theoretical entrenchments can lead to intellectual myopia (Meehan, 1999; Peck, 2001). Binary models that attempt to separate the analyses of economic and cultural factors obscure the complexities of social experience, where the material and the symbolic inevitably mediate each other.[5] The tensions of mediation endure in nation branding as it seeks to commodify nationhood at the same time that it infuses market exchange with affective qualities. Furthermore, nation branding mediates the relationships between the national and the global.

The subtitle of this volume refers to the marketization of national identities as a way to suggest the mutually iterative relationships of identities and markets. This mutuality necessitates a refusal of the economy/culture binary and invites us to focus on the workings of power in society. Questions about the circulation and reproduction of social power are central to post-Marxist thought. Post-structuralists, inspired in the main by the work of Michel Foucault, have focused on "discourses" as constitutive of particular subjectivities, which structure lived experiences. For Foucault, discourses are systems for constructing meaning that delimit the range of possible truth claims. Discourses "are not about objects, they do not identify objects, they constitute them and in the practice of doing so conceal their own invention" (Foucault, 1972, p. 49). Within this framework, national identities—as well as other forms of identification, including gender, race, class, and so on—can be understood as discursively constructed and maintained. Nation branding as a discourse delimits the boundaries of possible truth claims about national identity. It privileges the logic of value exchange, while concealing alternative possibilities for narrating the nation. In that sense, the Foucauldian tradition has a lot to offer to a critique of nation branding.

Another influential approach has been informed by the work of cultural anthropologist and sociologist Pierre Bourdieu. Bourdieu argued that, although discourses constitute social meaning, the full complexity of human experience needs to be examined in relation to social practice (including discursive practice). Individuals and groups act within the constraints of preexisting social structures, but are nevertheless creative agents, capable of transforming these structures. Bourdieu's later studies focused especially on the "social structures of the economy" (Bourdieu, 2005) and mounted a critique of neoliberalism (Bourdieu, 1998, 2002), which is relevant to the critique of nation branding. This approach helps us move beyond analyses of the narrations of national identity and the subjectivities created by branded nationhood. Rather, it uses a "political economy of practice" (Wacquant, 1992, p. 4) to reveal the vested interests of various actors engaged in nation branding as a field of social practice.

Both of these approaches share important commonalities, which have informed the outlook of this volume. To begin with, both recognize that social meaning and social power are relational. Importantly, this requires researchers to exercise reflexivity and acknowledge their own positionality within the systems of social relations they attempt to study. Furthermore, by paying attention to the way social power operates, both of these approaches allow scholarship to recapture the political dimensions of economic and cultural processes. This is particularly important to analyses of nationhood. To study nationhood without reference to power and politics would be an exercise in obfuscation as the nation continues to be an important form of political identification and national governments are still "central sites of power" (Curran, 2002, p. 183).

Despite all the talk of globalization, one's nationality still makes a great deal of difference in the way we experience the world. For instance, to be Palestinian is not the same as to be American, especially if you want to travel to Israel. At the same time, national identification is not insular—it is complicated by many other factors. Holding a French passport does not guarantee that people will see you as French, especially if you are a Muslim woman who covers her head. Furthermore, one's personal loyalties to the nation may shift with changing circumstances. You may have grown up calling yourself Yugoslav, but discovered later that your ethnic Albanian heritage was worth killing or dying for.

Writing at the height of the Cold War, American sociologist C. Wright Mills was keenly aware of the centrality of the nation-state in shaping political subjects:

> As the history-making unit, the dynamic nation-state is also the unit within which the variety of men and women are selected and formed, liberated and repressed—it is the man-making unit. That is one reason why struggles between nations and between blocs of nations are also struggles over the types of human beings that will eventually prevail in the Middle East, in India, in China, in the United States; that is why culture and politics are now so intimately related; and that is why there is such need and such demand for the sociological imagination. (Mills, 1959, p. 158)

Mills's insights have an enduring relevance today as the legacies of the Cold War continue to shape the world in a variety of ways. He proposed that the main tool of social inquiry and critique was the "sociological imagination," which he described as a "quality of mind" that enables its possessor "to grasp history and biography and the relations between the two within society" (p. 6). This tool seems fitting for the examination of the problems of post-communist national identities as they are felt at the level of personal experiences, while inescapably tied to large-scale historical transformations. The sociological imagination is a key weapon that critical scholars can rely on as they seek to understand and unmask the workings of the branded imagination.

THE CHAPTERS IN THIS VOLUME

As the preceding discussion suggests, the work of the sociological imagination is concerned with the analysis of real, lived experiences. This task should not be restricted within the narrow boundaries of academic disciplines. A strong measure of interdisciplinarity in the study of nation branding is also required by the expansive nature of the phenomenon under study. As I have argued earlier, nation branding sits at the intersection of political, economic, and cultural practices and discourses; moreover, it implicates local and global mediations of identity. Because of this, the chapters in this volume represent diverse approaches, and their authors come from a variety of disciplinary backgrounds, including media and communication studies, film studies, sociology, politics and international relations, and musicology. Nevertheless, the chapters that follow share a common interest in examining the discourses and practices of nation branding in an empirically grounded, historically situated, and theoretically informed manner.

The first section of the volume, titled *Promises and Problems of Post-Communist Nation Branding*, is intended to lay out a broad framework for a critically informed inquiry into this subject. The chapters by Sussman and Saunders pick up on two of the main themes I have outlined here—namely, the dimensions of nation branding as practice and as discourse—and explore them in relation to empirical evidence from a multiplicity of branding projects across the CEE region.

Gerald Sussman's chapter is informed by political economy and examines the incorporation of branding principles into foreign policy in the context of globalization. As part of his discussion, Sussman considers how the United States has employed branding strategies to sell its own image to international audiences. He then examines the processes through which Western European- and U.S.-funded institutions have imported branding into CEE as a way to bring former communist countries into the fold of Western economic and military structures. He argues that "the principal forms of Western intervention in the CEE region in the most recent decade (i.e., post-1999) have not been guns or bombs, but rather technologies of propaganda" (Sussman, this volume, p. 23). Focusing more specifically on the "branded revolutions" in Serbia, Ukraine, and Georgia, Sussman traces the influence of external funders and political actors in these events. Among other things, he finds that branding has been used in the region as a way to obscure the vested transnational interests behind political regime change.

His analysis raises important questions about the impact of branding on democratic processes in the region and establishes the relationship between branding strategies and the economic motivations of global capital.

Robert Saunders focuses, in turn, on the narrative dimensions of national identity construction and explores how these have shifted in the context of globalization and media liberalization after the end of the Cold War. Saunders documents the emergence of a number of "alternative narrators"—external to the nation—who have acquired the power to enter into the domain of discursive construction of national identity via mediated communication. Their narratives are not necessarily found in overt propaganda campaigns, but are located in popular culture artifacts that reflect long-standing stereotypes and mental maps associated with the Cold War. Through an analysis of a rich body of media texts, Saunders illustrates the increased porosity of national identity narratives and the complex negotiations this engenders. Importantly, he provides a glimpse into the way governments in former communist countries perceive the discursive interventions of external narrators as undermining their own control over the images of their countries. In his account, nation branding is—among other things—a response to the boundlessness of global mediation and a defensive strategy that nations can employ, albeit with varying degrees of success.

The remaining chapters in the volume present seven country-specific studies of nation branding, organized in two sections based on the two main foci sketched out in Part I. Part II is titled *Agents, Institutions, Practices*, and includes three chapters that present historical accounts of the evolution of nation branding as a field of social practice in Estonia, Bulgaria, and Poland, respectively. Sue Curry Jansen's chapter builds upon her previous research on Estonia's branding initiatives, strategies, and programs and covers a period of 18 years. One of the first CEE countries to adopt and apply the ideas of nation branding, Estonia is an important case to examine as it is often given as an example of forward economic thinking in the region. Jansen's analysis documents the engagement of Western and domestic brand consultants in the production of brand Estonia and discusses the relationship of branding to neoliberal globalization. She questions the ability of branding to live up to its promises; her most incisive critique concerns the "monologic, hierarchical, reductive" character of branding communication, which, she argues, is antithetical to democratic governance (Jansen, this volume, p. 92).

The chapters by Paweł Surowiec and myself draw heavily on the theoretical work of Pierre Bourdieu and discuss nation branding as a field of practice. My own account of the emergence of a Bulgarian field of nation branding between 2001 and 2005 illustrates the complex interactions between public- and private-sector actors. I propose that one of the key resources struggled over in the field of nation branding is a new form of legitimacy for post-communist elites, which emerges from the fusion of nationalism and market ideology. This speaks to the reasons why nation branding has been so attractive to a wide range of actors as they seek to gain access to power in the post-communist environment, where many social relations are being re-negotiated.

Surowiec adopts a similar theoretical and methodological approach to discuss the rise of nation branding in Poland from the late 1990s to present day. His analysis outlines the key institutions in Poland's private and public sectors who perpetuate the ideas and practices of nation branding in that country, noting that Polish academics have also had a role to play in this process. Surowiec offers the term "corpo-nationalism" as a way to describe a new form of identity politics that emerges from the marriage of national sentiments with the imperatives of global competition and marketing ideology, and argues that this mode of thinking about nationhood has thoroughly permeated Polish political culture.

Despite the geographic, historical, and sociological differences among these three country cases—with Estonia representing a Baltic state and a former Soviet republic, Bulgaria commonly classified as a Balkan nation and also the poorest nation in the EU, and Poland being the largest former communist nation in Central Europe and in the EU—some common patterns emerge from these chapters. The central involvement of Western brand consultants in each country is one important commonality. Another is a common desire of a new formation of local actors to present themselves as experts in their countries' engagement with globalization and marketization. Finally, in each case we can witness the ways in which branding works to depoliticize the processes of national identity construction, while at the same time infiltrating structures of governance.

Part III of the volume is titled *Representations, Mediations, Narrations*, and includes four studies on Slovenia, Romania, Hungary, and Serbia, respectively. The focus of these chapters shifts more explicitly toward analyses of the texts and narratives produced by branders, and the processes of meaning-making that originate with them. These chapters examine the symbolism of representations in a wide range of cultural artifacts, but also address the roles played by particular agents in struggles over the production of representations and meanings.

The chapter by Zala Volčič looks at the case of Slovenia—the most affluent of the former Yugoslav republics and the first to secede from the federation, and among the first post-communist nations to join the European Union in 2004. Volčič argues that nation branding in Slovenia is connected to the country's need to develop a unified sense of national identity, which is important in the post-Yugoslav era. At the same time, she points out that branding transforms national identity by way of translating nationalist ideas into the language of commercial appeals. This, Volčič argues, does not necessarily imply that modern "political nationalism" is somehow better than branding's "post-political commercial nationalism," but it illustrates that "the shortcomings of nationalism themselves change with the way in which nationalism reproduces in accordance with political, social, and economic logics" (Volčič, this volume, p. 149).

Next, Alice Bardan and Anikó Imre examine the image struggles of post-communist Romania. These authors argue that, despite the country's aspirations to the contrary, Romania continues to occupy a symbolic space on Europe's map as a repository of darkness, backwardness, and barbarity. Images of fictional vampires, bloodthirsty dictators, and widespread poverty are symbolically conflated in the Western imagination and reproduced in a number of popular culture narratives. Bardan and Imre discuss in details four recent and widely popular examples of Western imaginings of Romania. They then contrast them with the Romanian government's own efforts to counteract this form of "negative branding" of the country through state-sponsored communication campaigns. However, the authors argue, the government's efforts are predestined for failure as they do not engage the wide support of the Romanian population and, in the end, are aimed at producing narratives that satisfy the desires of a Western gaze more than anything else.

The following chapter by Laszlo Kulcsár and Young-ok Yum turns its attention to nation branding in Hungary and puts into question the proposition that a unified national brand is feasible in practice. Kulcsár and Yum trace the various institutional forms that nation branding has taken in post-communist Hungary since the 1990s and relate them to particular types of engagement with the problem of articulating a national identity for Hungary. As the authors' analysis illustrates, the branded narratives of national identity in Hungary have changed in parallel with the political agendas of ruling parties. Discourses of unity and homogeneity prevail when conservative, right-wing governments are in power, while liberal, left-wing politicians opt for more diffuse, place- and product-oriented forms of country branding. Another source of tension in the branding narratives concerns their tendency to overemphasize urban over rural articulations of identity. Kulcsár and Yum conclude that, in the case of Hungary, such tensions may be more productively resolved within the context of cultural initiatives led by nonpartisan organizations, rather than through top-down, centralized brand strategies.

This latter point is also central to the analysis in the final chapter of the volume, which focuses on Serbia's efforts to re-invent itself through music. Musicologist Brana Mijatović describes the rise to international prominence of a Serbian "world music" genre and two Serbian music festivals. Mijatović argues that world music has provided a cultural alternative for the articulation of more hopeful narratives of national identity, which depart from the politically charged discourses that have defined conflict-torn, post-communist and post-Yugoslav Serbian society. At the same time, she illustrates that Serbian politicians were quick to co-opt the popularity of this music phenomenon into a discourse of nation branding that transcends the realm of popular culture. Again, this chapter demonstrates the impossibility of separating the cultural from the political and documents the complex ways in which nation branding factors in their interconnections.

As in the previous section, the chapters in Part III of the volume highlight several common themes. First, they illustrate the multiplicity and complexity of symbolic manifestations of nationhood and speak to the difficulty of maintaining unified narratives of national identity. Further, they show the conflictual nature of global and local articulations of identity and illuminate the role of mediation in their interactions. Finally, these chapters remind us that symbolic practices are necessarily political practices and that national identity continues to have a central role as a mobilizing focus of collective passions.

LOOKING AHEAD

Above all, the chapters in this volume are intended to invite further conversation and critical examination into the role nation branding plays in the cultural, political, and economic fortunes of post-communist Europe. This volume does not claim to offer an exhaustive examination of the topic, nor does it address the full range of branding activities in the CEE region. Many of the countries of the former Soviet Bloc, not discussed in this collection, have also engaged with nation branding and their experiences are equally worthy of study.

This collection illustrates the continued centrality of the problems of national identity in post-communist Europe. Sociologist Michael Kennedy (1994) writes:

> The process of identity formation after communism is ironic. Politicians, activists, and analysts emphasize the unprecedented fact of communism's end. At the same time, however, its subjects insist that they want no more "experiments"—they only want what has been proven to succeed. They want to be normal . . . Despite the unprecedented transformation they are living through and the "aberration" of history that led to it, East Europeans want unproblematic identities. (pp. 3–4)

The chapters in this collection show that nation branding is not likely to deliver such "unproblematic identities" to its post-communist clients. In that respect, the complex mosaic of agents, practices, symbolic articulations, and mediations that emerges from these chapters provides a critical alternative to the marketing-dominated literature on nation branding which promises (but fails to deliver) simple solutions.

At the same time, the enduring crisis of representations will continue to provide new openings for branders to exert their influence and to extract profit from the identity struggles of post-communist nations. Thus, critical scholarship needs to continue to question the particular ideological work that nation branding does in the post-communist environment and beyond. Who gets to speak on behalf of the nation, and for what purpose? What are the consequences of the increased marketization of nationhood? What does this process imply about the fate of nationhood as a central form of collective identification, and of nation-states as the chief mechanism of political organization and governance still prevalent today? Most importantly, what can we do—as critical scholars, national subjects, and global citizens—to understand and transform the social conditions in which we find ourselves? Such are the questions that engage the flights of the sociological imagination and animate the chapters in this volume.

NOTES

1. For reviews of the marketing literature see, for example, Hanna & Rowley (2008), Kavaratzis (2005), Papadopoulos (2004).
2. For a more comprehensive review of the literature on nation branding, which discusses consistencies and contradictions among different approaches across disciplines, see Kaneva (2011).
3. Bulgarian cultural scholar Alexander Kiossev (2002) goes as far as to argue that, in the case of the Balkans, nationality would not have emerged at all without the presence of an idealized Western Other that could be emulated and admired.
4. For a comprehensive explanation and a critique of the precepts of shock therapy as it was deployed in Eastern Europe, see Gowan (1995).
5. Raymond Williams (1977) pointed out that a more nuanced reading of Marx would re-direct our attention from questions of "determination" to questions of "mediation" and return us to an examination of "specific and indissoluble real processes" (pp. 81–82).

REFERENCES

Anholt, S. (2007). *Competitive identity: The new brand management for nations, cities and regions.* New York: Palgrave Macmillan.

Anholt, S. (2008). From *nation branding* to *competitive identity*—the role of brand management as a component of national policy. In K. Dinnie (Ed.), *Nation branding: Concepts, issues, practice* (pp. 22–23). Oxford, UK: Butterworth-Heinemann.

Aronczyk, M. (2007). New and improved nations: Branding national identity. In C. Calhoun & R. Sennett (Eds.), *Practicing culture* (pp. 105–128). New York: Routledge.

Aronczyk, M. (2008). "Living the brand": Nationality, globality and identity strategies of nation branding consultants. *International Journal of Communication, 2,* 41–65.

Baker, C. (2008). Wild dances and dying wolves: Simulation, essentialization, and national identity at the Eurovision Song Contest. *Popular Communication, 6*(3), 173–189.

Bennett, W. L., & Lagos, T. (2007). Logo logic: The ups and downs of branded political communication. *Annals of the American Academy of Political and Social Science, 611*(1), 193–206.

20 Nadia Kaneva

Bernhard, M. (2010). The revolutions of 1989: Twenty years later. *Angelaki: Journal of the Theoretical Humanities, 15*(3), 109–122.

Bjelić, D. I., & Savić, O. (Eds.). (2002). *Balkan as metaphor: Between globalization and fragmentation.* Cambridge: MIT Press.

Bourdieu, P. (1984). *Distinction: A social critique of the judgment of taste.* Cambridge, MA: Harvard University Press.

Bourdieu, P. (1998). *Acts of resistance: Against the tyranny of the market.* New York: The New Press.

Bourdieu, P. (2002). The politics of globalization. *Global Policy Forum.* Retrieved March 14, 2002, from http://www.globalpolicy.org/ngos/role/globdem/globgov/2002/0220bourdieu.htm

Bourdieu, P. (2005). *The social structures of the economy.* Cambridge, UK: Polity Press.

Burawoy, M., & Verdery, K. (1999). Introduction. In M. Burawoy & K. Verdery (Eds.), *Uncertain transition: Ethnographies of change in the postsocialist world* (pp. 1–17). Lanham, MD: Rowman & Littlefield.

Cosgrove, K. (2007). *Branded conservatives: How the brand brought the right from the fringes to the center of American politics.* New York: Peter Lang.

Curran, J. (2002). *Media and power.* London: Routledge.

Dinnie, K. (2008). *Nation branding: Concepts, issues, practice.* Oxford, UK: Butterworth-Heinemann.

Ditchev, I. (2000). Европа като легитимация [Europe as legitimation]. *Социологически Проблеми, 32*(1/2), 87–108. Sofia, Bulgaria: Sociology Institute of the Bulgarian Academy of Science.

Dzenovska, D. (2005). Remaking the nation of Latvia: Anthropological perspectives on nation branding. *Place Branding and Public Diplomacy, 1*(2), 173–186.

Einstein, M. (2008). *Brands of faith: Marketing religion in a commercial age.* New York: Routledge.

Fan, Y. (2005). Branding the nation: What is being branded? *Journal of Vacation Marketing, 12*(1), 5–14.

Foucault, M. (1972). *The archeology of knowledge and the discourse on language.* New York: Harper & Row.

Gandy, O. (Ed.). (1995). Colloquy. *Critical Studies in Mass Communication, 12*(1), 60–100.

Genov, N. (2002). Facing the future: Eastern Europe in the global context. *Sociological Problems, 34*(Special Issue), 11–20. Sofia, Bulgaria: Sociology Institute of the Bulgarian Academy of Science.

Gilboa, E. (2008). Searching for a theory of public diplomacy. *Annals of the American Academy of Political and Social Science, 616*(55), 55–77.

Gowan, P. (1995, September/October). Neo-liberal theory and practice for Eastern Europe. *New Left Review, 1*(213), 3–60.

Hanna, S., & Rowley, J. (2008). An analysis of terminology use in place branding. *Place Branding and Public Diplomacy, 4*(1), 61–75.

Hearn, A. (2008). Variations on the branded self: Theme, invention, improvisation and inventory. In D. Hesmondhalgh & J. Toynbee (Eds.), *The media and social theory* (pp. 194–210). London: Routledge.

Hearn, A. (2010). "Through the looking glass": The promotional university 2.0. In M. Aronczyk & D. Powers (Eds.), *Blowing up the brand: Critical perspectives on promotional culture* (pp. 195–218). New York: Peter Lang.

Jansen, S. C. (2008). Designer nations: Neo-liberal nation branding—Brand Estonia. *Social Identities, 14*(1), 121–142.

Kaneva, N. (2007). Meet the "new" Europeans: EU accession and the branding of postcommunist Bulgaria. *Advertising & Society Review, 8*(4).

Kaneva, N. (2011). Nation branding: Toward and agenda for critical research. *International Journal of Communication, 5*, 117–141. Retrieved January 10, 2011, from http://ijoc.org/ojs/index.php/ijoc/article/viewFile/704/514

Kavaratzis, M. (2005). Place branding: A review of trends and conceptual models. *Marketing Review, 5*(4), 329–342.

Kennedy, M. (1994). An introduction to East European ideology and identity in transformation. In M. Kennedy (Ed.), *Envisioning Eastern Europe: Postcommunist cultural studies* (pp. 1–45). Ann Arbor: University of Michigan Press.

Kiossev, A. (2002). Notes on self-colonizing cultures. In I. Znepolski, K. Tchervenkova, & A. Kiossev (Eds.), *Rethinking the transition* (pp. 361–369). Sofia, Bulgaria: St. Kliment Ohridsky University Press.

Knight, G. (2010). Activism, branding, and the promotional public sphere. In M. Aronczyk & D. Powers (Eds.), *Blowing up the brand: Critical perspectives on promotional culture* (pp. 173–194). New York: Peter Lang.

Lury, C., & Moor, L. (2010). Brand valuation and topological culture. In M. Aronczyk & D. Powers (Eds.), *Blowing up the brand: Critical perspectives on promotional culture* (pp. 29–52). New York: Peter Lang.

Meehan, E. (1999). Commodity, culture, common sense: Media research and paradigm dialogue. *Journal of Media Economics, 12*(2), 149–163.

Mills, C. W.(1959). *The sociological imagination.* New York: Oxford University Press.

Moore, L. (2008). Branding consultants as cultural intermediaries. *Sociological Review, 56*(3), 408–428.

O'Reilly, D. (2006). Commentary: Branding ideology. *Marketing Theory, 6*(2), 263–271.

Papadopolous, N. (2004). Place branding: Evolution, meaning and implications. *Place Branding, 1*(1), 36–49.

Peck, J. (2001, Spring). Itinerary of a thought: Stuart Hall, cultural studies, and the unresolved problem of the relation of culture to "not culture." *Cultural Critique, 48*, 200–249.

Rupnik, J. (1996). The reawakening of European nationalisms. *Social Research, 63*(1), 41–75.

Said, E. (1978). *Orientalism.* New York: Pantheon Books.

So much gained, so much to lose. (2009, November 7). *The Economist*, 11–12.

Spassov, O. (2000). *Преходът и медиите: Политики на репрезентация (България 1989–2000)* [The transition and the media: Politics of representation (Bulgaria 1989–2000)]. Sofia, Bulgaria: St. Kliment Ohridsky University Press.

Sussman, G. (2010). *Branding democracy: U.S. regime change in post-Soviet Eastern Europe.* New York: Peter Lang.

Szondi, G. (2008). Public diplomacy and nation branding: Conceptual similarities and differences. *Discussion Papers in Diplomacy.* Hague, Netherlands: Clingendael Netherlands Institute of International Relations.

Thrift, N. (2005). *Knowing capitalism.* London: Sage.

Todorova, M. (1997). *Imagining the Balkans.* New York: Oxford University Press.

Twitchell, J. B. (2004). School daze: Higher Ed, Inc in an age of branding. In J. B. Twitchell, *Branded nation: The marketing of Megachurch, College, Inc., and Museumworld* (pp. 109–192). New York: Simon & Schuster.

Van Ham, P. (2001). The rise of the brand state: The postmodern politics of image and reputation. *Foreign Affairs, 8*(5), 2–6.

Van Ham, P. (2002). Branding territory: Inside the wonderful worlds of PR and IR theory. *Millennium: Journal of International Studies, 31*(2), 249–269.

Verdery, K. (1993). Whither "nation" and "nationalism"? *Daedalus, 122*(3), 37–46.

Volčič, Z. (2005). The notion of "the West" in the Serbian national imaginary. *European Journal of Cultural Studies, 8*(2), 155–175.

Volčič, Z. (2008). Former Yugoslavia on the World Wide Web: Commercialization and branding of nation-states. *International Communication Gazette, 70*(5), 395–413.

Wacquant, L. J. L. (1992). Toward a social praxeology: The structure and logic of Bourdieu's sociology. In P. Bourdieu & L. J. D. Wacquant, *An invitation to reflexive sociology* (pp. 1–60). Chicago: Chicago University Press.

Wang, J. (2006). Managing national reputation and international relations in the global era: Public diplomacy revisited. *Public Relations Review, 32*(2), 91–96.

Wang, J. (2008). The power and limits of branding in national image communication in global society. *Journal of International Communication, 14*(2), 9–24.

Wernick, A. (1991). *Promotional culture: Advertising, ideology and symbolic expression.* London: Sage.

Widler, J. (2007). Nation branding: With pride against prejudice. *Place Branding and Public Diplomacy, 3*(2), 144–150.

Williams, R. (1977). *Marxism and literature.* Oxford, UK: Oxford University Press.

Wolff, L. (1994). *Inventing Eastern Europe: The map of civilization on the mind of the Enlightenment.* Stanford, CA: Stanford University Press.

Znepolski, I. (1997). *Езикът на имагинерния преход* [The language of the imaginary transition]. Sofia, Bulgaria: Literaturen Forum.

2 Systemic Propaganda and State Branding in Post-Soviet Eastern Europe[1]

Gerald Sussman

INTRODUCTION

The informational economy, on which the United States and other leading industrial states have staked the future, is profoundly implicated in a broad range of transformations, similar in scope to the radical changes brought about by the era of the industrial revolution. Transnational capitalism is continually reorganizing not only the system of production, but also the spheres of politics, social relations, knowledge, and cultural practice. Embedded in neoliberal economic and organizational restructuring, the digital mode of development (Castells, 1996) has altered relations among nations in ways that have broken traditional boundaries, territorial and other forms, and the spatial-temporal order of things. Digital capitalism, still mainly headquartered in the West and focused on the informational functions of production, circulation, and consumption, enables those in the promotional fields to push the frontiers of consumerism and the commodification of consciousness. The "sacred" character of nations and states poses no barrier to those wishing to bring them into the fold of spectacular consumption. And the new instruments of communication and informational and symbolic transfer excite such possibilities.

This chapter examines the political economic foundations of nation branding over the past decade. It looks at America's branding strategy employed to sell both its own image abroad and other efforts used to integrate the Central and Eastern European (CEE) region[2] within the Western economic and military alliance structure. Within a discursive strategy of "branded democracy" (Sussman, 2010), the principal forms of Western intervention in the CEE region in the most recent decade (i.e., post-1999) have not been guns or bombs, but rather technologies of propaganda. Before considering the attempts to sell "Brand America" and the U.S. engagement in the "color revolutions" of Eastern Europe, it is important to first discuss the political economic context in which promotional activities have accelerated and come to permeate key aspects of its foreign policy.

SELLING SOCIETIES

It is now well understood that Western capitalist economies, particularly that of the United States, have shifted their base from manufacturing and agriculture to informational goods and services. It remains somewhat problematic as to what the informational economy actually means—a topic which I discussed in an earlier book (Sussman, 1997). However, there is no question that a substantial part of what was once the American industrial system is now located overseas (although still heavily under American ownership). The advent of digital communications has been central to the restructuring of the economy in organizational and technological terms, and the ongoing shift from government to private-sector regulation has enabled higher concentrations of capital to dominate domestic and overseas markets.

One of the most crucial functions of the informational economy lies in the *selling* of symbolic goods (images, data, visual games, media, and other immaterial commodities). This requires a greater emphasis on consumerism, as the prevailing "religion," and the "opening up of more and more of the spaces of everyday life to promotional activity" (Moor, 2008)—from the branding of stadia and streetcar stops to advertisements printed on theater and bus tickets. Most popular manufactured consumer goods (clothing, footwear, toys, computers, phones, television sets, hardware, and many other items) are produced offshore, while domestic industry has come to concentrate on advertising, marketing, and other promotional occupations. In the last half of the 20th century, manufacturing employment in the United States was reduced from more than one-third of the total number of jobs to just over one-tenth, while service employment rose to about 80% (Hagenbaugh, 2002). The leading structural change in the United States, as well as in other leading capitalist economies, is a concentration in the marketing (promotion) of material and entertainment culture, rooted in a growing network of production, supplier, and consumer linkages.

The informational economy is lodged at a more "superstructural" level within the regime of neoliberalism, a top-down, supply-side legal regime and discourse about generating wealth through networked sub-centers and flows of capital, while dismantling or paring down the social welfare and other nonmilitary functions of the state. Under neoliberalism, a convergence of commercial and political propaganda finds its maturity in the post-Fordist (flexible, deterritorialized) economy. With the coming of post-Fordism (beginning in the 1970s), politics and public administration have been reconstituted, outsourced, and privatized through professional promotionalism, branding, and intensified consumerism for those with the means to pay for it (American elections are more than ever the best that money can buy). The promotional and propaganda "PR state," rooted in advertising and political marketing, incites visceral and mostly negative responses to government, while cultivating affective responses to commodities that are generally associated with the gratification of desires.

Once in power, the administration of George W. Bush stepped up the use of propaganda in its foreign and domestic policies. Its relief effort for the tsunami victims in Southeast Asia in 2005 was treated within inner government ranks less as a humanitarian gesture and more as an example of "successful public diplomacy" (Fouts, 2006, p. 15). Washington public diplomacy practitioners hailed it as changing the image of the U.S. government—as a correction to the prevailing negative foreign opinion toward Brand America. It is likely that U.S. action taken after the Haiti earthquake calamity in January 2010 will be viewed within the same moral framework. Naomi Klein (2007) has argued that crises such as these are exploited by the opportunistic and unabashed neoliberal policies of American "disaster capitalism."

SYSTEMIC PROPAGANDA

Contemporary techniques of commercial and political persuasion are nested in what has become a broader context of what I would call *systemic propaganda*. By this I mean that propaganda is not simply a policy and project outcome, but rather that it is now grounded in the system of production. The mutually constituted forces behind economic, financial, technocratic, and technological change have enabled the formation of a new international division of labor such that leading industrial countries, particularly the United States, have moved from being nations of producers to being nations of sellers and consumers. It is the seller-consumer relationship and the "offshoring" of manufacturing that compels a higher and more pervasive order of public persuasion, both commercial and ideological, which has deeply influenced social interaction and given rise to a broad set of promotional practices, from the ever more ubiquitous presence of advertising to the new forms of everyday self-promotion (via personal websites, Facebook, Twitter, and the like).

Before World War II, propaganda in the United States was largely associated with government efforts to "educate" and lead a public that nationally syndicated journalist and commentator Walter Lippmann (1927) derisively described as a "bewildered herd" (p. 155). Joseph Goebbels, Nazi Germany's Reich Minister for Propaganda and Popular Enlightenment—also a former journalist—shared such a notion and deeply admired the propaganda achievements of the United States. He declared, "Propaganda must label events and people with distinctive phrases or slogans" (Goebbels, n.d.). Yet Goebbels, although extremely sinister in his objectives, would be considered an amateur propagandist by current standards in terms of volume of output, reach, and technical sophistication.

Under the lead of the corporate commercial sphere, post-war propaganda became more deeply commodified. In 2008, even with declining revenues, total U.S. advertising investments were worth $232.9 billion (Myers, 2009), a figure significantly higher than the gross domestic product (GDP) of Nigeria (with some 155 million people) and, in fact, larger than the GDPs of all but 36 countries. Total U.S. investments in advertising, direct marketing, promotion, events, and public relations in 2008 were $751.8 billion (Myers, 2009), which when compared to national GDPs would make it the 18th largest "country." Modern systemic propaganda, political or commercial, does not rely on the imagination of professional marketers alone. Aided by advanced panoptic collection and sorting technologies, propaganda draws far more systematically on the surveillance of citizen-consumer databases to "co-construct" effective messages, though usually without the permission or awareness of the surveilled. Indeed, the tolerances and preferences of audience-responders in the data mining process are *intrinsic* in shaping promotions. This renders data providers (consumers) as indispensable, informal, and largely uncompensated *labor* in the value creation of the informational commodity, be it public policy or toothpaste.

A 2003 study by the U.S. Bureau of Labor Statistics calculated that over 15 million people worked in overall sales positions (Lambert, 2003). The U.S. Department of Labor estimated in 2008 that some 623,800 people were working in advertising, marketing, promotions, public relations, and sales management alone (U.S. Department of Labor, n.d.). But a study published by the Institute for Public Relations (Falconi, 2006) argues that the methods used by the U.S. Department of Labor grossly underestimate the number of public relations professionals. Indeed, many job classifications would not be counted in either index—check-out counter clerks, radio show hosts, call center employees, window display and graphic designers, commercial illustrators, professional athletes, and many others, including densely patched NASCAR drivers, who are required or incentivized, in at least part of their working lives, to pitch products and services. A *Wall Street Journal* article, for example, reported that in NFL (National Football League) games lasting an average of 185 minutes, playing time occupied only 11 minutes, while advertising took up an hour, which did not include the logos and stadium advertisements that informally show up on TV screens (Biderman, 2010). The branding of space and the people involved in it are taking up and conditioning ever greater proportions of our visual and cognitive space.

In the new promotional economy, among those U.S.-based transnational corporations still manufacturing tangible goods, many focus more of their energies on marketing and branding than on the actual production of goods. Pharmaceutical companies, for example, spend more on advertising costs than on research and development. In the public sector, with many of the state's functions now farmed out to private contractors, the business world has considerably more of a direct hand in influencing, if not managing, governmental affairs—from producing public informational goods, to providing mercenary soldiering abroad, to organizing the political campaign process. Intensive surveillance and analysis of citizens' personal data and consumer habits is conducted by companies, such as Acxiom,[3] and sold to private vendors and to political campaign consultants who then target customized, interest-focused direct mail to potential voters for their candidates.

The culture of consumerism also bears evidence of relentless profiteering through simulacra. There is a line of clothing malappropriately called "Society of the Spectacle," which not only treats spectacle as a fact of contemporary life but also claims to be responsive to "critical issues" in the world by "propagating social awareness" and offering "casual-luxury apparel designed for fashion savvy individuals" ("About S.O.S.," n.d.). Its entrepreneurial founders offer no reference on their website to the author of their eponymous rip-off, Guy Debord, who was anything but enthused about the image-conscious consumerist emphasis of fatuous modern bourgeois culture.

But this is not unusual within anything-goes postmodernist capitalist mores. An online clothing company markets its products under the label "Propaganda," while a UK-based branding and marketing firm for companies and their products also calls itself "Propaganda" and claims to have a registered trademark on the name. In Portland, Oregon, a department store, Meier & Frank (owned by May Co.), introduced a new line of women's clothing in 2003 called "Ideology" (McInerny, 2003, p. C-1). Far from Portland's shores, a Russian "political technology" consulting firm plies its campaign management talents under the name "Niccolo M" (for Machiavelli, of course). The corporate market has few scruples about stealing and reworking classics from historical memory, often into their signifying antonyms (as in the lexicon of the Ministry of Truth in Orwell's *1984*). Dozens of commercial advertisements have sampled the songs of such groups and performers as Led Zeppelin, The Monkees, Carole King, The Rolling Stones, The Who, Deep Purple, Jefferson Airplane, Alice Cooper, Eric Clapton, and the Beatles. Janis Joplin's plaintive lyrics assailing materialist culture in "Mercedes Benz" were appropriated many years later as an ad by the car manufacturer.

NATION BRANDING

One of the derivatives of neoliberalism and systemic propaganda is a hybrid of advertising and marketing—*branding*. Branding adds to the exchange value of a commodity, concept, person, space, or place by establishing a lifestyle identity and a loyalty among customers to the brand name. Branding specialist Wally Olins, who is chair of London-based Saffron Brand Consultants and celebrated within the promotional community for creating "Brand Poland," asserts quite candidly that "branding is propaganda . . . what it boils down to is manipulation and seduction. That's the business we're in. That's the business of life" (cited in Jansen, 2008, p. 133). Olins acknowledges that "the word brand excites a great deal of contentious discussion," and for this reason he prefers the term "reputation management" (Olins, 2005) to describe the spinning of the nation-state as a production unit and trade generator—as if that were less contentious. Such cavalier assertions represent the postmodern arrogance of an industry habituated to the exaltation of frivolous consumption and fetishization found in advertising and other promotional media. It recalls Guy Debord's critique of "the world of the autonomous image, where deceit deceives itself" (Debord, 1994, p. 12).

In its relentless pursuit of the conquest of spatiality, entrepreneurial branding is not limited to the promotion of consumption of material goods and intangible services. It is now part of a strategic set of discursive practices intended to bring more public land masses (and even rivers) under the regulatory and ideological administration of international capital. Branding spaces, indeed nations, is an aggressive assertion with legal and coercive underpinnings in what Lefebvre (1991) identified as the ownership over spaces of consumption and the consumption of spaces. The professional branding of space has extended itself beyond the spectacle of theme cities, with their convention, sports, and entertainment centers, urban renewal, high-rise condominiums, pedestrian-friendly commercial malls, new businesses, theaters, tourist amusements, restaurants, and other built amenities, along with heavy policing and surveillance intended to breathe life into the declining downtown districts of major metropolises. Branding activities reconceptualize the nation-state, denuded of much of its governing function, as a more dedicated partner in production or as an object of fancy or fantasy. Even charities, which take up much of the state's diminishing social assistance, employ branding, assisted by consultants who advise on the creation of institutional logos, campaign paraphernalia, tactics, and strategies (Moor, 2007). Capitalism, Lefebvre (1991) notes, has turned from production *in* space to the production *of* space. There is no limit to the marketing and commodification of place and space, much as the Italian *autonomista* Mario Tronti, writing in 1962, had anticipated:

> The more capitalist development advances . . . the more the production of relative surplus value penetrates everywhere, the more the circuit production-distribution-exchange-consumption inevitably develops . . . the relationship between capitalist production and bourgeois society, between the factory and society, between society and the state, become more and more organic . . . and the whole society becomes an articulation of production. In short, all of society lives as a function of the factory and the factory extends its exclusive domination over all of society. (Cited in Dyer-Witheford, 1999, p. 263, n2)

With the deepening of neoliberalism and the enabling capacities of new informational technologies, propaganda is increasingly undertaken by, or outsourced to, private commercial actors. A business-friendly image is regarded as a *sine qua non* to nations' survival as viable economic entities in a transnational corporate-dominated economic system. For PR firms, nation-states are now registered simply as "accounts," little different than beer producers or toy manufacturers. Simon Anholt, a British journal editor and international marketing adviser, runs an indexing service for governments that he calls the Nation Brand Index. He also claims to have invented the term "nation branding," which he defines as "the business of applying corporate marketing theory to countries" (Teslik, 2007).

Clearly, Anholt has put his résumé in the service of Western state and corporate interests and sees nation branding as part of a larger neoliberal economic strategy. But he is not simply a hired gun for industry. One journalist discovered that

> [Anholt] sits on the advisory council of Business for Diplomatic Action, a group of marketing, academic, and corporate veterans—which counts intellectual heavyweights like Joseph Nye and Jeffrey Garten, as well as corporate titans like McDonald's and GlaxoSmithKline, among its ranks—organized in 2004 to combat anti-Americanism abroad. (Risen, 2005)

Branding has become a booming business. A former PR specialist for Hill & Knowlton (a firm headquartered in New York and known for its work with pro-Western regimes, including autocratic governments in the Middle East and Africa)[4] in Budapest and London, and more recently a British business university lecturer in much demand on the international speaker circuit, György Szondi insists that nation branding or reputation management in CEE countries turns on their ability to institute neoliberal reforms, a precondition for attracting foreign capital. He writes, "Having a country brand is necessary to attract investors but not enough; there must be an infrastructure, a skilled workforce, favorable tax policies and returns on investment" (Szondi, 2007, p. 14). Szondi adds that "for countries whose image is better than reality (Poland, Czech Republic, or Romania), the challenge is to transform their superior image into concrete investment projects while the countries that score higher on reality than image (Hungary, for example) should improve their perception in the market and level of notoriety" (p. 15). Even better, he suggests that the Czech Republic would be well served to change the English version of its name to make it easier for foreigners to vocalize. Estonia, too, might have been well served to adopt the German name Estland (for its association with high-ranking Finland on the attractiveness scale) (p. 16).

A fellow traveler of Szondi, Simon Anholt identifies six main areas of nation branding interest: tourism, exports, governance, investment and immigration, culture and heritage, and people (summarized in Kaneva, 2007). Most typically, nation branding is used to promote tourism and foreign investment. Anholt insists that nation branding is a force for good, involving "the intelligent and judicious application of marketing and branding techniques upon countries [which] can be a powerful force for global wealth distribution and cultural as well as economic development" (Anholt, 2002, p. 59). There is simply no evidence that such an outcome has occurred. Indeed, the recession in Western Europe led to a meltdown in Eastern Europe. Five years after joining the EU, branded Estonia "has gone from boom to bust" (Stokes, 2009). Perhaps its economic results would have been more favorable had it followed the renaming strategy proposed by Szondi.

Some of Anholt's other findings are also rather murky. In partnership with the Roper marketing firm, his firm found in late 2009 that, on the basis of their selected markers, the United States was the world's most "beloved country"—which, he says, had much to do with Obama and the end of the Bush administration (Sherman, 2009). This finding is likely to have been overstated. In 2008, a U.S. Congress report found a precipitous drop in the image of the United States abroad during the George W. Bush administration (Subcommittee on International Organizations, Human Rights, and Oversight, 2008). Richard Lugar, former chair of the U.S. Senate Committee on Foreign Relations, wrote in February 2009 (already into the Obama administration) that polling in 21 countries indicated that 43% of respondents "had a negative view of the United States" (Lugar, 2009). It is unlikely that a country's image can radically switch in the space of just one year. Even if in some way correct, this merely indicates the fickle and unreliable character of such a finding. Moreover, Anholt's claim that the degree of branding success in a country correlates with economic improvement and wealth distribution does not appear to hold up in the case of the "beloved country," which continues to suffer from massive real unemployment and growing income inequality, the worst among the major industrial countries—even worse than Ukraine, whose real GDP fell by more than 7% in 2009 (World Bank, 2008).

Anholt nonetheless believes that nation branding starts with the marketplace and the consumer (Mayes, 2008, p. 127). He argues that the unyielding law of comparative advantage requires nations to compete for status and symbolic advantage in order to survive. A "brand strategy" and a "brand image" are a necessity if they want to be attractive to the transnational corporate community and compete as viable neoliberal economic entities. He even advises governments to develop cabinet-level branding ministers—which, indeed, could be seen as a postmodern equivalent of a ministry of propaganda. Anholt, though, is taken seriously by the corporate business community, which undoubtedly appreciates his devotion to the preservation of Western hegemony.

In Anholt's view, for many countries (*pace* Thatcher), there is no alternative: "Countries have to play the market rules just as companies do, like it or not" (cited in Kaneva, 2007). Otherwise, they are "doomed to fail"

(Anholt, cited in Mayes, 2008, p. 128). States find their place in the world economy by competing with one another to become a desirable destination. A "strong positive image has the potential of giving a powerful and distinct competitive advantage for a place" (Seppo Rainisto, cited in Andersson, 2007, p. 121). Anholt claims that up to a third of all global wealth is derivative of branding (cited in Jansen, 2008, p. 125). But, he admonishes, while "an economic tool of critical importance," nation branding is different from branding products and requires a higher order of representation (Anholt, 2005).

Nation branding is an extension of city branding and theme parks, involving a spectacle of promotion intended to attract foreign investment, tourism, and trade to states collaborating with international capital and development institutions. In each of these branded environments, social and cultural diversity is obliterated by the value put on homogenized spectatorship and consumption. A Dutch academic elaborates on how branding integrates the identity and business interests of the state:

> Tiny Estonia now not only takes exception to the label "post-Soviet state," it also dislikes being called a "Baltic" country. Toomas Hendrik Ilves, the country's foreign minister, refers to Estonia as a "pre-EU" or a "Scandinavian" country. Lacking blue-chip brands such as Finland's Nokia or Sweden's Volvo, Estonia may also try to push itself as a "green country" to attract environmentally conscious individuals and foreign direct investment. Poland's Ministry of Foreign Affairs, meanwhile, has set up a special promotional program aimed at improving the country's image, which most EU citizens still associate with devout Catholicism, backwardness, and conservatism. (van Ham, 2001, p. 4)

Efforts at nation branding have the effect of depoliticizing the nation and decoupling it from the authority of the state. Nation branding disregards internal conflicts that inhabit all nations; it attempts to neutralize what is, at a nation's core, difference and often discord. Indeed, nation branding is not as much about (re)constructing a nation as creating a spectacle by which transnational elites attempt to reappropriate nationhood as a signifier of consumption values. Nation branders are like missionaries who represent not a people and their culture, but the nation as an appendage, a surface environment for generating exchange value.

Nation branders and state diplomats alike operate as extension agents within the larger context of neoliberalism, which fosters the interests of transnational corporations (TNCs) over other aspects of international relations. According to the former director of the University of Southern California's Center on Public Diplomacy, the American diplomat is expected to be "part activist, part lobbyist, and part street-smart policy entrepreneur" (Fouts, 2006, p. 22). Nation branding and other private and state PR initiatives serve to lay the groundwork to make new regional markets safe for foreign investment. To that end, an international accounting and auditing firm, Ernst & Young, conducts "attractiveness surveys" for CEE countries to assist them in attracting TNC capital.

Has the idea of the nation been transformed into intellectual property? What exactly is a nation? For Anthony Smith (2001), it is a named people usually living in a historic territory (or homeland) with a common language and ancestry, as well as shared myths and a sense of unique history. In other words, the nation is an internal "imagined," if not organic, affinity. For Benedict Anderson (1993), the nation is a sense of "community" constructed largely out of a vernacular literature, derivative of "print capitalism" (and therefore a modern evocation). Nation is not a "branded" identity that can be organized by professional wordsmiths or image makers. It is a set of social, cultural, and political (not professional or economistic) relationships, a collective expression of its people.

Instead of people defining themselves, nation branding is outsourced to domestic and foreign corporations, enabling the latter to determine national identity: the "Brand Estonia" account was handled by British Interbrand (a branch of Omnicom Group, one of the world's largest advertising conglomerates) and designed and developed in New York City (Jansen, 2008, p. 123). What branding firms do for nation-states is deliver them to the forces that seek to denationalize them economically while boosting their national identities for the purpose of pushing international competition and patron-client relations—not unlike the way that a political system brings in foreign consultants to promote and manage a money-driven electioneering process and build links to international capital.

NATION BRANDING AND U.S. PUBLIC DIPLOMACY

Those who find nation branding an effective way to alter a state's image tend to regard public consciousness, per Lippmann, as a *tabula rasa* waiting to be inscribed by propagandists. But even the United States, an advanced center of the promotion industries, had little success in a "public diplomacy" strategy called "Brand America," created by the George W. Bush administration and backed by a Congressional budget appropriation of $520 million. Billed as "the biggest public-relations effort in the history of United States foreign policy," it was part of an effort "to 'sell' America to the world" through a media propaganda blitz in the Middle East and South Asia (Snow, 2003, p. 24). This particular propaganda project rested on advertising executive Charlotte Beers, a seasoned Madison Avenue pro, who, with no previous foreign policy portfolio, was chosen by then Secretary of State Colin Powell to be Under Secretary for Public Diplomacy and Public Affairs (PDPA) (Critchlow, 2004, pp. 85–86). Beers brought her background as a former executive at three ad agencies, J. Walter Thompson,[5] Tatham-Laird & Kudner, and Ogilvy & Mather.

In 2002, Beers initiated a particular State Department propaganda effort, officially called the "Shared Values" Initiative (SVI). This program focused on trying to counter the highly critical views of U.S. policy in the Arab region. The idea was to try to win over hearts and minds toward U.S. military initiatives, focusing mainly "on beaming U.S. propaganda into the Muslim world, much of it directed at teens" (Cockburn & St. Clair, 2004, p. 320). At a cost to taxpayers of some $15 million, one of SVI's objectives was to purchase local broadcast time on Arab channels to promote a favorable image of the United States as a country as well as its foreign policy (Kendrick & Fullerton, 2004, p. 297).

To assist her, Beers brought in Cari Eggspuehler, head of the American private-sector interest group Business for Diplomatic Action ("Brand America," 2004/2005). She also hired the consumer marketing services of advertising agency McCann-Erickson Worldwide to help produce television spots about American and Muslim "shared values." These were intended for on-air circulation in various Islamic countries. Beers described the project as "the most elegant brand I've ever had to work with" (Kuchment, 2001).

By almost all accounts, "Brand America" was a flop. There is little evidence to show that the Middle East's negative opinion of the U.S. invasion and occupation of Iraq, with the extraordinary violence that ensued (over 600,000 Iraqi violent deaths by mid-2006, according to the British medical journal *Lancet*),[6] has been placated by U.S. attempts to persuade people in the region of America's good intentions. With few stations willing to run the commercials, the U.S. mainstream media reported that SVI was poorly received ("Brand America," 2004/2005). SVI ads were soon suspended and Beers promptly resigned her post, citing personal reasons.

The State Department's misguided attempts to convince the Arab world of its positive objectives "likely stemmed," Klein argued, "from the fact that Beers views the United States' tattered international image as little more than a communications problem" (Klein, 2002). Beers's preparation for foreign policy work was based on her established reputation as a brand specialist for Uncle Ben's rice and Head & Shoulders dandruff shampoo (Dumenco, 2001). However, marketing products or working previously with Powell as fellow board directors at Gulf Airstream Aircraft were entirely different matters from pitching the story of America's good intentions in the Middle East. Against critics, Powell defended her appointment, insisting, "We are selling a product. We need someone who can re-brand American foreign policy, re-brand diplomacy" (cited in Klein, 2002). Beers remained in the PDPA position from October 2001 until March 2003. Powell lasted another year.

Beers's replacement, Margaret Tutwiler, had little more success with "public diplomacy" initiatives in the Middle East. Prior to assuming the PDPA assignment, Tutwiler had worked on media relations for the Cellular Telecommunications Industry Association, a trade lobbyist for the wireless communications industry. In 2000, she coordinated media for George W. Bush from Florida as the vote counting controversy was unfolding. She lasted only six months at PDPA, abruptly departing, just as the Abu Ghraib scandal became public, to assume a position as a government relations specialist with the New York Stock Exchange. She passed seamlessly through the revolving door between government and big business to ply her contacts in the convergent public and private worlds. Tutwiler also lent her talents to the International Republican Institute, which is the overseas "democracy promotion" branch of the Republican Party. In 2007, she became communications director at Merrill Lynch.

Tutwiler's replacement was Karen Hughes, a former communications adviser to then Governor of Texas, George W. Bush. A member of the White House Iraq Group, she, together with spin master Karl Rove, Republican political consultant Mary Matalin, and others, had helped design and market the rationale for the 2003 invasion of Iraq. John Brown, a 22-year foreign service veteran, who quit the State Department in protest over the invasion, described Hughes as a "key person in the creation of the crude propaganda that led our country into war" ("The People's Diplomat," 2006). Inheriting the hopeless "public diplomacy" task from Beers and Tutwiler, Hughes's photo ops and PR "listening tours" in the Middle East and other Islamic countries did no more to stop the plunging reputation of the United States in the Muslim world than her predecessors had (Barber, 2007, p. 207; Giraldi, 2007; Rich 2006, p. 223). With plummeting support among Arabs for the U.S. intervention, Hughes resigned her position as coordinator of war public relations at the end of 2007. In 2008, she joined the PR firm Burson-Marsteller, headed by Hillary Clinton's former chief presidential campaign strategist Mark Penn, to return to her more familiar role as a domestic political spinstress.

Benjamin Barber (2007) writes that the PDPA "not only treats America as a brand, but argues that the country's fortunes may depend less on policy realities or traditional identity and behavior, than on brand marketing by experienced advertising and marketing executives" (p. 200). The migration of branding to foreign policy and politics in general reflects the enormous influence of the informational and marketing economy and the authority of agencies of the neoliberal state to privatize and professionalize these critical public domains. Foreign policy is conceived as a selling activity, as if it was just another product to be pitched, like Cola-Cola. The State Department and key congressional members involved in foreign policy are expected to support a privately organized marketing model of politics that deprives citizens of the right of public deliberation (Barber, 2007, p. 205). There is no precise measure of how much the U.S. government spends on "public communications" overall, but, according to a minority staff report, private PR firms (not including projects performed by internal government agency employees) received $88 million in public relations contracts in 2004 alone (Kosar, 2005, pp. 7–8). The State Department's budget for public diplomacy for FY 2009 was $37 million ($36 million in FY 2008) (White House, 2009). The official congressional budget for all forms of public diplomacy in 2005 was increased to $1.2 billion (Johnson, Dale, & Cronin, 2005).

BRANDING EASTERN EUROPEAN "REVOLUTIONS"

The Bush administration had more success in putting propaganda to work in Eastern Europe. In the uprisings that took place in the region starting in 2000, symbolic forms of protest took center stage in Western-assisted efforts to sequentially depose vulnerable and recalcitrant nationalistic political leaders in Serbia, Georgia, and Ukraine without recourse to armed intervention. With the direct advice and financing of numerous U.S. "democracy promotion" groups (and some support from Germany and Britain), local youth activists were taught how to tactically use posters, buttons, logos, graffiti, slogans, citizen mobilization, a revolutionary-sounding lexicon, and the branded term "color revolution," which created a sense that the momentum was not just a political campaign but, rather, a transformational movement.

Working closely with Western European and American agents and advisers, the youth movements *Otpor* [Resistance] in Serbia, *Kmara* [Enough] in Georgia, and *Pora* [It's Time] in Ukraine, which precipitated a set of nonviolent *coups* against, respectively, Slobodan Milošević, Eduard Shevardnadze, and, at least momentarily, Viktor Yanukovych, are now all but vanished, some of their leaders having taken on establishment political identities of their own. Gone are the silhouette clenched-fist logos, the catchy slogans, the Gene Sharp–inspired nonviolent political destabilization tactics,[7] and the numerous other marketing tactics that the rebellious youth took to heart with a lot of support from USAID, Freedom House, the U.S. National Endowment for Democracy (NED), the International Republican Institute (IRI), the National Democratic Institute (NDI),[8] George Soros and his Open Society Institute, and other American institutions.

The democracy promoters' "revolutionary" template involved a "flexible" array of political, financial, technical, branding, and marketing tactics to foment a militant public mood, get people into the streets, and force either an election or a post-election surrender of power to rid the region of the West's undesired incumbents (Sussman & Krader, 2008). As a Kazakhstani researcher analyzed it, political marketing tactics operate in the following fashion:

> The "branding" technology is a tool of psychological manipulation. The counter-elite works hard to synchronize public consciousness by imposing behavioral and identification matrices on society as a form of fashionable behavior: external and internal forces employ psychological,

semiotic, and other mechanisms to plant conscious and subconscious identification with the opposition and its aims in the minds of the people. This makes it much easier to plant political ideas later. (Tastenov 2007, p. 40)

In advance of the elections that were to be held in the three countries, Serbia (2000), Georgia (2003), and Ukraine (2004), IRI helped instigate and choreograph large street demonstrations, as well as design branded symbols of resistance, such as the clenched fist (Traynor, 2005). IRI's Iraq program personnel in fact received *their* training through the institute's CEE programs (National Endowment for Democracy, 2006, p. 36). The uprisings and their icons were reported by jingoist mainstream American media as indicators of a sweeping popular, pro-Western tide. The same media, often acting as much like handmaidens to government as the semi-authoritarian-controlled press that they criticized, all but ignored the massive street protests in the United States, Britain, and many other countries on the eve of the U.S. invasion of Iraq.

The first of the color revolutions took place in Serbia shortly after NATO prepared the ground with a massive air assault designed to destabilize the country, support the breakaway Kosovo region, and bring about the arrest of Milošević. Serbia's *Otpor* youth movement leader, Srdja Popovic, boasted that the struggle for power centered on the manipulation and control of branding and "propaganda":

A battle for "media space" began, with *Otpor* producing low-cost propaganda materials, such as posters, handouts, stickers, and graffiti, using only black and white shades on all propaganda material to solidify "brand recognition." The movement was able to cover every available physical space and "managed to a surprising extent to shape, if not to control, the 'terms of the debate'" . . . The strategy of presenting *Otpor* as the national victim of government repression drew conversions, as stated here, even from within the ranks of the government. (Popovic, 2001)

In the branding and propaganda effort, *Otpor* was not alone. With the support of American PR firms, which generated most of the "news" about the Yugoslavian crisis (Salander, 2007), *Otpor's* political campaign was toasted in the West for its masterful marketing and branding techniques.[9] In fact, the slogans that *Otpor* activists recited and spray-painted on walls were pretested by opinion polls and vetted by American advisers. *Otpor* and Democratic Opposition of Serbia (DOS) spokespeople were tutored on how to handle journalists and "stay on message." DOS marketing specialist, Milan Stevanovic, acknowledged the joint nature of the propaganda effort: "The foreign support was critical . . . This was the first campaign where our strategy was based on real scientific research" (quoted in Dobbs, 2000). Some of the "scientific" campaign tactics behind *Otpor* came from the Serbian company, Strategic Marketing (currently a joint venture with the American market research firm A.C. Nielsen, and British PGM Consulting), "which ran a series of focus groups on behalf of the opposition coalition and the *Otpor* student resistance movement with financial support from Western democracy groups" (Dobbs 2000).

Strategic Marketing displayed the markings of an American-style branding campaign. Each of *Otpor*'s and the other opposition groups' pretested "core messages" was designed to "sell" regime change in much the same way that soft drinks are marketed. The CEO of Strategic Marketing, Srđan Bogosavljević, declared, "We approached the process with a brand to sell and a brand to beat . . . The brand to sell was Koštunica. The brand to beat was Milošević" (quoted in Dobbs, 2000).

Among the keys to a good "revolution" brand were logos. *Otpor* graffitied a black-and-white fist logo on walls, printed it on stickers, and emblazoned it on t-shirts—an image and set of tactics later copied by Georgia's *Kmara* youth movement. USAID paid for 80 tons of stickers reading, "*Gotov je*" ["He's finished"], which young *Otpor* activists pasted on flat surfaces throughout Belgrade and other Serbian cities (Dobbs, 2000). Peter Ackerman and associates, American producers of a propaganda film about the fall of Milošević, *Bringing Down a Dictator* (2002), boasted on the film's website: "*Otpor* became a ubiquitous brand-name, as familiar as Coca-Cola and Nike" ("The Story," n.d.; Sussman, 2010). Ackerman was concurrently head of an interventionist group called the International Center on Nonviolent Conflict and later became board chair of Freedom House. *Otpor*'s co-founder, Ivan Marovic, echoed Ackerman: "Our idea was to use corporate branding in politics . . . The movement has to have a marketing department. We took Coca-Cola as our model" (quoted in Traynor, 2005).

Reasoning that brands were more critical to success than even charismatic but vulnerable leadership, *Otpor* organizers enlisted 20 or so revolving surrogates (Stefanovic, 2000) who took turns standing in for the organization with prepared logos and rehearsed messages. Marovic told National Public Radio's Bob Garfield the following:

> In the 20th century, branding was done by connecting a movement to the leader, so everybody remembers Lech Walesa, or Nelson Mandela, or Mahatma Gandhi. In Serbia, Georgia, and Ukraine, branding was done not by connecting to leaders. Leaders could have been blackmailed or bribed or even maybe killed. You can't do that with brands or ideas. (Garfield, 2004)

That is to say, brands are more durable than citizen organizers and people can be more efficiently mobilized by canned inanimate symbols than by a living, breathing, and vulnerable leader.

Figure 2.1 Logo of the *Otpor* movement in Serbia.

Figure 2.2 Logo of the *Kmara* movement in Georgia.

The "revolution" brand soon became used as a transferable template. In its training of the youth movements in Georgia (*Kmara*) and Ukraine (*Pora*), *Otpor* reproduced the marketing tactics it employed in Serbia. *Pora*, "supported by the [British] Westminster Foundation, brought in Serbian agitators to train 200 [Ukrainian] activists" (Lane, 2009, p. 129). *Otpor* activist, Aleksandar Maric, boasted: "We trained them [Ukrainian youth opposition] in how to set up an organization, how to open local chapters, how to create a 'brand', how to create a logo, symbols, and key messages" (quoted in Bransten, 2004). Freedom House provided *Pora* with $500,000, while another Ukrainian opposition group, *Znayu*, received $50,000 from Freedom House and an additional $1 million from the U.S.-Ukraine Foundation to initiate a teaser-type advertising campaign in 17 Ukrainian cities. "*Znayu* was one of our larger projects in terms of visibility, but it was really just a small part of our whole work," explained an election specialist from Freedom House in Kiev, Juhani Grossman (quoted in MacKinnon, 2007, p. 174).

A Canadian Broadcasting Corporation reporter, Carol Off, who helped produce a CBC documentary, *Anatomy of a Revolution* (2005), looked at the events in 2004–2005 that led to the Ukraine uprising and subsequent election of Yushchenko. She found that foreign money, especially from the United States, was central to that "revolution," which she described as a "carbon copy" of the events staged a year earlier in Georgia. This had much to do with the "Madison Avenue–style branding" efforts of professionals from the United States. When Serbian, Georgian, and Ukrainian student leaders were brought together in Hungary to study techniques of nonviolent conflict, the funding and technical support came from the International Republican Institute, George Soros, and Colonel Robert Helvey, a former U.S. military intelligence expert. In Kiev, Off found that "so many of the same tactics, so many of the same kind of procedures happened in Serbia, but I [also] realized that so many of the same people were there, so many of the same funding agencies were there" (Off, 2005).

What these interventions mean for regional democracy and national sovereignty will take some years to determine. But the early evidence, based on the political behavior of the Western-backed successors to power, does not suggest that the color revolutions lived up to their promise. Indeed, there was nothing at all actually revolutionary about the uprisings in these countries, as they can be seen as little more than intra-elite transfers of power, world capitalist integration of their economies, and expectations of their membership in NATO. There were no radical social or political transformations to justify calling them "revolutionary." The appropriation of the term in these cases is merely promotional in character.

Since the "orange revolution" in Ukraine, the election of Yushchenko, and the government's turn toward joining the EU, Ukrainian state leaders have more actively taken up the baneful art of modern political promotion. Leading up to the scheduled 2010 election, all three major candidates for the presidency—Yushchenko, the prime minister Yulia Tymoshenko, and former prime minister Viktor Yanukovych—imported heavyweight American political consultants to manage or advise their image campaigns. Tymoshenko had the services of the consulting firm AKPD Message and Media, founded by David Axelrod, which ran Barack Obama's 2008 presidential campaign. She also brought in American pollsters John Anzalone and Jeff Link of Link Strategies. Incumbent president Yushchenko employed the services of the American polling and political strategy firm Greenberg Quinlan Rosner and political consultant Jordan Lieberman, and, as of 2009, had advisers in his camp who are linked to Bill Clinton. Yanukovych, the *bête noire* of the Americans in 2004, hired the Washington-based, high-powered Republican Party firm of Paul Manafort, which advised the 2008 presidential campaign of John McCain. The persuasive lobbying power of these firms in Washington is clearly a major factor in their selection (Stern, 2009; Sussman, 2010). But in 2010, it was Yanukovych who prevailed, and his presidential victory was sweet revenge for the humiliation he previously suffered, ending the saga of the U.S.-backed "orange revolution."

BRANDED STATE IDENTITIES IN CENTRAL AND EASTERN EUROPE

Central and Eastern Europe's national identities, subdued in certain respects, but not suppressed during the Soviet period despite the communist parties' official "internationalism," have been refocused in recent years. Most states in the region seek either a more Europeanized identity or realignment with the center of the former Soviet Union, the Russian Federation. Many people in the region still associate national identity with a time when social welfare was an accepted public function of the state. With the onslaught of privatization, the notion of "public" has been largely discarded through the commercialization and "balkanization" of public spaces and institutions, a conversion to private automobile transportation, largely unplanned, big box consumerist culture and institutions, and a garish importation of corporate logos. In recent years, most Eastern European cities, for example, have experienced a dramatic reduction of public transit, leading to "increasing levels of congestion, pollution, and social isolation" (Stanilov, 2007, p. 277). The so-called free market has taxed the poorer Eastern European states in ways unimagined in the initial eagerness of several state leaders for liberalization.

Nation branding among the CEE countries began to take off with the collapse of the Soviet Union and its allied regimes, creating an almost unobstructed pathway to neoliberal penetration of the region. From the public relations industry perspective, what the CEE countries immediately required in order to integrate with the West was an image makeover in order to remove the taint of socialism, bureaucratism, and the Western "orientalizing" of its "balkanized" cultures. The region now has the fastest advertising growth rate in the world ("World Media 2007," 2007). CEE's nationhoods are circumscribed by the prevailing desire of state leaders to integrate their economies with that of the EU and the larger transnational economic order. Nation branding is part of this strategic initiative. From the EU perspective, branding also serves to modify historical nationalism, particularly of Eastern European states, thereby "contributing greatly to the further pacification of Europe" (van Ham, 2001, p. 3). However, it also forces the region's nations to compete against each other for branded supremacy, inducing each to outdo and denigrate the other.

Most of the CEE countries have attempted to refashion themselves to appeal to the EU members, to the larger foreign investment community, to tourist trade, and to other industries. In 1998, the Hungarian government briefly created a "Country Image Centre" to help promote itself abroad, but it lasted only until the next government came to power, which dismissed the initiative as not nation but political branding (Kulcsár & Yum, this volume; Szondi, 2008, p. 201).

Of all the countries in the region, Russia clearly remains the holy grail of the international business community as well as the principal target of U.S. geopolitical *realpolitik*—a term with which nation brander Simon Anholt identifies his work (Jansen, 2008, p. 133). Russia's absorption into the world economy has been made more certain by the presence of transnational consumerist enterprises, including Coca-Cola, McDonald's, IKEA, American Express, Nestlé, Wrigley, Proctor & Gamble, Unilever, Nike, Levi Strauss, PepsiCo, Philip Morris, GM, and others. These corporations, in turn, are supported by the consumer marketing data delivered by such brand research companies as WPP's TGI and TNS Gallup (O'Leary, 2008). People such as Rory Davenport, a leading Western PR consultant in the region and managing director of the Washington-based Qorvis Communications, are a major reason for Russia's accelerating market status. Russia's annual advertising market expanded at an average rate of 41% from 2000 to 2006, when it reached sixth place internationally ("World Media 2007," 2007).

With an eye to joining the competitive surge in attracting foreign investors and tourist currency, branding and place marketing have become important concerns of CEE state policy. In the Czech Republic, for example, this is aided by "a group of internationally renowned consultancies and producers in the form of the Association for Foreign Investment" (Capik, 2007, p. 156). Poland has an Institute of Polish Brand, with close ties to the government, which has collaborated with the British branding company, Saffron, to sell Poland's national image (see Surowiec, this volume).

Kaneva (2007), who looked at how Bulgaria attempted to burnish a brand image, targeted at both Bulgarians and Western Europeans, to make the country a desirable candidate for EU membership (which it achieved along with Romania in 2007), expressed skepticism about the compelling necessity of nation branding. For one thing, as she found, a country's actual social conditions and relations of power matter little to image makers. Nation branding, she argued, ignores the historical foundation of the state: "Generally, the goal of marketing research is *not* to critique social relations but, rather, to identify modes of action that would improve the strategic positions of agents within specific competitive fields" (italics in original). State-sponsored advertising that sells the nation to EU audiences is lodged within certain assumptions about Western Europe as a "developed" and "civilized" model to which Bulgaria must aspire and thus represents a form of "self-colonization," an assimilation to a notion of a unified, albeit superficial, "Europeanness." But, as another author put it, "Nation branding does not allow for citizens to play a significant [civic] role in the branding process" (Widler, 2007, p. 144).

BRANDED NATIONS, SOVEREIGNTY, AND DEMOCRACY

The maintenance of the corporate state requires an intensification of public persuasion through various forms of promotional speech and text in order to divert citizens from the cognitive dissonance that follows from the unwillingness of the neoliberal state to protect public interests. Producers and consumers, more than citizens, are the constitutive elements of a neoliberal state. Indeed, the notion of consumer is becoming convergent with labor, as the informational economy breaks down the separation by treating the data extracted from, and produced by, citizens as a (largely uncompensated) form of created value intrinsic to informational goods and services. It is but one more step to treating the nation as a commodity branded for consumption.

Branding is an attempt to bring order in a networked informational economy that is unleashed from the more structured nexus of Fordist-era production and consumption and requires a stable system of networking to maintain and expand its reach and power (Lash, 2002, pp. 149–150). As such, there can be no genuinely organic or democratic character to nation branding as it reconstitutes the state as the "intellectual property" of an integrated, elite set of domestic and external actors. As nation branding is intended primarily for external legitimation, there are important implications about its use with regard to state sovereignty and domestic democratic development.

For many, nation branding represents a profaning of the sacred idea of national identity. Its use is premised on the identification of a country by calculations of its most competitive image, not what its own people regard as the useful pursuits of their state. The principal objectives of nation branding are concerned with attracting foreign investment, encouraging trade, and supporting tourism. The trade and investment designs of branding clearly point to a small class of transnational executives and stock owners seeking networked profit opportunities through ties with local compradors who are likely to engage in corrupt practices to secure the relationship. And tourist-oriented branding is "conducted from uneven power bases as encoded in commodified identities," fortifying hegemonies of class, race, and gender (Mayes, 2008, pp. 127–128).

Nation branding involves techniques similar to polling. It's regarded by its defenders as a means of capturing authentic internal and external images of a country. But as external polling is not a substitute for, or even a supplement to, deliberative democratic discourse, neither can branding be a genuine reflection of what images citizens wish to project of themselves, or whether citizens even desire to sell themselves through marketing measures to outsiders. Branding can only simplify and homogenize; CEE nations are a vast imbricated mosaic of peoples, cultures, histories, and nations within nations that require sophisticated understandings of their great diversity and internal struggles for identity.

It is hard to determine how seriously to take nation branding as it appears to be an exaggerated extension of neoliberal globalization and commodification—the notion that everything is for sale and that the potential market value of a nation (which some economists actually calculate) can be traded on international exchanges like stock equity. The presumption is that if the brand value of the nation declines, so does the nation itself. As more wisely chosen U.S. government officials might have discovered, it is all the more difficult to sell a "democratic" image of the United States and defend the rationale for invasion in the Middle East and elsewhere when unemployment is growing, income for the majority is falling, higher education and medical care are the most expensive in the world, and where nearly 20% of children live in poverty. The real "product" of a nation is derived from the energy discharged by its citizens, not the fetishized logos and ideological objectifications of marketers. Nations with happy and well-cared-for citizens do not need to have themselves marketed or branded. Their actions and degree of well-being speak much louder than their images. As Henri Lefebvre (1991) noted, drawing on Hegel and Marx, "there can be no thought, no reflection, without language, and no language without a material underpinning" (p. 402).

Moreover, the severe recession in the world economy in recent years has had a devastating impact on Central and Eastern Europe, leading to spiraling downturns in production, exports, finance, tourism, investment, and GDP, not unlike the trauma unleashed by "shock therapy" in the years immediately following the collapse of the Soviet Union. Since 2008, tourism and foreign direct investment (FDI), two critical sources of hard currency in the region, have badly suffered. This is not a favorable condition for nation branding efforts—or for advertising and marketing of any kind, where spending, in fact, has declined in recent years. The economic downturn and political repression have also led to greater skepticism about the democratic claims of the "color revolutions," resulting in the delegitimation of several governments in the region, including Saakashvili in Georgia and Yushchenko in Ukraine, who lost the presidency in 2010. What their initial elections demonstrated is that marketing and branding do not have lasting impacts when the claims of leadership itself are found suspect.

However, pressure on the region toward economic integration with the West, particularly among those states not already members of the European Union, will continue to drive competitive, externally oriented marketing initiatives, including nation branding. In light of the 2010 Greek economic debacle, this strategy is bound to fail and leave most people in the region worse off than they were before global market fundamentalism was introduced. Citizens across most of Central and Eastern Europe and the governments that assert their leadership would be better served concentrating on the substance of democracy and development rather than on creative images that mask current real conflicts, inequalities, human suffering, lack of political freedom, and the decline of social services.

NOTES

1. This chapter draws in part from my book *Branding Democracy: U.S. Regime Change in Post-Soviet Eastern Europe* (Peter Lang, 2010). I wish to thank my colleague, Dr. Evguenia N. Davidova, for her thoughtful comments on an earlier draft of this chapter.
2. The definition of the CEE region varies from one list to another. In this chapter, I am including, for geographically descriptive purposes, Ukraine and Georgia under this classification, two countries that seek membership in the European Union.
3. In November 2001, the Acxiom Corporation offered to conduct for the U.S. Department of Justice surveillance of websites dealing with sensitive political issues, such as abortion, white power, religion, immigration, and foreign policy and to include contact information from such sites. In 2003, the company passed on personal data on millions of JetBlue and other airline customers, without their consent, to a firm conducting an anti-terrorism study for the U.S. Department of Defense (Gunn, 2006).
4. In Uganda, for instance, Hill & Knowlton had performed services for the state at a cost of $650,000. Uganda's per capita GDP in 2004 was a mere $300. CNN also cashed in by contracting with the Ugandan government, under president-for-life Yoweri Museveni, an advertising purchase of $1 million (Kahn, 2006, p. 90).
5. Richard Nixon's close political advisers, H. R. Haldeman, John Ehrlichman, and Charles Coulson, had come from J. Walter Thompson. All three were eventually convicted for their illegal activities in the Watergate scandal.
6. A study written for the journal found that 655,000 Iraqis had died between March 2003 and June 2006 (see Burnham, Lafta, Doocy, & Roberts, 2006).
7. Gene Sharp's most influential work, and the one used in Serbia to instruct the youth movement on nonviolent methods of overthrowing governments, is *From Dictatorship to Democracy* (1993/2002).
8. The IRI and NDI are foreign-focused "democracy promotion" organizations of the two respective U.S. political parties, which in turn receive their money from the government-funded National Endowment for Democracy and from private corporate sources.
9. Peter Ackerman, while on the Albert Einstein Institution board, praised the symbolic actions of *Otpor* in his made-for-television documentary *Bringing Down a Dictator* (2002). He later became more actively involved in the region through his strategic nonviolent action training organization, the International Center on Nonviolent Conflict.

REFERENCES

About S.O.S.: Overview. (n.d.). Society of the Spectacle. Retrieved December 16, 2010, from http://www.societyofthespectacleclothing.com/joom/about-sos.html

Anderson, B. (1993). *Imagined communities: Reflections on the origin and spread of nationalism*. London: Verso.

Andersson, M. (2007). Region branding: The case of the Baltic Sea region. *Place Branding and Public Diplomacy, 3*(2), 120–130.

Anholt, S. (2002). Nation branding: A continuing theme. *Brand Management, 10*(1), 59–60.

Anholt, S. (2005). Plug into your national brand: Interview with Simon Anholt. *International Trade Forum, 4.* Retrieved December 16, 2010, from http://www.tradeforum.org/news/fullstory.php/aid/948/Plug_into_Your_National_Brand.html

Barber, B. (2007). *Con$umed: How markets corrupt children, infantilize adults, and swallow citizens whole.* New York: Norton.

Biderman, D. (2010, January 15). 11 minutes of action. *The Wall Street Journal.* Retrieved December 16, 2010, from http://online.wsj.com/article/SB100014240 5274870428120457500285205556140 6.html

Brand America: Yankee Doodle branding. (2004/2005, December/January). *Brand Strategy.* Retrieved December 16, 2010, from http://www.businessfordiplomaticaction.org/news/articles/yankeedoodlebrandingarticle.pdf

Bransten, J. (2004, December 20). Ukraine: Part homegrown uprising, part imported production? *Radio Free Europe/Radio Liberty.* Retrieved October 9, 2007, from http://www.rferl.org/featuresarticle/2004/12/be8e5d97–7eaf-404e-8e91-e21723ff74b6.html

Burnham, G., Lafta, R., Doocy, S., & Roberts, L. (2006, October 11). Mortality after the 2003 invasion of Iraq: A cross-sectional cluster sample survey. *Lancet.* Retrieved December 16, 2010, from http://brusselstribunal.org/pdf/lancet111006.pdf

Capik, P. (2007). Organising FDI promotion in Central-Eastern European regions. *Place Branding, 3*(2), 152–163.

Castells, M. (1996). The rise of the network society. Cambridge, MA: Blackwell.

Cockburn, A., & St. Clair, J. (2004). *Imperial crusaders: Iraq, Afghanistan and Yugoslavia.* New York: Verso.

Critchlow, J. (2004). Public diplomacy during the Cold War: The record and its consequences. *Journal of Cold War Studies, 6*(1), 75–89.

Debord, G. (1994). *Society of the spectacle.* New York: Zone Books.

Dobbs, M. (2000, December 11). U.S. advice guided Milosevic opposition. *The Washington Post.* Retrieved December 24, 2010, from http://www.washingtonpost.com/ac2/wp-dyn?pagename=article&contentId=A18395-2000Dec3

Dumenco, S. (2001, November 12). Stopping Spin Laden. *New York Magazine.* Retrieved December 16, 2010, from http://nymag.com/nymetro/news/media/features/5379

Dyer-Witheford, N. (1999). *Cyber-Marx: Cycles and circuits of struggle in high-technology capitalism.* Urbana: University of Illinois Press.

Falconi, T. (2006). How big is public relations (and why does it matter?): The economic impact of our profession. Institute for Public Relations. Retrieved December 12, 2010, from http://www.instituteforpr.org/files/uploads/Falconi_Nov06.pdf

Fouts, J. (2006). Executive summary. In J. Fouts (Ed.), *Public diplomacy, practitioners, policy makers, and public opinion* (pp. 8–19). Los Angeles: USC Center on Public Diplomacy. Retrieved December 12, 2010, from http://uscpublicdiplomacy.org/pdfs/USCCPD_PublicDiplomacy_WPO_2006.pdf

Garfield, B. (2004, December 3). Revolution, Inc. [Transcript of broadcast]. *On the media.* National Public Radio. Retrieved December 12, 2010, from http://www.onthemedia.org/yore/transcripts/transcripts_120304_revolution.html

Giraldi, P. (2007, March 7). Clueless in Gaza: Karen Hughes and the collapse of American public diplomacy. *Antiwar.com.* Retrieved December 14, 2010, from http://www.antiwar.com/orig/giraldi.php?articleid=10632

Goebbels, J. (n.d.). Goebbels' principles of propaganda. Retrieved December 24, 2010, from http://www.psywarrior.com/Goebbels.html

Gunn, A. (2006, February 2). Acxiom pitched feds on large-scale Web-surveillance project. *Computerworld*. Retrieved December 16, 2010, from http://www.computerworld.com/s/article/print/108348/Acxiom_pitched_feds_on_large_scale_Web_surveillance_project

Hagenbaugh, B. (2002, December 12). U.S. Manufacturing jobs fading away fast. *USA Today*. Retrieved December 16, 2010, from http://www.usatoday.com/money/economy/2002-12-12-manufacture_x.htm

Jansen, S. C. (2008). Designer nations: Neo-liberal nation branding—Brand Estonia. *Social Identities, 14*(1), 121–142.

Johnson, S., Dale, H., & Cronin, P. (2005). Strengthening U.S. public diplomacy requires organization, coordination, and strategy. *The Heritage Foundation*. Retrieved December 16, 2010, from http://www.heritage.org/Research/Public-Diplomacy/bg1875.cfm

Kahn, J. (2006, November/December). A brand-new approach. *Foreign Policy*, pp. 90–92.

Kaneva, N. (2007). Meet the "new" Europeans: EU accession and the branding of Bulgaria. *Advertising & Society Review 8*(4). Retrieved October 20, 2010, from http://muse.jhu.edu/journals/asr/v008/8.4kaneva.html

Kendrick, A., & Fullerton, J. (2004). Advertising as public diplomacy: Attitude change among international audiences. *Journal of Advertising Research, 44*(3), 297–311.

Klein, N. (2002, March 10). Brand USA: America's attempt to market itself abroad using advertising principles is destined to fail. *Los Angeles Times*. Retrieved December 10, 2010, from http://articles.latimes.com/2002/mar/10/opinion/op-klein

Klein, N. (2007). *The shock doctrine: The rise of disaster capitalism*. New York: Henry Holt.

Kosar, K. (2005). *Public relations and propaganda: Restrictions on executive agency activities*. [CRS report for Congress]. Congressional Research Service. Retrieved October 10, 2010, from http://www.fas.org/sgp/crs/misc/RL32750.pdf

Kuchment, A. (2001, November 26). Selling the U.S.A.: Old-style propaganda meets Madison Avenue spin as America gears up to reinvent its image in the Muslim world. *Newsweek*, p. 66.

Lambert, B. (2003). *In the marketing mix*. Unpublished paper presented at the Professional Sales Symposium of the United Professional Sales Association, Washington, DC, November 24.

Lane, D. (2009). "Coloured revolution" as a political phenomenon. *Journal of Communist Studies and Transition Politics, 25*(2/3), 113–135.

Lash, S. (2002). *Critique of information*. Thousand Oaks, CA: Sage.

Lefebvre, H. (1991). *The production of space*. Cambridge, MA: Blackwell.

Lippmann, W. (1927). *The phantom public*. New York: Macmillan.

Lugar, R. (2009, February 26). To win hearts and minds, get back in the game. *Foreign Policy*. Retrieved October 12, 2010, from http://experts.foreignpolicy.com/posts/2009/02/26/to_win_hearts_and_minds_get_back_in_the_game

MacKinnon, M. (2007). *The new Cold War: Revolutions, rigged elections, and pipeline politics in the former Soviet Union*. New York: Carroll & Graf.

Mayes, R. (2008). A place in the sun: The politics of place, identity and branding. *Place Branding and Public Diplomacy, 4*(2), 124–135.

McInerny, V. (2003, April 29). Presenting a new ideology the clothing line aims for style and quality without designer prices. *The Oregonian*, C-1.

Moor, L. (2007). *The rise of brands*. New York: Berg.

Moor, L. (2008). Neoliberalism and promotional culture. *Soundings*. Retrieved October 20, 2010, from http://www.lwbooks.co.uk/journals/soundings/cultures_capitalism/cultures_capitalism10.html

Myers, J. (2009, September 14). No advertising industry recovery anticipated until 2011. *The Huffington Post*. Retrieved December 16, 2010, from http://www.huffingtonpost.com/jack-myers/media-economist-jack-myer_b_285911.html

National Endowment for Democracy. (2006). *The backlash against democracy assistance*. A report prepared by the National Endowment for Democracy for Senator Richard G. Lugar, Chairman of Committee on Foreign Relations, United States Senate. Retrieved December 24, 2010, from http://www.ned.org/docs/backlash06.pdf

O'Leary, N. (2008, February 1). The rise of BRIC: How Brazil, Russia, India and China are reshaping the marketing world. *Adweek*. Retrieved December 16, 2010, from http://www.adweek.com/aw/content_display/special-reports/other-reports/e3ibd2a4d5f94f9578bb5e64247c12ae3b1?pn=4

Off, C. (2005, February 16). Anatomy of a revolution [Interview by Rick Maccinnes-Rae]. *Dispatches*. Canadian Broadcasting Corporation.

Olins, W. (2005, December 3). *Nation branding in Europe*. Retrieved December 1, 2009, from http://www.sbs.ox.ac.uk/news/archives/EMBA/National+branding+in+Europe.htm

The people's diplomat: An interview with John H. Brown. (2006, January 11). *Press Action*. Retrieved October 12, 2010, from http://www.pressaction.com/news/weblog/full_article/brown01112006

Popovic, S. (2001, January 31). An analytical overview of the application of Gene Sharp's theory of nonviolent action in Milosevic's Serbia. *The Communication Initiative Network*. Retrieved December 16, 2010, from http://www.comminit.com/en/node/274331/348

Rich, F. (2006). *The greatest story ever sold: The decline and fall of truth—from 9/11 to Katrina*. New York: Penguin.

Risen, C. (2005, March 13). Re-branding America. *The Boston Globe*. Retrieved December 12, 2010, from http://www.boston.com/news/globe/ideas/articles/2005/03/13/re_branding_america?pg=full

Salander, T. (2007). How the public is led into wars [Book review]. *Current Concerns*. Retrieved December 16, 2010, from http://www.currentconcerns.ch/index.php?id=439

Sharp, G. (2002). *From dictatorship to democracy: A conceptual framework for liberation*. Boston: Albert Einstein Institution. (Original work published 1993) Retrieved December 16, 2010, from http://www.aeinstein.org/organizations/org/FDTD.pdf

Sherman, L. (2009, October 16). World's most well-liked countries. *Forbes*. Retrieved December 16, 2010, from http://www.forbes.com/2009/10/05/well-liked-countries-lifestyle-real-estate-tourism-america.html

Smith, A. (2001). *Nationalism: Key concepts*. Cambridge, UK: Polity Press.

Snow, N. (2003). *Information war: American propaganda, free speech and opinion control since 9–11*. New York: Seven Stories Press.

Stanilov, K. (2007). Democracy, markets, and public space in the transitional societies of Central and Eastern Europe. In K. Stanilov (Ed.), *The post-socialist city: Urban form and space transformations in Central and Eastern Europe after socialism* (pp. 269–283). Dordrecht, Netherlands: Springer.

Stefanovic, N. (2000, May 13). What is *Otpor*? Fist in the eye of the regime. *Vreme*. Retrieved October 10, 2007, http://www.ex-yupress.com/vreme/vreme72.html

Stern, D. (2009, October 30). Can US political consultants sway Ukrainian voters? *Globalpost*. Retrieved December 12, 2010, from http://www.globalpost.com/dispatch/ukraine/091030/akpd-consulting-ukrainian-presidential-campaign

Stokes, M. (2009, October 7). Estonia economic outlook, Q4 2009. *Roubini Global Economics*. Retrieved December 12, 2010, from http://www.roubini. com/analysis/96203.php

The story. (n.d.). *Aforcemorepowerful.org*. Retrieved December 24, 2010, from http://www.aforcemorepowerful.org/films/bdd/story/index.php

Subcommittee on International Organizations, Human Rights, and Oversight. (2008, June 11). *The decline in America's reputation: Why?* [Report]. House Committee on Foreign Affairs, U.S. House of Representatives. Retrieved December 12, 2010, from http://foreignaffairs.house.gov/110/42566.pdf

Sussman, G. (1997). *Communication, technology, and politics in the information age*. Thousand Oaks, CA: Sage.

Sussman, G. (2010). *Branding democracy: U.S. regime change in post-Soviet Eastern Europe*. New York: Peter Lang.

Sussman, G., & Krader, S. (2008). Template revolutions: Marketing U.S. regime change in Eastern Europe. *Westminster Papers in Communication and Culture*, 5(3), 91–112.

Szondi, G. (2007). The role and challenges of country branding in transition countries: The Central and Eastern European experience. *Place Branding and Public Diplomacy*, 3(1), 8–20.

Szondi, G. (2008). Country promotion and image management: The case of Hungary. In K. Dinnie (Ed.), *Nation branding: Concepts, issues, practice* (pp. 201–205). Oxford, UK: Butterworth-Heinemann.

Tastenov, A. (2007). The color revolution phenomenon: From classical theory to unpredictable practices. *Journal of Social and Political Studies*, 1, 32–44.

Teslik, L. (2007, November 6). Anholt: Countries must earn better images through smart policy [Interview with Simon Anholt]. *Council on Foreign Relations*. Retrieved December 12, 2010, from http://www.cfr.org/publication/14719/ anholt.html?breadcrumb=%2F

Traynor, I. (2005, June 6). Young democracy guerrillas join forces. *The Guardian*. Retrieved December 16, 2010, from http://www.mjaft.org/pdf/the_guardians_activism_festival.pdf

U.S. Department of Labor. (n.d.). *Occupational outlook handbook, 2010–11 edition*. Bureau of Labor Statistics. Retrieved December 1, 2010, from http://www. bls.gov/oco/ocoS020.htm#emply.

Van Ham, P. (2001). The rise of the brand state: The postmodern politics of image and reputation. *Foreign Affairs*, 80(5), 2–6.

White House. (2009). Detailed information on the Public Diplomacy assessment. *ExpectMore.gov*. Retrieved December 12, 2010, from http://www.whitehouse. gov/omb/expectmore/detail/10004600.2006.html

Widler, J. (2007). Nation branding: With pride against prejudice. *Place Branding and Public Diplomacy*, 3(2), 144–150.

World Bank. (2008). *World development indicators, 2008*. Washington, DC: International Bank for Reconstruction and Development.

World Media 2007: Rich man poor man. (2007, March 30). *Campaign*. Retrieved December 16, 2010, from http://www.campaignlive.co.uk/news/login/647732

3 Brand Interrupted

The Impact of Alternative Narrators on Nation Branding in the Former Second World

Robert A. Saunders

INTRODUCTION

In 1991, the USSR's union republics gained independence, birthing 15 new countries across two continents. In 1993, Czechoslovakia's "velvet divorce" added two more nation-states to the map. During the Wars of Yugoslav Secession (1991–2000), the Socialist Federal Republic of Yugoslavia's constituent republics won their freedom, contributing half a dozen new members to the international community. These states have debuted at a rather complicated juncture in history, one in which deterritorialized information and communication technologies (ICTs) have become nearly ubiquitous, economic interdependence is a daily reality, and cultural hybridization is the norm. According to Vladimir Lebedenko (2004), Deputy Director of Russia's Ministry of Foreign Affairs, "Most of these newly independent states were faced with the need for self-identification and assertion of their image in the international arena" (p. 71).

As a consequence of these changed circumstances, some authors claim that the community of nations has come to function as a marketplace where states must define and differentiate themselves in order to attract foreign direct investment (FDI), add value to their export products, promote tourism, and develop their diplomatic and strategic alliances (Anholt, 2007; van Ham, 2001). This set of activities is most commonly identified as nation branding, and the political elites of many post-totalitarian countries have taken up this mantle with pride and purpose. However, in a world where CNN has displaced the diplomatic pouch, where YouTube trumps the *International Herald Tribune*, and where Bono wields greater influence than the president of Nigeria, it is painfully evident that any country's branding strategy must anticipate, negate, and even accommodate its unwanted "branding" by alternative actors.

From the "belligerent branding" (Anholt, 2007) of academics like Stephen Kotkin (2002), who labeled the entirety of post-Soviet space as "Trashcanistan," to popular films like *The Terminal* (2004), which paints post-communist Europeans as naive, backward rubes, to *Our Dumb World: The Onion's Atlas of the Planet Earth* (Dikkers, 2007), which uses parody to revive old and create new stereotypes of the former Second World as a dangerous, xenophobic neverland, this chapter explores the impact of external narrators on the emerging "brand states" of post-totalitarian Europe and Eurasia. Special attention is paid to parody and response, particularly the often surreal battles between (Western) cultural producers and (Eastern European/Eurasian) national governments for the right to determine a given country's nation brand. In this chapter, I focus particularly on the cases of Kazakhstan, Slovakia, and Albania.

In addition to country-specific studies, I also interrogate the Western tendency to lump all post-communist/post-Soviet states together into an unknown but instantly recognizable whole, lacking distinction or difference, and how such trends interrupt the branding efforts of individual states. Here, I focus on the spoof travel guide *Molvanîa: A Land Untouched by Modern Dentistry* (Cilauro, Gleisner, & Sitch, 2004) and related projects, including the country's (fake) Eurovision entry, Zladko "Zlad" Vladcik's "Elektronik Supersonik" video and single. I also discuss the continuing use of the former Second World as a propitious location for the generation and/or hosting of villains in popular literature and films, from J. K. Rowling's forbidding "Albania" to Austin Powers' fatuous "Kreplachistan," and how such *praxes* both reflect and advance Cold War frames of thought.

This study, which relies heavily on discourse analysis, is grounded in literature and analytic methodologies drawn from the fields of nation branding, popular geopolitics, and media studies. I employ a constructivist approach to international relations, that is, one which focuses on the socially constructed nature of world politics, particularly state-to-state interaction. The chapter attempts to add to the developing field of postmodern diplomacy, with a particular focus on how relations between states are adapting to new information and communication paradigms that allow for nongovernmental organizations, individual actors, and transnational communities to make their voices heard. I problematize the proposition that national brands can be tightly controlled and managed by national governments. Rather, I argue that narratives of nationhood—whether they are thought of as "brands" or not—are continually negotiated and, moreover, that in the era of globalized media flows, these negotiations have come to include new, extra-national actors and narrators.

ON NATIONAL IMAGE AND NATION BRANDING

National image has long been recognized for its impact on relations between countries. Likewise, a state's reputation is a vital tool for achieving foreign policy goals. In international politics, the practices of policymakers are girded by their own national self-image (*Selbstbild*), as well as how other nations or cultures perceive their country (*Fremdbild*). Frank Louis Rusciano (2003) argues that world opinion—or the "more or less consensual

perception" (p. 361) of a state's reputation—is integral to a country's negotiation of its national identity. Joseph S. Nye, Jr. (2004) suggests that a
positive national image provides the ability to entice and attract other
countries; such attraction often leads to acquiescence or imitation. Consequently, national image and country reputation are major components of
alliance-building and figure prominently in international conflict. While
older countries enjoy well-established national images at home and abroad,
the past century has seen the emergence of roughly 100 new nations that
face a double challenge. They are charged first with crystallizing a coherent
national image in the domestic realm. Secondarily, states carry the burden
of transmitting a positive country image to the world community.

Such concerns are especially heightened in the current global information age. The spread of ICTs, the purported victory of the neoliberal
system, and the deepening of complex economic interdependence have
made governments ever more attentive to their national images. Borrowing from the field of business management, international relations scholars
have begun to explore the management of national image through strategic policy initiatives, targeted public diplomacy, and discrete programs
intended to alter global perception on the elite and mass levels. This new
field of inquiry investigates *nation branding*, a phenomenon that is distinct
from national image due to the active rather than passive nature of policy
elites in the shaping, changing, and maintaining of their country's image.
In short, nation branding is the practice of *brand management* applied to
a country's national image. Recognizing this distinction between national
image and nation branding, scholarship in the latter field has expanded
greatly over the past decade (see, e.g., Anholt, 2007; Aronczyk, 2009; Dinnie, 2008; Morgan, 2002). However, it should be noted that there is much
disagreement among scholars as to the implications of rethinking nationhood through the prism of brand mangement.

In nearly every corner of the globe, polities are now actively engaged in
the building, maintenance, and protection of their national brands. Peter
van Ham (2001) argues that the importance of creating a "brand state"
through effective image projection and maintenance of a dependable reputation is now the paramount concern of the postmodern political system.
Simon Anholt (2002), who coined the term "nation branding" in 1996, suggests that brands are gradually becoming "the dominant channel of communication for national identity" (p. 233), and Melissa Aronczyk (2009)
argues that "brand has become the dominant genre by which the nation is
expressed" (p. 292). State branding is particularly important for reinforcing positive images and blunting or negating unflattering ones. Effective
branding depends on the content, resonance, and reception of a country's
image abroad. Like any product, a country's image is "multifaceted and
may carry large amounts of both factual and affective information" (Papadopoulos & Heslop, 2002, p. 296). This brand plays a pivotal role in the
decision-making process for those nations, firms, or individuals interested

in doing business in said country. However, unlike brands in the corporate world where imitation is the norm, nation brands are unique properties; that is, no two nations are exactly alike (Jaworski & Fosher, 2003). Furthermore, national brands must reflect reality and avoid contradictions in messaging; failure to do so leaves the state open to charges of cynicism or hypocrisy and may result in severe damage to its reputation (Grimes, 2005). Lastly, states must increasingly deal with alternative narrators of their national identities and state brands, a troubling reality that has disproportionately affected the world's newest countries.

THE PROBLEMS OF NATIONAL IMAGE
IN THE POST–SECOND WORLD

The past two decades have seen the emergence of a plethora of new, relatively unknown nations. Elsewhere (Saunders, 2008), I have described these as the "Third Wave" of countries that gained independence during the 20th century. In the wake of the Great War (1914–1918), the demise of the Ottoman, Habsburg, and Romanov empires launched a host of new nations onto the world stage, including Iraq, Czechoslovakia, and Latvia. After World War II, decolonization in the so-called Third World nearly doubled the number of internationally recognized states, with former colonies such as Tunisia, Ghana, and Indonesia winning their independence from the Western European imperial powers.

Most recently, the dissolution of the federal states of the Union of Soviet Socialist Republics (USSR), Yugoslavia, and Czechoslovakia produced 23 new countries; it is this collection of states that I will focus on in this chapter. This "Third Wave" of newly independent states face a host of challenges, which were undreamed of by their counterparts in the "first" (1917–1932) and "second" (1946–1975) waves of decolonization and imperial dissolution during the 20th century.

These new countries must grapple with the difficulties posed by the triple threat of global economic interdependence, cultural hybridization, and the ebbing of state sovereignty wrought by the increasing power of non-state actors, including multinational corporations (MNCs), intergovernmental organizations (IGOs), international financial institutions (IFIs), private military companies (PMCs), supranational judicial systems, and global civic networks. In such an environment, these new states have had to accept that marketing, advertising, and branding have become integral components of statecraft. As one scans the vast political geography of the post–Second World, it quickly becomes evident that even the most unsavory regimes have become obsessed with nation branding, as evidenced by Abkhazia's "I Love Abkhazia" campaign and Belarus' decision to hire British public relations firm Bell Pottinger to improve its image (see Walker, 2007, 2009).

The Newly Independent States of Eurasia (NISE), which once made up the Soviet Union, share a set of particular challenges as they seek to brand (or re-brand) themselves. First, these new polities have had to grapple with the realization that the totality of the Soviet Union's national image was greater than the sum of its parts due to the cessation of the "remarkable ability of Moscow's totalitarians to project such a dynamic and imposing image" (Dobriansky, 1963, p. 129). Consequently, each post–Cold War successor state enjoys less, not more, brand awareness than they did as union republics of the USSR. This projection factor is echoed by other authors:

> Given the closeness of the Soviet information space, the level of [Western] interest in the Soviet social experiment was determined not so much by the country's real accomplishments as by the way they were reflected in information provided by information channels specially created for the purpose (the Cominform, Sovinformbureau, TASS, and others). (Semenenko, Lapkin, & Pantin, 2007, p. 80)

One country, the Russian Federation, is partially exempt from such brand space attrition as it is—for good and ill—the political, military, economic, cultural, and ideological successor of the defunct Soviet Union (though the country's internationally recognized weakness under Boris Yeltsin certainly weakened Russia's "Q score" around the world).[1]

In his 2002 essay "Trashcanistan," Stephen Kotkin famously described the entire post-Soviet region as a "dreadful checkerboard of parasitic states and statelets, government-led extortion rackets and gangs in power, mass refugee camps, and shadow economies" (p. 27). This tendency is clearly exemplified in the James Bond films of the 1990s, which updated stereotypes of Russians without abandoning Cold War ideological orientations (Dodds, 2003), thus making them into what Mark Lipovetsky calls, "former Soviets" rather than "post-Soviets" (Lipovetsky & Leiderman, 2008, p. 200). In *GoldenEye* (1995), one of the principal villains is the Georgian-Russian Xenia Onatopp (played by Famke Janssen), a *femme fatale* who achieves sexual satisfaction through killing her victims, notably by "gleefully crush[ing] her adversaries with her nutcracker thighs" (Malanowski, 2000). Onatopp personifies the hypersexualized archetype of the post-Soviet Russian woman (one of the few exports to the West during the calamitous years of Russia's "shock therapy"), combined with a political pedigree (she was a Soviet Air Force fighter pilot) and criminality (she is now a member of the fictional transnational crime syndicate Janus). In *The World Is Not Enough* (1999), Victor Zokas, a.k.a. Renard the Anarchist (Robert Carlyle), is assisted by a rogue nuclear scientist from Kazakhstan in his convoluted plot to make the Bosphorus uninhabitable, thus benefiting his lover, Elektra King (Sophie Marceau), an Azeri-American businesswoman who controls the premier pipeline conducting Eurasian oil to Europe.[2] Furthering the Bondian branding assault on post-Soviet space, the intervening film, *Tomorrow Never Dies* (1997), begins "on the Russian border" at a terrorist arms bazaar, underscoring Kotkin's critique of the region.

Such belligerent branding creates imposing hurdles for the post-Soviet states in a world where the "reputation of a country has a direct and measurable impact" on its engagement with other countries and assumes a "critical role" in the economic, social, political, and cultural progress of a given state (Anholt, 2007, p. 9). While Kotkin (2002) engages in hyperbole, his characterization of post-Soviet space does reflect a pervasive view of the region in the West, which is the primary target market for nation branding efforts. Furthermore, when it comes to developing a nation brand, the countries of the former Soviet Union must immediately confront the dominant paradigm afflicting their image: corruption (Garelli, 2006). Beyond the problem of corruption, the second most important issue facing the NISE is twofold: (1) overcoming ignorance of their very existence as states, and (2) differentiating from one another and from Russia.

Whereas Russia possesses one of the world's most deeply ingrained national images, other countries possess almost no historical referents as independent states. As such, they have suffocated under the post-Soviet moniker, which carries with it a number of unattractive tropes including "backwardness," "irrationality," and "xenophobia" (Lipovetsky & Leiderman, 2008), as well as places where the transitological paradigm has resulted in life which is "insecure and uncomfortable" (Semenenko et al., 2007, p. 81). Although we should not read too much into parody, the political content of films, such as *Borat: Cultural Learnings of America for Make Benefit Glorious Nation of Kazakhstan* (2006), *The Terminal* (2004), and the James Bond films of the late 1990s, have important roles to play in shaping the reception of branding efforts of post-Soviet nations.

Published in 2007, *Our Dumb World: The Onion's Atlas of the Planet Earth* also provides a fruitful field of data for analysis of the challenges facing the non-Russian post-Soviet republics of Eurasia. As the site of the worst effects of the Chernobyl disaster, Belarus is declared "inhabitable by 2307," Ukraine is marketed as the "bride basket of Europe," while Moldova is the continent's "basement." Armenia is a country where the population digs mass graves for "old times' sake," and Turkmenistan is home to the "world's greatest dictator" (Dikkers, 2007, pp. 167, 181–182, 205, 207). Each of these nuggets evinces a bit of the Second World stigma that dogs the former Soviet republics, which—through a mixture of triumphalist *Schadenfreude* and chance—have become a running punch line for many Westerners or been subsumed within an unreal, but instantly recognizable, post-Soviet neverland.

Ukraine, while increasingly branded as an independent state, still grapples with the problems associated with its "Little Russia" image. The problem of distinction without difference from Russia is, however, not confined to Ukraine; Moldova and Belarus similarly fit into this category and have confronted difficult realities *vis-à-vis* nation branding, which have been multiplied by domestic political problems. Elsewhere, ancient peoples like the Georgians and Armenians—two of the earliest Christian nations—have some extant advantages in developing their countries' national brands (particularly via the influential Armenian diaspora), but have made little headway in achieving the level or type of international recognition they seek for their nation brands. For the various Central Asian Republics (CARs)—all whose names end in the Persian affix -*stan* (land)—the challenge is perhaps the greatest, as they must define themselves in a world where "Stans" are afflicted by war, tribal violence, Islamist terror, endemic poverty, and dramatic levels of gender inequality. The perceived similarity in their names often stands as a further barrier to recognition.

In sharp contrast, the Baltic republics of Estonia, Latvia, and Lithuania have made formidable progress in developing brand recognition in the West despite their post-Soviet heritage (e.g., "E-stonia," "Latvia: The Land That Sings," and "Lithuania the Brave"), due in large part to their admission into the European Union (EU) and the North Atlantic Treaty Organization (NATO). Despite their heritage as former Soviet republics, the Baltic states are increasingly viewed as part of the "Other Europe," rather than "Eurasia," a term that is inevitably linked with the lands that comprised Soviet Russia (1918–1922) and the USSR prior to 1940. However, inclusion in the zone populated by the states of the former Eastern Bloc comes with its own set of nation branding and country image headaches. In *The Other Europe: Eastern Europe to 1945*, E. Garrison Walters (1988) writes:

> Eastern Europe is far more a political expression than a geographical one . . . This is true both within the area itself and its relationship to the surrounding regions . . . Perhaps the only definition that could approach unanimous support is the one that simply points out that the solidly Russian areas to the east and the solidly German and Italian lands to the west are not part of Eastern Europe. (p. xi)

The protean nature of Europe between the Italo-Teutonic "center" and the Russian "orient" remains a vexing problem for the states that connect the Balkan Peninsula to the Baltic Sea. Part of the problem lies in the history of the region as an imperial crossroads. The meeting place of the Ottoman (1299–1923), Romanov (1613–1917), Habsburg (1526–1918), and Hohenzollern (1701–1918) empires—and thus an eternal zone of conflict and mutative politics—the "Other Europe" served to ignite the passions and fears of Western Europeans for centuries, while invariably being characterized as inchoate and amorphous. From Lord Byron—who wrote of the Balkans in 1809, "All countries are much the same in my eyes" (quoted in Goldsworthy, 1998, p. 14)—to Bram Stoker (1897), who described Transylvania as "a country which is full of beauty of every kind" and doomed to its location in "one of the wildest and least known portions of Europe" (p. 2), where maps are of virtually no use—the liminal space, or the "European backyard," between Vienna and St. Petersburg came to function as an "oriental palimpsest" on which myths may be written, revised, erased, and rewritten at will (Wallace, 2008, p. 47). Adapting Edward Said's (1979) theory of orientalism, Maria Todorova (1997) has argued that a Western gaze has constructed the region, particularly the Balkans, as tribal, backward, primitive, dangerous, and barbaric, that is, Europe's quintessential "other" (as if it did not already have enough such "others," e.g., the Muslim world, Russia, America, etc.). As I will discuss in the conclusion of this chapter, this embedded tendency toward exoticization remains a significant factor in the generation of images from the outside and is increasingly made manifest through a sort of "self-exoticism for Western consumption," particularly when it comes to nation branding (Volčič, 2008, p. 409). Given these issues, burnishing the images of the countries of the former Eastern Bloc presents nearly as many challenges as is the case among the former Soviet republics.

In addition to being a site of danger and barbarism, Europe at its periphery has also become highly sexualized, a cultural process that has its origins in the "limber Eastern European gymnast" trope of the 1980s (see Hall, 2007b). This fact is underscored by *The Onion*'s description of Hungary as "adult-film capital of the world," where nearly three-quarters of the population is employed in the pornography industry and one must be "18 years or older to enter" (Dikkers, 2007, p. 171). Sadly, if the average Western European (particularly a Briton or Irish) is branded by the various nations of the region, the most common association is likely to be that of the stag/hen party. Tallinn, Prague, and Budapest are all touted as destinations for such bacchanalia, with these and other Central and Eastern European cities recently being featured as the backdrop for the television series *Boozed Up Brits Abroad* on Bravo TV. The tour company Pissup, which arranged nearly all of the filming venues and recruitment of reality TV "stars" for the program, features—alongside scantily clad Central European women—a map of Europe on its webpage with Estonia, Latvia, Lithuania, Poland, the Czech Republic, Slovakia, Hungary, Germany, and the Netherlands highlighted. Of Pissup's selected city itineraries for boozing romps, only one—Amsterdam—is not found in the former Second World; the others include such unlikely sites as Gdańsk and Brno. Pissup Tours' motto, "Beers, Babes and Bullets," neatly summarizes the reductionist tendency in the West (or at least Western media) to view the region as a site of unrepentant inebriation, unceasing fornication, and gratuitous violence, that is, a sort of "Wild West" in the east of the continent.

Figure 3.1   The homepage of UK tour operator Pissup Tours, brands East-Central Europe as a site of sex, drunkenness, and gunplay. *Source*: Screen captured on December 12, 2010, from http://www.pissup.com.

The "unknown" factor also hangs heavily on the countries of the Other Europe. As Larry Wolff (1994) has pointed out, there was little difference between Enlightenment-era imagined travelogues (like those of Baron Munchausen and Montesquieu's "Usbek") and genuine travel memoirs, as protagonists in both instances always find themselves in an "unknown land, disoriented" (p. 115). The dissolution of the three socialist federations during the 1990s led to a dramatic increase in European countries in a rather short period of time. Contributing to the bewilderment that some Western Europeans and North Americans experienced as they attempted to master this new political geography was a certain similarity among the nomenclature of the new states, for example, Slovenia/Slovakia, Macedonia/Montenegro, and Latvia/Lithuania.

In fact, the "-ia" ending is so common across the space that it led some nation branders to consider a complete name change in English. For instance, Estonia toyed with adopting either its German name (Estland) or the Estonian-language rendering, Eesti (J. Faro, personal communication, May 11, 2009). Similarly, Lithuania is still considering adopting the indigenous name for the country, Lietuva, to differentiate it from its northern neighbor, Latvia (Vaiga, 2008),[3] or, alternatively, opting for Lituania (pronounced *Lit-oo-ania*) to stress the country's historic association with the Latin language, which was used in the Polish-Lithuania Commonwealth's parliament during the late Middle Ages (D. Bankauskaite, personal communication, May 26, 2009). Regardless of such nominal legerdemain, the supposed "confusion" associated with Central and Eastern European countries is reflective of a failure to achieve resonance, rather than a genuine structural hurdle, because, as Anholt (2007) points out, Iceland and Ireland sound alike but are never conflated or confused with one another.

Inevitably, such conflation leads to a perception of the region as homogenous in its supposedly unfathomable heterogeneity (i.e., so diverse that it is unknowable and thus need not be known, at least intimately). This, in turn, allows for subreption by alternative narrators, including filmmakers, comedy writers, and other producers of Western popular culture, who interrupt the branding efforts of the countries in the region, reflecting Anholt's maxim: "The alternative to managing national image is *not* managing it; allowing somebody else to manage it for you" (2007, p. 41, emphasis in original). This tendency is reinforced by preexisting structures embedded in the framework of a "power imbalance between East and West, where the East is clearly placed in a dominated subject position" (Kaneva, 2007). I focus on such branding both on the *individual* level (through the targeting of specific countries, e.g., J. K. Rowling's "Albania" and Sacha Baron Cohen's "Kazakhstan"), as well as on the *collective* level (through parodied Eastern European/post-Soviet figments of imagination that bear fictitious, albeit somewhat familiar, names, e.g., Molvanîa, Krakozhia, Kreplachistan, Absurdisvanï, etc.).

TARGETING THE REAL: SUBVERTING THE IMAGES OF ACTUAL COUNTRIES

In this section, I explore the use of "real" countries in the former Second World for comedic or dramatic purposes by Western cultural producers.[4] My primary case study is Sacha Baron Cohen's use of Kazakhstan as a comedic vehicle for his Borat character (after first trying and then rejecting Moldova and Albania) from 2000 until the premiere of *Borat* in 2006.[5] I then explore similar employment of post-communist nations by writers and filmmakers, and how such usage impugns the nation brands of these states. I begin with the "battle over Borat."

Lacking a historically well-defined country image beyond its borders, the Kazakhstani government has worked hard to build a unique, recognizable, and credible national brand. Its elites and the masses both see Kazakhstan as categorically different from its troubled fellow "Stans" to the south (Uzbekistan, Kyrgyzstan, Turkmenistan, and Tajikistan) and are predictably uncomfortable with their country being categorized alongside Afghanistan, which possesses an entirely different historical and socioeconomic character. According to Roman Vassilenko, Kazakhstan's press secretary in the United States, "It is frustrating when we are lumped together with a country where girls were prevented from going to school for a decade and where the *burqa* is worn. The confusion with countries like Pakistan is also annoying" (personal communication, April 13, 2007). Kazakhstan's quiddity is based on being a resource-rich, multicultural, and stable outpost in an otherwise troubled region of the globe. Uncomfortable with the "Central Asian" stereotype, which combines Soviet and Islamic legacies of autocracy and authoritarianism, the Kazakhstani government has sought numerous venues to present a positive image to the world, including hosting the 2011 Asian Winter Games and close cooperation with NATO.

It is not surprising then that Sacha Baron Cohen, the British comedian and creator of the fictitious Kazakhstani reporter Borat Sagdiyev, touched a raw nerve with his increasingly high-profile parodies of Kazakhstan as a medieval backwater and its people as benighted *homo post-Sovietici*. Writing about the changing nature of diplomacy in a networked world, Elizabeth Hanson (2008) states: "The stage of world politics is so crowded that it is sometimes difficult to see who the main characters are . . . occasionally minor characters lurking in the background, or even previously invisible ones, leap to the center of the stage" (p. 179). Such was the case with Borat.

After several years of modest success on British and American television with *Da Ali G Show*, the character rose to global stardom with an eponymous feature-length film in 2006. The *Borat* motion picture unexpectedly provided Kazakhstan with a precipitous increase in its global profile, though one which came at a hefty price. The premiere of the film signaled the high-water mark in the postmodern conflict between a British comedian and the leadership of the world's ninth largest country. The feud dates back to 2000, when the Kazakhstani diplomat Talgat Kaliyev condemned Borat's portrayal of his country stating: "We can take a joke like anyone else. But this has gone too far—it's a form of racism. We want Borat banned" (quoted in Harris, 2000). Over the next few years, Astana's condemnation of Baron Cohen's parody escalated. In 2005, the foreign ministry threatened legal action if the British prankster did not cease his use of Kazakhstan as a prop for his humor. Paradoxically, the ensuing controversy helped Kazakhstan develop its tourism industry: despite Borat's disinformation campaign, many young Westerners realized that Baron Cohen's "Boratistan" was purely a plot device for his strange brand of humor and wished to learn more about the real Kazakhstan.

Kazakhstan's embassy in the United Kingdom reported record numbers of visa applications from British tourists in the wake of the MTV awards show, which ambassadorial staff readily attributed to Borat's burlesque. This unintended outcome is not trivial; according to Nigel Morgan, "Branding is perhaps the most powerful marketing weapon available to temporary destination marketers confronted by increasing product parity, substitutability and competition" (Morgan, 2002, p. 336). As the debut of *Borat* approached, Roman Vassilenko cheerily took on a role as Borat's alter ego, parlaying every media controversy into an opportunity to advance Kazakhstan's brand.[6] Likewise, Kazakhstan's ambassador to the United Kingdom, Erlan Idrissov, who had initially condemned Baron Cohen's characterizations of his country as "racist and slanderous" (Idrissov, 2006a), penned an editorial after the film's premiere thanking Baron Cohen for drumming up the "kind of media attention of which previously I could only dream" (Idrissov, 2006b). Despite the government's "educational" advertising about Kazakhstan and its people, Idrissov admitted, "The reality is that the only thing many millions of people in the West know about Kazakhstan—or think they know—comes from Borat," finally concluding that Borat had "put Kazakhstan on the map" (2006b).

In an idealized statist world, Kazakhstan's national brand would be primarily determined by the work of the government in the realms of politics, economics, science, sport, and culture. In the postmodern, interconnected world of MTV, iPods, and YouTube, Kazakhstan has to deal with the likes of Borat as well, an alternate and unwelcome narrator of Kazakhness. As Philip Kotler and David Gertner (2002) point out, "The entertainment industry and the media play a particularly important role in shaping people's perceptions of places, especially those viewed negatively" (p. 251). Unlike their counterparts in Turkmenistan and Uzbekistan, who appear to care little about global opinion, Kazakhstani

Figure 3.2   Sacha Baron Cohen as Borat at the film's premiere in Cologne, Germany in 2006. Photo by Michael Bulcik, SKS Soft GmbH Düsseldorf.

elites seek international respect and membership in the club of First World nations.

Under international media scrutiny, there came a realization that a new (and certainly un-Soviet) *realpolitik* was required for dealing with external threats to national identity. In the words of Anholt (2002), "Having a brand means living in the limelight, with all the benefits and obligations this confers" (p. 60). To its credit, Kazakhstan, as a country worried about world opinion, treated Baron Cohen quite well. The managers of Brand Kazakhstan essentially took lemons and decided, after painful consideration, to make lemonade. In this case, the state (Kazakhstan) and the cultural producer (Sacha Baron Cohen) ultimately entered into a symbiotic relationship in which both benefited. However, the relationship is not always so balanced.

In a case that somewhat parallels that of the battle over *Borat*, the American director Eli Roth incurred the wrath of the Slovakian state for his portrayal of the country in his 2005 horror film *Hostel*. In Roth's own words, the film depicts Slovaks as "a bunch of insane, chainsaw-wielding maniacs who torture people" (BBC, 2006). The subject of the film is a hostel whose guests become fodder for a pay-to-play torture chamber. The themes that gird the narrative are European anti-Americanism and American fears of the unknown and primitive "East" (though the principal villain is, in fact, an accomplished, globetrotting Dutch executive and most of the torturers are Westerners, not locals). Bratislava's ambassador to the United States, Ratislav Káčer, described the characterization as "unfair" and an insult "touching the pride of the nation" (PRI, 2006). Slovakian MP Tomáš Galbavý stated, "I am offended by this film. I think that all Slovaks should feel offended" (BBC, 2006). Clearly trying to protect his state's brand, he went on to describe the film as a "monstrosity that does not at all reflect reality [and does] damage the good reputation of Slovakia" (BBC, 2006). In response, Roth was unapologetic in his choice of the Central European republic as the backdrop for his gruesome film; "I set it in Slovakia especially because Americans don't know anything about that country . . . But you know what, at least Americans know the country now. That's a start" (PRI, 2006). However, Roth ultimately traveled to Slovakia to meet with journalists and politicians who condemned the choice of their country as a "haven of torment" (Sacks, 2007).

Interestingly, Milan Kňažko, a prominent Slovakian politician, actor, and intellectual, accepted a small role in the sequel, *Hostel: Part II* (2007), also set in Slovakia. A former Minister of International Relations, Kňažko is no stranger to the challenges his country faces in adapting to the flows of globalization and determining its own path forward within Europe. In an essay in *The Slovak Republic: A Decade of Independence (1993–2002)*, he states: "Considering its historical cultural profile and the actual value orientation of its society, Slovakia cannot remain on the margin of these processes and contexts" (Kňažko, 2003, p. 111). Going even further than Roman Vassilenko, Kňažko's actions suggest that working with foreign cultural producers, even on negative subject matter, can help a country's brand.

In addition to Slovakia's depiction as a den of abject evil, the country was also marked as an impoverished backpacker's nightmare/fantasy in the teen film *Eurotrip* (2004), directed by Jeff Schaffer. In the motion picture, four Americans unwittingly end up in Bratislava rather than Berlin, where they encounter sprawling Khrushchev-era *mikrorayons*, downtrodden peasants bathing in the streets, and a dog holding a severed human hand in its maw. Shortly after despairing, "We are in *Eastern* Europe!" the foursome encounters the congenial Tibor (Rade Serbedzija), who enthusiastically informs them that Slovakia recently got the 1980s crime drama *Miami Vice* on television and is now building its first train.[7] These characterizations are especially ironic, given Bratislava's current situation as a veritable suburb of Vienna, the Austrian capital, which lies only 60 kilometers away. Holiday disaster, however, is averted when the gang realizes that the exchange rate will allow them to live like kings in the Slovakian capital. Despite this serendipitous turn of events, the film reinforces negative stereotypes of the unknown "East" as a place inhabited by impoverished and desperate people, groping for a few pennies from beneficent Westerners.

Another country that has faced mass-mediated attacks on its brand in Anglophone popular culture is Albania. Just as the infamous reclusive communist country was seeking to open relations with the West in 1990, Matt Groening featured an Albanian exchange student in his fabulously popular television cartoon series *The Simpsons*. The 11th episode of the first season, titled "The Crepes of Wrath," saw Adil Hodxa—a character with the same surname as the country's late dictator Enver Hodxa—engaging in industrial espionage by transmitting photos and plans of Springfield's nuclear power plant back to his country via a fax line installed in a tree in Bart Simpson's tree house.

Whereas much of America's Generation X, that is, those born between 1961 and 1981, discovered Albania via *The Simpsons*, their younger counterparts likely learned of the country from J. K. Rowling, the author of the *Harry Potter* fantasy series. According to Gëzim Alpion, the British author employs a tried-and-true literary device of setting a portion of her epic series in the unknown and always ominous Balkans; however, unlike other writers who tend to obscure the exact location, Alpion (2005) states, "Rowling has no qualms in using the name of Albania in her *Harry Potter and the Chamber of Secrets* (1998) and *Harry Potter and the Goblet of Fire* (2000) as the country where the evil 'Dark Lord' and his dedicated followers find a perfect hideout" (p. 11). Elsewhere, Alpion (2002) writes:

> I do not know why, of all countries, Rowling has chosen Albania as the place that harbors evil creatures. If she has done this for a laugh, then this is a cheap and irresponsible laugh at the expense of a European country that has become small, "insignificant" and "voiceless" largely as a result of political witchcraft and wizardry practiced beyond its artificially drawn and imposed borders. I am inclined to believe that

Rowling's choice of Albania is an indication of the intellectual arrogance and ignorance often displayed by Western authors when writing about, to borrow Edward W. Said's phrase, "lesser peoples." (pp. 33–34)

Another example of this phenomenon is Barry Levinson's satirical film *Wag the Dog* (1997). The plot centers on the staging of a fake war between the United States and Albania. Orchestrated by presidential spin doctor Conrad Brean (Robert DeNiro) and Hollywood producer Stanley Motss (Dustin Hoffman), the conflict is meant to deflect voters' attention from a sex scandal involving a sitting president in the days before his reelection. Albania is chosen specifically for its geopolitical anonymity and the fact that its people are, in the words of Motss, "a bunch of wogs." In the wake of the film's premiere, Albania's then-Prime Minister Fatos Nano was forced to comment on its plot (and, by extension, the power of popular geopolitics), stating that war between the two countries "will never happen" (*Christian Science Monitor*, 1998). The choice of Albania underscored the fact that the country had both a weak and generally negative brand, as even a poorly thought of country like Iran or a well-known country like Brazil would have been too difficult to involve in the preposterous spin job.

The pervasiveness of Albania's unsavory brand came across in June 2007, when Jon Stewart, host of Comedy Central's satirical news program *The Daily Show*, referred to the southeastern European country as "a poor man's Kazakhstan." Embedded within this seemingly throwaway comment, meant to frame the enthusiastic (and sometimes ecstatic) reception the "Albaniacs" gave George W. Bush on his visit to the country, Stewart placed the Mediterranean country on a plane equal to that of the impoverished Central Asian countries of Tajikistan and Kyrgyzstan. Such a characterization should not be taken lightly given that Stewart has been named as "the single most important newscaster" in the United States (Baym, 2005, p. 260).[8]

Taken collectively, Rowling's "Albania," Roth's "Slovakia," and Baron Cohen's "Kazakhstan" reflect the ability of entertainers, comedians, and filmmakers to create spurious national stereotypes out of whole cloth. In today's world of overstimulated, undereducated, culturally confused youth, a country's image seems to be only as good as its last reference in popular culture (not forgetting Pierre Bourdieu's timeless maxim, "When one speaks of 'popular culture,' one is speaking about politics" [1978, p. 118]). Given such unhappy realities, a nation's image-makers would be unwise to ignore Baron Cohen, Roth, Rowling, or any other interlopers in their spatial and conceptual territory, but, at the same time, they are unable to do otherwise. Assisted by global flows of information and entertainment, nonstate actors can influence millions (if not billions) with their "art." Employing a real country in one's aesthetic creation has serious ramifications, as the previously mentioned nations have learned in recent years. Prior to the advent of the purported global village, a country's image was determined by factors that were predominately under the control of its national elites.

This is less true today than at any time in the past; consequently, national pantomime is no laughing matter.

TARGETING THE IMAGINARY: THE GEOGRAPHY OF ABSURDIA

In the wake of World War II, the visual arts, film, drama, literature, radio, and television all became sites for cultural production that shaped American and European perceptions on a host of topics, from the "fragility of liberty" to the "onslaught of totalitarianism" (Jacobson, 2006, p. 39). Infused with ideological vigor, Eastern Europe could now be portrayed as the quintessential "Other" through popular geopolitics, while serving the political interests of one's home country. Popular geopoliticians have shown how comics, pulp fiction, and other pop culture texts "contributed to hegemonic representation of national identity" through representation of the geographies of the Cold War (Dittmer & Dodds, 2008, p. 443). If this subversion was funny, it proved even more effective, because as Dodds (2005) states, "The spatial symbolic of humor can often challenge and even subvert dominant boundaries of national sovereignty and the nationalist scripting of place" (p. 96).

Sequential artists were particularly fond of developing instantly recognizable effigies of communist states with fanciful and fictitious names. Perhaps the most famous was Disney studio animator Carl Barks' "Brutopia," a hostile country bent on world domination, and which—not coincidentally—occupied the eastern third of Siberia (see Parker, 2008). Used in the *Donald Duck* and *Scrooge McDuck* comics, Brutopia sent its minions around the world claiming resources and intimidating the weak, saying all the while: "What Brutopia wants, Brutopia takes." Other pseudo–Eastern European nations with dark intentions for the West included Marvel Comics' "Latveria," home to the arch-villain Dr. Doom; "Borovia," the Eastern European communist nation in the *G.I. Joe* comic book series; "Pottsylvania," the home of the bumbling spies Boris Badenov and Natasha Fatale in *The Adventures of Rocky and Bullwinkle and Friends*; and Hergé's communist, totalitarian "Borduria," depicted in *The Adventures of Tin Tin*. Cold War culture producers in other fields also saw fit to create their own neverlands beyond the Iron Curtain (as if there were not already enough), including Alex Leister of the BBC who crafted "Boloxnia," an Eastern European communist country permanently situated in the year 1957; "Moldavia," a "mysterious" Eastern European country referenced in the Reagan-era ode to capitalism *Dynasty* (the show aired on ABC from 1981 to 1989); and the amazingly unimaginative "East European Republic," an anti-American power from the *Mission: Impossible* television series in the 1960s.

Although the Cold War officially ended more than two decades ago, cultural biases associated with the conflict continue to linger. These prejudicial predilections appear as frames, that is, political guidance embedded in media content via contextual clues, which in turn "evoke distinct patterns of judgment and opinions surrounding the issue" (Lenart & Targ, 1992, p. 341). As Nancy Condee (2006) attests, Cold War tropes continue to dominate cultural production; through these comforting, if inaccurate, lenses, Americans are able "to make sense of the former Soviet Union, the ex-socialist expanse from Brest to Vladivostok." In certain instances, it is thus possible to do away with "real" countries altogether, opting instead for constructs that embody all the desired elements of post-Soviet/post-communist space. Here, I provide a close reading of several of these fabrications and their quasi-ideological ramifications.

I begin with "Krakozhia," the fictional Slavic country employed in Steven Spielberg's motion picture *The Terminal* (2004). The plot of the film centers on a good-hearted traveler, Viktor Navorski (Tom Hanks), who becomes a "citizen of nowhere" when he is stranded in JFK International Airport after his passport is invalidated as the result of a coup in his homeland, "the tiniest country in the region . . . [which] has been involved in a civil war throughout the late 80s and 90s as it has tried to transition from Communist rule."[9] Politically, Krakozhia is thus an effigy of the so-called TAKO nations of post-Soviet space (i.e., Transnistria, Abkhazia, Karabakh, and Ossetia), which have declared sovereignty from their respective Commonwealth of Independent States (CIS) countries but have yet to achieve international recognition, or to paraphrase Navorski's apprehending border control agent in *The Terminal*, "Technically, these places do not exist."

Describing Navorski as "part-genius, part-idiot, at once the hero and victim of globalism," Jim Hoberman (2007) belittles Spielberg's choice to create an "imaginary Balkan country" rather than give his film a "political edge" by making the character a Middle Easterner or South Asian (pp. 128–129). Hoberman thus supports the impetus behind Lipovetsky's rhetorical question (posed in his essay, "Angel, Avenger or Trickster?" which compares Navorski and Borat): "After all, who cares about the Second World?" (Lipovetsky & Leiderman, 2008, p. 200). Although the answer is not immediately forthcoming (other than, of course, to the authors and readers of this volume), it is clear that—at least geopolitically speaking—the region has been declawed and is thus appropriate for parody.[10] With this in mind, I turn to highly parodic and decidedly apolitical *Molvanîa: A Land Untouched by Modern Dentistry* (2004).[11]

The first in the faux *Jetlag Travel Guide* series ("Taking You Places You Don't Want To Go"), *Molvanîa* is a full-length travel guide to a fake post-communist country, which combines exaggerated but somewhat plausible descriptions of the seedier, sadder, and insalubrious aspects of the old Eastern Bloc. Originally published in Australia as the brain-child of comedy writers Santo Cilauro, Tom Gleisner, and Rob Sitch, the book became a surprise hit and achieved worldwide distribution. *Molvanîa* has spawned a number of video projects as well, including a 30-minute video segment about the country, which was shown on Australian carrier Qantas' international flights, and two music videos by Zladko "Zlad" Vladcik.

Molvanîa is a landlocked country supposedly located "north of Bulgaria and downwind from Chernobyl." The artistry of the writers comes across in the ambiguity of space, placing Molvanîa in the Baltic region on one page and in the Balkans on another, thus hammering home the lack of need for specificity among Western audiences when dealing with the "European backyard." *Molvanîa* provides an enticing simulacrum of Eastern Europe through its use of genuine photos culled from across the region, including gold-toothed Aeroflot stewardesses, egg-painting peasants in traditional garb, and dour accordionists. Hotel and restaurant reviews are surprisingly detailed, for example, that of *Romajaci* in the capital "Lutenblag," which has a menu with "something for everyone—provided you like pork" (Cilauro, Gleisner & Sitch, 2004, p. 53). Such use of real images makes the book a more effective parody than *Borat: Touristic Guidings to Minor Nation of U.S. and A. and Touristic Guidings to Glorious Nation of Kazakhstan* (Hines & Baron Cohen, 2007), Sacha Baron Cohen's sloppy textual accompaniment to his film, which employs staged or doctored ethnoscapes to portray Kazakhstan as a medieval backwater.[12] *Molvanîa* also differs in intent from Baron Cohen's Boratistan imaginarium, which was, at times, calculated to infuriate Astana; according to Gleisner, "We decided to make up a country so we wouldn't offend anybody" (BBC, 2004). Former UK Minister for Europe Keith Vaz criticized the book, suggesting that *Molvanîa* reflects anti–Eastern European prejudices which are "taking root" in Western Europe (BBC, 2004). At the same time, Vaz gave the book kudos for unveiling the glaring ignorance of Westerners toward the post-communist "East."

Drawing a link to Borat, Richard Andrew Hall (2007a) describes the phenomenon of portraying "European white trash" (e.g., the denizens of Borat's "village" and the average Molvanîan) via the use of pseudo-cultural dispatches from a generic "Post-(card) Commiestan" (p. 6) as endemic in contemporary media. "In this way not much has changed from Bram Stoker's time: the need to find a setting that is simultaneously exotic and yet familiar, that acts as a prop but not distraction from the underlying goal of the art form" (Hall, 2007a, p. 6). Playing on Benedict Anderson's (1991) seminal analysis of national identity in the modern era, Hall describes these fictional places as "'really imagined communities' in the form of fictional countries placed in the post-communist space" (2007a, p. 7). Such anti-branding is neatly evinced in the country's fake standard, a "trikolor" with only two colors ("communist" red and yellow) emblazoned with the hammer, sickle, and—a Molvanîan innovation—the trowel.

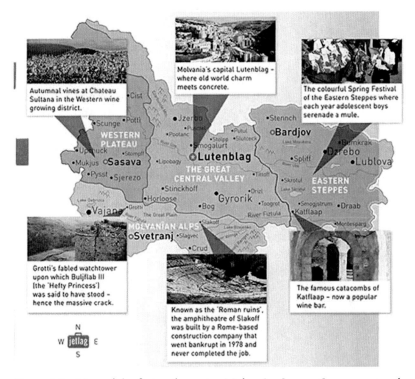

Figure 3.3   Map of the fictional country Molvanîa. *Source*: Screen captured on December 12, 2010, from http://www.molvania.com.au/molvania/map.html.

Figure 3.4   Coat of arms on Molvanîa's fictional flag. *Source*: Immanuel Giel and Ariane Schmidt, downloaded December 12, 2010, from http://en.wikipedia.org/wiki/File:Molvania.svg.

Moving beyond the actual text of *Molvanîa*, a curious addendum to the project—namely, Zladko Vladcik's "Elektronik Supersonik"—coyly reflects a current obsession in nation branding among the lesser known states of the former Second World: Eurovision.[13] According to Vasyl Myroshny-chenko, a branding consultant who has worked with Ukraine and Georgia, Eurovision is one of the quickest ways to put a positive patina on a small Eastern European nation brand. With access to an average of 2,500 journalists from all around Europe, it provides an opportunity to promote a state's flag and history, as well as market a country as a contributor to Europe's cultural patrimony (V. Myroshnychenko, personal communication, January 9, 2009). However, unlike Ukraine's 2004 victory and hosting of Eurovision in 2005, Molvanîa failed to improve its brand with its (faux) 2004 entry "Elektronik Supersonik" (Molvanîa's purported Eurovision entry remains quite popular on YouTube with its more than 2 million views).[14] The song—which is performed by *Molvanîa* co-author Santo Cilauro looking like a 1980s Borat (replete with a massive "mullet" hairdo and a futuristic silver tracksuit) and delivering jaw-dropping lyrics like "I put my butt plug in your socket"—was disqualified when the 23-year-old singer was arrested at Istanbul's Ataturk International Airport and immediately deported. According to the *Molvanîa* website: "While Eurovision does not normally test for recreational drugs, unfortunately for Vladcik, Turkish Customs do" (Molvanîa, 2004). The song's brilliant 3:06 minute video presents a vivid burlesque of 1980s European synth-pop, combined with the *Kitsch und Drang* of Eastern European attempts to embrace the West in the waning days of the Cold War (Vladcik's ungrammatical constructions often outdo those cooked up by Sacha Baron Cohen, as do his cultural malapropisms, such as "Darth Vapor").[15]

Whereas the Molvanîan artifice is relatively bereft of political content (though quite resonant in cultural terms), American author Gary Shteyngart's bestselling and well-reviewed *Absurdistan: A Novel* (2006) contributes to the belligerent branding of post-Soviet space in a self-cognizant and frequently normative fashion.[16] Much of the action takes place in the post-Soviet, Caspian republic of "Absurdsvanï." Ethnically divided between the "Sevo" and "Svanï," the "cretins of the Caucasus" (Shteyngart, 2006, p. 125), the post-Sovietesque neverland is a jolting bricolage of new wealth and crushing poverty, thus serving as a paragon of what Parag Khanna (2008) calls the "new Second World," which is "*both* first- and third-world at the same time" (p. xxv). The Absurdi capital, described as "a miniature Cairo after it had crashed into a rocky mountain" (Shteyngart, 2006, p. 134), is awash in investment from American multinationals, particularly oil conglomerates and designer clothiers, while the country ranks "slightly below Bangladesh" on the UN Human Development Index (p. 138). Trapped in a vicious cycle of rapacious leaders bent on establishing dynastic rule, Russian and American malfeasance, and civil and ethnic conflict, Absurdistan is a straw man for the post-Soviet republics of Georgia, Armenia, and

Azerbaijan, while not actually being any of them.[17] Unlike Steven Spielberg, Eli Roth, and Sacha Baron Cohen, Shteyngart's keen "awareness of the former Soviet Union" (Lee, 2008, p. 32) allows a genuine level of verisimilitude in his anti-branding of the post-Second World.

Similar to *Absurdistan* in critique of both post-Soviet banana republics and the American companies that love them (Dick Cheney's Halliburton, or "Golly Burton" as it is known to the Absurdis, is as much of a target for Shteyngart as is any regime in the region) is G. B. Trudeau's *Tee Time in Berzerkistan: A Doonsebury Book* (2009). The bound collection of comic strips recounts the attempts by President-for-Life Trff Bmzklfrpz (pronounced "Ptklm") to improve the status of "Greater Berzerkistan" in Washington with the help of high-paid lobbyists. Intentionally or not, Trudeau's book is a sublime, graphic rendering of Ken Silverstein's *Turkmeniscam: How Washington Lobbyists Fought to Flack for a Stalinist Dictatorship* (2008), which uncovered K Street's complicity in gussying up Saparmurat Niyazov's unsavory regime.[18] *Tee Time* opens with a former terrorist (now Berzerkistan's foreign minister) chatting with lobbyists about how to overcome the association of his country with genocide, torture, drug trafficking, and tyranny. The lobbyists lead with the obvious: "The goal of the campaign would be to rebrand your pariah state as valued partner in the global war on terror so that you'd qualify for a military aid package of, say, $25 billion" (Trudeau, 2009, p. 10). Next they advise the minister on how to "manage" the ethnic cleansing issue: "gentrification" associated with housing issues. Dealing with the president, however, proves more difficult as he refuses to abandon his Hitlerian haircut *cum* mustache because it "scares the homosexuals and gypsies" (Trudeau, 2009, p. 23). While Trudeau directly targets D.C. insiders, Central Asia gets caught in the crossfire as the region is made out to be something much worse than it actually is.

CONCLUSION

In the current era of deterritorialized media products and transnational information flows, cultural producers are instrumental—one might even argue *key*—in maintaining post-communist/post-Soviet Eurasia as what Maria Todorova (2005) refers to as a *marked* category. This is done through a constant reinforcing of pre-/post-Cold War "mental maps" (Todorova, 2005, p. 64), which maintain occidental Europe as the norm and oriental Europe as the absurd, the offensive, and/or the dangerous. In effect, Borat, Bond baddies, hostile hosteliers, Krakozhian and Absurdi coups, and "Elektronik Supersonik" all allow the West to maintain its borders with the "East" long after the fall of the Iron Curtain, even as these peoples, states, and lands are becoming "Europe/European" in the eyes of those who refused them this designation during the Cold War, without the addition of the heavily loaded "Eastern" or "communist" modifiers.

Whether on a conscious or subconscious level, cultural producers, such as Sacha Baron Cohen, J. K. Rowling, G. B. Trudeau, and Santo Cilauro, engage in mass-mediated objectification of the region. In their treatments of the former Second World, we can tease out the same streams of anxiety, narcissism, and fetishism that characterize various post-colonial discourses evident in the West's relationship with the Global South (see Yan, 2009). As is the case with many developing countries, the post-communist/post-Soviet world, hoping to profit from its status as the "Other," has seen some nation branders embrace auto-exoticism in order to be noticed in the global marketplace, for example, Transylvania's embrace of the Dracula myth (see Chelminski, 2003) and Macedonia's reflexive description as a "unique patchwork of cultures, where Balkan bloodlines have mixed with other more exotic still" (Volčič, 2008, p. 409). Such trends reflect an extension of the theory in popular geopolitics that nationalism is a form of fandom (Dittmer & Dodds, 2008), in that international relations is now turning into a competition for the equivalent of "Facebook friends." Nadia Kaneva (2007) has identified another pattern of activity, namely, denial of difference (and thus eradication of quiddity) as a mechanism to achieve a brand that will allow for a smooth integration into Europe (and avoid alienation and/or marginalization).

In an intensely connected and cosmopolitan world marked by what can be called—using Durkheim's language—an organic solidarity in international relations, states must differentiate themselves and provide value through their specificity. This truism has a direct impact on national identity production in post–Second World states, particularly those within the EU, and perpetuates the power disparity between "Old" and "New" Europe. In the crowded arena that currently constitutes the field of international relations, it is starkly evident that images are more important than ever. Although British comedians, American filmmakers, and Australian travel writers may not carry diplomatic credentials, it is increasingly clear that they and other "alternative narrators" have a role to play in determining nation brands, both in and outside of the former Second World.

NOTES

1. According to Duane E. Knapp (2008), Q scores are ratings that are often used for judging athletes and celebrities. The score is based on two factors: familiarity and how much the entity in question is liked or disliked (p. 190).
2. The plan provides a sort of nihilistic update to the 19th-century British fear of Russian control of the Turkish Straights, while taking into account current issues of Russian dominance of Central Asian and Caucasian hydrocarbon exports.
3. In fact, Lietuva is used in the country's tourism branding campaigns.
4. For the purposes of this chapter, I employ Abu-Lughod's definition of cultural producers, that is, those who are "working within structures of power

and organizations that are tied to and doing the work of national or commercial interests" (quoted in Mahon, 2000, p. 469).

5. For an analysis of how *Borat* has impacted the image of another post-communist country, Romania, see Bardan and Imre's chapter in this volume.

6. Vassilenko even posted a series of short, professionally produced videos about Kazakhstan on YouTube, which lauded the country as prosperous, stable, and tolerant.

7. Throughout the film, a tabletop is used as an ersatz map to show the current location of the quartet. Whereas Italy is symbolized by a plate of spaghetti and a glass of wine stands in for France, Slovakia is rendered as a messy ashtray and an unidentifiable brown stain on the tablecloth.

8. More recently, Albanians were besmirched by the kidnap-for-white-slavery film *Taken* (2008), which marks the Albanian mafia as so nefarious that "even the Russians give these guys a wide berth."

9. The "Krakozhian" language spoken by Tom Hanks is gibberish with a few Slavic-like utterances, but, according to the actor, is phonetically and structurally based on Bulgarian. Regarding the language and the positioning of Krakozhia, Hanks stated in an NPR interview: "Well, we started with a Slavic beginning to it and a Cyrillic-alphabet language; and Krakozhia means that it comes from one of those nations with an "-ia" at the end of it: Estonia, Latvia, Yugoslavia" (NPR, 2004).

10. Whereas satire is driven by a desire for positive change, parody does not necessarily need to contribute to political discourse (Gray, Jones, & Thompson, 2009). In effect, the post–Second World is now "safe," unlike the Muslim world, which poses—in the words of former U.S. President George W. Bush—an "existential threat" to contemporary (Western) civilization.

11. If the authors are to be believed, it was not a trip to the former Eastern Bloc that stimulated the idea for the book (and the ensuing series), but a vacation to Portugal, which ironically hosts the continent's most occidental point, Cabo da Roca (Latin: *Promontorium Magnum*).

12. At the time of writing, Baron Cohen's fake travelogue was selling roughly as many copies as the leading travel guide to the country, Paul Brummell's *Kazakhstan: The Bradt Travel Guide* (2008), on Amazon.com.

13. In good nation branding fashion, Vladcik ends the song with "Long live Molvanîa!"

14. By comparison, Georgia's withdrawn 2009 entry for Eurovision, Stephane & 3G's "We Don't Wanna Put In," which gained worldwide recognition via the BBC and other media outlets, has only been viewed a few hundred thousand times.

15. In 2005, Vladcik won the right to represent Molvanîa a second time with "I Am the Anti-Pope." However, his hopes for worldwide fame were once again dashed due to another disqualification on the grounds that "Satanism has no place at Eurovision," the one-line statement issued by the Kiev press office (Molvanîa, n.d.).

16. Shteyngart was born in Leningrad, but relocated with his family to the United States in 1979. His first novel, *The Russian Debutante's Handbook* (2003), was written after a visit to Prague and is partially set in "Prava," a fictional European city.

17. The term "Absurdistan" has, in fact, been in use for some time to make reference to the "border republics" of the CIS, symbolizing a "recognition of just how tragically comic life had become" in these post-communist states (Buchanan, 2002, p. 3).

18. Silverstein (2007) originally recounted his controversial strategy of posing as a shill for Ashgabat, and the startling results, in a *Harper's Magazine* article.

REFERENCES

Alpion, G. (2002). Images of Albania and Albanians in English literature from Edith Durham's *High Albania* to J. K. Rowling's *Harry Potter*. *BESA Journal, 6*(2), 30–34.

Alpion, G. (2005). Western media and the European "Other": Images of Albania in the British press in the new millennium. *Albanian Journal of Politics, 1*(1), 4–25.

Anderson, B. (1991). *Imagined communities: Reflections on the origin and spread of nationalism*. London: Verso.

Anholt, S. (2002). Forward. *Brand Management, 9*(4/5), 229–239.

Anholt, S. (2007). *Competitive identity: The new brand management for nations, cities, and regions*. New York: Palgrave Macmillan.

Aronczyk, M. (2009). How to do things with brands: Uses of national identity. *Canadian Journal of Communication, 34*(2), 291–296.

Baym, G. (2005). *The Daily Show*: Discursive integration and the reinvention of political journalism. *Political Communication, 22*(3), 259–276.

BBC. (2004, April 2). Molvanîa spoof mocks travel books. *BBC News*. Retrieved December 22, 2009, from http://news.bbc.co.uk/2/hi/europe/3592753.stm

BBC. (2006, February 27). Slovakia angered by horror film. *BBC News*. Retrieved May 10, 2010, from http://news.bbc.co.uk/2/hi/entertainment/4754744.stm

Bourdieu, P. (1978). *Le handicap socioculturel en question*. Paris: ESF.

Brummell, P. (2008). *Kazakhstan: The Bradt travel guide*. Bucks, UK: Bradt Travel Guides.

Buchanan, D. A. (2002). Soccer, popular music and national consciousness in post-state-socialist Bulgaria, 1994–96. *British Journal of Ethnomusicology, 11*(2), 1–27.

Chelminski, R. (2003). The curse of count Dracula. *Smithsonian, 34*(1), 110–115.

Christian Science Monitor. (1998, March 13). Etceteras. *Christian Science Monitor, 90*(74), 2.

Cilauro, S., Gleisner, T., & Sitch, R. (2004). *Molvanîa: A land untouched by modern dentistry*. Woodstock, NY: The Overlook Press.

Condee, N. (2006, November 12). Learnings of Borat for make benefit cultural studies. *Pittsburgh Post-Gazette*, p. H6.

Dikkers, S. (Ed.). (2007). *Our dumb world: The Onion's atlas of the planet earth* (73rd ed.). New York: Little, Brown.

Dinnie, K. (2008). *Nation branding: Concepts, issues, practice*. Oxford, UK: Butterworth-Heinemann.

Dittmer, J., & Dodds, K. (2008). Popular geopolitics past and future: Fandom, identities and audience. *Geopolitics, 13*(3), 437–457.

Dobriansky, L. E. (1963). The nuclear test-ban treaty and the Cold War. *Ukrainian Quarterly, 29*(2), 125–132.

Dodds, K. (2003). Licensed to stereotype: Geopolitics, James Bond and the spectre of Balkanism. *Geopolitics, 8*(2), 125–156.

Dodds, K. (2005). *Global geopolitics: A critical introduction*. Harlow, UK: Prentice Hall.

Garelli, S. (2006). *Top class competitors: How nations, firms, and individuals succeed in the new world of competitiveness*. Hoboken, NJ: Wiley.

Goldsworthy, V. (1998). *Inventing Ruritania: The imperialism of the imagination.* St. Edmunds, UK: St. Edmundsbury Press.

Gray, J., Jones, J. P., & Thompson, E. (2009). The state of satire, the satire of state. In J. Gray, J. P. Jones, & E. Thompson (Eds.), *Satire TV: Politics and comedy in the post-network era* (pp. 3–36). New York: New York University Press.

Grimes, W. (2005). Japan as the "indispensable nation" in Asia: A financial brand for the 21st century. *Asia-Pacific Review, 12*(1), 40–54.

Hall, R. A. (2007a). *Borat: Orientalist satire for make glorious debate Western intelligentsiya.* Retrieved December 22, 2009, from http://homepage.mac.com/khallbobo/RichardHall/pubs/boratslavicreview022807.pdf

Hall, R. A. (2007b). *Images of Hungarians and Romanians in modern American media and popular culture.* Retrieved December 22, 2009, from http://homepage.mac.com/khallbobo/RichardHall/pubs/huroimages060207tk6.pdf

Hanson, E. (2008). *The information revolution and world politics.* Lanham, MD: Rowman & Littlefield.

Harris, J. (2000, April 26). When Ali G went to Kazakhstan. *Independent,* p. F1.

Hines, A., & Baron Cohen, S. (2007). *Borat: Touristic guidings to minor nation of U.S. and A. and touristic guidings to glorious nation of Kazakhstan.* New York: Doubleday/Flying Dolphin Press.

Hoberman, J. (2007). Laugh, cry, believe: Spielbergization and its discontents. *Virginia Quarterly Review, 83*(1), 119–135.

Idrissiov, E. (2006a, October 4). Offensive and unfair, Bourat's antics leave a nasty aftertaste. *The Guardian.* Retrieved December 11, 2010, from http://www.guardian.co.uk/commentisfree/2006/oct/04/comment.television

Idrissov, E. (2006b, November 4). We survived Stalin and we can certainly overcome Borat's slurs. *The Times.* Retrieved May 10, 2010, from http://www.timesonline.co.uk/tol/comment/columnists/guest_contributors/article1086792.ece

Jacobson, M. F. (2006). *What have they built you to do?: The Manchurian candidate and Cold War America.* Minneapolis: University of Minnesota Press.

Jaworski, S. P., & Fosher, D. (2003). National brand identity and its effect on corporate brands: The nation brand effect. *Multinational Business Review, 11*(3), 99–113.

Kaneva, N. (2007). Meet the "new" Europeans: EU accession and the branding of Bulgaria. *Advertising & Society Review, 8*(4). Retrieved May 10, 2010, from http://muse.jhu.edu/journals/asr/v008/8.4kaneva.html

Khanna, P. (2008). *The second world: Empires and influence in the new global order.* New York: Random House.

Knapp, D. E. (2008). *The brand promise: How Ketel One, Costco, Make-A-Wish, Tourism Vancouver, and other leading brands make and keep the promise that guarantees success.* New York: McGraw-Hill Professional.

Kňažko, M. (2003). Culture and politics—rivals or allies? In M. M. Stolarik (Ed.), *The Slovak Republic: A decade of independence (1993–2002),* (pp. 109–118). Wauconda, IL: Bolchazi-Carducci.

Kotkin, S. (2002). Trashcanistan. *New Republic, 226*(14), 26–38.

Kotler, P., & Gertner, D. (2002). Country as brand, product, and beyond: A place marketing and brand management perspective. *Journal of Brand Management, 9*(4/5), 249–261.

Lebedenko, V. (2004). Russia's national identity and image-building. *International Affairs, 50*(4), 71–77.

Lee, S. S. (2008). Borat, multiculturalism, *mnogonatsional'nost'. Slavic Review, 67*(1), 19–34.

Lenart, S., & Targ, H. R. (1992). Framing the enemy. *Peace & Change, 17*(3), 341–362.

Lipovetsky, M., & Leiderman, D. (2008). Angel, avenger, or trickster? The "Second-World man" as the other and the self. In S. Hutchings (Ed.), *Russia and its other(s) on film: Screening intercultural dialogue* (pp. 199–219). Basingstoke, UK: Palgrave Macmillan.

Mahon, M. (2000). The visible evidence of culture producers. *Annual Review of Anthropology, 29*(1), 467–492.

Malanowski, J. (2000, August 20). A scene stealer's big score. *The New York Times.* Retrieved December 10, 2010, from http://query.nytimes.com/gst/fullpage.html?res=990CE5DB1E3FF933A1575BC0A9669C8B63

Molvanîa. (2004). Molvanîa disqualified from Eurovision. *Molvanîa.com.* Retrieved December 22, 2009, from http://www.molvania.com/molvania/eurovision_2004.html

Molvanîa. (n.d.). Molvanîa disqualified from Eurovision . . . again. *Molvanîa.com.* Retrieved December 22, 2009, from http://www.molvania.com/molvania/eurovision.html

Morgan, N. A. (2002). New Zealand, 100% pure. The creation of a powerful niche destination brand. *Brand Management, 9*(4/5), 335–354.

NPR. (2004, June 18). Tom Hanks discusses his new film "The Terminal." Interviewed by M. Norris. [Radio broadcast episode]. *All Things Considered.* National Public Radio.

Nye, J. S. (2004). *Soft power: The means to success in world politics.* New York: Public Affairs.

Papadopoulos, N., & Heslop, L. (2002). Country equity and country branding: Problems and prospects. *Brand Management, 9*(4/5), 294–314.

Parker, P. M. (2008). *Siberia: Webster's quotations, facts and phrases.* San Diego, CA: ICON Group International.

PRI. (2006, January 25). Slovakian reaction to the film "Hostel" [Radio broadcast]. *The World.* Public Radio International.

Rusciano, F. L. (2003). The construction of national identity—A 23-nation study. *Political Research Quarterly, 56*(3), 361–366.

Sacks, E. (2007, June 4). A "Hostel" audience of one. *New York Daily News.* Retrieved December 10, 2010, from http://www.nydailynews.com/entertainment/movies/2007/06/04/2007-06-04_a_hostel_audience_of_one.html

Said, E. (1979). *Orientalism.* New York: Vintage.

Saunders, R. A. (2008). *The many faces of Sacha Baron Cohen: Politics, parody, and the battle over Borat.* Lanham, MD: Lexington Books.

Semenenko, I., Lapkin, V., & Pantin, V. (2007). Russia's image in the West (formulation of the problem). *Social Sciences, 38*(3), 79–92.

Shteyngart, G. (2006). *Absurdistan: A novel.* New York: Random House.

Silverstein, K. (2007, July). Their men in Washington: Undercover with D.C.'s lobbyists for hire. *Harper's Magazine.* Retrieved December 10, 2010, from http://www.harpers.org/archive/2007/07/0081591

Silverstein, K. (2008). *Turkmeniscam: How Washington lobbyists fought to flack for a Stalinist dictatorship.* New York: Random House.

Stoker, B. (1897). *Dracula: A mystery story.* New York: W. R. Caldwell.

Todorova, M. (1997). *Imagining the Balkans.* Oxford, UK: Oxford University Press.

Todorova, M. (2005). Spacing Europe: What is a historical region? *East Central Europe, 32*(1/2), 59–78.

Trudeau, G. B. (2009). *Tee time in Berzerkistan: A Doonesbury book.* Riverside, NJ: Andrews McMeel.

Vaiga, L. (2008, January 30). Lithuania ponders brave new image . . . and name. *The Baltic Times.* Retrieved December 10, 2010, from http://www.baltictimes.com/news/articles/19740

Van Ham, P. (2001). The rise of the brand state: The postmodern politics of image and reputation. *Foreign Affairs, 80*(5), 2–7.

Volčič, Z. (2008). Former Yugoslavia on the World Wide Web: Commercialization and branding of nation-states. *The International Communication Gazette, 70*(5), 395–413.

Walker, S. (2007). Young rebels. *Monocle, 1*(6), 31–41.

Walker, S. (2009). Fresh Minsk. *Monocle, 3*(23), 23–28.

Wallace, D. (2008). Hyperrealizing "Borat" with the map of the European "Other." *Slavic Review, 67*(1), 35–49.

Walters, E. G. (1988). *The Other Europe: Eastern Europe to 1945*. Syracuse, NY: Syracuse University Press.

Wolff, L. (1994). *Inventing Eastern Europe: The map of civilization on the mind of the Enlightenment*. Stanford, CA: Stanford University Press.

Yan, G. (2009). "China Forever": Tourism discourse and self-Orientalism. *Annals of Tourism Research, 36*(2), 295–315.

Part II
Agents, Institutions, Practices

4 Redesigning a Nation
Welcome to E-stonia, 2001–2018[1]

Sue Curry Jansen

INTRODUCTION

Nation-states are relatively recent, post-Enlightenment inventions. They impose common administrative systems upon broad expanses of territory inhabited by heterogeneous populations, which frequently have diverse ethnicities, histories, customs, and cultural values. As a result, nations are, in Benedict Anderson's (1981) resonant phrase, "imagined communities." National identities are forged through representational practices that are historically and socially conditioned, dispersed, often incongruous, and frequently tension laden.

Nation branding seeks to eliminate the messy inconsistencies and cacophony of the multilayered social transactions involved in developing national identities. Branders lighten the burdens of history by rationalizing, disciplining, and instrumentally channeling the processes of imagining or, more precisely, re-imagining national identity. Nation branding consultants mobilize expertise in public relations, marketing, and design in concerted attempts to enhance a nation's positioning within the global economy. To this end, nation branders select, simplify, and promote those traits of a country's culture, commerce, geography, and natural resources that advance its instrumental agendas in the marketplace and international relations. But branding does not just promote what is—the best of what a country has to offer—it also includes aspirational elements that encompass a nation's ambitions: a vision for an even brighter future. Insofar as possible, branders also de-emphasize, ignore, or censor information that does not advance the brand.

The primary audiences (customers or consumers) targeted by nation branders are international tourists, foreign investors, and potential trading partners, as well as the citizens of the branded nation. Although branding consultants prefer to describe citizens as "partners" in the branding process, empirical evidence demonstrates that they are, at best, limited partners, as well as primary targets of branding initiatives. Nation branders recognize that messages to citizens must be strategic and motivational rather than direct and transparent because, as one brander put it, "We have to sell it internally . . . We can't talk about branding in market terms—people don't understand it" (Mändmets, quoted in Collier, 2008). Internal messages serve multiple purposes: (a) to minimize skepticism about and criticism of the use of public funds for branding; (b) to mobilize public participation and solidarity in branding-related activities such as festivals and pageants and to encourage use of the branding design elements in various civic and commercial contexts, and other brand-related activities; or, more directly (c) to overtly propagandize the population in the interests of the political and economic elites who commission branding initiatives (Collier, 2008; Nimjean, 2005, 2006).

In most cases, nation branding is also designed to enhance a nation's profile with international organizations such as the EU, NATO, the UN, or the WTO. In recent years, nation branding techniques have also played a role in public diplomacy: a nation's attempts to influence public opinion in other nations—that is, its propaganda efforts. One of the most widely publicized public diplomacy efforts in recent years was the United States' failed "Shared Values" campaign, undertaken in the wake of the 2001 terrorist attacks on New York, Washington, D.C., and Pennsylvania, in an attempt to improve public perceptions of the United States among Muslim populations around the world (Jansen, 2005; Plaissance, 2005; U.S. Department of State, 2003).

Although destination and place branding have been profitable public relations specialties for decades, nation branding *per se* is a recent development. The Irish Republic's "Young Europeans" campaign in the 1970s and 1980s, which promoted Eire's young educated workforce to the EU and the United States, and Spain's transformation of its image after the death of Franco, provided the prototypes for nation branding (Fanning, n.d.; Gilmore, 2002; Olins, 1999). The "Cool Britannia" project (Leonard, 1997) of the early Blair years was the first nation branding campaign to attract significant press coverage and controversy, with some critics describing the concept of nation branding as superficial and silly (Freely, 1998).

Nation branding advocates quickly came to the defense of their product. Wally Olins's *Trading Identities* (1999), which argues that nation branding is widely misunderstood and unfairly maligned in the press, was the first major contribution to this effort as well as the most literate and persuasive apology for the practice. Others quickly followed, with Simon Anholt (2003, 2007) establishing himself as the most prolific promoter and practitioner of nation branding and related products and services, including a pro-branding academic journal, *Place Branding and Public Diplomacy*.

END OF THE COLD WAR AND INTEGRATION
OF GLOBAL MARKETS

Nation branding was fortuitously positioned in the 1990s to meet the ideological and pragmatic challenges confronting nation-states and transnational corporations during that decade. The abrupt end of the Cold War created a global geopolitical identity crisis, forcing nations on both sides of the historic divide to rethink their alliances and positioning in the world. The master narrative of "globalization" was quickly instantiated in Western policy circles. Within this new narrative, "market" was intended to replace "war" as the foundational metaphor. Globalization encouraged devolution of the nation-state, promoted privatization of public services, and sought to integrate the world market by reducing trade barriers—reflecting the tenets of what came to be known as "the Washington consensus" (Williamson, 1990). Under the new order, a nation's power and prestige would, at least in theory, be a function of its performance in the marketplace rather than on the battlefield (van Ham, 2001). Countries that possessed global super-brands like Coca-Cola, SONY, and Microsoft—the United States, Western Europe, and Japan—were favorably positioned to thrive under the new regime, while other nations, especially smaller ones, faced the challenge of leveraging the visibility of their identities and products.

As Olins (1999) put it, before long, countries and products were "trading identities." Companies recognized that positive national identities attracted investments, tourists, and demand for exports. Conversely, government leaders, seeking to increase exports, began to promote the national brands of their countries' private companies. The convergence of interests produced the public-private partnerships that make nation branding possible and attractive to many governments and corporate leaders. In this context, Olins, Anholt, and firms like Interbrand were well positioned to take the process to the next level by "trading in identities"—that is, selling a nation an image of itself that the nation could, in turn, resell to the world.

The break-up of the former Soviet Union in 1991 proved to be a particularly attractive market for traders in identities. Nations that had literally disappeared behind the shadow of the USSR for almost a half-century, as well as the new nations that emerged out of former Soviet territories, faced unique challenges in their transition into the neoliberal global market economy. Not only did they require radical reorganization of their political and economic infrastructures, they also needed to be introduced or re-introduced to the world. To ensure the flow of international resources required for social and economic transformation, these nations required sustained international visibility; that is, national identities that could be tailored to meet the demands of global markets.

ENTER BRAND ESTONIA

Estonia was the first former Soviet state to undertake a comprehensive branding initiative. It is also regarded as an exemplary case in the branding literature (Dinnie, 2008; Gardner & Standaert, 2003). Estonia's success— the relatively rapid economic development of Western Estonia, especially the capital Tallinn—has, in effect, functioned as an advertisement for nation branding in Central and Eastern Europe, even though nation branders, rather disingenuously, caution against drawing easy parallels.

The role nation branding actually played in Estonia's rapid integration into the world market is open to question. The initial Estonian branding initiative was actually a short-term undertaking within the much larger economic development program of Enterprise Estonia (EE). Enterprise Estonia is a public, government-affiliated, nonprofit company that was established in 2000 to promote business and entrepreneurship, provide financial advice, assistance, training, and research centers to grow new companies, improve exports, and facilitate product development. Its supervisory board is composed of leading entrepreneurs and top government officials. The Estonian branding initiative built upon the momentum of EE's broader transformative efforts; it represented the icing on the cake of post-Soviet Estonian capitalism. Yet, there is no hard evidence that the branding effort produced the "Baltic Tiger." Hard evidence is, generally, difficult to come by in the nation branding business, although suggestion, implication, and hype abound.[2]

Brand Estonia was developed by Interbrand, a subsidiary of global communication giant Omnicom, in partnership with Emor, an Estonian marketing firm. When directly queried, Interbrand executives describe their achievements in modest terms (Lewis, 2002), but as the story gets retold within the industry, the impression is cultivated that Brand Estonia produced Estonia's transformation rather than benefited from and amplified it. The view from within EE is more circumspect. In a 2008 interview, EE's brand manager, Leitti Mändmets, who, with Erki Peegel, EE's director of public relations and marketing, helped oversee Brand Estonia said:

> Estonia has done very well over the last seven years. Our economy is good, our tourist sector was booming until last year and all of this was thanks to the launch of Brand Estonia—of course that isn't true! Probably we did play a part, but how big a part is really, really hard to measure. (Quoted in Collier, 2008)

Estonia, like other former Soviet states, faced historic challenges in transforming its economy, reclaiming its national identity, and establishing a position within the global community. Estonia was, however, better prepared than most other former Soviet states for the transition. Smaller than many European cities, with a population of just over 1.3 million people (2008 estimate), Estonia was an independent country from 1918 until the Soviet takeover in 1940. During the Soviet era, Estonia's oppressed intellectual elite and its vocal champions abroad actively sought to preserve its identity, characterizing it as a "captive nation" with a Western orientation and values. With a westward Baltic Sea coastline, Estonia's language, culture, and traditions do bear some close affinities to those of Scandinavia, especially Finland, its closest Western neighbor. Moreover, during the Soviet era, Estonia had access to Finnish broadcasting; as a result, modern Western values, democracy, capitalism, and consumerism were familiar to ethnic Estonians in the urban west, who have been the primary beneficiaries of recent Estonian prosperity.

Although the Estonian peoples' struggles for freedom should not be underestimated, theirs was a bloodless revolution, part of the four-year long "Singing Revolution" (1987–1990), which also included Latvia and Lithuania. As a result, after the revolution Estonians were in a position to begin organizing recovery immediately. Estonia had another advantage—a Soviet legacy that nation branders are not inclined to emphasize. In the 1950s, the Soviets set up scientific institutes in the Baltic countries and, by chance, Estonia wound up with the Institute of Cybernetics, which gave it a significant head start among former Soviet client states in developing its computer industry—the pride of *E*-stonia (Landler, 2005). Finally, Estonia is strategically positioned as the northern coastal gateway between Russia and the West; this was a serious strategic liability during the Cold War, but it became an economic asset after 1991. Today, Russia is a primary target of EE's marketing initiatives (Priks, 2008).

Despite these advantages, Estonia also faced major challenges. During the Soviet occupation, a program to Russify Estonia was undertaken, which included large-scale Russian immigration to Estonia, accompanied by forceful deportation of ethnic Estonians, so that by 1989 ethnic Estonians comprised only 61.5% of the population, while the Russian population had risen to 30.3%. When Estonia regained independence in 1991, the Russians went from being the politically dominant group to a minority without the rights of citizenship, creating a situation ripe for conflict. Russians were confronted with three choices: return to Russia, become naturalized citizens, or remain a stateless minority. By 2000, the Russian population had declined to 25.5% as a result of migration and higher mortality rates among Russians (Leinsalu, Vågerö & Kunst, 2004), although most Russians who remained in Estonia were subsequently re-enfranchised and rigid naturalization rules were relaxed.

Tensions remain, however, as was evident in May 2007 when a cyber attack was launched against Estonia's paperless government in response to the government's removal of a World War II–era statue of a Russian soldier from a park in Tallinn. The targets of the attack were the Estonian president and parliament, most of the government ministries, political parties, three of the country's top news organizations, two of the biggest banks, and firms specializing in communications (Traynor, 2007). The Estonian government accused the Kremlin of launching the cyber attacks, claiming that the attacks originated in Russia and came from Russian government IP addresses. A spokesman for the Estonian Defense Ministry compared the attacks on his country to the September 11 terrorist attacks on the United States. The Russian government denied involvement but refused to cooperate in an investigation of the attacks. While NATO officials described it as a concerted attack, not the work of a few lone individuals, they stopped short of attributing it to the Russian government (Traynor, 2007). Only one individual, an ethnic Russian Estonian student, was prosecuted for participating in the attacks ("Estonia Fines Man," 2008). Both Estonian and Russian responses to the cyber attacks indicate that, despite current economic ties, historical wounds have not healed and relations between the two nations are still fragile.

Estonian separation from the Soviet Union was accompanied by a severe economic crisis. Estonia immediately lost its primary market (92% of its trade had been with Russia), and state industries collapsed. In 1992, the inflation rate was more than 1000%, GDP fell by 30%, and unemployment (unknown in the Soviet period) approached 30% (Laar, 1996). With support from the West, Estonia undertook radical political and economic reforms under the leadership of its young prime minister, Mart Laar, who served in this post from 1992 to 1994 and again from 1999 to 2002. Laar is popularly known as "Margaret Thatcher's grandson" for his commitments to what George Soros (1998) calls "market fundamentalism" (p. xxvii). Laar (1996) describes his embrace of market fundamentalism as "shock therapy" for socialism (p. 98).

Specifically, under Laar, Estonia ratified a new constitution and legal system, which reduced the role of the government in the economy. The government fast-tracked privatization, introduced a stable currency that was soon made the equivalent of the Deutschemark, eliminated price controls, sold off state properties, underwrote business loans in lieu of unemployment benefits, created employment retraining programs, especially in information technologies, introduced a flat tax, and eliminated tariffs. The government also looked to the West for capital as well as political and military support, and launched a lobbying campaign for membership in the EU and NATO.

Laar's shock therapy produced the intended neoliberal outcomes. Estonia's economy recovered more quickly than other post-Soviet economies and continued to grow rapidly, moving from a negative GDP in 1994 to a 10% growth rate in 2006 (Bank of Estonia, n.d.). Tallinn had the most developed real estate market in the Baltics, with housing prices rising by 28%—the highest in Europe—in 2006, although Estonia has been hit especially hard by the global collapse of the real estate bubble.

Economic shock therapy is always painful (Klein, 2008). In Estonia, the human costs were high, including the creation of wide gaps between the winners and losers, the "haves" and "have-nots," as well as disenchantment among broad segments of the population, especially in the rural interior of the country and among older workers, trained for Soviet heavy industries, who became cast-offs of the Estonian "miracle" (Sosin, 2007). Disillusionment with Laar and his economic reforms led to his defeat in the 1995 elections. He was, however, returned to a second term as prime minister during a fiscal crisis in 1999. He responded to that crisis by further cutting welfare programs, business taxes, and trade barriers. Winner of the 2006 Cato Institute Milton Friedman Prize for Advancing Liberty, Laar claims Friedman's *Free to Choose*, the bible of neoconservative market fundamentalism, provided the playbook for his reforms (Cato Institute, 2006).

Estonia's nation branding initiative took place well after Laar's economic reforms were in place. In 2002 Estonia was scheduled to host the Eurovision Song Contest, which meant that it would receive extensive international media coverage that year. Seeking to amplify the effects of this attention, Enterprise Estonia decided to launch a nation branding campaign and to have a "branding book" ready before the song contest (Collier, 2008). As Laar (2002) put it at the time, "We are no longer knocking on Europe's doors but are going there singing" (p. 21).

The Eurovision Song Contest is a major trans-European media spectacle—a "festival of nations"—that rivals World Cup soccer and the Olympics in popularity and audience size (Aksamija, n.d., p. 3). Broadcast from Iceland to Israel, it has been described as "one of the most watched events on the planet" (Coleman, 2009). Symbolically, it was an ideal venue for Estonia, a shining star of the "Singing Revolution," to launch its debut on the world economic stage. Moreover, Estonia did not just host the 2002 song contest; to the surprise of audiences everywhere, it won it. The unexpected victory greatly amplified Estonia's international visibility; it also resonated closely with the branding message that framed Estonia as a small but talented, competitive, and innovative nation.

THE BRAND: *WELCOME TO ESTONIA*, 2002

Estonian poet and cultural critic, Jaan Kaplinski (2002), captured the essence of Brand Estonia when he said, "World market is our gospel" (p. 21). That gospel was inscribed in the brand book, *Welcome to Estonia*, which told the world Estonia had been transformed and was open for business. Interbrand's challenge in 2001–2002 was to put Estonia on the map for tourists and international investors; in Estonia's case, this was a literal challenge because research indicated that foreigners did not know where Estonia was located and frequently confused it with its neighbors. With a budget of 13.31 million Kroon (€850,000), Interbrand developed promotional materials, including the "Welcome to Estonia" logo; a photographic style, color palette, and graphics; promotional materials, including short video documentaries, a PowerPoint presentation, pamphlets, and a CD-Rom; as well as an outdoor display campaign and press events (Petrone, 2003; "Welcome to Estonia," n.d.). Estonian national airlines, airports, shipping docks, emerging tourist industry, and many businesses adopted the Brand Estonia campaign (Emor Marketing, 2002; Interbrand, n.d.).

Figure 4.1 "Welcome to Estonia" logo, created by Interbrand for Enterprise Estonia.

A promotional video, *Welcome to Estonia*, produced for Enterprise Estonia in 2002 and still available on YouTube, conveys the essential themes of the original vision, although it is not clear whether the video was produced as part of the Interbrand campaign or as a separate initiative of EE.[3] Three sets of messages are presented on screen in large type; these graphics fold over and repeat against a backdrop of colorful photographs of the old (pre-Soviet) and the new (post-Soviet) Estonia; the soundtrack consists of upbeat, feel-good music. The video begins and ends with the message, "Estonia, Positively Transforming." The "Welcome to Estonia" logo also bookends each of the three sets of messages. The first set of messages targets tourists with the slogans, "Nordic With a Twist," "Ecological Haven," and "Structured for Tourism." The second set—"Quality and Reliability" and "Flexibility and Personal Approach"—as well as the third—"No Establishment," "Innovative Solutions," "Adaptable Self-Starter," "Competitively Growing," "E-government," and "Europe's Freest Market"—are aimed at international investors and the EU. The old and new are conveyed with images of medieval and 21st-century buildings, people in folk costumes and business suits, computers, young blond women, coastal scenery, modern hotels, upscale restaurants and nightclubs, more computers, and many attractive young people. Young, dynamic, competent, and business-friendly is the salient message; images, texts, and subtexts combine to convey to investors in the highly regulated economies of Western Europe that Estonia is a capitalist haven where they can escape business regulation, strong labor unions, and high taxes.[4]

What was initially left unsaid by Interbrand's and Enterprise Estonia's campaign materials, and was actively censored by the government, is that unleashing the "Baltic Tiger" seriously exacerbated social problems in Estonia. Social scientists were chastised in 2002 by Prime Minister Siim Kallas and former Prime Minister Laar for proposing a research project on the "Two Estonias" ("Estonian Politicians Rebuke," 2002). Specifically, Kallas and Laar referred to the 2001 *Estonian Human Development Report*, which pointed out that "it is not possible for the integration propaganda to bridge the chasm of segregation of Russian and Estonian communities which had only deepened through the decades" (Aarelaid, 2001, p. 87). The report indicated that the transformation "divided the nation into winners and losers: those whose yearly income is measured in millions and those who have lost hope of ever getting out of unemployment and poverty" (p. 88).

By 2006 Mati Heidmets, editor of that year's *Estonian Human Development Report*, identified weaknesses in the Estonian system that could no longer be silenced because Estonia's admission to the EU in 2004 made it subject to international reporting and accountability. The 2006 report, as well as the EU's own assessment, indicated that Estonia has the lowest life expectancy for men in the EU—65.8 years, which is 10 years younger than men in Italy, for instance. It has the highest HIV/AIDS rate in the EU—1.3% of the population, as compared to 0.1% in Germany. It also has the widest wage gap in the EU and allots only half of the EU average for social expenditures (Bender, 2007). In a realistic assessment of the country's current situation and future prospects, Heidmets contends Estonia "must understand that it is not only a business machine" (quoted in Bender, 2007). The 2006 *Estonian Human Development Report* concludes, "Estonia has reached the stage in its development where fast growth can no longer occur at the expense of social development—progress in these areas must occur simultaneously" (Bender, 2007).

There is some evidence that once Estonia's accession to the EU and NATO seemed assured, the country's political elites became more sensitive to internal pleas for social justice. Marju Lauristin (2003) contends that Estonia faced the possibility of a "legitimation crisis" (in Habermas's sense of the term) as a result of its social contradictions, and speculates that "this could be a main reason for the discursive change in public communication on social issues" (p. 11; see also Habermas, 1975). It is, however, expected that it will take Estonia 15 to 20 years to fully implement EU standards of social policy. This projection predates the worldwide recession, which has hit Estonia's high risk economy much harder than other EU nations: Estonia's GDP declined 15.1% between June 2008 and June 2009 (Statistics Estonia, n.d.). Although the economy grew by 2.6% in the fourth quarter of 2009, the Bank of Estonia forecast an overall decline of 14.2% for 2009 and warned that "the effects of the economic crisis have not yet passed" (Tere, 2010).

BRAND E-STONIA, THE NEXT STAGES: EST_IT@2018

Responding to the recession, Estonian President Toomas Hendrik Ilves says, "Estonia must take time for serious reflection" (Valner & Pitk, 2008). He further contends, "All ideas for creating a more favorable climate for business are welcome, presuming, of course, that they do not involve loss of revenue for the state, at least not in a longer perspective" (Valner & Pitk, 2008). Part of EE's effort to reenergize Estonia's "business machine" is to renew the branding initiative. According to brand manager Mändmets, "There has been no grand strategy behind it [Brand Estonia] for the last six years" beyond using the branding book to attract tourists and investments (quoted in Collier, 2008). She believes that "now is the time to renew these stories because over the years lots of things have changed" and these changes "should add value" (in Collier, 2008). Mändmets offers a preview of what the update of Brand Estonia will look like:

> We are working on this right now. One key point is always innovation: e-government, e-tax system, Skype, cyberwars, e-banking—that's one side. Nature on the other side. We have working groups considering these stories in tourism, business and education. (Quoted in Collier, 2008)

Erik Peegel, director of marketing and public relations for Enterprise Estonia, adds that education "is one new aspect of renewing Brand Estonia" (quoted in Collier, 2008). The current initiative will emphasize activities in education and science; Peegel points out that most nation brands are now focusing more attention on education. Brand Estonia's latest incarnation is also refining and more precisely targeting its communications to specific countries as well as positioning itself to take advantage of any unexpected opportunities that may arise. Enterprise Estonia has been especially effective in capitalizing on serendipitous developments.

A few examples illustrate Enterprise Estonia's agile opportunism. Baruto, a famous Japanese Sumo wrestler, was born in Estonia (his Estonian name is Kaido Hoovelson); Enterprise Estonia forged an arrangement with Baruto, whereby he acts as a goodwill ambassador for Estonia in Japan (Collier, 2008).

Estonia's e-government had the dubious distinction of being the first confirmed victim of cyber warfare (Landler & Markoff, 2007), but Estonia turned adversity into opportunity. Although the crisis actually exposed the vulnerability of Estonia's vaunted e-government, Estonia managed to leverage the accompanying global publicity, and its strategic geographic positioning as the gateway to Russia, to its apparent advantage. In 2008 NATO established a Cooperative Cyber Defence Centre of Excellence in Tallinn ("NATO Opens New Centre," 2008) and Estonians are now developing and promoting their expertise in cyber security.

Skype was created by Estonian software developers for a company founded by a Swede and a Dane, and subsequently sold to eBay in 2005, which resold it to a group of international investors in 2009. Yet, Enterprise Estonia continues to successfully leverage the Estonian connection, so much so that an article in the *New York Times* asked, "What is it about Estonians that makes them the Baltic's answer to Bill Gates?" (Landler, 2005).

As part of its renewal efforts, in 2008 Enterprise Estonia launched a major new initiative in anticipation of the country's 100th anniversary— the Development Fund's 2008 Foresight Project, which has working groups in three sectors: Industry Engines 2018 (manufacturing), EST_IT@2018 (information technologies), and Service Economy 2018. According to the Estonian Development Fund's website, "The Estonian Growth Vision 2018 seeks an answer to the question: what will bring us wealth and prosperity at the time when the Republic of Estonia is celebrating its 100th anniversary?" ("Growth Vision 2018," n.d.). The site indicates that the project is ongoing and explicitly states that it is committed to avoiding answers that are "superficial and slogan-like." To date, no concrete plans are posted for the manufacturing group, but EST_IT@2018 and Service Economy 2018 have outlined areas for development. EST_IT@2018 has identified six areas for growth in the development of information technologies: financial services, ICT security systems, education, manufacturing, energy supply and efficiency, and health care. Service Economy 2018 recommends focusing on knowledge-based services, which they perceive as the most profitable businesses in the service economy, including telecommunication services, financial mediation, consulting services, exportable health care and education services, transportation and logistics, and creative industries.

Enterprise Estonia and the Estonian Tourist Board are also revitalizing their branding efforts; their 2008–2010 goals included building a positive image of Estonia abroad, creating positions of strength in more markets, spreading business beyond Tallinn, growing the tourist business in the off season, and increasing the length of tourist visits (Priks, 2008).[5] The plan calls for using the following channels to attract tourists: campaigns, booklets and other informational materials, press trips to Estonia, regular newsletters, information seminars and study tours for travel agencies, as well as study tours to Estonia for journalists. The 2002 slogans, "Nordic With a Twist" and "Ecological Haven" are retained, but their associated stories are being more fully developed, and the following slogans are added: "There Is More to Estonia than Tallinn," "Appropriate for a Tourist Country," and "Unconventionally Chic" (Priks, 2008, slide 15).

Estonian tourist revenue for 2007 was €1.05 billion; however, despite its aggressive promotion, Estonia does poorly in international rankings of tourist destinations: it ranks 47 out of 50 countries (Tubalkain-Trell, 2009). The low ranking is attributed to continued lack of international visibility. Estonia will have another opportunity to enhance its international profile, at least among Europeans, in 2011 when Tallinn, along with Tartu, Finland, is scheduled to serve as the EU's European Capital of Culture. Embracing the slogan, "Tallinn: Everlasting Fairytale," Estonian organizers, who plan to spend €7 million on the project, complain that the "EU is a bit stingy . . . donating a mere 1.5 million Euros" (Kloss, 2007, p. 2).[6] Considering that Brand Estonia 2002 was commissioned for less than €1 million, "Tallinn 2011" is an ambitious undertaking indeed, especially in the wake of the global recession and Estonia's, as yet, unrealized social policy objectives.

As part of its renewal effort, Estonia has greatly expanded its presence on the web as well as the sophistication of that presence. While there are multiple user-friendly sites promoting tourism, investment, and living conditions in Estonia, the official website (Estonia.eu), which uses the slogan "Official Gateway to Estonia," is the premier portal. It is a virtual encyclopedia of Estonian government, culture, commerce, trade, education, history, science, and information technology, with hundreds of informational links that would fill a bookshelf if translated into the retro-world of paper. The multimedia interactive site prominently features a podcast by President Toomas Hendrik Ilves welcoming visitors to Estonia and encouraging them to follow him on Facebook. It includes news feeds, videos, a video contest, a contest to win a free trip to Estonia, links for citizens to conduct the transactions of everyday life with their e-government, and an introduction to learning Estonian. The site also offers assurances that, in addition to Estonian, English is a primary language and German and Russian are well represented among the languages of the people of Estonia. In short, Estonia.eu is, as EST_IT@2018 promises, both an innovative and creative representation of *E*-stonia.

THE *MY ESTONIA* INITIATIVE

An interesting populist or quasi-populist variation on developing national identity took place in Estonia on May Day 2009. The organizers of *My Estonia* claim it was an independently developed civil society initiative staffed by unpaid volunteers ("Frequently Asked Questions," n.d.).[7] The project did receive funding from a number of public and private organizations, including the government, although these appear to have been small grants.

The *My Estonia* project recruited more than 100,000 Estonians to take part in a day-long, nationwide brainstorming session to consider how to build a better Estonia. Instead of waiting for the government to solve problems, the organizers see their mission as creating innovative venues, think tanks, "brainstorming bees," and online discussions, exploring answers to such questions as, "How do we deal with unemployment?" and "How can we tackle stress levels?" Intended to be an ongoing project, not just a one-day extravaganza, *My Estonia* organizers claim that they plan to put the best ideas into practice. It is, as yet, unclear whether *My Estonia* is a genuinely populist effort to reclaim the power to name, claim, and shape Estonia's future, as its organizers contend, or, as cynics might assume, whether it is an orchestrated ideological distraction designed to placate a populace in the throes of a severe economic contraction. The discursive frame is nonetheless much broader and far more open to pluralistic messages and interventions than Brand Estonia 2002's reductive "gospel of the market."

CONCLUSION

The methodologies of nation branding are antithetical to the assumptions and communication practices of genuinely democratic civil society initiatives. Commercial ambition is the *raison d'être* of place branding. Nation branding transforms civic space into real estate, that is, into "calculative space" (Cronin, n.d.) that is constituted by marketing data and instrumental decision making rather than conceived in terms of social relations and democratic governance. Sociologist Anne Cronin maintains that, by constantly reiterating the commercial nature of public space, calculative space can produce a "new type of reality" and cultivate new orientations to that reality (n.d., p. 18). That is, it can be culturally transformative because public space is not just privatized and the rules governing its use altered, it is also commodified and liquefied, that is, turned into capital.

The new reality, created by place branding, instantiates the reductive logic of market fundamentalism. Ironically, in the interests of global capitalism, it valorizes a form of economic determinism that comes closer to realizing the conditions that inspired Karl Marx's critique of 19th-century capitalism and his apology for socialism than the forms of capitalism that prevailed in his own time. Critics of Marx, even critics like Max Weber, Georg Lukács, and members of the Frankfurt School, who were deeply influenced by his work, contend that Marx's economism—his premature version of "market fundamentalism"—overstates the case. The *bête noire* of Marx's theory of dialectical materialism was, of course, Adam Smith's *Wealth of Nations* (1776). Unlike 20th-century market fundamentalists and shock therapists like Friedman and Laar, Smith never entertained the illusion that markets could produce justice, truth, social well-being, or morality.[8] His theory of economics was a sequel to his *Theory of Moral Sentiments* (1859). Marx's reductive diagnosis more accurately describes current neoliberal theories and practices of market fundamentalism than the philosophical views and conditions prevalent in 19th-century Europe. According to Marx's theory of historical materialism then, Brand Estonia is now well positioned to begin the march toward socialism. Irony aside, even Estonian leaders now seem to acknowledge that the shock therapy economy is not sustainable.

Elsewhere (Jansen, 2008), I have argued that nation branding is problematic for a number of reasons, quite apart from whether it works or not—that is, whether or not it increases tourism, foreign investments, and demand for exports. First, despite the fact that citizens/consumers are consulted by being subjected to marketing studies, the methodology of nation branding, *qua methodology*, is not democratic. It is, to use Umberto Eco's (1995, p. 12) term, "ur-fascist," not liberal or even neoliberal. Nation branding is a monologic, hierarchical, reductive form of communication that is intended to (a) privilege one message; (b) require, insofar as possible, that all voices of authority speak in unison; and (c) silence or marginalize dissenting voices. It is telling, in this regard, that in the East West Communications Global Index 200, which monitors favorable coverage of nations in international media, Singapore, with its rigid media censorship and authoritative government, ranks as the number one global nation brand (Frost, 2008).

Whereas nation branding messages are, by design, hyper-visible, the decision making involved in arriving at them and the multiple agendas incorporated within them are neither legible nor visible (Sennett, 1980). Or, as Wally Olins put it more succinctly, "branding is propaganda . . . what it boils down to is manipulation and seduction. That's the business we're in. That's the business of life" (quoted in Cook, 2007, p. 2).

According to Richard Sennett (1980), however, legitimately constituted democratic authority requires transparency: Rules governing democratic processes and decision making must be legible—clear, unambiguous, amenable to renegotiation by citizens—and visible—open to public inspection and debate. Propaganda—the business Olins is in—fails the test on both counts.[9]

Second, if brand development fails to meet democratic standards of legibility and visibility, brand management is overtly totalitarian. It requires strict control. Anholt (2003) is very forthright on this point. He advocates tight, hierarchal control over the brand, "making sure that every single message that comes out of a country . . . plays unerringly on the same basic themes" (p. 135). He draws an analogy to the "despotic management styles" involved in corporate branding and warns that unless nations can develop "the same single-minded sense of purpose and control," their branding efforts are "doomed to fail" (p. 135). Fortunately for those who still believe in free speech, branders have far less control over people and places than they do over products. A quick search of the Internet and YouTube does bring up images of Estonia as "Nordic With a Twist" and "Ecological Haven" and references to Estonian links to Skype, but it also yields advertisements for Estonian girls, many references to "boring" Estonia, and a vast array of other messages that run counter to and, in some cases, deliberately invert the themes of Brand Estonia.

Third, once market fundamentalism establishes itself as the ruling cosmology and globalization becomes the controlling metaphor of geopolitics, nations like Estonia are pressured to participate. Branders tell them that they will face futures of economic and political marginality and cultural invisibility if they don't brand their national identities. As Olins (1999) put it, "Once it [nation branding] takes off it will become unstoppable" (p. 23). And nation branding has taken off; in late 2006, *The Economist* reported that Anholt claimed "a country a week" was seeking his services ("Nation Branding: A New Sort of Beauty Contest," 2006). Anholt accepts and celebrates the inevitability of a world in which brands rule; he maintains that brands will "gradually become the dominant channel of communication for national identity" (2003, p. 139) and characterizes this as "an immutable law of global capitalism" (p. 145).

To be sure, branders exaggerate their powers and the powers of their product: Olins (2004) readily acknowledges this, albeit with a sly wink, in his criticisms of Naomi Klein, author of *No Logo* (1999), whom he dismisses as a naive outsider who has been seduced by the branding industry's hype (Olins, 2001). Anholt (2007) posits a similar claim when he warns that nation branding can potentially be "dangerous" because public relations firms tend to oversell and overcharge for their services. Such candor notwithstanding, the promotional hype, totalizing logic, and fear tactics of nation branders have successfully pressured nations of the former Soviet Union—who did not want to be left behind—to succumb to Anholt's immutable law.

Fourth, whether it is effective in achieving its publicly stated objectives or not, nation branding is a successful mechanism for transferring public funds and authority into private hands. It thereby contributes to advancing and naturalizing market fundamentalism. The illusions of community and solidarity that nation branding cultivates, by crafting images of a shared heroic history and common cultural icons, tend to function ideologically to position nation branding as a pro-social force, which enhances the public sphere. More often than not, however, its agenda is to deplete (privatize) and supersede the public sphere. The apparent triviality of many branding activities, colors, logos, and slogans—even the fact that they may appear to be a waste of money—may actually enhance nation branding's effectiveness as an agent of neoliberalism because potential critics may regard nation branding as too inane to warrant serious and sustained scrutiny.

Fifth, nation branders traffic in stereotypes. They trivialize public discourse, reduce history and culture to a few sound bites, and thereby foster anti-intellectualism. Moreover, they claim that their services are needed to distinguish nations from one another as the world becomes increasingly homogenized; yet, the proliferation of nation branding services, with their formulaic repertoire of logos, colors, slogans, and promotions, actually accelerates the homogenizing processes of neoliberalism by encouraging nations to conceive of their identities in reductive market terms. In short, nation branders are marketing fool's gold: The shiny surface conceals the deeper erosion of cultural distinction that nation branding sets into motion.

Enterprise Estonia wisely purchased just enough fool's gold to add some glitter to its own considerable transformative efforts in 2001–2002. Estonia 2018 seems to be seeking a more substantive vision for a sustainable Estonian economy and society than the superficial slogans, colors, and stories nation branding confects. Stripped of the theoretical pretensions its promoters spin so effectively, nation branding is only a specialized form of public relations and advertising. If a nation has undergone significant political or economic transformations, it may make good sense to showcase its accomplishments to international audiences. This does not, however, mean that it has to fabricate a new national identity, reduce civil space to calculative space, embrace the gospel of the market, or dumb down its public discourse.

NOTES

1. This chapter builds upon and considerably expands on my earlier research reported in "Designer Nations: Neo-liberal Nation Branding—Brand Estonia" (Jansen, 2008). That article used Estonia's 2001 branding initiative as a case study within a much broader theoretical analysis of nation branding practices throughout the world.
2. There are methodologies that measure global nation brands in terms of public perceptions of nations: Anholt's Nation Branding Index, launched in 2005, and, more recently, the East West Global Index 200, which measures how nations are perceived/covered in international media. As these indexes accumulate data and reliability over time, at least in theory, it may be possible in the future to measure the effects of nation branding campaigns.
3. The video can be viewed at http://www.youtube.com/watch?v=F7VszESIDX8. Many other promotional videos can be found on the Estonia.eu website.
4. Data from 2008 indicate that less than 10% of the eligible workforce in Estonia is unionized—the lowest in the EU ("Trade union membership 2003–2008," n.d.).
5. Elin Priks is a destination marketing consultant for Enterprise Estonia and the Estonian Tourist Board. She is also the consultant for Latvia and Lithuania.
6. "Tallinn 2011" is, of course, inconsistent with the Estonian Tourist Board's effort to get visitors to think beyond Tallinn.
7. The *My Estonia* group is an outgrowth of an earlier initiative—"Let's do it!"—which brought together 50,000 volunteers to clean up litter in Estonian forests and countryside ("How It All Started," n.d.).
8. In fact, Smith's moral theory is an important constituent of economist Amartya Sen's (2009) influential theory of justice (see also Sen, 2010).
9. The lack of legible and visible authority is evident in Olins' admission that some of the work he has done for countries has been "very confidential" because "it's an issue a lot of countries find very sensitive and don't like talking about, because they feel people may think it's a waste of public money" (Olins, n.d., p. 1). Similarly, as we have seen, Mändmets acknowledged that in Estonia, the branding initiative has to be presented in other terms internally because "we can't talk about branding in marketing terms—people don't understand it" (quoted in Collier, 2008). Although Mändmets is surely right that many people may not understand the specifics of the protocols of marketing methodologies, nation branding itself is a fairly simple idea that an "educated" and "innovative" population can surely grasp and assess.

REFERENCES

Aarelaid, A. (2001). The identity of Estonians and *cairos*. In R. Vetik (Ed.), *Estonian human development report 2001* (pp. 86–88). Retrieved December 5, 2010, from http://www.tlu.ee/~teap/nhdr/2001/EIA2001Inglise.pdf

Aksamija, A. (n.d.). Eurovision Song Contest: Between symbolism of European unity and a vision of the wild, wild East. *Europelostandfound.net*. Retrieved April 19, 2010, from http://www.europelostandfound.net/files/elf/Eurovision.pdf

Anderson, B. (1981). *Imagined communities: Reflections on the origins and spread of nationalism*. London: Verso.

Anholt, S. (2003). *Brand new justice: The upside of global branding*. Oxford, UK: Butterworth-Heinneman.

Anholt, S. (2007). *Nation branding potentially dangerous* [Podcast]. Retrieved May 28, 2010, from http://www.cfr.org/publication/14748/anholt.html

Bank of Estonia. (n.d.). *Annual indicators of Estonian economy*. Retrieved December 5, 2010, from http://www.eestipank.info/dynamic/itp2/itp_report_2a.jsp?reference=503&className=EPSTAT2&lang=en

Bender, R. (2007, September 12). Risk factor "boomtown." *Café Babel: The European Magazine*. Retrieved June 12, 2009, from http://www.cafebabel.com/eng/article/22187/risk-factor-boomtown.html

Cato Institute. (2006). *Mart Laar's biography*. Retrieved January 4, 2010, from www.cato.org/special/friedman/laar/index.html

Coleman, N. (2009, May 17). Norway's Alexander Rybak wins Eurovision Song Contest. *Courier Mail*. Retrieved May 28, 2010, from http://www.couriermail.com.au/entertainment/norwegian-sweeps-eurovision/story-e6freq7f-1225713009268

Collier, M. (2008, July 21). About Brand Estonia. *Baltic Times*. Reposted on *Nation-branding.info*. Retrieved April 28, 2009, from http://www.nation-branding.info/2008/07/21/about-brand-estonia

Cook, J. (2007, January). Packaging a nation. *Travel and Leisure*. Retrieved July 12, 2007, from http://www.travelandleisure.com/articles/packaging-a-nation

Cronin, A. (n.d.). *Calculative spaces: Cities, market relations and the commercial vitalism of the advertising industry*. Online paper, Department of Sociology, Lancaster University, UK. Retrieved May 28, 2010, from http://www.lancs.ac.uk/fass/sociology/papers/cronin-calculativespaces.pdf

Dinnie, K. (2008). *Nation branding: Concepts, issues, practice*. Oxford, UK: Butterworth-Heinneman.

Eco, U. (1995, June 22). Eternal fascism: Fourteen ways of looking at a blackshirt. *New York Review of Books*, pp. 12–15.

Emor Marketing. (2002, February 2). The results of the Brand Estonia project. Retrieved January 9, 2005 from http://www.emor.ee/and/arhiiv.html?id=863

Estonia fines man for "cyber war." (2008, January 25). *BBC News*. Retrieved April 17, 2010, from http://news.bbc.co.uk/2/hi/technology/7208511.stm

Estonian politicians rebuke social scientists over "two Estonias." (2002, April 22). *Estonian Review*. Estonian Ministry of Foreign Affairs. Retrieved December 5, 2010, from http://www.vm.ee/?q=en/node/3749

Fanning, J. (n.d.). William Butler Yeats Nobel laureate; branding guru. *McConnells Advertising*. Retrieved January 9, 2005, from http://www.mcconnells.ie/branding/yeats050704.html

Freely, M. (1998, June 30). Scrambled eggheads. *The Guardian*. Retrieved 18 July, 2007, from http://www.guardian.co.uk/politics/1998/jun/30/thinktanks.comment

Frequently asked questions. (n.d.). *Teeme ära! Minu Eesti* [Let's do it! My Estonia]. Retrieved December 5, 2010, from http://www.minueesti.ee/?lng=en&leht=88,291

Frost, R. (2008). Rating nation brands: What really counts. *Brandchannel.com*. Retrieved April 27, 2010, from http://www.brandchannel.com/features_effect.asp?pf_id=443

Gardner, S. & Standaert, M. (2003, March 3). Estonia and Belarus: Branding the old Bloc. *Brandchannel.com*. Retrieved January 5, 2005, from http://www.brandchannel.com/print_page.asp?ar_id=146&section=main

Gilmore, F. (2002). A country—can it be repositioned? Spain—the story of country branding. *Journal of Brand Management, 9*, 281–293.

Growth vision 2018. (n.d.). Estonian Development Fund. Retrieved December 4, 2010, from http://www.arengufond.ee/eng/foresight/growth

Habermas, J. (1975). *Legitimation crisis*. Boston: Beacon Press.

How it all started. (n.d.). *Teeme ära! Minu Eesti* [Let's do it! My Estonia]. Retrieved June 19, 2009, from http://www.minueesti.ee/?lng=en&leht=88

Interbrand. (n.d.) Portfolio details, Estonia Tourist Board. Retrieved January 9, 2005, from http://www.interbrand.com/portfolio_details.asp?portfolio=2089

Jansen, S. C. (2005). Foreign policy, public diplomacy, and public relations: Selling America to the world. In L. Artz & Y. R. Kamalipour (Eds.), *Bring em on: Media and politics in the Iraq War* (pp. 51–66). Lanham, MD: Rowman & Littlefield.

Jansen, S. C. (2008). Designer nations: Neo-liberal nation branding—Brand Estonia. *Social Identities, 14*(1), 121–142.

Kaplinski, J. (2002). Quoted in *Eesti elu* [Estonian life]. Retrieved December 5, 2010, from http://web-static.vm.ee/static/failid/273/Eesti%20elu.pdf

Klein, N. (1999). *No logo: Taking aim at the brand bullies*. New York: Picador.

Klein, N. (2008). *The shock doctrine: The rise of disaster capitalism*. New York: Henry Holt.

Kloss, K. (2007, December 9). Tallinn 2011: Fairytales spin gold. *Cafébabel.com: The European Magazine*. Retrieved June 12, 2009, from http://www.cafebabel.com/eng/article/22128/tallinn-2011-fairytales-spin-gold.html

Laar, M. (1996). Estonia's success story. *Journal of Democracy, 7*(1), 96–101.

Laar, M. (2002). Quoted in *Eesti elu* [Estonian life]. Retrieved December 5, 2010, from http://web-static.vm.ee/static/failid/273/Eesti%20elu.pdf

Landler, M. (2005, December 13). Hot technology for chilly streets in Estonia. *The New York Times*. Retrieved May 28, 2010, from http://www.nytimes.com/2005/12/13/technology/13skype.html

Landler, M., & Markoff, J. (2007, May 24). Digital fears emerge after data siege in Estonia. *The New York Times*. Retrieved January 3, 2010, from www.nytimes.com/2007/05/29/technology/29estonia.html

Lauristin, M. (2003, Fall). Social contradictions shadowing Estonia's "success story." *Demokratizatsiya*. Retrieved June 17, 2009, from http://findarticles.com/p/articles/mi_qa3996/is_200310/ai_n9310188/pg_11/?tag=content

Leinsalu, M., Vågerö, D. & Kunst, A. E. (2004). Increasing ethnic differences in mortality in Estonia after the collapse of the Soviet Union. *Journal of Epidemiology and Community Health, 58*, 583–589.

Leonard, M. (1997). *Britain: Renewing our identity*. London: Demos.

Lewis, E. (2002, June 3). National pride and prejudice. *Brand Strategy*, 20–25.

Nation branding: A new sort of beauty contest. (2006, November 9). *The Economist*. Retrieved December 4, 2010, from http://www.economist.com/node/8147055

NATO opens new centre of excellence on cyber defence. (2008, May 14). NATO OTAN. Retrieved June 19, 2009, from http://www.nato.int/docu/update/2008/05-may/e0514a.html

Nimjean, R. (2005). Articulating the "Canadian way": Canada and the political manipulation of the Canadian identity. *British Journal of Canadian Studies, 18*(1), 26–52.

Nimjean, R. (2006). The politics of branding Canada: The international-domestic nexus and the rethinking of Canada's place in the world. *Revista Mexicana de estudios Canadienses 11*, 1–15.

Olins, W. (1999). *Trading identities: Why countries and companies are taking on each others' roles*. London: Foreign Policy Center.

Olins, W. (2001, September 8). The case for brands. *The Economist*. Retrieved May 28, 2010, from http://www.wallyolins.com/includes/ecn_reprint1.pdf

Olins, W. (2004). *Wally Olins on brand*. London: Thames & Hudson.

Olins, W. (n.d.). Brand leader. *Dorchester Group Magazine, 10*. Retrieved June 15, 2005, from http://www.wallyolins.com/my_latest_book/includes/interview.pdf

Petrone, J. (2003, March 13). Brand Estonia project shaping up positively. *Baltic Times*. Retrieved September 6, 2004, from http://www.baltictimes.com/news/articles/7730

Plaissance, P. L. (2005). The propaganda war on terrorism: An analysis of the United States' "Shared Values" public-diplomacy campaign after September 11, 2001. *Journal of Mass Media Ethics, 20*(4), 250–268.

Priks, E. (2008). *Destination Estonia. Activities through branding 2008–2010* [PowerPoint presentation]. Estonia Tourist Board, Enterprise Estonia. Retrieved May 28, 2010, from http://www.tourism.lt/informacija/PTO%202008%20 vasaris/ELIN%20PRIKS%20-%20DESTINATION%20ESTONIA%20-%20 VNO%2028-02-08.ppt

Sen, A. (2009). *The idea of justice*. Cambridge, MA: Harvard University Press.

Sen, A. (2010, April 23). The economist manifesto. *New Statesman*. Retrieved May 28, 2010, from http://www.newstatesman.com/ideas/2010/04/smith-market-essay-sentiments

Sennett, R. (1980). *Authority*. New York: Knopf.

Soros, G. (1998). *The crisis in global capitalism: Open society endangered*. New York: Public Affairs.

Sosin, N. (2007, September 13). Internet mad E-stonia. *The European Magazine*. Retrieved June 12, 2009, from http://www.cafebabel.com/eng/article/22145/internet-made-e-stonia.html

Statistics Estonia. (n.d.). Most requested statistics. Retrieved May 28, 2010, from http://www.stat.ee/main-indicators

Tere, J. (2010, March 3). Bank of Estonia: Effects of the economic crisis have not passed. *The Baltic Course: International Magazine for Decision Makers*. Retrieved April 18, 2010, from http://www.baltic-course.com/eng/analytics/?doc=24274

Trade union membership 2003–2008. (n.d.). Report of the European Foundation for the Improvement of Living and Working Conditions. Retrieved December 4, 2010, from http://www.eurofound.europa.eu/docs/eiro/tn0904019s/tn0904019s.pdf

Traynor, I. (2007, May 17). Russia accused of unleashing cyberwar to disable Estonia. *The Guardian*. Retrieved May 28, 2010, from http://www.guardian.co.uk/world/2007/may/17/topstories3.russia

Tubalkain-Trell, M. (2009, May 26). Estonia does poorly in ranking as tourist destination. *Baltic Business News*. Retrieved June 17, 2009, from http://www.balticbusinessnews.com/Default.aspx?PublicationId=d0585a58-ba6c-472f-9-c1b-88e3d1167da2

U.S. Department of State. (2003, January 16). *U.S. reaches out to Muslim world with Shared Values initiative* [State Department briefing]. Retrieved May 28, 2010, from http://www.america.gov/st/washfile-english/2003/January/20030116185938skaufman@pd.state.gov0.3441126.html

Valner, S., & Pitk, M. (2008, June 19). President Ilves: "Estonia must take time for serious reflection." *President.ee*. Retrieved December 5, 2010, from http://www.president.ee/en/media/interviews/3308-president-ilves-qestonia-must-take-time-for-serious-reflection-q-interview-to-maaleht-19-june-2008/index.html

Van Ham, P. (2001, September/October). The rise of the brand state: The postmodern politics of image and reputation. *Foreign Affairs*, 2–6.

Welcome to Estonia. (n.d.). Story sheet. Retrieved January 10, 2005, from http://www.tvlink.org/enlargement/docs/Estonia/EST%203%20-20%Branding.doc

Williamson, J. (1990). What Washington means by policy reform in Latin America. In J. Williamson (Ed.), *Latin American adjustment: How much has happened* (pp. 5–38). Washington, DC: Institute for International Economics.

5 Who Can Play This Game?
The Rise of Nation Branding in Bulgaria, 2001–2005

Nadia Kaneva

INTRODUCTION

In the spring of 2005, I was returning to Bulgaria for extended fieldwork on the country's nation branding activities. Although I had been researching the topic remotely for over a year, there were moments when I was still not sure that nation branding was, in fact, a substantive phenomenon. Was there a clear set of ideas and practices that constituted nation branding? Or was this just a lot of hype? My uncertainty was somewhat abated almost immediately upon arrival. After landing at Sofia Airport, the first thing I saw from a friend's car, as we drove away, was a giant billboard with the official Bulgarian national logo that had been recently approved by the Council for European Integration. The billboard seemed a bit odd; it simply displayed the large logo—an abstractly painted smudge in orange and yellow, intended to resemble a rose, and the word "Bulgaria" written in green under it—against a white background. There was no slogan because, as I would find out later, none had been agreed upon. Although the purpose of this billboard was unclear to me, something made its existence on the side of the highway possible and meaningful. That *something* was exactly what I had come to investigate.

This chapter sets out to describe the emergence of a Bulgarian field of nation branding between 2001 and 2005. My approach follows Bourdieu's field theory[1] and conceptualizes nation branding as a field of social practices and discourses in which institutional and individual actors are jockeying for position and struggling over desired resources. In this context, the account in this chapter has three main goals. First, it maps out the institutional and political-economic landscape of the Bulgarian field of nation branding. Second, it provides detailed descriptions of two paradigmatic branding projects—*Branding Bulgaria* and *Promotion Bulgaria*—that were instrumental in establishing a local discourse of nation branding. Third, it discusses the implicit rules for participation in the field, as they emerge from ethnographic observations and interviews with field actors, and outlines three main themes used to legitimate the field's existence. Ultimately, my aim is to unmask the strategic motivations of actors for establishing a Bulgarian field of nation branding and for participating in it.

A peculiar characteristic of the field of nation branding in Bulgaria, as well as in other former communist nations, is its project-driven nature.[2] The project format for structuring public and private initiatives was introduced in Bulgaria after 1989, with the influx of foreign funds—from organizations such as the U.S. Agency for International Development (USAID), the EU, the Open Society Institute, and others—that are typically administered by nongovernmental organizations (NGOs) or special quasi-governmental agencies on a short-term basis. The project format has been increasingly adopted by various branches of state and local administrations as a way to take advantage of foreign funds.[3]

Discussing the differences between a pre-1989 "communist bureaucratic culture" and an accession-motivated "European bureaucratic culture," Ditchev (2000) points out that "the first is the culture of five-year *plans*, the latter is the culture of *projects*: plans are imposed from the top and presuppose a constant upward transferring of responsibility; projects are related to individual planning, reports, time-tables, responsibility" (p. 102, emphasis in original). The ability to apply for and win project funding has become important in government and in the new NGO sector. NGOs, in particular, become incubators for a new elite of bureaucrats with the relevant grant-acquisition skills. At the same time, Ditchev notes that it would be an exaggeration to argue that the communist bureaucratic culture has completely disappeared.

My observations of the field of nation branding confirm Ditchev's description. Many of the examples I discuss in this chapter are of short-term projects which, though often unrelated, were usually aware of each other's existence. Thus, field actors were conscious of the competitive nature of the field and structured their activities in response to that assumption. The main institutional actors in the field between 2001 and 2005 can be divided into three categories: (a) government institutions, (b) NGOs and business associations, and (c) private marketing and branding consultants and agencies. These groups came to the field with various priorities and interacted in complex ways to further their agendas. However, they shared certain discourses of legitimation, used to explain the necessity of nation branding for Bulgaria. Moreover, as I will argue, participation in the field of nation branding was a form of seeking legitimacy for their claims to power in the post-communist environment. This is not surprising, given that nation building, and subsequently national image, are driven by elites and associated closely with the power of the nation-state. Thus, I understand nation branding is a subfield of the "field of power," which is synonymous with the power of the state in modernity (Bourdieu, 1994, p. 5).

INSTITUTIONAL AND POLITICAL-ECONOMIC DIMENSIONS OF THE FIELD

A number of government ministries, agencies, and offices have been involved in efforts to brand Bulgaria. Given the origins of nation branding within the disciplines of marketing and economics, it is not surprising that government activities that were most explicitly defined as nation branding were carried out by the Ministry of the Economy (ME) and two of its executive agencies: The National Agency for Advertising and Information (later renamed as the State Agency for Tourism), charged with tourism promotion, and the Bulgarian Investment Agency (later renamed as InvestBulgaria Agency), charged with attracting foreign direct investments.

The international images of countries are also linked to their political activities, and this dimension of image management became particularly relevant in light of Bulgaria's aspirations for EU accession. In that context, the Ministry of Foreign Affairs (MFA) became another important institutional actor in the field of nation branding, as it was tasked with coordinating Bulgaria's communication activities leading up to EU accession. In February of 2002, the Bulgarian Council of Ministers approved a Communication Strategy for Bulgaria's Accession to the EU (CS), produced by the MFA. The CS, and its related Action Plan for Communication Activities, focused on the period between 2002 and the accession on January 1, 2007, and aimed at "bringing Bulgarian citizens closer to the everyday dimension of EU membership, while at the same time making concerted efforts to raise the knowledge of European citizens about Bulgaria" (Communication Strategy, 2002).

The CS had a yearly budget of 5 million Bulgarian leva (approximately $3.1 million) in 2003 and 2004, used to fund a range of communication efforts directed at internal and external audiences. The funding protocol required ministries to provide an annual program for activities related to CS goals, which had to pass a set of approvals before moneys were allocated. In turn, each ministry held public auctions and accepted bids from private contractors interested in executing communication projects from the ministries' programs. This process established a framework of client-service relations between government institutions and private contractors, including branding and advertising consultants and agencies, and has been an important structural characteristic of the field of nation branding. Ministry-initiated public auctions, related to communication campaigns, have continually been in the focus of the media and were often described as ridden by corruption, with a few favored agencies winning most of the major bids ("Foreign Gives 1 Million," 2003; Iliev, 2004; Kandov, 2004a).[4]

Generally, MFA rhetoric described advertising campaigns funded by the CS as "public diplomacy," and there was an effort to distinguish CS projects from branding campaigns. An MFA official, who had authored the text of the CS, explained:

> If you are speaking in a more political, more strategic plan, when you are trying to establish Bulgaria as, let's say, a factor of stability in the region and, well, a predictable and reliable partner within NATO and the EU, then it is more difficult to talk about branding because we are talking of expectations of a strategic nature. (Personal interview, July 7, 2005)

However, despite the MFA's seeming aversion to the language of branding, the CS funded at least one initiative that self-identified as a "nation branding" project—*Promotion Bulgaria*, executed by the ME in 2004. This project, in fact, produced the Bulgarian national logo (which I encountered upon my arrival in Sofia) that will be discussed in detail later in this chapter. Another major initiative, widely touted as "the largest PR [public relations] campaign for Bulgaria," was the country's participation in the Europalia festival in Brussels in 2002; this initiative was also funded from the CS budget.

The case of *Europalia Bulgaria* deserves some attention because of the significant media attention it received, as well as the fact that it was frequently mentioned by my informants as an early, though ill-conceived, attempt at nation branding. The annual Europalia festival in Brussels has existed since 1969 and is organized by Europalia International, a nonprofit entity set up by the Belgian government. Bulgaria's participation was negotiated by the Bulgarian Ministry of Culture in 2001 during the government of the Union of Democratic Forces (UDF). The Ministry of Culture was also put in charge of preparing the country's festival presentation. However, after the 2001 parliamentary elections, the UDF lost power and the new government neglected preparations for Europalia. Four months before the festival's starting date, this lapse was discovered, and the MFA was urgently tasked with setting up a mechanism that would ensure the country's proper participation. The MFA allotted 1.8 million leva (approximately $1.2 million) from the CS budget for this purpose and set up an emergency National Europalia Committee, headed by journalist and cultural critic Emmy Barouh. These last-minute measures resulted in a program biased toward the arts, which included art exhibitions, concerts, literary conferences, dance performances, theatrical presentations, and films (Barouh, personal interview, July 20, 2005). Unlike other countries presenting at Europalia, Bulgaria did not showcase its business sector—it featured no tourism or export promotions (Butzev, 2003). Thus, despite record-high attendance of all festival events in Brussels, the lack of coordination between government and business was seen by Emmy Barouh, Commissary General of the National Europalia Committee, as a failure.

Europalia Bulgaria was mentioned by my informants as an example of the piecemeal, *ad hoc* approach toward national promotion that characterized the early Bulgarian efforts at nation branding. It was seen as symptomatic of the lack of a national vision and coordination, and an illustration of the outdated understanding of national image-building as predicated on displaying the country's high culture exemplars but unconnected to trade and marketing promotion. Indeed, many of the other projects discussed in this chapter emphasized their superior understanding and application of branding and marketing principles.

Although many projects in the field of nation branding were initiated and housed by government institutions, few were solely state funded and executed. A project could be initiated and coordinated by a ministry but be partially or fully funded with international money funneled through an NGO. For example, the Open Society Institute contributed funds to *Europalia Bulgaria* (Europalia: The Traces Remain, 2003), and USAID funded the production of promotional materials for the Bulgarian Investment Agency. The foreign funding entities that were mentioned most often in interviews in relation to communication and publicity activities were the EU (through its structural funds) and USAID. Foreign participation also included the activities of the British Council, which funded a project titled *Branding Bulgaria,* which will be discussed in detail later in this chapter.

The foreign sources of funding also influenced the field in terms of introducing external (Western) branding consultants, invited through institutional channels to give expert advice on various projects. In that sense, foreign-funded NGOs served as sales agents for Western brand consultants seeking new business opportunities in Eastern European markets. Further, NGOs operated as mediators between the public and private sectors. This is illustrated by the case of the Bulgarian information and telecommunication industry (ICT), which was identified as a priority sector for economic development.

As a result of the globalizing market for ICT services and a trend of outsourcing to countries with lower labor costs, Bulgaria gained a share of the global ICT market, supporting a healthy local ICT industry. Bulgaria's appeal as an outsourcing destination was proudly cited by government institutions, such as the Bulgarian Investment Agency, and business associations in the ICT sector as a measure of the country's economic success.[5] The ICT sector was among the first in Bulgaria to develop a strategy for promotion and development, which included a section on country branding ("Strategy and Action Plan," 2004). The logic behind the inclusion of nation branding in the strategy was that a better image for the country would give its ICT industry a global economic advantage and help individual companies in their sales efforts. As one industry executive stated, "Every time we make a client presentation we have to start by explaining where Bulgaria is. We first have to sell Bulgaria, then the sector, and only then our companies" (personal interview, July 29, 2005).

The branding efforts of the Bulgarian ICT sector were financially and logistically supported by USAID, under a program for encouraging economic competitiveness. They led to the creation of a lengthy strategic document, a logo and slogan for the ICT industry ("ICTalent"), and the establishment in 2004 of the Bulgarian ICT Cluster, an NGO charged with coordinating development and promotional efforts. The consortium of companies and business associations represented by the ICT Cluster sought active support from the government for the development of the sector. However, in interviews with ICT executives, I discovered a general skepticism about the partnership between business and government as well as a sense of frustration with the lack of coordination between private and public efforts to promote the country. Nevertheless, most informants maintained that nation branding should be a priority and that the government should take the lead and provide the bulk of the funding.

PARADIGMATIC NATION BRANDING PROJECTS

Having outlined the broader boundaries of the field, I focus next on two projects that self-identified explicitly as nation branding initiatives. These paradigmatic projects—with the suggestive names *Branding Bulgaria* and *Promotion Bulgaria*—bear several important similarities. First, both aimed to influence public opinion in Bulgaria about the need for national promotion and consciously worked to generate media publicity and public debate about the international image of the country. Second, both attempted to re-imagine Bulgaria—the nation—as a total brand, rather than focusing on a separate industry or aspect of economic or cultural activity. In addition, both invited advice from international branding consultants and were, to a significant extent, influenced by their ideas and recommendations.

At the same time, the projects bear several important differences, which can be summarized along the lines of institutional basis and approaches to participation. *Branding Bulgaria* was initiated by a non-native NGO, the British Council, and relied on a broad-based network of participants recruited from various institutions. By contrast, *Promotion Bulgaria* was a state-sponsored initiative that operated within the bureaucratic structure of the ME, was funded by the CS, and was less open to broad participation from external groups.

Branding Bulgaria (BBG) began in 2001 and concluded in November 2004. The project was headed by Leah Davcheva, Head of the Department of Cultural Studies and Literature at the British Council in Bulgaria, who had supervised a number of British Council projects on intercultural exchange and education prior to her work on the BBG project. Davcheva explained that, although the main mission of the British Council was "to promote the UK," the BBG project went beyond the boundaries of traditional cultural exchange and education. The BBG project used the idea of *mutuality*, a central tenet in the overall strategic vision of the British Council, to justify the logic of its activities. This meant that the rationale for the project was framed in terms of an exchange of ideas between Bulgaria and the United Kingdom, where British expertise and experience, particularly in the area of nation branding, could be shared with Bulgaria in the context of mutual enrichment (personal interview, July 18, 2005).

BBG was steered by an initiative group of volunteers, which varied in number from 10 to 15 individuals during different phases of the project. The group consisted of representatives of government, business, NGOs, the media, and the intellectual elite who had been selected with an eye to including "as much as possible, professionals and individuals representing state and private organizations/institutions directly involved in and responsible for image building" (Davcheva, personal interview, July 18, 2005). Davcheva, who had been the main convener of the initiative group, explained that she also tried to include people from different generations in order to get a variety of viewpoints. Generational differences turned out to be a significant factor in the workings of the initiative group, with younger participants being more receptive to the ideas of branding.

In addition to the initiative group, a wide network of other participants from the private and public sectors were involved in the project's activities. Participation at different events varied from 15 to 50 attendees, and the list of those invited continued to change over the three years of the project. Overall, attendees included government officials, business executives, NGO officers, university professors and graduate students, journalists, advertising and PR professionals, and visual artists.

The total budget of the project was approximately £30,000 over three years from funds of the British Council. This budget covered retainer fees for three British consultants; a fee for the author of the project's final report, published as a booklet, *Take It Easy!* (Mineva, 2003); a salary for an additional project manager during the second phase of the project; and payment for two research reports on internal and external public opinion about Bulgaria. In addition, the budget covered administrative expenses, catering costs for a number of events, production costs for promotional materials and the final booklet, as well as the production costs for an informational website about the project's activities. In its last phase in 2004, BBG also received a £4,000 grant by the Open Society Institute in Bulgaria, which was used for the development of a promotional web portal.[6] In-kind support was provided by the Euro-Bulgarian Cultural Center, a nonprofit funded by the Ministry of Culture and the EU's PHARE program, which was an official partner in the BBG project and hosted some of its public events.[7]

BBG went through two distinct phases. The first phase (March 2001– March 2003) involved a series of public discussions on the national image of Bulgaria. The project also commissioned a study, conducted by a subdivision of Gallup International in Bulgaria, on existing perceptions among young Bulgarians about the ways in which the country is perceived by Western Europeans (Balkan British Social Surveys, 2002). In addition, two workshops, led by British consultants, were held in November 2001 and February 2002. The November 2001 workshop was moderated by branding consultants Anneke Elwes and Yvonne McClean, and one of its main goals was "to bring together the key people who could articulate and shape the future brand of Bulgaria in order . . . to excite them about the possibilities of national branding and to give them a sense of ownership over the process" (Elwes, 2001).

This workshop was modeled on business and advertising workshops. It included structured exercises and brainstorming sessions that introduced the nation branding paradigm and elicited ideas about possible areas that should be included in the construction of a national brand for Bulgaria. The participation of Anneke Elwes is notable because she is the author of an influential report, titled *Nations for Sale* (Elwes, 1994)—one of the earliest texts that introduces the idea of nations as brands, widely cited in the professional literature on nation branding. Many of the project participants mentioned this workshop in interviews and pointed out Elwes' involvement as crucial in their introduction to the ideas of nation branding. According to Davcheva, Elwes' contribution "gave structure to the whole project" and the title of her workshop, "Branding Bulgaria," gave the project its name (personal interview, October 6, 2005).

The second workshop, held in February 2002, took a shift toward a broader discussion of national identity and cultural representations, although some time was devoted to generating ideas for a possible brand slogan for Bulgaria. According to the workshop's facilitator, Dr. Alan Durant of Middlesex University, a major reason for this shift was that Elwes and McClean had declined further participation in BBG and his own expertise was more academic than business oriented (personal interview, October 12, 2005). One outcome of the second workshop was the decision to produce a written document that would summarize the themes and findings from previous discussions. The writing of this text was assigned to Mila Mineva, then a Doctoral Candidate in Sociology and Assistant Professor of Cultural Studies at Sofia University, who had been an active participant in the discussion groups. The first phase of the project concluded in March 2003 with the publication and public presentation of Mineva's text, titled *Take It Easy! Towards a Strategy for Representing Bulgaria* (Mineva, 2003). Arguably, this document contains the first systematic local effort to make the case for nation branding in Bulgaria. The booklet, published in a combined Bulgarian and English language volume, was distributed free of charge among governmental, nongovernmental, and business institutions in Bulgaria and some copies reached the United Kingdom via the institutional channels of the British Council.

The project's second phase involved the development and execution of a tourism-oriented web portal and a pilot advertising campaign to promote it. During this phase, the initiative group continued to meet and discuss the project's progress. A second project manager, Boris Deliradev, was added to the team and charged with coordinating web production and advertising. The target group for the website was determined as British college students, and a research report was commissioned from the Manchester School of Business, which measured this group's knowledge of Bulgaria (Manchester Business School, 2003). The website was designed with a focus on attracting young, affluent British travelers who were not interested in "organized tourism" but wanted to explore Bulgaria on their own. The advertising campaign to promote the site ran in the spring of 2004 on five college campuses in Britain (Manchester University, Oxford University, Cambridge University, Glasgow University, and University College in London) and consisted of posters and free postcards. Using the headline, "Where on Earth is Bulgaria?" and images of young travelers, the campaign aimed to drive traffic to the website, where students could learn more about Bulgaria and register to win one of four grand prizes (a week-long trip to the country).

Despite the fact that the final product of BBG was a small-scale, short-lived advertising campaign, the project had significance for establishing a public discourse of nation branding in Bulgaria, which would then be picked up by various other institutions and projects. BBG accomplished this by maintaining a high public profile in the media and by making a number of concerted efforts—through events, public discussions, publications, and so on—to generate a wider debate about the need for Bulgaria to brand itself. The majority of my informants who had not been involved in BBG had heard or read about it in the media and were aware of its purposes. The project involved both the private sector and government institutions, with varying success. It had been quite successful, for instance, in collaborating with private companies in the development of its promotional materials and its web campaign. However, its attempts to involve the MFA in larger discussions about the presentation of Bulgaria abroad were unsuccessful (Davcheva, personal interview, July 18, 2005). Some of the participants in BBG seminars and workshops later participated in other branding projects organized by government institutions. Leah Davcheva and Boris Deliradev were invited to consult in other branding-related activities and participated in an advisory capacity in *Promotion Bulgaria*, the second paradigmatic project, which I will discuss next.

Promotion Bulgaria (PBG) was administered by the ME between July 2004 and February 2005. Its total budget was 243,662 leva (approximately $149,000) and came from the budget of the CS for EU accession (Bulgarian Telegraph Agency, n.d.). PBG was managed by Ekaterina Vitkova, a former journalist and PR practitioner who, at the time, served as head of the political cabinet of the Minister of the Economy.[8] In the course of the project, expertise was provided by Dutch nation branding consultant Hans Cornelissen, who had advised the Dutch government on branding issues. He supplied the main theoretical framework of nation branding and was instrumental in pushing the idea for creating a "copy platform" for the presentation of Bulgaria, modeled on the Dutch copy platform (Bulgarian Ministry of the Economy, 2004a).[9] The one-page "Copy Platform for Presentation of Bulgaria Abroad" outlined a few main ideas that Bulgaria was to communicate in its international promotion. However, this document did not lead to further substantive actions.

In its conception, PBG anticipated to continue operations in 2005 (Communication Strategy 2004 Annual Report, 2005), but it was cut short by a political reshuffling at the ME in February 2005, when Minister Lydia Shuleva was pulled out of office, and the political cabinet, including Ekaterina Vitkova, was replaced. Despite its short existence, however, the project was significant because it constituted an ambitious effort by a state institution to come up with a unified frame of visual and textual representation for Bulgaria, intended to become the basis for a broad national policy. PBG accomplished several things; most notably, it managed to create and approve a national logo for Bulgaria.

The history of the logo's birth speaks to the institutional battles that *Promotion Bulgaria* had to navigate. In March 2004, the Bulgarian Council for Economic Growth (CEG), an interinstitutional group with participation from several ministries and major business associations, convened to discuss the need for improving the international image of Bulgaria. The goal of the meeting was to discuss Bulgaria's "national advertising," whose aims were understood as the following:

> Establishing a positive image of Bulgaria abroad through national advertising; Expanding the list of Bulgarian exports of goods and services . . . ; Preserving positions in markets where Bulgarian goods are traditionally exported and entering new promising markets; Increasing the volume of export and improving its content (finished products with higher added value, instead of raw materials). (Bozhinov, 2004)

As a result of decisions made at the CEG meeting, the ME was entrusted with holding a public competition among young people, aged 16 to 29, for a national logo and slogan to be used in future promotional efforts. The competition was announced on March 31, 2004, and allowed only a month (until April 30, 2004) for submission of proposals (Bulgarian Ministry of the Economy, 2004b). The rationale for the quick turnaround time and for restricting entrants to a narrow age bracket was not discussed in any of the press releases of the ME. The competition was successfully completed, and the winning entries were announced in June 2004. Although widely publicized, the winning logo and slogan were never used in official promotional materials. Instead, they were replaced by another logo, created in a closed procedure, overseen by the *Promotion Bulgaria* project that had been launched in July 2004, shortly after the conclusion of the competition.

In fall 2004, the ME formed "an informal group including representatives of academic circles and the arts," whose goal was to come up with ideas for a "representational platform" for Bulgaria (Kandov, 2004b). During this phase, PBG organized a series of seminars and workshops with intellectuals, representatives of local and national government, media, and marketing practitioners. The project also commissioned a survey of perceptions about Bulgaria among 200 foreigners living in the country, executed by Bulgarian research company Vitosha Research in November 2004. The survey included a list of specific symbols that could represent Bulgaria and elicited responses from respondents about each symbol's relevance. The rose was identified as one of the symbols with highest relevance[10] and was selected to be the symbol featured in the national logo (Vitosha Research, 2004).

Figure 5.1 Bulgaria's national logo, created by artist Emil Vulev.

The new national logo was created by Bulgarian artist Emil Vulev and executed in the Cyrillic and Roman scripts by the private company Design-BG.[11] This logo was approved by the Bulgarian Council for European Integration in December 2004 (Bulgarian Ministry of the Economy, 2004c), only a couple of months before PBG's abrupt end in February 2005. The logo was originally met with little popular support, and the process for its creation was seen by some as an example of top-down, government action and clientelism. Despite oppositional sentiments, however, the logo was put into use almost immediately in the various promotional materials of government institutions, state-funded tourism brochures, and on the labels of some export products (BulgarianIndustry.bg, 2005). PBG also commissioned a number of promotional materials, such as brochures and CD-ROMs, with the new logo and graphic standards. Their execution was awarded to private companies selected through public auctions in accordance with Bulgarian administrative laws. The materials were published in several Western European languages and covered such topics as Bulgaria's historical and cultural heritage and its nature.

Despite the large quantity of materials produced, however, they had limited distribution abroad. Materials were given to Bulgarian diplomatic offices abroad and to other ministries internally, where they often remained in boxes and found no further use. Vitkova explained this with the bureaucratic mindset in government institutions. As she put it, "Once you are out of the system you can't rely that these bureaucrats will keep things going. Simply, this is not their cause and they don't care" (personal interview,

July 6, 2005). Another important reason for the project's limited effectiveness was the lack of long-term planning and continuity across administrations after the 2005 parliamentary elections, in which the ruling party lost.

THE LOGIC OF THE FIELD: *EMIC* EXPLANATIONS

The complex dynamics of the field of nation branding entail internal rules of participation and an understanding of the key resource over which field actors struggle. Although these are rarely laid out in explicit terms, they are tacitly understood and accepted by actors in the field and, therefore, can be inferred from their ideas about hierarchy, responsibility, and purpose for participation. In this section I attempt to unmask the implicit rules of the field of nation branding as they emerge from my ethnographic interviews with participants. I first focus on the way interviewees described the structure of the field. Second, I analyze how informants justified the appeal of nation branding and the need for its introduction in the local context. In short, this section primarily presents the *emic* explanations of actors in the local field of nation branding.

The most common complaint repeated in most of my interviews was the chaotic nature of nation branding in Bulgaria. As one informant put it, "Everyone is doing something . . . producing piles of logos" (personal interview, July 29, 2005). This chaos was attributed to a number of factors, including a "bureaucratic mindset," "lack of funds," or lack of sufficiently evolved political and business thinking. Another informant suggested, with sarcasm, that the only way to explain the goings on within the field was to apply chaos theory. As he put it,

> This is rather a question of making a mathematical model . . . of the chaos that exists in the field of advertising in Bulgaria right now; then you attack the model with random events like, pop! a new logo appears from the Ministry of the Economy, and what would be its effect on the rest of the system? (Personal interview, July 6, 2005)

This comment was intended to convince me that there were many hidden interests behind the public displays of nation branding projects. In this sense, it represented an effort to preserve the opacity of the internal dynamics of the field and protect its unspoken rules of participation.

Although I do not claim to have exposed all of the interests that came into play within the early field of nation branding, a few were readily identifiable by looking at its political-economic dimensions. Perhaps the most obvious competition in the field was among marketing and advertising agencies bidding for the budgets of various branding projects. While agency practitioners were often skeptical about the effectiveness of such projects, they were happy to produce logos, brochures, and all sorts of other materials as long as the money kept flowing. As one advertising executive stated, "There is some money we can get our hands on—isn't that nice?" (personal interview, June 6, 2005).

The overall impression of chaos in the field, however, was a sign of a more important struggle for political influence among institutional actors. This was illustrated in the cases of both paradigmatic branding projects described earlier. The political struggles were commonly acknowledged by informants who argued that many nation branding projects came about as "internal PR campaigns," that is, as short-term tactical efforts to raise the public visibility of a particular ministry or government agency. By demonstrating concern for the international image of the country, government bureaucrats could appear patriotic and attract votes from the population or larger spending quotas from the state budget. It is hard to present empirical evidence that such tactics were successful, but the multiplicity of branding projects suggests this is a plausible interpretation. One BBG participant summarized, "The problem is that . . . everything happens in the shape of some small circles and simply some of these circles are in power, others are not . . . but these circles do not want to communicate with each other" (personal interview, July 20, 2005).

The struggles of political interests were further complicated by the emergence in the post-communist context of a new, professional elite of "cultural intermediaries" (Bourdieu, 1984), drawn from media and communication, PR, marketing, and advertising experts. This group was making a claim on the power to define the image of the nation and, in that sense, its identity. This shifted the balance of power away from traditional intellectual elites (previously loyal to the communist regime) and into the direction of agents whose alignment was with business and market interests. The field of nation branding attracted members of both groups: representatives of older generations, who had been associated with power during communism, were trying to reposition themselves in the new social situation in order to retain their privileges; representatives of the emerging group of marketing experts, by contrast, were interested in improving their strategic positions within the field of power. The resulting lack of homogeneity in the composition of the nation branding field is evident in the discursive clashes between different groups, manifested in the form of chaotic and sporadic activity as well as in conflicting strategies for defining the social relevance of a Bulgarian national brand.

On the one hand, the national brand was presented as something that should be handled by experts and not of great importance to the average citizen. As one informant argued,

> It is not necessary for people to be able to recognize an effort and a product and to identify it and name it with its proper scientific or applied term in the way experts conceived it or in the way experts evaluate it. . . . For the ordinary person . . . from the street this is not so

important. . . . Each of us does our work and makes our efforts at a specific level of competency, among our reference group and when everyone does their work well at that level somehow half of the common work is done. (Personal interview, June 21, 2005)

In this view, nation branding—much like national identity building—was an elite project, hardly concerned with inclusion and democratic participation. If inclusion was considered at all, it was at the superficial level of "representation" in the advertising messages or through the mechanisms of market research on "perceptions." Thus, average citizens were cut out from the construction of a new national identity through branding on the grounds that they lacked the competency necessary to participate in the process.

An opposing view held that the national brand belongs to everyone and, hence, public opinion could not be ignored. At the same time, the role of the state and political elites was still seen as instrumental. In the words of one BBG participant:

[Nation branding] cannot be done [only] by some professions because . . . every one of us has the right to do it. Every citizen, regardless of profession, has the right to participate in the understanding of the country in which he lives. You can't prevent him from having a vision of his country, of course. And because of this, I say that this is a political decision, in other words, there has to be a political will from some elites and, honestly, I don't think it has to be a consensus decision. (Personal interview, July 20, 2005)

This quote captures a key contradiction in the internal discourse on nation branding—its simultaneously populist and elitist ambitions. Shaping the national image was understood, on the one hand, as the right of every citizen. On the other, it was the privilege of political elites, who had the power to make the "political choice" to procure a national brand, and it was the prerogative of professional experts in symbolic manipulation to create and popularize it.

One reaction to the agonistic structure of the field was to argue in favor of centralized structures and activities related to branding. Centralization scenarios, described by interviewees, included the creation of a state executive agency reporting to the "highest level of government," an independent NGO, or the hiring of a large international advertising and PR agency. Whereas the proposed mechanisms of centralization differed based on actors' institutional affiliations and positions in the field, the sentiment in favor of strong, top-down authority was consistent and could be seen as inherited from the statist culture under communism.[12] In this sense, nation branding could be understood as a mechanism through which political, economic, and cultural elites sought new *legitimacy* (a key resource in the field) for their privileged positions, while reproducing the narrative of a strong state inherited from the past and, at the same time, adapting it to the conditions of marketization. In sum, the field of nation branding became a site upon which the legitimacy battles of various elites were being fought out.

To get at the nature of these legitimacy battles, my interviews with informants included a number of questions about the meaning of branding and its social relevance for Bulgaria. I was interested in the justifications informants would provide for the existence of the field and their participation in it. The broad answer that emerged repeatedly in interviews was that nation branding represented a "new way of thinking." This new thinking had many dimensions, but they can be summarized under three broad themes: *modernization*, *marketization*, and *mediatization*. These intertwined processes were seen as pressures that demanded a re-thinking of the nation as a brand. Moreover, they justified the need to shift some of the responsibility for the construction of the national image from its former place within the politicized structures of the communist state to a technocratic "team of professionals, people who know how to make a brand" (personal interview, July 18, 2005). In the following pages I briefly show how these themes emerged from the interviews.

One of the earliest statements of the role of nation branding as a means of "modernizing" the country's image was made by Kevin Lewis, then Director of the British Council in Bulgaria, when he inaugurated the *Branding Bulgaria* project at a tourism conference in Sofia in January 2001. Lewis (2001) framed the benefits of nation branding in the following terms:

> There is frustration that misleading stereotypes are not doing justice to the people of the country. There is a strong desire that the very positive aspects of contemporary Bulgaria should be made known. In the longer run [nation branding] will bring all sorts of benefits. In the commercial area; in diplomacy and foreign relations; and in building up national self-confidence, without which the reform process will not get near its potential.

As this quote illustrates, the post-communist transition provided a discursive framework of reference within which the need for nation branding could be legitimated.

Yet the formulations of what nation branding meant in practice were often vague and differed among respondents. Definitions of nation branding, elicited in interviews, included broad statements, such as "simply communications," referring to process; "a comprehensive message we want to give," referring to content; or more strategic formulations, such as "the effective communication of a nation's identity, long-term priorities and unique selling points to an international audience." The commonality among most definitions was that they did not question the ability of nation branding to deliver results. It was simply seen as a tool that had to be mastered and applied to the problem at hand. The idea of branding as a tool that could be skillfully administered by "experts" enforced its status as a modernizing discourse.

In the particular case of the *Branding Bulgaria* project, the modernizing potential of nation branding was summarized in the first pages of the project's final document:

> In the mid-nineties, the tag "national image" was replaced by "national brand." This illustrates a more modern approach to marketing countries globally. National brands "sell" the country as a product and lifestyle. (Mineva, 2003, p. 7)

This quote suggests that the proposed modernization should occur both in terms of using a different language to talk about the nation and in terms of thinking differently about the essential qualities of the nation. The need for this modernization was tacitly accepted by participants in the BBG project and explained in reference to the post-communist transition. In short, because the country had changed, its image had to change as well, and the "modern" way to communicate that change was through branding. Thus, nation branding was charged with two tasks: it had to first create the new national identity and then communicate it to the outside world.

The second major theme in respondents' elaborations of the need for nation branding was the social shift toward liberalized market relations, often linked to the idea of globalization. Markets were seen as carriers of the "modern" and "new" and not as specific institutions, such as financial or commodity markets, for instance. Rather, "the market" was a metaphor for a new way of organizing society, associated with a new mode of thinking, opposed to the obsolete (i.e., communist) social order. Consider, for example, the following interview excerpt:

> *Interviewer:* Tell me about the significance of speaking about the nation as a brand.
>
> *Respondent:* In the contemporary world, in order to be relevant or adequate to the thinking of contemporary people from different corners of the world, in order not to sound archaic or to propagandize or not to remain at the level of the purely educational or PR representations of the country, you need to think precisely in the categories of the modern, in the categories of marketing, in the categories of advertising, so that you can present and sell, in the good sense of the word, something recognizable, something that is easily associated with who you are. (Personal interview, June 21, 2005)

This statement demonstrates how "the modern" is equated with "the categories of marketing and advertising." Because the modern world as a whole was understood as defined by markets (in this broader sense), the ability of Bulgaria to be integrated and recognized within this global picture depended on its ability to articulate its identity in marketing and advertising terms. In other words, nation branding's main appeal was based on the perception that the world had changed and now operated according to the logic of markets—a reality that no country could ignore. The re-articulation of national identity in marketing terms, then, was a matter of evolution and even survival.

Subsequently, criticisms of nation branding were phrased mainly in terms of a lack of sufficient local expertise and a lack of an evolved "thinking in terms of products." One of my informants put this bluntly when he explained that "we [in Bulgaria] don't even know how to advertise chewing gum, let alone advertise the nation" (personal interview, July, 2004). The lack of a local "culture of branding" was, in turn, linked to the chaotic and often self-serving nature of branding activities. In the words of a BBG respondent,

> What happens when we talk about branding is that it is thought of as a PR campaign and not as an investment in something beyond the logo, beyond the image, beyond these things. And this is because it is done in a piecemeal way. Well, during socialism there were years and years and years of [image] work in the same direction. Now there is no such thing. There are no years. There is a project [*Branding Bulgaria*], which lasts a maximum of three years. After these three years pass, something else happens. (Personal interview, July 20, 2005)

This argument is significant because of the parallel to the image-building activities of the communist state. It speaks to a larger question about the changing dynamics of national identity construction after communism and the role of nation branding in these changes. There is an important ambivalence in the fact that, on the one hand, the national image constructed by the communist state for internal and external circulation was seen as outdated, yet, at the same time, the totalizing identity-building framework inherited from communism could still be used as a model for national image building. The heritage of the communist period and the "communist way of thinking" also demarcated a generational line among respondents, where people from the generation that had come of age during the post-communist transition period were more likely to embrace and call for "new," that is, market-oriented thinking, whereas older generations were more likely to think about national identity in terms of cultural and historical heritage.

The generational split carried over into attitudes toward the impact of globalization on national identity as well. For older informants, the changes in the global landscape tended to represent new realities that simply had to be accepted. For the younger generation, these changes suggested a liberatory potential because they provided a more fitting framework within which one could make sense of everyday experiences in a consumer society than the narratives of the nation's glorious past. This theme is evident in the following interview excerpt:

> *Interviewer:* So, what exactly . . . appealed to you in this idea [of nation branding], in this way of thinking about the presentation of the nation?
>
> *Respondent:* The first thing which made me like it is that it seems to me that the logic in which today's world is being constructed is very different from the logic in which nation-states were constructed once upon a time . . . At the moment, the world is different, you know, you can't go on with a representation that is from the 19th century. From here the question follows, what could be the new representation? And because I think that the world is market-oriented . . . then the representation should also be market-oriented. (Personal interview, July 20, 2005)

It is interesting to note in this quote the implication that Bulgarian nationhood itself was in some way anomalous in its current state, because it was not in sync with the "market-oriented" world. Thus, once again, nation branding was seen not only as a tool for updating the country's image, but also as a means by which the nation itself could be re-imagined through the market metaphor.

The final theme concerns the role of the media in justifying the need for nation branding. The media were described by respondents both as the mirror in which Bulgaria's new national identity could be discovered and as the channels through which it could be changed. The understanding of the media as a mirror was evident in a constant concern among informants with the way Bulgaria was represented in the foreign press. A persistent view that the foreign media only published negative information about the country was common among informants and they often referred to particular examples they had encountered. Interestingly, this view is not corroborated by content analyses of Western media coverage of Bulgaria (e.g., Iordanova, 1995; MarketLINKS, 2005a, 2005b). In fact, these analyses conclude that the local media minimize positive and neutral coverage of Bulgaria in the foreign media, while consistently overemphasizing negative coverage.

The myth of the malevolent foreign media became particularly virulent in the context of Bulgaria's EU accession. Bulgarian media perpetuated the idea that critical Western observers continually scrutinized Bulgaria's image and charged that the government was not doing enough to counter negative perceptions. For example, a radio journalist cornered Meglena Kuneva, then Minister for European Integration, in an on-air interview with the question, "Why does Bulgaria fail to place its good sides within Western eyesight and we attract the attention of other Europeans mainly with negative news and comments?" (Bulgarian National Radio, 2005). The minister's answer was quite telling. After disclaiming that the question was too large to be answered in simple terms, she stated: "Bulgaria lacks an integrated strategy, if I must speak formally, about promoting ourselves abroad" (Bulgarian National Radio, 2005).

Against this backdrop, the stated goals of most nation branding projects included efforts to counter negative media coverage in "the West" with positive information about Bulgaria. The positive coverage of *Europalia Bulgaria* in the Belgian media, for example, had been hailed as a success for the image of the country, despite the fact that its longer term impact was questioned. Nevertheless, respondents argued that, as Bulgaria was thrust into a globalized media environment, nation branding was one way to intervene in the international media dialogue with a controlled message about the country. Many of the branding projects involved media professionals in their activities to a lesser or greater extent, and that, once again, demonstrated the significance of an emerging professional class of symbol handlers, who had a particular role to play in the articulation and dissemination of a national brand.

CONCLUSION: *ETIC* OBSERVATIONS

In conclusion, what is the significance of this examination of early nation branding activities in Bulgaria? I propose that by looking at the dynamics of the field, it is possible to address the question: How does a global market ideology, embedded within the discourse of nation branding, become integrated and legitimized at the level of local discourses and practices? The answer to this question concerns the relationships between power struggles and social change in post-communist Bulgaria. Fairclough (1995) identifies two significant trends in late modern societies, which are relevant to theorizing the field of nation branding and can put the preceding descriptive analysis into perspective. The first trend is the "marketization of discourse," which Fairclough defines as "the reconstruction on a market basis of domains which were once relatively insulated from markets, economically, in terms of social relations, and in terms of cultural values and identities" (1995, p. 19). As my data suggest, the discourse of nation branding clearly worked to marketize the domain of national identity construction and, from a global perspective, the nation-state itself.

Second, marketization is closely linked to another trend, which Fairclough terms "technologization of discourse," and explains as a process through which discourses become naturalized. He argues that the technologization of discourse is "an important resource in attempts by dominant social forces to direct and control the course of the major social and cultural changes which are affecting contemporary societies" (1995, p. 91). Discursive technologization involves a combination of three main types of activities:

(i) research into the discursive practices of social institutions and organizations, (ii) redesign of those practices in accordance with particular strategies and objectives, usually those of managers or bureaucrats, and (iii) training of institutional personnel in these redesigned practices. (p. 91)

Following Fairclough, then, nation branding in Bulgaria became naturalized as a legitimate subfield of national identity production through a process of discursive technologization. By reviewing the history of branding projects in Bulgaria, it is evident that they followed almost exactly the three types of technologizing activities described by Fairclough. Both *Branding Bulgaria* and *Promotion Bulgaria* began with conducting research on the nation's image; they later included some form of training seminars where people were encouraged to re-think the image of the nation in terms of branding; finally, they drafted strategic statements about the national brand. In the course of all this, they set up bureaucratic entities, albeit temporary ones, to oversee the process, and they proposed permanent structures to manage the national brand in the long term.

It is important to note that both of these projects were greatly influenced by the advice of Western consultants to whom the technological aspects of the nation branding discourse were already well familiar. By contrast, the structuring process of discursive technologization was not followed so strictly in some of the other projects—particularly those run by government institutions, where the bureaucratic models of the state were still firmly in place and where the influence of foreign advisors was minimal. The most prominent example of this latter case was the state's handling of *Europalia Bulgaria*.

Fairclough's theory of technologization also helps to explain the significance of calls for experts and institutionalization expressed by many of my informants. The technologization of discourses is consistent with an aspect of bureaucratic rationality, which Weber has identified as central for modern nation-states. As such, it is not alien to the fabric of Bulgarian institutions. However, it could be argued that discursive technologization increased in the context of EU accession because Bulgaria had to implement a number of bureaucratic requirements and procedures defined by the EU administration. These necessitated the retraining of bureaucrats within the state institutions, the introduction of strategies and objectives, and the increased use of research instruments and statistical reports. In that sense, nation branding was related to a general process of "Europeanization" that post-communist Bulgaria had consciously undertaken.

However, as I have argued elsewhere (Kaneva & Popescu, 2011), none of these processes provide the necessary space for a genuine social debate on the post-communist crisis of national identity. In fact, nation branding exacerbates the national identity crisis because of the demands for standardization of messages and communication strategies it places on the state. In other words, the discursive technology of nation branding leads to the construction of a superficial, performative discourse of a stable and homogenous national identity, suitable for external consumption, that does not necessarily reflect the popular sentiments of the citizenry.[13]

At the same time, it cannot be concluded that the consultants and government officials who introduced the technology of nation branding in Bulgaria were acting with a deliberate intention to harm the nation. For proponents of nation branding (both globally and locally), the hegemony of the market is not an object of contestation but a matter of common sense—a sign of hegemony at work. Fairclough (1995) recognizes this when he writes about the relationship between technologization and domination:

> There are clear tendencies at national and even transnational levels which can be linked to state and dominant class (including capitalist multinational) interests without too much difficulty; yet it is not possible to trace them to one or even several particular moments or locations of central policy formation. Rather the policies and planning which underlie processes of discourse technologization have been determined at different levels and different times, in many different institutions and organizations, within the private domain as well as within the public domain. (p. 92)

At the same time, informants are fully aware that mastery of the discursive technology of nation branding gives them additional social capital and power. Thus, their legitimation strategies, presented in this chapter, should be understood as deriving from their own particular interests in the field.

As the descriptive data presented here suggest, the field of nation branding in Bulgaria was bustling with activity between 2002 and 2005. A look at the sources of funding for various branding projects confirms that the lines between the national government, international NGOs and transnational bodies, and international and domestic business interests are intertwined in complex ways. Despite the apparent intractability of state bureaucracy, the insularity of the state in its actions and decisions aimed at controlling national identity production is undermined. In other words, nation branding indicates a shift within the national field of power.

The analysis also demonstrates that pressures exerted on national identity by processes of marketization, Europeanization, and mediatization were absorbed and adapted by local elites in opportunistic ways that served their internal political purposes. Local actors used their familiarity with, and access to, Western ideas and discursive technologies (such as nation branding) to establish their status as "experts" in the field and thus legitimate their claims to power. Thus, a key resource, struggled over in the field of nation branding, is a new form of legitimacy for the stratum of cultural intermediaries. Through a process of discursive technologization, local actors attempted to naturalize the prescriptions of nation branding. By extension, they enhanced the ability of a global market ideology to infiltrate the domain of national identity construction and the field of state power, which had been largely independent from market principles under communism. In this way, the legitimacy struggles of new local elites in the post-communist context also benefit the interests of global capital.

NOTES

1. Bourdieu's field theory was elaborated throughout his voluminous body of work (e.g., 1984, 1994, 1996), but a synthetic account of its main tenets can be found in Swartz (1997). See also Surowiec (this volume).
2. Similar dynamics are described in some of the other chapters in this volume, including the chapters by Bardan and Imre, Kulcsár and Yum, Jansen, and Surowiec.
3. European Union funds to aid accession countries, such as the funds administered under the EU's PHARE program, were central in this process in Central and Eastern Europe.
4. One journalistic account reported that as many as half of all government public auctions between 2000 and 2004 were won with the help of a bribe (Russev, 2005).
5. According to a report by A. T. Kearney, a consultancy that publishes an annual ranking of the top 40 outsourcing destinations, Bulgaria holds the dubious distinction of entering the rankings for the first time in 2005 at rank 15 (Sofia News Agency, 2005). This statistic was widely reported in the business press and highlighted on the Bulgarian Investment Agency's website.
6. Both websites produced by BBG are no longer available. Their original URLs—www.image.bg and www.experiencebulgaria.org—are now occupied by unrelated companies.
7. Budget details were provided by Leah Davcheva in a personal interview on July 18, 2005. A newspaper article lists the project's budget as £20,000 for the period of 2001 to 2003 (Hristova, 2002).
8. The term "political cabinet" refers to ministry officials who are appointed by, and are directly subordinate to, the minister. The staff of the political cabinet is generally recruited from the political party represented by the minister. In a coalition government, different ministries are headed by representatives of different parties, and their political cabinets are reflective of these differences. This often leads to conflicting positions among the ministries. The political cabinet typically includes the deputy ministers, a parliamentary secretary, a head of cabinet, and a public relations officer.
9. A copy platform is "a statement prepared by the advertiser (often in association with an advertising agency) setting forth the advertising strategy, a summary of the rationale for the strategy, and related background information" (*AMA Dictionary of Marketing Terms*, n.d.).
10. Bulgaria is a major producer of natural rose oil, and the rose has long been an important symbol of national identity. The Rose Valley, where oil-giving roses are grown, hosts an annual Festival of the Rose. Rose oil vials in folk-art containers are a staple gift for foreign visitors.
11. Explanations, cited in the media, for discarding the winning logo from the public competition stated that its thin lines made it difficult for reproduction in various graphic formats ("The Logo of Bulgaria," 2004).
12. Kulcsár and Yum (this volume) make a similar argument in the case of Hungary.
13. Iordanova (2007) and Bardan and Imre (this volume) make similar arguments in relation to Romania.

REFERENCES

AMA Dictionary of Marketing Terms. (n.d.) Copy platform. Retrieved December 8, 2010, from http://www.marketingpower.com/_layouts/dictionary.aspx?dLetter=C

Balkan British Social Surveys. (2002). *Branding Bulgaria project: Group discussions* [Research report]. Sofia, Bulgaria.

Bourdieu, P. (1984). *Distinction: A social critique of the judgment of taste.* Cambridge, MA: Harvard University Press.

Bourdieu, P. (1994). Rethinking the state: Genesis and structure of the bureaucratic field. *Sociological Theory, 12*(1), 1–18.

Bourdieu, P. (1996). *The state nobility: Elite schools in the field of power.* Stanford, CA: Stanford University Press.

Bozhinov, B. (2004). *Проект за създаване на специален фонд за финансиране на национална реклама в чужбина* [Project for the creation of a special fund for financing national advertising abroad]. Bulgarian Chamber of Commerce. Sofia, Bulgaria.

Bulgarian Ministry of the Economy. (2004a). *Промоцията на България в чужбина— какво, къде, как? Еднодневен семинар по брендинг. 30 Септември, 2004* [The promotion of Bulgaria abroad—what, where, how? One-day branding seminar. September 30, 2004]. Unpublished seminar materials. Sofia, Bulgaria.

Bulgarian Ministry of the Economy. (2004b). *Стартира конкурсът за лого и мото на България* [The competition for Bulgarian logo and slogan starts]. Retrieved December 10, 2005 from http://www.mi.government.bg/news.html?id=3674

Bulgarian Ministry of the Economy. (2004c). *Съветът за европейска интеграция одобри националното лого на България* [The Council for European Integration approved the national logo of Bulgaria]. Retrieved September 12, 2005, from http://www.mi.government.bg/news.html?id=4152

Bulgarian National Radio. (2005, December 23). *Интервю с Меглена Кунева: На България ѝ липсва цялостна стратегия за промоцията ни навън* [An interview with Meglena Kuneva: Bulgaria lacks a complete strategy for promotion abroad]. *"Нещо повече," Програма Хоризонт* ["Something More" show, *Horizont*].

Bulgarian Telegraph Agency. (n.d.). *България и Европейския Съюз* [Bulgaria and the European Union]. Retrieved January 12, 2006, from http://www.bta.bg/site/bulgaria-eu/html/eu-enlargement/bg-eu-history.htm

BulgarianIndustry.bg. (2005, February 24). *30 български фирми износителки избраха логото на България* [30 Bulgarian export firms selected the logo of Bulgaria]. Retrieved August 23, 2005, from http://www.bulgarianindustry.bg/bg/news/archive/news2005?common_news=2496219846773935664

Butzev, H. (2003, March 7). *Културата е динамика на настоящето, не статика на миналото: Интервю с Еми Барух* [Culture is the dynamic of the present, not the stasis of the past: An interview with Emmy Barouh]. *Култура* [*Kultura* newspaper].

Communication Strategy. (2002). *Комуникационна стратегия за подготовка на членството на Република България в Европейския съюз* [Communication strategy for the preparation of the membership of the Republic of Bulgaria in the European Union]. Retrieved December 8, 2010, from http://europe.bg/upload/docs/Communication_Strategy.pdf

Communication Strategy 2004 Annual Report. (2005). *Отчет за изпълнението на Работната програма за 2004 година в изпълнение на плана за действие 2002–2006 г. на Комуникационната стратегия за подготовка на членството на Република България в ЕС* [Report for the execution of the 2004 Working Program under the 2002–2006 plan for action of the Communication Strategy for the preparation of accession of the Republic of Bulgaria to the EU]. Bulgarian Ministry of Foreign Affairs.

Ditchev, I. (2000). *Европа като легитимация* [Europe as legitimation]. *Социологически Проблеми, 32*(1/2), 87–108. Sofia, Bulgaria: Sociology Institute of the Bulgarian Academy of Science.

Elwes, A. (1994). *Nations for sale.* London: BMP DDB Needham.

Elwes, A. (2001). *Branding Bulgaria.* Unpublished workshop report. British Council. Sofia, Bulgaria.

Europalia: The traces remain. (2003). *Европалия: Следите остават . . . Или как държавата гради своите образи пред света* [Europalia: The traces remain . . . Or how the state builds its images for the world]. Sofia, Bulgaria: Valentin Trayanov.

Fairclough, N. (1995). *Critical discourse analysis: The critical study of language.* London: Longman.

Foreign gives 1 million. (2003, August, 6). *Външно дава 1 млн. лева на 4 фирми за реклама на евроинтеграцията* [Foreign gives 1 million Leva to four firms to advertise Eurointegration]. *Всеки Ден [VsekiDen.com].* Retrieved December 8, 2010, from http://217.75.128.36/asp2/s3nArt.asp?media=70&artno=1&artdate=2003/8/6&CDLANG=BG

Hristova, R. (2002, July 25). Bulgaria branded. *SofiaEcho.* Retrieved August 12, 2005, from http://www.sofiaecho.com/article/bulgaria—branded/id_4975/catid_5

Iliev, P. (2004, March 30). *Обществените поръчки—голямата лапаница продължава!* [Public auctions—the feeding frenzy continues!]. *Всеки Ден [VsekiDen.com].* Retrieved February 28, 2006, from http://www.vsekiden.com/news.php?topic=3&id=4731

Iordanova, D. (1995). Media coverage of Bulgaria in the West and its domestic use. In F. L. Casmir (Ed.), *Communication in Eastern Europe: The role of history, culture, and media in contemporary conflicts* (pp. 223–246). Mahwah, NJ: Erlbaum.

Iordanova, D. (2007). Cashing in on Dracula: Eastern Europe's hard sells. *Framework, 48*(1), 46–63.

Kandov, B. (2004a, December 12). Déjà vu *в Агенцията по туризъм* [Déjà vu at the Tourism Agency]. *Капитал [Kapital* newspaper].

Kandov, B. (2004b, December 11). *Министерството на икономиката прие ново лого, но без стратегия* [The Ministry of the Economy approved a new logo but without a strategy]. *Капитал [Kapital* newspaper].

Kaneva, N., & Popescu, D. (2011). National identity *lite*: Nation branding in postcommunist Romania and Bulgaria. *International Journal of Cultural Studies, 14*(2), 191–207.

Lewis, K. (2001). *Branding Bulgaria: Changing perceptions of Bulgaria.* Presentation at the First International Conference on Tourism in Bulgaria, January 9–11, 2002. Hilton Sofia, Sofia, Bulgaria.

Manchester Business School. (2003). *Perceptions of Bulgaria and preferences for travel abroad.* Unpublished research report.

MarketLINKS. (2005a). *Образът на България в чуждестранните медии: Количествено проучване* [The image of Bulgaria in foreign media: A quantitative study]. Unpublished research report. Sofia, Bulgaria.

MarketLINKS. (2005b). *Чуждестранните медии за България през погледа на Българските медии. Количествено проучване* [The foreign media about Bulgaria through the eyes of Bulgarian media: A quantitative study]. Unpublished research report. Sofia, Bulgaria.

Mineva, M. (2003). *Take it easy! Towards a strategy for representing Bulgaria.* Sofia, Bulgaria: British Council.

Russev, V. (2005, February 23). *Рушвет за всяка втора обществена поръчка!* [A bribe for every other public auction!]. *Монитор [Monitor* newspaper]. Retrieved December 8, 2010, from http://www.monitor.bg/article?id=30765

Sofia News Agency. (2005, November 24). Bulgaria among top locations for "offshore" work. *Novinite.com*. Retrieved December 8, 2010, from http://www.novinite.com/view_news.php?id=55664

Strategy and action plan for Bulgarian competitiveness in world ICT Markets (version 5). (2004). Unpublished ICT Cluster records. Sofia, Bulgaria.

Swartz, D. (1997). *Culture and power: The sociology of Pierre Bourdieu*. Chicago: University of Chicago Press.

The logo of Bulgaria approved, the sea is missing. (2004, December 8). *Логото на България одобрено, морето го няма* [The logo of Bulgaria approved, the sea is missing]. *Netinfo.bg*. Retrieved January 10, 2005, from http://news.netinfo.bg/?tid=40&oid=670466

Vitosha Research. (2004). *Образът на България сред чуждестранните граждани и бизнесмени: Аналитичен доклад* [The image of Bulgaria among foreign citizens and businessmen: An analytical report]. Unpublished research report. Sofia, Bulgaria.

6 Toward Corpo-Nationalism
Poland as a Brand[1]

Paweł Surowiec

INTRODUCTION

This chapter offers a reflexive case study of the introduction and enactment of nation branding in Poland. I draw on Pierre Bourdieu's social theory, as well as nationalism scholarship, to reveal the "imposition" of and "invasion" of social space by neoliberal ideologies (Bourdieu, 2003). The discussion investigates the neoliberal agenda of the Polish state and its adoption of a promotional discourse of branding. Applying a critical perspective on branding, the chapter sets out to reveal how and why nation branding comes to occupy social spaces in Poland, and argues that this process leads to the emergence of *corpo-nationalism*—a neoliberal form of national identity politics.

In recent years, scholars of nationalism have moved beyond ideology-driven theorizations and toward approaches that focus on social practices. Brubaker (1996) understands nationalism as "interlocking and interactive," or, put simply, as susceptible to influences from other areas of practice. Following Brubaker, I consider nation branding in performative terms, that is, as a category of practice where nationhood is an institutionalized cultural and political form and "nationness as a contingent event or happening" (p. 21). On a discursive level, however, I regard nation branding as ideological "social cement"—an interpellating force—that is contested by institutions responsible for Polish propaganda overseas and is channeled structurally via the discourses and performative actions of nation branders.[2]

According to a structuralist view of nationalism (e.g., Hobsbawm, 1990), propaganda is at the heart of national identity construction. A discursive re-contextualization of propaganda as nation branding—a movement rooted in self-advantaging promotional culture—fits into a growing body of literature demonstrating the corporatization of public and foreign affairs (Taylor & Kent, 2006). However, nation brand conceptualists (e.g., Anholt, 2005; Olins, 1999) take this process of corporatization further and make ideological promises of national development and modernization that exceed the existing evidence on the advantages that marketing can deliver in a global competition for capital.

The signification of Poland as a "brand" results in a qualitative shift in the understanding of Polish national identity dynamics. Although multiple Polish identities endure in ethnic form (Porter, 2002), and the development of liberal nationalism in Poland is well under way (Auer, 2004), the reinvention of Polish national identity through branding can be understood as part of the marketing indoctrination of a post-communist nation. However, the introduction of nation branding into Polish public discourse is not as straightforward and unproblematic as marketing professionals would argue. Rather, it re-opens a discussion on the relationship between the Polish state and the purpose of national identity construction in post-Soviet Poland.

My analysis in this chapter is informed by Bourdieu's empirical, relational, and reflexive approach to research and seeks to trace the relationships between agents who attempt to form a Polish field of nation branding and, by extension, alter the processes of national identity construction.[3] I analyze Polish government documents that outline promotional policy, corporate documents and online sources, and secondary sources (research reports, presentations, featured media artifacts, and videos) in order to contextualize the emergence of nation branding in Poland. In addition, I draw on data from 47 qualitative interviews, conducted in Poland and the United Kingdom between July 25, 2009, and August 3, 2010. The interviews provide the basis for my claims about the views of Polish government technocrats, communication managers, corporate business managers, and nongovernmental organization (NGO) managers in relation to their interpretative practices of nation branding. The chapter also gives a flavor of particular promotional artifacts used by the state. However, a detailed analysis of these artifacts is beyond the scope of this chapter. Although the full complexity of promotional discourse and of agency in the field of nation branding cannot be reconstructed here, my goal is to offer insights into branding ideology as a structuring mechanism and a motivating factor for a professional class of technocrats in Poland.

NEOLIBERAL *DOXA* AND BRANDING AS IDEOLOGY

A departure point for a discussion of the Polish nation branding discourse is the recognition of branding's pervasive, universalizing, totalizing, and revisionist aspects. As critical scholars of marketing point out, marketing refers to the beliefs and collective representations of its practitioners. Marion (2006) asserts that "marketing ideology works as a collective action frame of marketers and the extreme generalizations of marketing vocabulary show its pervasiveness" (p. 247). For Marion, marketing ideology produces *legitimacy* for accepting the market logic, while at the same time producing a *legitimization* of marketing practices by the continuous reiteration of marketing concepts.

In addition, marketing relies on inventing new ideological concepts. According to O'Reilly (2006), branding ideology—committed to the production of capitalist meaning—is dependent on an expansionist, linguistic, acquisition-by-merger strategy. He views the ideological discourse on branding, and its growing portfolio of referents, as "accommodating signifiers in order to legitimate itself within the language" (p. 269). This process has been supported by the revisionism of marketing professionals who seek to rewrite the historical contexts of propaganda in a way that incorporates it into the new linguistic terms of branding ideology (see, e.g., Olins, 2002). This revisionism enables the market-driven principles of branding to overwrite propaganda as a traditional apparatus for national identity formation and projection (Taithe & Thornton, 1999).

According to Bourdieu (2003), efforts to apply neoliberal solutions to governance represent an attempt to impose a universal economic model that has its roots in the political economy of the Anglo-Saxon world. He points out that neoliberal discourses have resulted in "insidious impositions representing a whole set of presuppositions imposed as self-evident" (Bourdieu, 1998, p. 34).Thus, Bourdieu (1998) insists that it is important to understand how the neoliberal *doxa* is produced as its marketing apparatus threatens democratic politics. The ideological, globalizing impositions of neoliberalism are based on the implementation of "structural adjustment" policies developed by a "transnational capitalist class" (Sklair, 2001). Neoliberalism is, above all, an intellectual project, which according to Bourdieu and Wacquant (1999) is reproduced and imposed within the setting of a particular state by a small group of people, typically with centrist political affiliations, gathered around "think tanks" that aim to develop neoliberal policies. (An example of such a think tank in Poland is the Institute of the Polish Brand, which will be discussed in more detail later.)

The deterministic, free market agenda of neoliberalism is present in the writings of nation branding proponents. In a critical account of this literature, Jansen (2008) proposes that nation branding aims to transform social space into "calculative space" (p. 122). She further explains how nation branding functions within the context of a neoliberal political economy:

> Some constituents of nation branding that contribute to the production of calculative space are: a) overt embrace of commercial language, practices, and assumptions, reflecting the post-Cold War ascent of the logic of "market fundamentalism"; b) formation of public-private partnerships to advance specific trade, industry or corporate interests along with national agendas, policies and ideologies; c) use of private contractors to determine the salient features of a nation's identity, based upon what can be marketed to tourists, international investors, and potential trade partners; and d) reduction of the input of citizens to what can be measured by market research. (pp. 122–123)

In this way, nation branding creates a specific type of social space in which social agents enact their vision of national identity construction.

This view corresponds with Bourdieu's understanding of society as comprised of autonomous, but structurally homologous, fields of production, cultural practice, and consumption of various cultural and material resources (Swartz, 1997). Bourdieu's field theory also fits with Sztompka's (1993) paradigmatic division of social theories into those fitting a "system model" and those fitting a "field model." Sztompka speaks of the "field image," where the underlying axiom is that societies are dynamic entities and therefore susceptible to change. Although stable elements can be identified, as in the organic system model, societies in this view are endlessly subjected to influences determined by events and sequences of actions.

Field is a fundamental analytical unit in Bourdieu's sociological analysis. It describes a social space within which two other key categories of social practice are embedded—*habitus* and *capital*. Fields denote particular areas of social agents' production, circulation, and appropriation of goods, services, knowledge, and status, and the comprehensive positions held by actors in their struggle to monopolize different forms of capital. Bourdieu (1990) sees fields as social spaces competing over different aspects of representation.

Bourdieu explicitly connects the functions of the state in contemporary societies to what he terms "the field of power." Within the field of power, elites struggle over "statist capital," which is a form of meta-capital that "enables the state to exercise power over the different fields and over the rates of conversion between them and thereby over the relations of force between their respective holders" (Bourdieu, 1994, p. 4). Henceforth, Bourdieu argues that power struggles among dominant groups ultimately need to be fought out within the structures of the state. Thus, the state dominates principles of legitimating power in any given society. For Bourdieu, the state is also "a field of ideological production" (Swartz, 2004, p. 6). Hence, appeals to universality by various dominant groups are nothing more than disguises for the ideological interests of those groups as they strive for legitimacy within the field of power. Indeed, Bourdieu argues that dominant elites (located in subfields) are engaged in a complicit relationship with the state whereby various agents contribute to the legitimation of the field of power but "only by taking their 'cut' of the profits, by seeking to divert to their advantage whatever quantum of power they capture" (Wacquant, 1993, p. 36).

Finally, Bourdieu (1984) notes the entry of "cultural intermediaries" as newcomers into the political field. Cultural intermediaries form a class of professionals circulating particular knowledge representing "formerly sealed-off areas of culture" (Featherstone, 1991, p. 10), and their actions are shaped by a professional marketing *habitus* (Bourdieu, 1984). Following this view, the field of nation branding can be seen as a subfield of the field of power, where technocrats and various professionals struggle to enforce their *vision* of Poland, reflected in *division* of its branding-driven representations of Polishness.

Bourdieu's structuralist-agentic view of social reality combines readily with structuralist and constructivist theories of nationalism. Structuralist theses regard nationalism as a project of elites and emphasize the power of state influence over national identity formation (Gellner, 1983; Hobsbawm, 1990; Rokkan, 1975). This view is in line with Bourdieu's (1994) understanding of the state as the possessor of meta-capital and the holder of power over different social fields.[4] From this perspective, the power of the Polish state can be seen as manifested "in the realm of symbolic production" where its grip "is felt most powerfully" (Bourdieu, 1994, p. 2). I would argue that, by adopting the nation branding discourse, the neoliberal Polish state redefines the purpose of its national representations within the broader community of nations.

NEOLIBERAL STATISM AND NATION BRANDING IN POST-COMMUNIST POLAND

Poland, an aspiring political leader in Central and Eastern Europe, has in recent years been subjected to discourses attempting to redefine national identity in terms of corporate branding principles. The corporate-style branding exercise in Poland began in earnest in 2003, but the introduction of promotional discourse into Poland's public space dates back to the early 1990s. Promotional discourse surfaced in the context of political and economic changes after 1989 from a Soviet-style authoritarian regime and a central command economy to a pluralist democracy, confusedly equated with a neoliberal market logic (Puchalska, 2005). The emergence of a neoliberal hegemony in the 1990s reinforced an agenda of Polish market competitiveness and required a redefinition of national identity that fit with that framework.

Neoliberal "transitology" was introduced into Poland in two waves: in 1990 by "shock therapy," and later through selectively chosen aspects of Europeanization (Shields, 2008). However, changes to Poland's political economy lacked a strong dimension of economic nationalism, historically present in advanced capitalist societies (Greenfeld, 2003). In addition, since 1989, democratic institutions in Poland were strongly influenced by Western consultancy culture. This trend also affected the institutional field traditionally responsible for overseas propaganda on behalf of the Polish government.

Since the early 1990s, the Polish state's symbolic actions in the transnational milieu have grown in specialization. Among the most notable tactics are the use of media relations, advertising, featured articles and business reports, market research, cultural and business exchanges, lobbying, online communications, publicity stunts, exhibitions, and international broadcasting.[5] The professional narratives of decision makers and government communication managers reveal that the structural significance of such tactics has been redefined. One theme that emerges from interviews is that propaganda practices are associated with the "communist era," whereas post-communist Poland needs marketing-driven approaches to projecting its identity. At the same time, interview accounts do not clearly explain the difference between propaganda and marketing communications. This morphogenesis is embedded in a promotional culture and defines the politics of promotional discourse on Poland.

The overarching discourse of promotion, derived from marketing ideology and practice, suits the post-Soviet mindset of Polish technocrats, for whom democracy and social progress mean modernization via marketization of social spaces. Their logic can be summed up as follows: First we had to build democratic institutions; now we need to modernize by building a brand. On the other hand, their attitude toward propaganda is dialectical and reflects how the Polish past is enacted in their contemporary practice: Propaganda carries a Sovietized stigma, whereas promotion is understood as performed for the political and economic benefit of all Poles.

The term "promotion" is explicit in the Polish public domain. Government communication officials refer to the institutional framework they oversee as "a system of Poland's promotion" (Piątkowska, personal interview, August 19, 2009). However, behind closed doors, these same officials acknowledge that the practices they are involved in are based on persuasive communication and are, therefore, propagandistic by their very definition (Moloney, 2006). This shift in language from propaganda to promotion is significant because it suggests the market-oriented nature of the field in which nation branding has been contested in Poland. How social agents involved in the field refer to their practice is determined by their "feel for the game" (Bourdieu, 1990), or their sense of a practical, context-dependent, intuitive approach to functioning in the field.

While promotional discourse is ongoing in the institutional structure of the Polish government, on the level of *praxis,* propaganda aimed at enhancing perceptions of Poland abroad has also been influenced by Westernization and, in particular, discourses underpinned by market-oriented social forces. For example, in September 2001, the Department of Promotion (later renamed as Department of Public and Cultural Diplomacy) in the Polish Ministry of Foreign Affairs issued a set of guidelines titled *ABC of Marketing in Public Diplomacy*, which emphasized the importance of a marketing toolkit for the diplomatic representation of Poland by "professionals managing this task, but also those embassy employees, who in their official and informal contacts with foreigners can be considered as a source of information about Poland" (Polish Ministry of Foreign Affairs, 2001, p. 2).

Between 2000 and 2004, most of the promotional campaigns produced or commissioned by state officials in Poland or overseas were justified with Poland's accession to the European Union (Szondi, 2009). Today, the overall purpose of their practice has been reduced to one common denominator: exchange value. Policy data reveal that Polish technocrats within state structures unanimously define the logic of the market as giving *legitimacy* to their practice. "Competitiveness" is embedded in the policy documents guiding the direction of promotional campaigns. For instance, a policy document of the Department of Public and Cultural Diplomacy at the Polish Ministry of Foreign Affairs (2010) indicates that the department's practice is aimed at increasing Poland's competitive advantage; the Polish Tourism Organisation (2008), according to its marketing strategy document, strives to achieve competitive advantage by marketing Polish tourism products; the Polish Ministry of Economics (2010) embraces branding as a means to improve Poland's competitive identity, and its subsidiary Polish Investment and Information Agency follows suit. Similarly, two communication strategy documents by the Adam Mickiewicz Institute (2009, 2010)—a government-sponsored organization responsible for promoting Polish culture overseas—reproduce the branding ideology and subject Polish culture to further commercialization.

Since 1989, the imperatives of development, modernization, and competitiveness have played a significant role in the formation of a neoliberal political space in Poland (Sidorenko, 1998). In the context of Poland's promotional discourse, those imperatives operate as buzzwords expressing the aims of the Polish technocratic class and their significance for, what they define as, national progress. This legitimacy narrative is disclosed in a contemporary government policy outlining considerations for perception management:

> Poland shall define its image and promote it professionally and in a consistent way abroad; this image is coherent with regard to identity and value with the image promoted inside the country, so as to—on the one hand—support the Polish citizens abroad in their positive identification with the home country and with each other, and on the other hand create a positive image of Poland as a modern, dynamically developing country amongst foreigners. Such activities are especially crucial in the era of global capital and investment competition. (Chancellery of the Prime Minister of Poland, 2008, p. 34)

Nevertheless, at the level of *praxis*, the enactment of Poland's perception management, at home and abroad, relies on propaganda techniques. Nation branding has come forward as one of the competing solutions for Poland's perception management. The crossover between government propaganda and corporate-like branding implies an ongoing corporatization of government structures and the indoctrination of Poles into the virtues of marketing.

OUTLINE OF THE POLISH FIELD OF NATION BRANDING

Bourdieu and Wacquant (1992) argue that every field analysis should begin with a mapping out of the agents in the field as well as establishing their relationship to the field of power. There are several public and private institutions in Poland forming a social space in which nation branding is debated as a means to national identity formation. Over the last few years this field has grown in complexity.[6]

Attempts to form a field of nation branding in Poland were closely aligned with the Polish field of power. As mentioned earlier, the government institutions involved in the discourse of nation branding so far include the Polish Ministry of Foreign Affairs and its Department of Public and Cultural Diplomacy, the Ministry of Economics Department of Economic Promotion, the Polish Information and Investment Agency and its Department of Economic Promotion, the Polish Tourism Organization and its Departments of Marketing Tools and Strategic Planning, the Polish Agency for Enterprise Development, the Polish Ministry of Culture and National Heritage and its Adam Mickiewicz Institute. Their work is tied to governmental structures by the Council of Poland's Promotion—a ministerial body, which is involved in promotional policy development.

Senior and middle management in these state structures recognize nation branding as a concept. For example, the Deputy Chairmen of the Polish Tourism Organisation (Walas, personal interview, August 31, 2009) and of the Adam Mickiewicz Institute (Potoroczyn, personal interview, April 22, 2010) express desire to "manage brand Poland." The work of their departments, however, is not always characterized as nation branding. The day-to-day administrative practices and campaigns produced by those institutions bear the hallmarks of nation branding but are not related to an overarching integrated nation branding strategy. As it stands, their practices are limited to statutory bureaucratic commitments in accordance with the Polish legal system, their financial abilities, and their institutional goals.

The second group of actors involved in the nation branding discourse includes Polish business, research centers, and the marketing and public relations industry, which accept the nation branding discourse but do not always agree with the ways nation branding initiatives in Poland have been initiated and developed. The key players in that group include trade organizations, such as The Polish Chamber of Commerce and its offshoot, the Institute of the Polish Brand; marketing consultancies, such as DDB Corporate Profiles, Brief for Poland, New Communications, Stafiej and Partners, Eskadra, Communication Unlimited, and Orbita; and research organizations, such as the Institute of Public Affairs (a public policy research organization) and Maison (a consumer research firm).[7]

A Polish national logotype—using the country's name spelled in Polish and an image of a red-and-white kite—was produced by advertising agency DBB Corporate Profiles as part of a campaign called "Poland: Europe Is Bigger." This artifact materialized in response to the government's promotional discourse and was formalized in an agreement between the Polish Ministry of Foreign Affairs and DDB Corporate Profiles in August 2001. One of this campaign's aspects was to produce a standard for visual representation of "brand Poland." The significance of the logo to nation branding discourse in Poland is twofold: It indicated the formal beginning of a marketing makeover of national identity, and it was later considered for incorporation into a broader nation branding program (more on this program later in the chapter).

Although the introduction of nation branding in Poland is associated with the self-proclaimed expertise of British brand consultants, such as Simon Anholt and Wally Olins, its growing popularity has also served to mobilize Polish marketing and public relations consultants to seek opportunities in the field. Their agency has been enacted through participation in public bids for consultancy projects as well as production of materials used in domestic and international communications by government departments promoting Poland. This is evident in the proliferation of various "bottom-up" attempts to market Poland by the Polish marketing and public relations industry, which welcomed the nation branding discourse as it coincided with its expertise and *habitus*. Several of those projects failed because of political changes in the public administration, funding issues, and limited trust on the side of the Polish public administration. However, the multiplicity of initiatives demonstrates the reproduction of the nation branding discourse in Poland and its compliance with Western consultancy culture.

A few examples of such industry-driven initiatives are worth mentioning. In 2000, a few Polish marketing industry leaders formed a coalition attempting to establish a professional platform for marketing Poland as a tourist destination. The idea underpinning the partnership was to unify industry expertise and prevent fragmentation of campaigns in the area of tourism promotion. This alliance of marketing consultancies and media agency representatives operating in the Polish market was initiated with a brainstorming session titled *The Session of the Century*. The management of participating organizations offered expertise and services to set the foundations for the systematic promotion of "the tourism dimension of brand Poland" (Zmyśony, personal interview, August 31, 2009). This project was formalized in the institution of the Advertising for Poland Association. Although strategic and creative planning began soon after the association's establishment, politically originating changes among the senior management of the Polish Tourist Organization led to the failure of the initiative. Further attempts to revive the association were unsuccessful, and its leaders moved their attention to Polish city councils to seek other consultancy opportunities, or undertook work on marketing campaigns at the government level.

A similar scenario unfolded in the case of the Polish public relations consultants' initiative *Public Relations 4 Poland*. In 2006, public relations professionals formed a coalition that aimed at counseling the Polish government on the strategic direction for Poland's promotion. After a few months, this initiative lost its momentum, and initial negotiations held with the Head of the Promotion Department at the Polish Ministry of Foreign

Affairs did not yield results. The management of the Ministry's Department of Promotion at that time was particularly distrustful of external strategic consultancies and finalized minor tactical tasks itself.

For Polish marketing and public relations professionals, engagement in nation branding carries the symbolic capital of prestige and social recognition. These projects are considered as high profile. Professional accounts present the previously mentioned initiatives as "consultancy free of charge," implying that the struggle for economic capital is secondary to the marketing and public relations actors in the field. This mechanism has been, to an extent, reinforced by Polish technocrats. For example, DBB Corporate Profiles charged the Polish state a symbolic sum of PLN 1 (approximately 25 cents) for their "Poland: Europe Is Bigger" campaign. How long industry professionals were prepared to work for free is not discussed in their professional accounts.

NATION BRANDING IN POLAND:
A GREAT PROMOTIONAL ROBBERY?

A large-scale nation branding initiative, introduced as the Program of National Marketing, began in Poland in 2003; it will be the focus of this section. The analysis of this program reveals how nation branding clashed with political reality in Poland from 2003 onward. A special role in the struggle to reinvent Poland as a brand was enacted by the Polish Chamber of Commerce and by British agency Saffron Brand Consultants, whose chairman is Wally Olins. Both organizations were the *spiritus movens* behind a paradigmatic nation branding program for Poland. Their efforts to reinvent Polish national identity as a brand were pompously propagated as "the biggest nation branding project of all times" (Saffron Brand Consultants, 2007).

Initially, this program began as a bottom-up process: Nation branding climbed up from the mezzo-societal level of Polish business into the macro-level, penetrating the Polish Ministry of Foreign Affairs, the Ministry of Economics, governmental agencies, and the Polish Parliament (the *Sejm*). Before the instigation of a nation brand building program, the Polish Chamber of Commerce—an association of private business—established the Academy of Brands—a commercial scheme that served the purpose of professionalization and popularization of branding (Institute of the Polish Brand, 2010). The scheme awarded "flagship brand" status to corporate businesses, which, as the academy argued, had further potential to be used in national marketing campaigns. One example of this endorsement is evident in a 2001 campaign for Poland with the slogan, "Poland. The Heart of Europe," commissioned by the Chamber of Commerce. A print advertisement, produced for this campaign and featured in the August 20–27, 2001, issue of *Time Magazine*, used discursive intertextuality and presented the corporate logos of businesses certified by the Chamber of Commerce. A call for action accompanying the Academy of Brands was the slogan "Support what is strong!" ["*Co mocne podeprzeć!*"]. This scheme was officially recognized by the Polish Ministry of Economics. The search for successful symbols of Polish capitalism was in progress. So was the search for new consultancy and project opportunities.

The Polish Chamber of Commerce tried to dominate the discourse of Poland's promotion, in line with the corporate self-interest of its members. While the Academy of Brands laid the grounds for the vision of Poland as a brand, the remaining problem was to persuade Polish government technocrats that Poland needed a concerted branding program. The Chamber of Commerce embarked on informal negotiations with various government structures but was unsuccessful in securing their commitment. In turn, the chamber approached an external branding consultant, Britain's Wally Olins, and retained his services as a way to advance the branding agenda. Olins was seen as a holder of a higher level of symbolic capital in the field of nation branding, compared to the symbolic capital of the Polish Chamber of Commerce.

Although nation branding ideology initially had the compliance of the Chamber of Commerce senior management, its implementation over time encountered acts of resistance among the Polish public administration. The Head of the Institute of the Polish Brand, Mirosław Boruc, became a key "compliant professional" (Cialdini, 1993), who embraced the discourse of British brand consultants like Olins and struggled to use it as a way to capitalize on his own self-proclaimed branding expertise. His familiarity with the subject, influenced by the quasi-academic publications of nation brand consultants, and his co-operation with Saffron became a source for upholding the nation branding ideology. The institute facilitated the spread of this ideology by translating and publishing key nation branding texts by British consultants into the Polish language. This effort was aimed particularly at Polish youth and was billed as an act of education. The Institute of the Polish Brand also relied on the Nation Brand Index, started by Simon Anholt and a recognized selling tool for nation branding consultancies, in its efforts to legitimize a large-scale branding project. This made possible the indoctrination of Polish government technocrats.

On June 14, 2003, the Polish Parliament hosted a conference, which was an attempt to publically introduce the Program of National Marketing masterminded by the Polish Chamber of Commerce. The purpose of this conference was to move the nation branding agenda forward. This conference received the patronage of the Parliament Speaker and other interested parties (including the Ministry of Foreign Affairs, the Ministry of Economics, the Polish Information and Investment Agency, and the Polish Tourist Organization), and was a stepping stone to receiving financial and political backing from the top level of the Polish government for the launch of a large-scale nation branding program.

In December 2003, the Polish Chamber of Commerce commissioned Saffron Brand Consultants to work on this nation branding program. The plan was to implement a long-term branding strategy under the patronage of the Polish President and under management by the Institute of the Polish Brand. Due to its five years tenure, the Polish presidential seat was seen as stable and, therefore, it was speculated that implementing a long-term strategy with the support of the president would yield better economic outputs. At the outset, to obtain support for the program, the Chamber of Commerce relied on a network of personal contacts developed by its management amongst politicians aligned with the Social Democratic Party (SLD). In fact, their cooperation with the Polish Presidential Palace began when President Aleksander Kwaśniewski declared his patronage of their scheme to propagate the value of product and corporate brands for the Polish economy (Boruc, 2001). However, the Polish president never fully endorsed the nation branding program.

Nevertheless, between 2003 and 2007, Saffron and Olins coordinated work on Poland's nation branding program. First, Olins' team aimed at establishing contacts with representatives of the Polish state, seeking further political support. Second, they conducted an audit that revealed overseas perceptions of Poles and their own self-perceptions. This examination, similarly to corporate branding audits, revealed a set of generalizations which, in Saffron's opinion, represented the national features of Poles. The audit was based on the participatory observations of a single Briton traveling to Poland, interviews and focus groups with Polish media and marketing professionals, and Polish technocrats (Olins, 2004). While this investigation generated some empirical data, the team of Saffron and the Chamber of Commerce also relied on secondary data collected by the Institute of Polish Affairs (Kolarska-Bobińska, 2002) to understand external perceptions of Poland. Saffron's work did not bring to light the origins of Polish stereotypes outside Poland or the roots of Poles' auto-stereotypes. Rather, through oversimplified analysis and methodological unreliability, the Saffron audit ended up articulating another layer of stereotypes of Polishness.[8]

Although works on Polish national identity are widely present in academic as well as popular discourse, they were not taken into consideration by Saffron's auditors, as their research was another contractual service. Saffron drew up a report, titled *A Brand for Poland—Advancing Poland's National Identity* (Olins, 2004), which spelled out the results of the audit and Saffron's "diagnosis" of Polishness. The conclusions of this report were to be used as a semiotic guide informing the development of promotional campaigns for Poland. The report argued that the "older generation" in Poland "maintains a deeply pessimistic vision of reality. It is preoccupied with history, they view themselves in messianic terms, they are defensive, protective, resentful, and distrusting" (Olins, 2004, p. 51). Moreover, the report characterized Poles as suffering from an "inferiority complex," "believing in traditional culture and values," having a "traumatized national consciousness," and revealing "positivist and romantic streaks" (pp. 50–51). On the other hand, the "younger generation" of Poles, according to the report, "feel like Europeans," they are "modern" and "view Poland as a contemporary nation," they are committed to the market economy, "find nationalism passé," hold "anti-establishment" views, maintain a "cautious optimism" about the future and "face fully West" (pp. 51–53).

The nation branding team generalized features of Polishness and categorized them into positive traits, including "individualism," "resourcefulness," "imagination," "resilience," "nonconformism," and "openness," and negative traits, such as "lack of self-esteem," "undervalued," "misunderstood," "short-termism," "westernism," and "gloominess" (Olins, 2004, pp. 48–53). These traits then became a basis for generating what the marketing industry calls "a big idea"—a solution to the made-up marketing problem: namely, the lack of recognition of Poland overseas. Moreover, it was argued, this problem was largely due to poor coordination of promotional efforts by the Polish government.

This so-called diagnosis was labeled *Creative Tension* and outlined three dimensions, which form an overall celebration of Polish neoliberal capitalist values. These dimensions are: (1) *individualism*—signifying this trait of Polishness as an attractive feature for investors and tourists; (2) *work in progress*—defining Poland as a growing, expanding state, which, thanks to the dreams and aspirations of Poles, can be leveraged into investor relations, and, on the other hand, the liveliness, trendiness, and buzz has the potential to be memorable for its visitors; and (3) *creative tension*—standing for the alleged polarity of Polish national traits: "Poland is part of the West and also understands the East, Poles are passionate and idealistic and also practical and resourceful, the Polish character is ambitious and down to earth" (Olins, 2004, p. 79).

These interpretations of Polishness reproduce the tenets of neoliberal ideology, which have been outlined by social theorists. Eagleton (2007) illustrates how individualism is a descriptor of neoliberalizing nations; Eyal, Szelényi, and Townsley (2000) demonstrate how noncapitalist elites in Central and Eastern Europe struggled to build a neoliberal version of capitalism; and the last component builds on a geopolitical myth of Polish post-Soviet past: Previously, Polish nationalism, fueled by populist explanations of the nation's history, has faced the need to construct a narrative of "Poland between the West and the East." The idea of *betweenness* is re-articulated in the context of Poland's integration in the European Union, where the divide between "old" and "new" Europe has been explicit in the Polish public domain (Galbraith, 2009).

In the second stage of the nation branding project, Saffron considered incorporating the existing logo designed by DBB Corporate Profiles in 2001. Although this logo was created using preexisting notions of Polishness, nation branders considered attributing to it a clearer semiotic connotation. Saffron reserved the right to develop a brand book and other visual communication materials for Poland that were to become part of implementing *Creative Tension* via Polish institutions managing Poland's perceptions overseas.

On December 6, 2004, *Creative Tension* was publically introduced. The Chamber of Commerce organized a second conference in the Polish Parliament, which aimed at presenting the foundations for the project. In the Chamber of Commerce's vision, the nation brand had to be a form of "social movement," whereby all Poles would share the vision of brand Poland as defined by *Creative Tension*. This vision is consistent with the totalizing character of ideology, described by Lukács (1971) as inherent to reification. Nevertheless, nation branding takes this process further: It depoliticizes selected aspects of nationhood, stripping off their original political, aesthetic, and cultural values by subjecting them to commodity fetishism logic.

The introduction of *Creative Tension* resulted in a discussion over the ways this idea could be implemented. The historically and culturally complex perceptions of Poland among different publics and Poles themselves were to be challenged via a synthesis of new signifiers of Polishness. Between January and September 2005 the Chamber of Commerce aimed at establishing a system of visual representation, developing a brand book and key campaign messages, and conducting an institutional audit in order to implement the project. The Chamber of Commerce also commissioned further consultancy work from Saffron, the outputs of which materialized in the form of an executive report, titled *A brand for Polska—Further Advancing Poland's National Identity* (Olins, 2007). This report claimed that, as far as nation brand building was concerned, Poland was ahead of the game:

> Poland has both first and second mover advantage. Poland started early and correctly, achieving that most elusive component of a successful branding programme: a viable core idea. This happened more than two years ago. The idea and the ambition of the national reputation and branding programme are well known now in certain circles; the pump is primed. (p. 33)

The report also indicated that because other nations undertake nation branding, so should Poland. The acts of compliance, inherent in promotional culture, have another strong dimension in Polish nation branding discourse: Its logic is, partly, justified by the fact that other states engage in nation branding and therefore Poland needs to jump on this bandwagon. A special role in this discourse has been played by Spain and Ireland whose economic propaganda, as featured in global media outlets, was presented as a model to follow. Both of those states have, purportedly, re-branded themselves and are showcases of how to enact nation branding.[9] Nation branders enthusiastically use them as examples, but the nation branding failures of Charlotte Beers in the United

States (Fitzpatrick, 2010) or of New Labour in the United Kingdom (Awan, 2007) are not addressed in legitimations of nation branding.

Soon after the release of Saffron's second report in 2007, Poland's branding initiative lost its momentum, as political elites were concerned with the formation of a new cabinet. In the democratic elections of October 2007, the Polish conservative party Law and Justice took power, and its leaders, Lech and Jarosław Kaczyński, had their own, more inward-facing, vision of Polish national identity than that of the Chamber of Commerce. For Olins, Poland's new political leaders became a scapegoat for the breakdown of his program. In a talk at the Birmingham Business School in April 2007, Olins took Polish politicians to task for their lack of interest in branding. At this stage, the imposition of a centralized nation branding program in Poland ceased, although, in 2009, Saffron worked again with the Adam Mickiewicz Institute on a visual identity for Poland's campaign in Britain called *The Polska Year*.

Nation branding activities in Poland between 2001 and 2007 left a legacy of marketing and advertising professionals wishing to capitalize on branding services to various branches of the government, a consultancy bill of €300,000 that was paid to Saffron (Przeslakowski, personal interview, July 27, 2009), and a cohort of Polish academics invested in reproducing nation branding ideology (e.g., Florek, 2006; Jasiecki, 2004; Ociepka, 2008). The Polish field of nation branding has evolved since its initial focus on symbolic capital and is now also motivated by the possibility of gaining economic capital. For example, in 2006 the Institute of the Polish Brand charged the Polish Ministry of Foreign Affairs PLN 900,000 (approximately $280,000) for a piece of consultancy exploring perceptions (opinion polling) of "brand Poland" overseas, followed by a set of general recommendations (Boruc, personal interview, August 17, 2009). The Institute of the Polish Brand also offered its consulting services to the Warsaw Borough Council in 2007 and to the Polish Tourism Organization in 2008. The struggle for economic capital in the field is largely enacted on the basis of self-proclaimed expertise in nation barding.

The resistance toward nation branding among Polish technocrats and government communication managers since 2007 has been largely the result of their perception of a conceptual weakness in *Creative Tension*. *Creative Tension* misses the point with regard to how Poland should be represented. Moreover, nation branders underestimated the workings of the democratic system, whereby changes in government often entail new management as well as means of representation of Polishness via promotional campaigns. While Polish government communication managers in the field offer reflexive insights into nation branding practice, the concept of "Poland as a brand" *per se* is not questioned. Saffron's nation branding program is seen as a step toward the professionalization of this practice, as it resulted in a homology of language used by technocrats and attempts to coordinate promotional campaigns.

There are also notable, culturally driven acts of resistance toward nation branding ideology, among them a disagreement with its value exchange principle ("selling Poland" has negative historical connotations going back to its partition in the 18th century). Another, self-reflexive theme emerging from the interview data indicates that resistance toward nation branding is a result of an ossified management of the field institutions, post-Soviet style bureaucratic mindsets, and reluctance to change.

An idealized corporate managerialism is present among the architects of the nation branding program. In Poland the market principles of nation branding were legitimized as "post-ideological" (Bell, 2000), whereby nation brand management should be bipartisan and therefore not serving any political party's interests; "post-political" (Žižek, 1999), as Poland is a commonwealth of all Poles; and "post-historical" (Gehlen, 1956), as it is time for the nation to move forward away from Poland's gloomy history of suffering. For nation brand ideologists, their project was a way out of a national inferiority complex, and this had to be free of self-interest. They strived to legitimize the nation branding program as a matter of national importance. In their view, corporate style managerialism was a way forward for Poland and enacted pragmatism as free of ideological connotations. Their misrecognition in this view is twofold: They do not fully recognize a link between the political economy and the purpose of the nation brand as they are driven by their own interest; on a practical level, they rely on verbal and quasi-academic accounts of nation branding stories in different nations and fail to accept the lack of empirical evidence of successes in nation branding.

CONCLUSION

Several conclusions arise from the Polish case. The local field of nation branding emerged in the context of discussions about Poland's identity projections as a means to develop a long-lasting national reputation. However, my analysis reveals little understanding of international power politics among the self-proclaimed nation branding experts and marketing and public relations practitioners in the field. National reputation is an extension of a specific dimension of mediated foreign politics and the behavior of a state as an actor in the international system. Social theory approaches to international relations explore this matter. For example, Mercer (1996) offers a middle range reputation theory of the state, and Sharman (2007) contextualizes the complexity of national reputation within rationalist and constructivist frameworks and discusses how powerful foreign policy making is for national reputation. This is a neglected area by those who developed nation branding ideology and attempted its practice in Poland. Given that nation branding in Poland does not address foreign policy matters in a strategic way, questions about its effectiveness and the credibility of nation branding consultants should be asked. Put simply, if a prevailing aspect of national reputation is a derivative of a specific dimension of foreign policy, nation branding consultants miss the point in their approach to "identity and image" politics.

Furthermore, in theory, nation branding appears intellectually closer to authoritarian regimes than to the democratic politics of pluralist nations. Its commitment to unification and synergy of identity projections is hardly viable in any democratic political system where institutional voices represent different interests. O'Shaughnessy (2009) demonstrates why the idea of branding is closer to the propaganda practices in totalitarian Nazi Germany, where unification of messages and the rhetoric of their projection were supported by terror. The imaginative writings of nation branding "textbooks" do not attempt to address the specificity of pluralist politics and different versions of nationalism existing in specific political, social, or cultural settings. Their generic and normative approach to the branding of nations demonstrates misrecognition in understanding the democratic process, whereby different institutions speak of Poland via their promotional campaigns in a context-dependent way.

The Chamber of Commerce in Poland and its Saffron team accuse the Polish public administration of "not promoting Poland" (Kłoczko, 2010) and of not merging promotional efforts, attempting to legitimize the concept of branding and increase the social prominence of macro-marketing practice in Poland. However, the problems of Poland's nation branders did not stem from a lack of political will for managing the perceptions of Poland. Rather, they were the result of the intellectual shortcomings of nation branding as a concept that underestimates the values of democratic politics, that is, a pluralism of "voices" driven by different versions of nationalism and represented via different propaganda genres and messages.

The case of Poland demonstrates, regardless of the claims of branding ideologists, that branding cannot be directly applied as per "handbook" into different social realms. However, nation branding has left its legacy in Poland. The field image we are left with is that of neoliberal *corponationalism*—a form of identity politics underpinned by global market competitiveness, which aims to enhance the sense of national identity via the application of marketing ideologies and practices. Paradoxically, the emergence of nation branding is symptomatic of a national identity crisis in Poland.[10] Compliance with promotional culture and the belief that Poland can be reinvented as a brand demonstrates that Polish technocrats struggle to offer new viable visions of Polishness. In sum, nation branding in Poland has emerged as an ideological discourse that mediates the power structures of government with corporate interests and has been used by Polish technocrats to legitimize the dominant neoliberal social order.

NOTES

1. The author acknowledges comments from readers of this chapter, including Carrie Hodges, David Alder, Mike Molesworth, and especially Kevin Moloney.
2. For a comprehensive definition of "nation branders," see Aronczyk (2008). My use of the term in this chapter is consistent with hers.

3. Kaneva (2007; this volume) has applied Bourdieu's field theory in relation to nation branding. She makes a distinction between global and local fields of nation branding. Following this approach, nation branding in Poland is classified as a local field in this chapter.

4. Although Bourdieu never discussed national identity construction, his oeuvre has been used by nationalism scholars (e.g., Helbling, 2007).

5. For a detailed account of Poland's overseas perception management efforts, see Szondi (2009).

6. Chong and Valencic (1999) note the multifaceted character of contemporary national perception management, which used to be regarded as "an exclusive interpretational discourse for the official exercise of foreign policy . . . However, over the past decade, a large scale change has evolved. Images are continuously and deliberately managed and targeted by and for a wide range of actors and purposes" (p. 3). For Moloney (2005), public institutions and other actors of the competitive game "speak multiple voices" (p. 551).

7. A third group of field actors, although not a driving force in the debate on nation branding, includes Polish NGOs and selected Polish artists. This group is not specifically discussed in this chapter.

8. It should be noted that in my interviews with Polish nation branders the term "stereotype" was avoided and replaced with marketing jargon, such as "nation brand image" or "Polish brand perceptions."

9. It will be interesting to see whether the current economic crises in Ireland and Spain will change in any way the way nation branders discuss them.

10. Girard (1999) encapsulates this argument in the following way: "Overall, one might say that the emergence of 'branding' is refracted through crisis" (p. 22).

REFERENCES

Adam Mickiewicz Institute. (2009). *Strategia komunikacyjna IAM oraz zasady działania wydziału ds. komunikacji* [Adam Mickiewicz Institute communication strategy]. Warsaw, Poland: Author.

Adam Mickiewicz Institute. (2010). Startegia IAM, 2010–2016. [Adam Mickiewicz Institute strategic plan, 2010–2016]. Warsaw, Poland: Author.

Anholt, S. (2005). *Brand new justice: How branding places and products can help the developing world* (2nd ed.). Oxford, UK: Butterworth-Heinemann.

Aronczyk, M. (2008). "Living the brand": Nationality, globality, and the identity strategies of nation branding consultants. *International Journal of Communication, 2*. Retrieved September 15, 2008, from http://ijoc.org/ojs/index.php/ijoc/article/view/218

Auer, S. (2004). *Liberal nationalism in Central Europe*. London: Routledge.

Awan, F., (2007). *Young people, identity, and the media: A study of conceptions of self-identity in Southern England* (Doctoral dissertation, The Media School, Bournemouth University, Bournemouth, UK). Retrieved December 9, 2010, from http://media.bournemouth.ac.uk/research/documents/fatimah_abstract.pdf

Bell, D. (2000). *The end of ideology*. Cambridge, MA: Harvard University Press.

Boruc, M. A. (2001). *An economy under its own flag*. Warsaw, Poland: Institute of the Polish Brand.

Bourdieu, P. (1984). *Distinction: A social critique of the judgment of taste*. Cambridge, UK: Polity Press.

Bourdieu, P. (1990). *The logic of practice*. Cambridge, UK: Polity Press.

Bourdieu, P. (1994). Re-thinking the state: Genesis of and structure of bureaucratic field. *Sociological Theory, 12*(1), 1–18.

Bourdieu, P. (1998). *Acts of resistance: Against the new myths of our time.* Cambridge, UK: Polity Press.

Bourdieu, P. (2003). *Firing back: Against the tyranny of the market.* London: Verso.

Bourdieu, P., & Wacquant, L. J. D. (1992). *An invitation to reflexive sociology.* Chicago: Chicago University Press.

Bourdieu, P., & Wacquant, L. J. D. (1999). On the cunning of imperialist reason. *Theory, Culture and Society, 16*(1), 41–58.

Brubaker, R. (1996). *Nationalism reframed: Nationhood and the national question in the New Europe.* Cambridge, UK: Cambridge University Press.

Chancellery of the Prime Minister of the Republic of Poland. (2008). *Poland 2030: development challenges.* Board of Strategic Advisors. Warsaw, Poland: Author.

Chong, A., & Valencic, J. (1999). Preface. In A. Chong & J. Valencic (Eds.), *The image, the state and international relations:Proceedings from the conference on 24 June 1999 at the London School of Economics and Political Science: Selected papers* (pp. 3–6). London: London School of Economics and Political Science.

Cialdini, R. (1993). *Influence: The psychology of persuasion* (2nd ed.). New York: Quill William Morrow.

Eagleton, T. (2007). *Ideology: An introduction.* London: Verso.

Eyal, G., Szelényi, I., & Townsley, E. (2000). *Making capitalism without capitalists: The new ruling elites in Eastern Europe.* London: Verso.

Featherstone, M. (1991). *Consumer culture and postmodernism.* London: Sage.

Fitzpatrick, K. R. (2010). *The future of U.S. public diplomacy: An uncertain faith.* London: Brill.

Florek, M. (2006). The country brand as a new challenge for Poland. *Place branding, 1*(2), 205–214.

Galbraith, M. H. (2009). Between East and West: Geographic metaphors of identity in Poland. *Ethos, 32*(1), 51–81.

Gehlen, A. (1956). *Urmensch und Spätkultur. Philosophe Ergebruisse und Augssagen* [Primitive man and modern culture: Philosophical results and conclusions]. Bonn, Germany: Athenaüm-Verlag.

Gellner, E. (1983). *Nations and nationalism.* New York: Cornell University Press.

Girard, M. (1999). States, diplomacy, and image making: What is new? Reflections on current British and French experiences. In A. Chong & J. Valencic (Eds.), *The image, the state and international relations:Proceedings from the conference on 24 June 1999 at the London School of Economics and Political Science: Selected papers* (pp.20–26). London: London School of Economics and Political Science.

Greenfeld, L. (2003). *The spirit of capitalism: Nationalism and economic growth.* Cambridge, MA: Harvard University Press.

Helbling, M. (2007, June 12–13). *Re-conceptualizing the construction of nations with Bourdieu's help. Nationalism and national identities today: Multidisciplinary perspective.* Paper presented at the Cronem Conference, Surrey, UK.

Hobsbawm, E. J. (1990). *Nations and nationalism since 1780.* Cambridge, UK: Cambridge University Press.

Institute of the Polish Brand. (2010). *Kim jesteśmy, i o co nam chodzi?* [Who are we and what are we getting at?]. Retrieved August 5, 2010, from http://www.imp.org.pl/o-nas/kim-jesteśmy-i-o-co-nam-chodzi.html

Jansen, S. C. (2008). Designer nations: Neo-liberal nation-branding—Brand Estonia. *Social Identities, 14*(1), 121–142.

Jasiecki, K. (2004). Rola marki w promocji wizerunku Polski i polskiego biznesu [The role of the brand in promoting Poland's image and business]. *Studia Europejskie, 1,* 63–85.

Kaneva, N. (2007). *Re-imagining nation as a brand: Globalization and national identity in post-communist Bulgaria* (Doctoral dissertation, School of Journalism and Mass Communication, University of Colorado at Boulder).

Kłoczko, M. (2010). *KIG: nikt nie promouje Polski* [Polish Chamber of Commerce: No one promotes Poland]. Interview for BankierTV. Retrieved August 1, 2010, from http://www.youtube.com/watch?v=nHo1YUrKeO4

Kolarska-Bobińska, L. (Ed.). (2003). *Obraz Polski i Polaków w Europie* [Perceptions of Poland and Poles in Europe]. Warsaw, Poland: Institute of Public Affairs.

Lukács, G. (1971). *History and class consciousness*. London: Merlin Press.

Marion, G. (2006). Marketing ideology and criticism: Legitimacy and legitimization. *Marketing Theory*, 6(2), 245–262.

Mercer, J. (1996). *Reputation and international politics*. Ithaca, NY: Cornell University Press.

Moloney, K. (2005). Trust and public relations: Center and edge. *Public Relations Review*, 31(4), 550–555.

Moloney, K. (2006). *Rethinking public relations* (2nd ed.). London: Routledge.

O'Reilly, D. (2006). Commentary: Branding ideology. *Marketing Theory*, 6(2), 263–271.

O'Shaughnessy, N. (2009). Selling Hitler: Propaganda as a Nazi brand. *Journal of Public Affairs*, 9(1), 55–76.

Ociepka, B. (2008). Re-branding Russia: A neighbor's perspective. *Russian Journal of Communication*, 2(2), 212–214.

Olins, W. (1999). *Trading identities: Why countries and companies are taking on each other's roles?* London: Foreign Policy Centre.

Olins, W. (2002). Branding the nation: The historical context. *Journal of Brand Management*, 9(4/5), 241–249.

Olins, W. (2004). *A brand for Poland—advancing Poland's national identity. Stage one: Creating the core idea.* London: Saffron Brand Consultants. Retrieved December 9, 2010, from http://www.imp.org.pl/images/stories//pdf/Raporty_Ollins/SAFF_Poland.pdf

Olins, W. (2007). *A brand for Polska—further advancing Poland's national identity.* London: Saffron Brand Consultants.

Polish Ministry of Economics. (2010). *Strategia umiędzynarodowienia gospodarki polskiej (wersja robocza z 19 stycznia 2010 r.)* [A strategy for internationalization of the Polish economy (work in progress, January 19, 2010, version)]. Warsaw, Poland: Ministry of Economics.

Polish Ministry of Foreign Affairs. (2001). *ABC marketingu w dyplomacji publicznej* [ABC of marketing in public diplomacy]. Department of Promotion. Warsaw, Poland: Author.

Polish Ministry of Foreign Affairs. (2010). *Kierunki promocji Polski do 2015 r. (wersja robocza, 8 kwietnia 2010)* [Directions of Poland's promotion until the year 2015 (work in progress version, April 8, 2010)]. Department of Public and Cultural Diplomacy. Warsaw, Poland: Author.

Polish Tourism Organization. (2008). *Marketingowa strategia Polski w sektorze turystyki na lata 2008–2015* [Poland's tourism marketing strategy between 2008–2015]. Warsaw, Poland: Author.

Porter, B. (2002). *When nationalism began to hate: Imagining modern politics in nineteenth-century Poland.* Oxford, UK: Oxford University Press.

Puchalska, B. (2005). Polish democracy in transition? *Political Studies*, 53(4), 816–832.

Rokkan, S. (1975). Dimension of state building and nation-building. In C. Tilly (Ed.), *The formation of nation states in Western Europe* (pp. 562–600). Princeton, NJ: Princeton University Press.

Saffron Brand Consultants. (2007). *Saffron clients.* Retrieved July 21, 2007, from http://saffron-consultants.com/the-usual/clients

Sharman, J. C. (2007). Rationalist and constructivist perspectives on reputation. *Political Studies*, 55(1), 20–27.

Shields, S. (2008). How the East was won: Transnational social forces and the neoliberalisation of Poland's post-communist transition. *Global Society*, 22(4), 445–468.

Sidorenko, E. J. (1998). *Neoliberalism after communism: Constructing a sociological account of the political space of post-1989 Poland* (Doctoral dissertation, University of London, UK).

Sklair, L. (2001). *The transnational capitalist class*. Oxford, UK: Blackwell.

Swartz, D. (1997). *Culture and power: The sociology of Pierre Bourdieu*. Chicago: University of Chicago Press.

Swartz, D. (2004, August 14–17). *The state as the central bank of symbolic credit*. Paper presented at the 99th annual meeting of the American Sociological Association, San Francisco, CA.

Szondi, G. (2009). Central and Eastern European public diplomacy: A transitional perspective on national reputation management. In P. Taylor & N. Snow (Eds.), *The Routledge handbook of public diplomacy* (pp. 292–313). New York: Routledge.

Sztompka, P. (1993). *The sociology of social change*. Oxford, UK: Wiley-Blackwell.

Taithe, B., & Thornton, T. (1999). *Propaganda: Political rhetoric and identity 1300–2000*. Phoenix Mill, UK: Sutton.

Taylor, M., & Kent, M. L. (2006). Public relations theory and practice in nation building. In C. H. Botan & V. Hazleton (Eds.), *Public relations theory II* (pp. 299–315). Mahwah, NJ: Erlbaum.

Wacquant, L. J. D. (1993). From ruling class to the field of power: An interview with Pierre Bourdieu on *La Noblesse d'État*. *Theory, Culture & Society*, 10(3), 1–17.

Žižek, S. (1999). Carl Schmitt in the age of post-politics. In C. Mouffe (Ed.), *The Challenge of Carl Schmitt* (pp. 18–37). London: Verso.

Part III

Representations, Mediations, Narrations

7 Branding *Slovenia*
"You Can't Spell Slovenia Without Love . . . "[1]

Zala Volčič

INTRODUCTION

The newly created nation-states of the former Yugoslavia have recently joined a number of other poorer nations around the world—from Nigeria and Rwanda to Romania and Turkey—that have become a hot market for so-called nation branders. Nation branders argue that smaller and poorer nations in particular need to work on developing their recognizable image in the global marketplace (Anholt, 2003, 2007; Holt, 2004; Kotler & Gertner, 2002; Olins, 1999; Papadopoulos & Heslop, 2002) in order to increase visibility, attract tourists and foreign investors, expand exports, promote their international profiles among members of international organizations, and, importantly, mobilize patriotism at home.

The former Yugoslav states, which are in the middle of adjusting to international capitalism, have also embraced nation branding as a strategy for self-promotion, economic development, and image diplomacy. Public relations and marketing—those adjuncts to capital—have become deeply embedded in these post-socialist nations as part of a mantra that all a country has to do in order to succeed in the global marketplace is to change its image internally and externally. The promise is that with a better image, other social problems can be addressed, that ultimately they are all tied to the economy, and the economy is tied to the national "brand." The hope is that the magic of branding might—as its promoters and highly paid Western and local consultants alike assert—work economic miracles, boosting tourism and attracting the bounty of foreign investment.

In the year 2009, most of the former Yugoslav states were extremely busy in their branding efforts. They all initiated some kind of branding campaign with the most recent, as of the time of writing, originating from the fledgling nation of Kosovo. With the well-paid commercial guidance of global advertising giant Saatchi & Saatchi, Kosovo introduced a promotional television spot that focuses on the collective spirit of the youth of Kosovo in building their new country. The Kosovo spot tries to change the nation's image from a war-torn country into a young, peaceful, and beautiful Balkan country ready to become another normal member of Europe.

The ad closes with the slogan, "Kosovo—The Young Europeans," which recalls Ireland's branding efforts of the 1980s. At the time, Ireland's international image was poor. The Irish Republic's "Young Europeans" campaign in the 1970s and 1980s promoted its educated, young workforce to European and American investors. As *The Irish Times* writes, "The Industrial Development Authority identified some of Ireland's key strengths: a young and well-educated workforce in plentiful supply in a member state of the European Union. It then ran a highly successful international advertising campaign: 'The Young Europeans'" ("Ireland Inc.," 2009). The similarity between the two campaigns is, perhaps, an example of the derivative and repetitive character of advertising and one more proof of how branding campaigns copy and recycle one another (and themselves).

The main focus of this chapter, however, is on the branding efforts of Slovenia. As is the case with most of the seven former Yugoslav states, after the collapse of the common state, Slovenia continues to be involved in the project of constructing a "unified" national identity. Government agencies and private enterprises alike focus on consolidating a sense of distinctive national identity and a national brand identity (Volčič, 2008). However, nations are complex, political entities, and national identities are created through political practices that are historically and socially conditioned and are multilayered. I will suggest that nation branding is a marketing practice that simplifies and borrows only those aspects of a nation's identity that promote a nation's marketability. Nation branding, as Jansen (2008, p. 122) argues, not only introduces different nations to the world but also reinterprets national identity in market, commercial terms and provides new narratives for domestic consumption.

That's especially important in the former Yugoslav context, where recent nationalisms have had devastating effects. The nation branding phenomenon cannot be understood apart from these concrete historical conditions because they emerge against the background of the collapse of socialism and the violent Yugoslav wars that resulted in an estimated 300,000 deaths and millions of refugees. Peter van Ham (2002) recognizes some problematic aspects of nation branding and juxtaposes national identity to nation brand identity. He argues that a nation brand, that is, a market-based form of national identity, is far less dangerous than the nationalistic identity formations that triggered various violent wars throughout the 20th century. However, nation branding and nationalism are connected (Aronczyk, 2007), and, as I will suggest, nation branding *is a part of* a "commercial nationalism," which refers to a twofold process whereby the creation of a sense of national identity is taken on by the commercial sector as a form of marketing, while the injunction to identify with the nation is equated with a form of consumption.

Of interest to this chapter is how nation branding campaigns, caught up in the shifting currents of post-socialist nationalism, underwrite what might be described as an emergent form of commercial nationalism that represents important transformations in the reproduction of the concept of nation. I will argue that commercial nationalism is a way of describing how nationalist ideas migrate from the realm of political propaganda to that of commercial appeals. If the nation brand has become a significant way in which the nation is articulated, it becomes increasingly important to address the ways in which this development impacts how we think about the reproduction of national identity.

This chapter will first briefly explain the historical and political context for understanding Slovenian national identity and introduce different branding campaigns in the Slovenian context, which is characterized by post-socialist forms of neoliberal economic policy. Next, the specific focus will be on presenting a critical analysis of the branding campaign "I feel S*love*nia." I will show how in this campaign, one notices the deployment of commercial language, stereotypes, and practices; the creation of public-private partnerships; and the use of private entities to create a nation's identity. I will critically reflect upon the celebratory claims that marketers make: that because the ordinary citizens are now invited to participate in the campaign, the recasting of national identity becomes an open, democratic process. In the last part, I critique the nation branding initiatives, arguing for the importance of distinguishing between the nation-state and consumer goods like toothpaste.

To investigate these themes and questions, I draw on a range of qualitative research methods. I carried out textual analyses of various strategic, operational marketing, branding, and public relations plans and proposals, and I analyzed images, final reports, and findings included in the documents created by branding consultants. Websites of the organizations engaged in different countries' promotion and nation branding were also analyzed. In addition, 11 in-depth interviews were conducted with Slovenian "consultants," practitioners, and officials who were involved in the branding process either directly or indirectly.[2]

Ultimately, I argue that nation branding relies on the conflation of citizen and consumer, promoting a sense of national identity as something to which the consumer has the individualized, choice-based relationship associated with consumption. Moreover, it configures the nation as a standing reserve—a "post-political" resource to be consumed, perhaps as part of a taste culture of consumption. By contrast, the creation of common national symbols and rituals associated with what might be described as political (or "pre-post-political") forms of national identity formation rely on a sense of collective nation building and the nation as a project rather than a standing reserve. This is not to say that the only choice is between a "good" political nationalism and a "bad" commercial nationalism. Rather it is to suggest that the shortcomings of nationalism themselves change with the way in which nationalism reproduces in accordance with political, social, and economic logics. As Jansen (2008) argues, nation branding fits well with a neoliberal, post-socialist context precisely because it embraces a logic that privileges market relations (market fundamentalism). Rather than addressing and dealing with the (sometimes dangerous) appeal of national identities, nation branding constrains national imaginaries within a logic of commodification, focusing on populist and commercially "efficient" national characteristics.

NATIONAL IDENTITY AND EARLY NATION BRANDING INITIATIVES IN SLOVENIA

The nation-state has been under attack by the forces of globalization for at least two decades now (Harvey, 2001). Historically, there were many mechanisms of how the nation-state fostered unity and identity—the state and its cultural apparatuses (including the media and the educational sphere) played a crucial part in this process. But during the 1990s, the nation started to be promoted and crafted as a brand, in commercial terms, by private and commercial entities. Different international PR and marketing agencies, such as Interbrand, Wolff Olins, and Kotler Marketing Group, promote and celebrate the idea that nations are like other commodities in need of carefully crafting their image if they want to survive in a competitive world. This shift clearly signals a change in how both nationalism and democracy are being understood and practiced.

The majority of current literature on nation branding is produced by advertising experts who continue to be engaged in the practice of collaborating with different international PR firms and consulting for their own governments. Most of these publications are rather applied (Dzenovska, 2005; Fan, 2006; Gilmore, 2002; Gilmore & Rumens, 2005; Konečnik & Lapajne, 2008; Szondi, 2007). These authors suggest that it is precisely through branding that national governments can make their nations attractive to transnational capital, subordinating national sovereignty to the logic of capital flows.

After the collapse of socialism, Slovenia, like other nations in the Balkans and Central and Eastern Europe, found itself facing the challenge of transforming its economy, (re)creating its national identity, and establishing its position as a new nation within the global community. Slovenia gained its independence and became a parliamentary democracy in 1991. The transition to capitalist democracy was accompanied by the rise of (neo)liberalism and its privileging of the marketplace. The "triumph" of nationalism and (neo)liberalism in the 1990s was marked by the gospel of individualism and a focus on commercialization (Zerdin, 2007, p. 8). At the beginning of the 21st century, Slovenia has radically reduced welfare programs and transferred certain duties of "the social" from the state to the citizenry (Kurnik, 2005, p. 92).[3]

There were several attempts during the mid-1980s and early 1990s by the Slovenian Ministry of Tourism to engage in comprehensive nation branding and recast Slovenia's (international) image. It was as early as 1986 that the Slovenian Tourist Board created its first campaign "Slovenia—my country"

[*Slovenija—moja dežela*] with the aim to "boost pride and love for Slovenia at home, since then we still didn't have our own country . . . Overall, this was the most successful campaign up until today" (personal interview, 2009; for more, see Pompe, 2003). Later, the slogan *"Turizem smo ljudje"* (roughly translating into "We are the people for tourism") was introduced, followed by "Slovenia, on the sunny side of the Alps" [*Slovenija na soncni strani Alp*] (Kovač, 2006; Petek & Konečnik Ruzzier, 2008, p. 53). According to one of my informants, the goal of these programs was to "position Slovenia . . . internationally . . . as a modern, fun, inexpensive, affordable, sunny and welcoming country" (personal interview, 2010).

Other efforts included campaigns and slogans, running from 1995 to 2004, such as "A miniature Europe," "Paradise in Europe," "The green piece of Europe," and "Green jewel of Europe" (Petek & Konečnik Ruzzier, 2008, p. 53). In 1996, the Centre for the Promotion of Tourism introduced a new logo to promote tourism in Slovenia—a bouquet of flowers referred to as a "bouquet of peace, greens, and love" that appeared alongside the word "Slovenia" spelled with the internal letters "love" emphasized: SLOVEnia. It's worth pointing out that these were mostly short-lived advertising campaigns, whose results tended to be disappointing for the wider public and businesspeople alike (Smolej, 2006).

During the late 1990s, Slovenia's image management attempted to become more formalized and strategic, leading toward a more coordinated attempt to develop "a serious nation brand." Debates such as "What kind of a story should Slovenia share with the world?" started among the elites, experts, and the wider public (Kovač, 2006). When Slovenia entered the European Union (EU) in 2004, the Slovenian Tourist Agency selected the slogan "Slovenia invigorates" [*Slovenija pozivlja*] to introduce Slovenia to the rest of Europe. But again, according to some, the campaign was not coordinated, and the slogan itself was misunderstood not only in the English-speaking world but especially in the Italian context where the slogan was basically nonsensical [*Slovenia rinvigorisce*]. In May 2006, the first international advertising video spot was made especially for global television channels, such as CNN. The original slogan "Slovenia: Your perfect getaway" (which in Slovene became *Slovenija. Popolna za pobeg od resnicnosti*, translating literally as "Slovenia: A perfect escape from reality") was replaced by "Slovenia. A diversity to discover" [*Slovenija. Raznolikost, vredna raziskovanja*], after criticism by the minister of foreign affairs (Smolej, 2006, p. 37).[4] The Slovenian Tourist Board spent a grand total of 187 million Slovenian tolars (about €780,000) on producing the spot and buying advertising time on CNN Europe, which led to the cancellation of many other promotional activities abroad. The spot was a collage of beautiful landscape impressions, various architectural points of interest, and flashes of prominent Slovenian athletes and artists. These scenes were accompanied with evocative messages such as "Be free," "Sail away," and "Ride off." Emotional music included a melancholic folk song, *Gizdava* [Conceited Woman].

Mostly, these campaigns were conscious attempts to detach Slovenia from the former Yugoslav, "Balkan" region and what it dominantly stands for: backwardness and instability. As Bakić-Hayden and Hayden (1992) argue, Slovenia has the "fear and suspicion" of the Balkans and views the Balkan region as undemocratic, wild, and less developed. Elsewhere I analyzed the official website of the Slovenian government, and I have shown how Slovenia places itself firmly within the broad center of the mainstream of European geography, culture, history, and economy (Volčič, 2008). It attempts to reinforce the imagery of historically and culturally being a part of a Western and "civilized" Europe by emphasizing its Habsburg heritage, Alpine associations, and contiguity with Austria and Italy. For example, Slovenia is about "delightful villages and warm and hospitable people, whose lives are still steeped in the traditions of centuries of Austrian rule" (cited in Volčič, 2008, p. 402). This should come as no surprise, as many authors have already explored how Slovenia attempts to distance itself from belonging to the Balkans (Allcock, 1991; Todorova, 1997; Wolff, 1994). Similarly, in my interviews in Slovenia, I would frequently hear statements such as the one below:

> Slovenia is a "new" country, and had to introduce itself to the rest of the world. Well, we did not have to "change negative stereotypes" about ourselves necessarily, since Europe and the world didn't really know us . . . Hungary, Bulgaria, or Poland, for example, struggled with different problems, because they had to reorient the stereotypes. What was important, however, was to connect Slovenia to Western Europe, and not to the rest of Yugoslavia. (Personal interview, 2009)

Overall, Slovenes, after 18 years of independence, continue to be concerned and almost obsessed with their national image (Smolej, 2006, p. 1; Sočan, 2003, 2004). The results of a survey that showed the (rather limited) extent of Slovenia's international recognition (especially in Western European countries, such as Germany and France) were hotly debated (Konečnik, 2006). Particularly striking and memorable to Slovenes was the finding that Slovenia routinely gets confused with Slovakia by Western Europeans (Smolej, 2006, pp. 25–26). Thus, most of my Slovenian informants claimed that the primary task of the nation branding campaign should be to spread information about Slovenia, because it is "still a rather unrecognized country" (personal interview, 2010).

Despite the often-inflated claims about the importance of branding, there has been little public expression of doubts, criticisms, or dilemmas about the process of nation branding in Slovenia.[5] The celebratory voices of PR, marketing, and advertising gurus dominate the public discussion in advocating and justifying branding. For example, the director of the advertising agency Imago, Borut Sočan (2004, p. 12), claims that nation branding is not about simplifying the idea of the Slovenian nation, but about creating a recognizable image of Slovenia that cuts through the clutter of an image- and information-saturated world. The informants I talked to whole-heartedly support and legitimize the nation branding process and would refer to other "stellar" examples abroad, citing, for example, branding campaigns in Estonia, Ireland, and Portugal because "these countries also had to deal with not being recognized . . . or they had to deal with negative stereotypes . . . and they faced troubles in the economy. But the branding campaigns helped them tremendously" (personal interview, 2010). One of the informants went so far as to claim that,

> Slovene national identity is very complex . . . its geography, and history, and culture . . . so we basically needed a simple and cute slogan to make sense of our national culture. To have a national brand is not just to advertise our touristic spots . . . to have a brand means that we can identify our own identity and frame a vision and a strategy for ourselves: Who we are, what we do, where as a nation we are excellent, where we actually want to go . . . It's extremely important that people, ordinary people, identify with this brand, since *they are the ones who are crucial in promoting the Slovene brand inside and outside the country.* (Personal interview, 2010, my emphasis)

AND FINALLY . . . "I FEEL SLOVENIA"

Slovenia's latest branding initiative coincided with the country's presidency of the EU. In February 2007, just before Slovenia started its presidency, the Ministry of the Economy unveiled a new branding campaign: first internally to the rest of the Slovenian government and then to the public at large. Before then, Slovenia had not had a coordinated national brand, but national elites had been devoted to creating one for several years (Konečnik, 2004; Volčič, 2008). Thanks in part to their efforts, the Slovenian government became convinced of the need to commercially craft its image and create a coordinated national campaign. The slogan "I feel Slovenia" (in English) was, according to one expert, an auspicious choice because it invoked "those natural senses and feelings that only Slovenes have and share" (personal interview, 2009). "I feel Slovenia" (in Slovene: *Slovenijo čutim*) was to be used systematically across the government sector, as well as by nongovernmental organizations, business organizations, and various associations and individuals in order to promote Slovenia to the domestic population, as well to foreign visitors, investors, and business partners in the cultural, political, and economic spheres. The aim of the campaign was both to craft a new national image for external consumption and to revive national unity and pride within the country. In 2008 alone, more than €400,000 was allocated to communicating the brand to local and foreign audiences, including different sponsoring shows and media campaigns (Ministry of Economy, 2008).

When conducting interviews with marketing and PR practitioners in Slovenia, I repeatedly heard a story of how Slovenia was in "desperate need to finally get an overall nation brand identity." As one informant put it,

> Slovenia is so small, so basically, we are cursed. If the country does not take care of its own brand identity . . . if it does not create it, then . . . the other countries have the power to craft a stereotypical image for it. Everyone is afraid of stereotypes, since these can lead to limited foreign investment. Slovenia needed a national brand identity. (Personal interview, 2010)

It was in 2006 that the government started to back what was the country's first long-term branding effort. In July 2006, it called for proposals, and in November 2006, the slogan "I feel *Slove*nia" (created by the Slovenian advertising company Nuit) was selected out of 250 possible alternatives, including SloVENIa, VIDI, VICI.[6] The campaign, from the start, found itself embroiled in rumor, controversy, and charges of corruption. The committee was criticized for including too many politicians (out of 10 members, there were 6 politicians and only 4 experts). Also, it was discovered that the government had apparently chosen a slogan before going through the motions of appointing a committee to choose one. This was revealed when a photo surfaced of then-Prime Minister Janez Jansa wearing a cap with the slogan on it two months before the public contest had been decided (Stritar, Čuk, & Ilovar, 2007). In the end, it appeared that the contest was little more than public relations: an attempt to make the people feel they had chosen a slogan, which had already been pre-selected for them. In other words, the branding gurus had devised an interactive marketing campaign for the slogan they had selected—but the campaign ran the danger of backfiring on them.

Figure 7.1 The "I feel *Slove*nia" logo is part of a nation branding campaign executed by communication consulting company Pristop.

In 2007, the Slovenian Ministry of the Economy invited marketing agencies to create an overall nation branding campaign for Slovenia on the basis of the slogan, "I feel S*love*nia." Pristop, a Slovenian PR and marketing agency, was announced as the winner responsible for crafting the campaign and Slovenia's "new" image. In order to do that, Pristop said it would use "a very complex methodology, including internal and external research . . . for example, surveys, that were sent to 900 'relevant' Slovenes . . . focus groups and interviews with elites, including roughly 30 experts" (personal interview, 2010; but see also Konečnik, Lapajne, Drapal, & de Chernatony, 2009).[7] Pristop also embraced the new marketing paradigm of "co-creation," which argues for the importance of including citizen-consumers in the production process as a means of ensuring they are already invested in the final product and to provide them with a sense of empowerment (Zwick, Bonsu, & Darmody, 2008). Pristop consistently emphasized the participatory focus of the brand-building campaign, noting,

> We included participants from three Ministries, the state Tourist Agency, and different experts in order to make the brand connected as much as possible with the Slovenian public at large. All Slovenian citizens were invited to participate in making the Slovenian brand over the Internet thanks to a dedicated website. (Personal interview, 2009).

According to Konečnik et al. (2009), who served as consultants in the branding process, "The branding approach for Slovenia was holistic because all the relevant stakeholder groups involved in executing the brand were invited to take part in the branding process" (p. 51). Such reports legitimize the promise that the ordinary citizen is a participant and co-creator in the branding process. However, as I will suggest later, one needs to be careful of this promise, as it has more to do with extracting free labor from citizens—including the labor of marketing to themselves—and less with a concern for either democratic participation or consumer value.

On the basis of their methodology, the marketing consultants revealed their findings that "Slovenia is green, it invigorates, it is elemental, and based on organic development and family" (Konečnik et al., 2009, p. 56). The simplistic character of these findings, based on costly research and complicated planning, demonstrates some of the shortcomings of the marketing industry as a whole, including the focus on generating messages that have such broad, non-controversial appeal that they come across as simple and a bit vacant. To drive this point home, the marketers also observed, "Slovenia does not identify itself with specific characteristics, such as . . . the highest mountain or the longest river . . . since, Slovenia is a special feeling above any functional promises . . . " (personal interview, 2010). According to one of the informants, "We wanted to create a brand for all Slovenes; despite the fact that the government requested it . . . The brand has functional, but also emotional and experiential dimensions" (personal interview, 2010). According to one of the scholars involved in the project,

"We . . . strove to develop a brand and marketing strategy that would be considerably different from branding strategies applied in other countries" (Konečnik, 2010). It seems that what's different about Slovenia and its brand promise is that "you can't show Slovenia simply with an image . . . you have to *feel* and *experience* Slovenia" (*Priročnik*, 2007, p. 7). Another informant added,

> The brand summarizes the key elements of Slovene identity, expresses a vision of the country, and conveys its symbolic promise. However, *one has to live it, feel it*—through words, sounds, colors, touch, actions and experience. *You cannot spell Slovenia without love* . . . [laugh] The mission is clear: going forward with nature, which means focusing on organic development, promoting a niche economy, welcoming diversity, and attracting the best technological and human potential. (Personal interview, 2010, my emphasis)

Pristop developed a set of national design elements and published them in a handbook referred to as a "brand style book" (*Priročnik*, 2007), which included interpretations of Slovenian stories, variations of the logo "I feel Slovenia" (a slogan that, not insignificantly, is based on an English language pun; the word "love" does not mean anything in Slovene), photographic styles, color palettes, and graphic devices. The core brand identity of brand Slovenia looks like a complicated science chart, with the words, "Slovene Green," "Pleasant Excitement," and "Elemental (Nature)" in the middle of the circle (surrounded by key defining categories, such as "values," "vision," "mission," "benefits," "distinguishing preferences," and "personality") (*Priročnik*, 2007). According to one of the informants, "for sure the brand represents the love that Slovenes have for their nature . . . we identify with it, we are close to the nature, and we are proud of our mountains, the Adriatic coast, and our lakes" (personal interview, 2010).

"Slovene green" forms the core of the Slovenia brand identity because Pristop has figured out, based on their research, that Slovenes feel very close to nature, "they are very conscious of nature" (personal interview, 2010). The creators explained:

> Green is more than a color in Slovenia. It is "*Slovene* green" that expresses the balance between the calmness of nature and the diligence of the Slovene people. It stands for intact nature and our focus to keep it that way, for lifestyle equilibrium and an orientation towards nature . . . "Slovene green" represents the harmony of all senses that help us to experience Slovenia. *One never remembers Slovenia in images, but as the scent of the forest, the murmur of a stream, the astonishing taste of spring water and the softness of wood.* (Lipovšek, 2007, my emphasis)

But, not surprisingly, many other countries in the world have green at their center, claiming nature as a core element of their national identity. From New Zealand to Australia, Germany, Ireland, Norway, and Estonia, many countries very aggressively try to market themselves as a "green country," attracting environmentally conscious people (van Ham, 2002, p. 257). In this regard, although the Slovene campaign ostensibly focuses on the uniqueness of Slovenia, it ends up reproducing those themes that marketers have decided are hot-button issues of the new millennium.

The campaign inevitably attempts to portray a unique image of Sloveneness, connected to nature. Stanković (2005) writes about the traditional construct of Sloveneness as something deeply related to nature and an idealized rural life. In this regard, the campaign demonstrates the way in which nation branding requires a *commercial* reappropriation of Slovenia's "natural" history. The campaign "I feel S*love*nia" is conceived as an evocation of traditional and modern motifs that lend it a certain sense of timelessness and connection to nature. As one informant explains, in what sounds like stream-of-consciousness marketing hype, perhaps tongue-in-cheek,

> Slovenia is full of contradictions . . . and one such contradiction is the dichotomy between rural and urban. The brand is not rural, it's green, it's eco . . . it's rural, in a way, but it's also industrial and cold at the same time . . . I love you in the cold . . . I am warm when it's green . . . Green in the middle of urban Ljubljana. (Personal interview, 2010)

The campaign produced promotional materials, including short video documentaries, a PowerPoint presentation, pamphlets, and a CD-ROM as well as an outdoor display campaign and press events (Ministry of Economy, 2008; "Slovenia: Znamka I feel S*love*nia," 2008). The promotional activities included advertising the slogan "I feel S*love*nia" on 85 London taxis and a touring truck called the *EU Road Show,* which stopped in every capital city of the EU. At these events, members of the touring crew played harmonica and offered traditional foods and drinks—typical populist practices.[8]

There were a couple of offspring campaigns coming from the overall brand campaign "I feel S*love*nia." For example, the Slovenian Tourist Board developed a "Slovenia-Friendly Office—Slovenia Green Office" project that seeks to encourage Slovenia's (tourism) industry and destinations to develop environmental standards. One of their pamphlets says, "Employees are encouraged to behave in a more environmentally friendly way in offices by stylish stickers specially designed to tie in with the 'I feel S*love*nia' brand" ("Pisarna prijazna Sloveniji," n.d.). There are other campaigns now taking place, designed specifically for the domestic population, such as "Close to home, close to the heart" [*Blizu doma, blizu srca*] that attempt to support and upgrade the brand "I feel S*love*nia." For the international market, the campaign "Slovenia . . . bet you will love it" has been developed.

In sum, the campaign attempts to position itself as something stable, simple, and as offering a clear and consistent narrative about Slovenia. I am not interested here in judging the success of the campaign itself, however it might be measured. Instead, I want to offer some arguments, using the case study of the "I feel S*love*nia" campaign, about how, at its heart, nation branding is a hierarchical, reductive form of communication that is intended to privilege a simplistic and reductionist message about a nation. I also want to argue that nation branding as a process amounts to a form of marketplace governance, a means of enlisting the populace to participate in and become invested in the marketing of the state as an extension of the entrepreneurialization of the self.

CRITICAL REFLECTIONS ON NATION BRANDING

The image, the brand of Sloveneness, becomes a powerful marketing tool, inviting all Slovenes to be involved in "feeling Slovenia," "co-creating Slovenia," and realizing profits for everyone in the country. It is crucial to address the question of what happens to national identity when it no longer necessarily links to political and state apparatuses for its construction, but comes to rely extensively on commercial forces for its (re)production. What we see is a shift from "official, classical, state-oriented" nationalism to a more commercial one that is based on stereotypical commercial symbols and markers. Nation branding is not just about consuming products, it's about consuming "nationalism" and reproducing its most commercial, simplistic dimensions. That goes hand-in-hand with the idea of "propagating" nationalism for the sake of profits. Consuming nationalism then, through nation branding initiatives, relies on the conflation of citizen and consumer and promotes a sense of national identity as something to which the consumer has the individualized, choice-based relationship associated with consumption.

There are two main concerns about nation branding that I want to reflect upon in this section. The first one has to do with a populist/commercial understanding of national identity, where we see different national characteristics being recycled, and exploited, for commercial purposes. For example, according to Konečnik et al. (2009, p. 57), different participants in the "I feel S*love*nia" campaign were asked to define what marks Slovenia. What are those crucial characteristics that would exclusively define Slovenes? According to their research, these are very stereotypical ones, connoting nature: the highest mountain Triglav, the picturesque lake Bled, the coastal city of Piran, the Postojna caves, and the Ljubljana castles, as well as, of course, the Slovene language, its unique culture, and food. Mostly, respondents shared that they want to live in an environmentally clean country and protect nature. The campaign adopts a set of clichés about Slovene national identity, telling the citizenry that "we" are "warm, hospitable, and 'green' people. We have historical sites, wine, nature, and delicious food" (personal interview, 2010). Marketing and branding specialists in Slovenia adopt a similar logic, focusing on stereotypical characteristics such as natural and cultural diversity in a small space, wine, quality of life, and the joyful and open spirit of the Slovene people (Pompe, 2003; Sočan, 2003, 2004; see also Jančič, 2006). What one sees here is the process whereby marketers borrow positive, "exotic" elements from well-established national stereotypes and exploit them by targeting Western consumers who are searching for some kind of "exotic" Other of Europe: a nearby country, but one that can be treated as an exciting, novel, and diverse other (without being too different). Other critical scholars of nation branding have reached similar findings when analyzing the branding efforts of Romania and Bulgaria (Kaneva & Popescu, 2011) or the self-presentation of former communist countries at the international song contest Eurovision (Baker, 2008).

This is further connected to the "participatory and emancipatory" promise of the branding campaigns—the promise that the citizens themselves are now invited to participate in the co-creation of a sense of national brand identity. In the post-socialist era, the transition is from state propaganda to advertising propaganda, from a top-down assertion of collective identity to an ersatz "bottom-up" investment in brand identity. The nation comes to stand as one more consumer choice (although for many, of course, the choices are severely limited) rather than a site of collective belonging and action. Marketing scholars (Firat & Dholakia, 2006; Firat & Venkatesh, 1995) have, for a long time, seen branding as liberating and as empowering consumers/citizens. Involving ordinary citizens from diverse layers of society in discussions about how to define the national self satisfies those who would criticize the practice's potential for elitism and exclusion.

This latest strategy of "co-creation" is a part of a larger marketing exercise by producers to reduce the distance between production and consumption, and to seek ways to control and appropriate the creativity of ordinary citizens. No wonder then that the Slovenian "branders" follow the "smart" marketers, claiming to defer to the empowered, free, and liberated consumer/citizen. Ordinary Slovenes were invited to "co-produce" the Slovenia brand on the Internet, and specifically, through a nationwide mail campaign seeking public feedback. Where once the invocation was to participate in *nation building*, in the new millennium this has given way to the injunction to share in *nation branding*. This is a distinct kind of responsibility, insofar as it positions citizens, as it were, between the state and its external consumers: tourists, international investors, and so on. Nation branding thus has a double audience: the "internal" population, so to speak, who are meant to relate to the brand as both a form of empowerment and a means of maximizing the resources available to them; and an external population, for whom the brand is to serve as both an enticement to spend and invest and a perception-controlling device.

To enlist the language of branding is to color international relations and internal national development with the brush of the economy. Even those aspects of diplomacy, for example, that are not strictly economic, are meant to be shaped by the public relations effects of "the brand." (Consider, for example, one of the U.S. responses to the 9/11 attacks: to hire a marketing expert to help re-brand the U.S. image in the Middle East, with the [specious] claim that the United States did not have a policy problem but merely an image problem.) For the internal population—the audience that participates in "building" the brand—taking responsibility for internalizing it becomes a condition for the prosperity of the nation and thus a form of incentivized work on the self. Offloading the labor of building brand identity onto the populace means assigning them the responsibility for its success and their own—and making the link between the two. So it was that in July 2008, Slovenes received the invitation to participate in a discussion about what they think about Slovenia and its "brand." The response was not uniformly positive, with some citizens pushing back against the equation of citizenship with marketing to oneself and to others. One blogger responded angrily to this invitation:

> Are you absolutely crazy??? They are inviting me to respond to questions about Slovene national characteristics, so that they will then measure my responses and supposedly come up with something new . . . come on! You can't measure Slovene identity, you can't "come up" with it and sell it like that . . . I don't want to participate in "co-creating" a national identity in this way . . . and for that, to win a T-shirt! ("Poceni kupovanje," 2008)

Many argue that the participatory branding campaign helped legitimate the idea that a national brand identity "represents the real nature of Slovenia rather than imposing one that feels artificial, that is, you know, top-down . . . the Slovenian brand builds national self-confidence and solidarity; and it promotes national cohesion" (personal interview, 2009). The connection of nation branding to the ideas of freedom, globalization, capitalism, solidarity, participation, and cohesion offers a way to talk about nationhood that is not connected to socialism, or "top-down" models for the creation of a sense of national identity. The model of "the national branded self" fits neatly with the participatory promise of the interactive era and echoes its logic: the invitation to participate not just in the marketing of oneself, but to "propagandize" to oneself. The market becomes a dominant platform not only for participation in a culture of exchange, but also for political participation in a democratic, national public sphere.

Which leads me to my second point. In the interviews, the necessity for citizens to "internalize the brand" was emphasized over and over again as a crucial element of successful nation branding. This idea is based on the assumption that Slovenes themselves have to accept the branded image as their own and start to "live the brand" (Konečnik & Go, 2008, p. 185). As the *Handbook of Brand Slovenia* puts it, "The power of the brand lies in the content and motivation of the Slovene citizens to live the brand" (*Priročnik* 2007, p. 5). Borrowing from the language of brand communities, the *Handbook* goes on to say,

> *We will all express and communicate the image of Slovenia* . . . but the brand will be used differently by different groups . . . for example, the businessperson will adjust the brand to his/her own needs . . . an athlete will translate the Slovene story into his/her own sports' story . . . there are as many Slovenes as there are Slovene stories . . . and everyone can use their own interpretation . . . but whoever will use the brand will need to think how to communicate the brand holistically, using all the senses. (*Priročnik*, 2007, p. 6)

I want to argue here that it makes a difference whether the portrayal of national priorities and characteristics is structured by the private sector for commercial purposes or by various state and public actors for political and cultural reasons. Thus, one needs to insist on the importance of highlighting the distinctive character of those forms of nationalism whose purpose is to mobilize a brand community around markers of national identity in order to drive ratings and sell products. For the purposes of my analysis of the nation branding phenomenon as it links to commercial nationalism, I would distinguish between recent attempts by nations to brand themselves, and, on the other hand, the use of nationalism by commercial entities to sell media products, including music, news, and entertainment programming (Volčič, 2009). In the latter case, national priorities are subsumed to market ones; in the former, the two realms become one: engaging in diplomacy and political action is understood as a form of marketing.

CONCLUSION: COMMERCIAL NATIONALISM AS SELLING THE NATION

I want to use the example of the Slovenian branding campaign to trace the outlines of several elements of what can be described as commercial nationalism—the phenomenon whereby commercial private institutions take on an increasingly important role in framing the nation in the era of globalization, neoliberalization, and, in Central and Eastern Europe (as elsewhere), the galloping commercialization of the media industries. My central interest, however, is in the way that commercial nationalism imports commercial imperatives into the version of nationalism it purveys—and that these imperatives may not fit comfortably with prior conceptions of state-oriented nationalism. The Slovenian case study illustrates the ways in which nation branding seeks to mobilize the populace to "live" the national brand and to promote it nationally and internationally. In a post-socialist, (neo)liberal context, nationalism becomes a form of consumption and citizenship a mode of "living the brand." The responsibilities of citizenship become intertwined with the productivity of branding: Citizens are now encouraged to embrace and promote the brand. The new Slovenian elites, eager to embrace the (neo)liberal regime, of course create specific ideologies of national identity within the larger discursive universe of available materials. These elites are involved in imaginative ideological labor that brings together cultural elements, selected historical memories, and interpretations of experiences; but most of all, their discourse about nation branding and forming national identity from below fits neatly with the post-socialist and (neo)liberal-state effort to offload certain duties of society onto the citizens themselves. This practice increasingly takes place within a context characterized by the accumulation of capital, and it further coincides with the triumph of (neo)liberal ideology. Thus, when new elites, including branding experts, attempt to resolve national identity construction, their own discourse is full of internal contradictions. One consequence of the adoption of nation branding is a particular type of populist form of commercial nationalism. If, once upon a time, shaping the national image was the privilege of political elites who relied upon experts in symbolic manipulation, nation branding, as new elites argue, promises to place the power of brand creation in the people's hands.

There is little reason to believe that repackaging national narratives for the global (and local) marketplace rids them of nationalistic elements. Nation branding promotes a particular type of nationalism that echoes the use of nationalist appeals to sell. From both sides, that of the state and that of the private sector, we see a convergence on what might be described as the formation of "commercial nationalism." For example, local producers and media outlets use nationalist appeals to sell, and the state enlists the logic of marketing as a strategy for national development, which, in turn, is understood largely in economic terms. I therefore propose two crucial elements of commercial nationalism as a starting point for thinking about shifting constellations of national (brand) identity in a globalized era.

First, and perhaps most obviously, commercial nationalism is a means to a very specific end: sales. For the private sector this means sales of goods and services; for the state it means GDP, trade balances, and economic development. As the private sector takes on forms of propaganda associated with the state, the state embraces the strategies of marketers. These developments are not, in themselves, new, but their conjunction in an era of neoliberal globalization marks a shift in the form and content of nationalism itself. To understand the imagined community of the nation through the mechanism of a brand identity is to reconfigure national identity as a strategic asset in the entrepreneurialization of the populace. "I feel **Slovenia**" mobilizes themes of national identity and authentic "Sloveneness" to gain profit and advertising revenues outside and inside Slovenia. On the side of the market, commercial nationalism is subordinated to a "higher" end—one that transcends loyalty to particular political formations, political representatives, government policies, and even, paradoxically, loyalty to the nation. Brand loyalty comes to represent a loyalty to the logic of the market. There is no clear political agenda attached to commercial nationalism, but in its commercial form it serves not solely as a point of national identification, but of brand loyalty. The allegiance is only secondarily to a sense of national community or identity and primarily to a brand and its authenticity.

Second, from the perspective of the state, commercial nationalism serves as a resource for public relations, public diplomacy, and propaganda; however, given its higher (or lower) allegiance to the profit motive, it can be a problematic or ambiguous resource. The tendency of commercial nationalism is to read the political through the lens of marketing—not just to view politics as one more form of salesmanship, but to offload forms of national identification onto the private sector. Indeed we might describe the advent of commercial nationalism as a kind of reflexivization of "imagined community" in an era characterized by anxiety over its fate in the face of fragmentation, mobility, and globalization. If, for example, the national newspaper helped create a sense of shared community traveling through time, commercial nationalism provides a point of identification in the face of the fragmentation of the public sphere in the era of the Internet and associated forms of mass customization. The recent tendency of political figures to appear as heavy supporters of branding campaigns—such as former Slovenian Prime Minister Janez Jansa wearing a hat with the slogan "I feel *Slove*nia" and widely promoting the brand—marks a further permutation of the relationship between politics and celebrity mediated by the notion of authenticity as a key component of national identification.

In a post-socialist, (neo)liberal order then, creating the nation brand becomes more than forming a particular commodity: it becomes a particular type of national belonging.

NOTES

1. This chapter is an output from a program of research funded by the University of Queensland's Early Career Grant. The author gratefully acknowledges UQ's support and especially thanks the Centre for Critical and Cultural Studies, and its director, Graeme Turner.
2. I met my informants in different public and private spaces, preferably cafés, and their offices. Significantly, at first, they all attempted to legitimize their own professional position as something extremely important for the national culture. Also, they would explain to me over and over again different "complex" methodologies they use in their work, mostly, the so-called SWOT analysis (identifying strengths, weaknesses, opportunities, and threats).

3. Moreover, other benefits, such as free higher education and housing, that for decades were provided by the state, are now being privatized (Kodelja, 2005).
4. The minister insisted the word "getaway" implies "fleeing a crime scene" and this was, therefore, an unacceptable way to promote Slovenia.
5. The only discussions were organized by the Slovene Society of Designers, but they revolved mostly around questions of design (see more in Stritar et al., 2007).
6. A logo was designed by Slovene design studio Luks and it contains a heart symbol, a drawing of the highest Slovene mountain Triglav, and the leaf of a tree. In February 2007 the government approved the slogan but said the logo was not satisfactory.
7. For its research work only, Pristop received €158,000 ("Slovenija bo prijetno vznemirjala," 2008).
8. After analyzing the *Handbook of Brand Slovenia*, it's clear that the advice of nation-branding guru Wally Olins (1999, pp. 23–24) was carefully followed, especially where he outlines a seven-step process, paraphrased as follows: 1. Creation of a group with representatives in government, industry, the arts, education and the media to help to legitimize and implement the branding initiative. 2. Adoption of qualitative and quantitative methods in order to find out how the nation is understood both within and outside. 3. Consultations with opinion-leaders regarding the nation's strengths and weakness. 4. Identification of the core strategy of the campaign and creation of the central idea around which the strategy is based. This is usually a slogan, around which the rest of the campaign is framed. 5. Development of a visual design and attaching it to everything that represents the nation. 6. Adjustment of the message to carefully target desired audiences: international tourists, internal and external investors. 7. Creation of a public-private group to launch the program. It's necessary to make it alive in government, commerce, industry, the arts, and media.

REFERENCES

Allcock, J. B. (1991). Constructing the Balkans. In J. B. Allcock & A. Young (Eds.), *Black lambs and grey falcons: Women travellers in the Balkans* (pp. 170–191). Bradford, UK: Bradford University Press.

Anholt, S. (2003). *Brand new justice: The upside of global branding.* Oxford, UK: Butterworth-Heinemann.

Anholt, S. (2007). *Competitive identity: The new brand management for nations, cities and regions.* New York: Palgrave Macmillan.

Aronczyk, M. (2007). New and improved nations: Branding national identity. In C. Calhoun & R. Sennett (Eds.), *Practicing culture* (pp. 105–128). New York: Routledge.

Baker, C. (2008). Wild dances and dying wolves: Simulation, essentialization, and national identity at the Eurovision Song Contest. *Popular Communication, 6*(3), 173–189.

Bakić-Hayden, M., & Hayden, R. M. (1992). Orientalist variations on the theme "Balkans": Symbolic geography in Yugoslav cultural politics since 1987. *Slavic Review 51*(1), 1–15.

Dzenovska, D. (2005). Remaking the nation of Latvia: Anthropological perspectives on nation-branding. *Place Branding and Public Diplomacy, 1*(2), 173–186.

Fan, Y. (2006). Branding the nation: What is being branded? *Journal of Vacation Marketing, 12*(5), 5–14.

Firat, A. F., & Dholakia, N. (2006). Theoretical and philosophical implications of postmodern debates: Some challenges to modern marketing. *Marketing Theory, 6*(2), 123–162.

Firat, A. F., & Venkatesh, A. (1995). Liberatory postmodernism and the reenchantment of consumption. *Journal of Consumer Research, 22*(3), 239–256.

Gilmore, F. (2002). A country—can it be repositioned? Spain—the success story of country branding. *Brand Management, 9*(4/5), 281–293.

Gilmore, F., & Rumens, R. (2005, October 10). No logo, no future. *Brand Strategy.* Retrieved March 20, 2010, from http://downloads.acanchi.com/Brand_Strategy.pdf

Harvey, D. (2001). *Spaces of capital: Towards a critical geography.* New York: Routledge.

Holt, D. (2004). *How brands become icons.* Boston: Harvard Business School Press.

Ireland Inc. (2009, September 9). *The Irish Times.* Retrieved April 22, 2010, from http://www.irishtimes.com/newspaper/opinion/2009/0919/1224254857870.html

Jančič, M. (2006). Slovenija brez turističnega logotipa [Slovenia without the touristic logo]. *Marketing Magazin, 301*(1), 16–19.

Jansen, S. C. (2008). Designer nations: Neo-liberal nation-branding—Brand Estonia. *Social Identities, 14*(1), 121–142.

Kaneva, N., & Popescu, D. (2011). National identity *lite*: Nation branding in post-communist Romania and Bulgaria. *International Journal of Cultural Studies, 14*(2), 191–207.

Kodelja, Z. (2005). Lavalova kritika neoliberalne doktrine izobraževanja? [Laval's critique of the neoliberal doctrine of education]. In C. Laval (Ed.), *Šola ni podjetje: Neoliberalni napad na javno šolstvo* [The school is not a corporation: Neoliberal attack on public schools], (pp. 313–336). Ljubljana, Slovenia: Krtina.

Konečnik, M. (2004). Slovenija kot blagovna znamka? Seveda. [Slovenia as a brand? Of course.]. *Finance, 139,* 8.

Konečnik, M. (2006). Ovrednotenje premozenja znamke Slovenije kot turisticne destinacije v oceh Nemcev in Hrvatov [Evaluation of Slovenia's brand as a touristic destination in the eyes of Germans and Croatians]. *NG 1*(2), 37–49.

Konečnik, M. (2010). *A follow-up to the Branding Slovenia story.* Retrieved April 22, 2010, from http://nation-branding.info/2010/01/20/a-follow-up-to-the-branding-slovenia-story

Konečnik, M., & Go, F. (2008). Tourism destination brand identity: The case of Slovenia. *Brand Management, 15*(3), 177–189.

Konečnik, M., & Lapajne, P. (2008, January/March). Uspeh slogana je odvisen tudi od komunikacijske strategije države [The success of the slogan depends also on the state's communication strategy]. *Turizem, 12*(92), 13.

Konečnik, M., Lapajne P., Drapal, A., & de Chernatony, L. (2009). Celotni pristop k oblikovanju identitete znamke "I feel Slovenia" [Whole approach to the creation of identity brand "I feel Slovenia"]. *Akademija MM, 2,* 51–62.

Kotler, P., & Gertner, D. (2002). Country as brand, product, and beyond: A place marketing and brand management perspective. *Journal of Brand Management, 9*(4/5), 249–261.

Kovač, B. (2006). Avtogol [Autogoal]. *Mladina, 47*(1). Retrieved April 22, 2010, from http://www.mladina.si/tednik/200647/clanek/slo-ekonomija—bogomir_kovac

Kurnik, A. (2005). *Biopolitika: Novi družbeni boji na horizontu* [Biopolitics: New social struggles]. Ljubljana, Slovenia: Sophia.

Lipovšek, L. (2007, November 23). Branding: I feel Slovenia. *Slovenia Times*. Retrieved April 22, 2010, from http://www.sloveniatimes.com/en/inside. cp2?uid=D1A4A0AB-1FB3-BC6C-BE2E-25B82D43B706&linkid=news&cid= 839A4F2D-F008-C37A-2CC9-4314C8A807ED

Ministry of Economy. (2008). *Komuniciranje znamke Slovenije (I feel Slovenia) v letu 2008* [Communicating a brand (I feel Slovenia) in 2008]. Retrieved April 22, 2010, from http://www.mg.gov.si/nc/si/splosno/cns/novica/article/11987/5930

Olins, W. (1999). *Trading identities: Why countries and companies are taking on each other's roles*. London: Foreign Policy Centre.

Papadopoulos, N., & Heslop, L. (2002). Country equity and country branding: Problems and prospects. *Journal of Brand Management, 9*(4/5), 294–314.

Petek, N., & Konečnik Ruzzier, M. (2008). Uvajanje znamke "I feel Slovenia" ali "Slovenijo Cutim" [Introducing the brand "I feel Slovenia"]. *Akademija MM, 2*, 49–60.

Pisarna prijazna Sloveniji [Friendly office to Slovenes]. (n.d.). *Slovenia.info*. Retrieved April 22, 2010, from http://www.slovenia.info/?ps_slovenia_green=0

Poceni kupovanje političnih točk [Cheap buying of political points]. (2008, July 3). *Zloba.si*. Retrieved April 22, 2010, from http://www.zloba.si/poceni-kupovan-je-politicnih-tock

Pompe, A. (2003). Kdo pravzaprav nima pojma o znamki slovenskega turizma? [Who actually understands the brand of Slovenian tourism?] *Marketing Magazin, 266*(1), 12.

Priročnik Znamke Slovenije [Handbook of Brand Slovenia]. (2007). *I feel Slovenia*. Ljubljana, Slovenia: Pristop.

Slovenia: Znamka I feel Slovenia, Slovenijo čutimo, iz teorije prehaja v prakso [Slovenia: Brand I feel Slovenia from theory to practice]. (2008, January 16). *E-turizam.com*. Retrieved April 22, 2010, from http://www.e-turizam.com/Turizam-Vijesti/Vijesti-iz-Slovenije/Slovenia-Znamka-I-feel-Slovenia-Slovenijo-cutimo-iz-teorije-prehaja-v-prakso.html

Slovenija bo prijetno vznemirjala [Slovenia will trigger emotions]. (2008, January 16). *Dobro Jutro*. Retrieved April 22, 2010, from http://www.dobrojutro.net/novice/slovenija/slovenija_bo_prijetno_vznemirjala/73380

Smolej, M. (2006). *Vpliv drzave na prepoznavnost Slovenije* [The effect of the state on the branding of Slovenia] (Master's Thesis submitted to the Faculty of Economics, University of Ljubljana, Slovenia).

Sočan, B. (2003). Blagovna znamka Latvija. Mislite, da se hecam? [Brand Latvia. Do you think I am joking?] *Marketing Magazin, 272*(1), 21.

Sočan, B. (2004). Evropa zdaj—Slovenija mora bogatiti Evropo [Europe now: Slovenia has to contribute to Europe]. *Marketing Magazin, 276*(2), 12.

Stanković, P. (2005). *Rdeci trakovi. Reprezentacija v slovenskem partizanskem filmu* [Red strip. Representation in Slovenian partisan film]. Ljubljana, Slovenia: Fakulteta za Druzbene Vede.

Stritar, J., Čuk, M., & Ilovar, R. (2007, August 24). Iz slogana v logotip [From slogan to logotype]. *Dmagazin*. Retrieved April 22, 2010, from http://www.dmagazin.si/2007/08/iz-slogana-v-logotip_24.html

Szondi, G. (2007). The role and challenges of country branding in transition countries: The Central and Eastern European experience. *Place Branding and Public Diplomacy, 3*(1), 8–20.

Todorova, M. (1997). *Imagining the Balkans*. New York: Oxford University Press.

Van Ham, P. (2002). Branding territory: Inside the wonderful worlds of PR and IR theory. *Millennium: Journal of International Studies, 32*(2), 249–269.

Volčič, Z. (2008). Former Yugoslavia on the World Wide Web: Commercialization and branding of nation-states. *International Communication Gazette, 70*(5), 395–413.

Volčič, Z. (2009). Television in the Balkans: The rise of commercial nationalism. In G. Turner & J. Tay (Eds.), *Television studies after "TV": Understanding television in the post-broadcast era* (pp. 115–124). London: Routledge.

Wolff, L. (1994). *Inventing Eastern Europe: The map of civilization on the mind of the enlightenment.* Stanford, CA: Stanford University Press.

Zerdin, A. H. (2007). Spremembe v notranjem krogu omrezja slovenske ekonomske elite v letih 2004–2006 [Internal changes within Slovene economic elites between 2004–2006]. *Druzboslovne Razprave, 23*(3), 7–25.

Zwick, D., Bonsu, S., & Darmody, A. (2008). Putting consumers to work: Co-creation and new marketing govern-mentality. *Journal of Consumer Culture, 8*(2), 163–196.

8 Vampire Branding
Romania's Dark Destinations

Alice Bardan and Anikó Imre

INTRODUCTION: THE "DRACULESCU" LEGACY

Ceauşescu really ruined it for Romania. His long, increasingly mad reign is proving to be a stubborn legacy for the country to shed. In the past decade, this legacy has been revitalized by Western tourism and media representations as a commercialized, exoticized relic of dark communism in a way that would have seemed insensitive in the years immediately following the Romanian revolution and the fall of the Soviet empire.

Of course, other Soviet-ruled countries had long-reigning dictators as well. But Tito, Brezhnev, Kádár, and Hoxha died before the regime's regional collapse, and Zhivkov, Honecker, and Husák eased their adherence to communist dogma before the end of the Cold War and peacefully gave up their leadership in 1989. In addition, communist rule in some countries was punctured by acts of popular resistance and revolt: 1956 in Hungary, followed by the "goulash communism" of the Kádár regime; 1968 in Czechoslovakia, followed by Václav Havel's dissident movement; and Lech Wałęsa's Solidarity movement in Poland after 1980. In comparison, Romania is plagued by a historical image of passive acquiescence to authoritarianism. Nicolae Ceauşescu was not only beloved by his people for the first half of his reign, but also held on to his absolute power uninterrupted until the bloody end. He was Secretary General of the Romanian Communist Party from 1967 and assumed the additional title of President from 1974, a total rule he and his wife Elena lost only in December 1989, when they were confronted by masses of demonstrators in Timişoara and Bucharest and hastily executed by the military.

The violence of the 1989 revolution turned TV cameras on Romania. CNN's round-the-clock coverage constructed a narrative of collective exhale and euphoria after a quarter century of oppression by a fanatic, who believed in his misguided ideals over the reality of a starving population (Borcila, 2003; Morse, 1998). The post-revolutionary coverage conveniently forgot that the United States and Western Europe supported Ceauşescu during his first decade in power, when he was still mistaken by the world for an anti-Soviet, Western-friendly maverick. The bloody spectacle of the

Romanian revolution justified the rational inevitability of global capitalism against the lunacy of communism represented by Ceaușescu's projects: his massive constructions; his rationing of food in order to pay back a large foreign debt; his plan to boost population growth by banning abortion and contraception, which led to a rise of orphaned children and a record number of HIV infections; and his forced urbanization and nationalization, directed explicitly at ethnic minorities. All of these atrocities were uncovered by U.S. and Western European news media in the 1990s as proof of communism's inherent inhumanity and ultimate failure.

In the 1990s, the Yugoslavian wars made Romania's problems pale in comparison at the same time as they further confirmed the popular international view of the primitive Balkans. By the 2000s, the morality tale of evil communism became less urgent to reiterate as the Bush and Blair administrations staged another global war elsewhere to evoke new terrors and reinforce the inevitability of U.S.-led neoliberal capitalism. This shift of international attention also allowed the ghost of Ceaușescu to take on a lighter, commodified life as a bloodsucking monster out of a horror movie, not unlike his predecessor Dracula.

Dracula, based loosely on Vlad Țepeș, the historical 15th-century ruler of Wallachia, was also borne out of the Western fascination with the primitive East,[1] where bloodthirsty rulers are given to torturing their people in order to nurture their own superhuman ambitions. Although Bram Stoker's novel, first published in 1897, which invented Dracula and placed the vampire in Transylvania, went untranslated in Romania until 1990, Ceaușescu's increasingly harsh regime repeatedly evoked associations in Western journalism between the dictator and the vampire in the 1980s (Light, 2007). Recent Western European and American docu-fictional representations, following the lead of Sacha Baron Cohen's *Borat* (Charles, 2006), have continued to link these two vampiric icons as Romania's main tourist attractions and contributions to global culture. At a remove of two decades from state socialism, this collapsing of recent history into medieval legend reduces the collective trauma left over by socialism into a themed attraction, rendering Romania as not only the most appropriate site for such a mystery tour into the past but also fair game for mockery as a land hopelessly left behind by civilization.

As we show in this chapter, the fact that Romania has continued to be a repository of Cold War imagery more than any other post-socialist country presents a significant obstacle to the state's own re-branding efforts. But a successful brand Romania faces yet another challenge: the nation's own skeptical population. Clearly, citizens have turned skeptical toward their governments all across the region due to the unfulfilled promises of the post-socialist transition and EU accession. The exploitation of the periphery in merciless neoliberal competition among states has contributed to a widespread sense of disappointment with the cultural effects of consumerism and has been readily exploited by the nationalist and religious right.

A string of recent local scandals, exposing corruption among state and local politicians, have further deepened post-socialist governments' crises of legitimacy. As a result, the gap between the attractive nation brands governments are trying to engineer and the people whose identities these brands allegedly reflect is exceptionally large in the region.

In this chapter, we assess the Romanian state's efforts to re-brand Romania as a tourist destination in the face of such external and internal obstacles. We start with an overview of four vivid cases of Western media representations that have drawn on Romania for caricatured, nostalgic evocations of the Cold War. We then put in historical context and track the recent preoccupation with branding Romania, characterized by disagreements between the state and the public, as these have registered in a number of state-sponsored marketing initiatives. We pay particular attention to the campaigns of infamous Romanian Tourism Minister Elena Udrea and analyze the reasons why they have failed to mobilize national pride among Romanians. Finally, we issue a critical commentary on the sense of optimism and inevitable progress with which branding and marketing experts and researchers tend to imbue nation branding. As our case study of Romania's plight shows, the "freedom" that the neoliberal market confers on countries to reinvent themselves as branded commodities favors state and corporate entities with strong brands and established power positions within the global economic network. Conversely, it severely restricts the options of small and economically weak countries, often forcing them to embrace and mobilize negative stereotypes.

DRACU-FICTIONS

Borat

As is well known, the "Kazakh" scenes of Sacha Baron Cohen's 2006 mockumentary were filmed in the Romanian Gypsy village of Glod. Kazakhstan, a post-Soviet republic, the ninth largest country in the world and its fifth oil exporter, engaged in a six-year diplomacy battle with MTV, and later with Baron Cohen himself, over the film's unfavorable portrayal of the fictional Borat's homeland. The government was understandably sensitive about the country brand it had carefully cultivated since the collapse of the USSR. The construction of a modernizing, multicultural country, different from the other "Stans," was tarnished by Borat, one of three regular characters Baron Cohen assumed on his *Da Ali G Show* (aired in the United Kingdom on Channel 4 in 2000 and in the United States on HBO in 2003–2004). However, the diplomacy war eventually mellowed into a reluctant acceptance of the Borat character when it turned out that the country was not known well enough for its image to be tarnished. In fact, Borat/Baron Cohen put Kazakhstan on the map, even if in the unflattering light of an extreme parody. Because the film generated curiosity and boosted the tourism industry, the Kazakh state eventually ended up playing along and even incorporated Borat as a publicity figure in the service of its own state-branding strategy (Saunders, 2008; see also Saunders, this volume).

At the same time, the actual, pseudo-documentary images of a cow in the living room, toothless men, muddy streets, incestuous families, and rampant anti-Semitism confirmed Cold War stereotypes of a backward Eastern Europe and attached these to Romania for comic purposes. After the film's 2006 release, the noise of protest by misled and undercompensated local Romanian extras was drowned out by the film's own publicity campaign and critical reception, which revolved around the United States as the film's real target of mockery. The producers' blithe use of rural Romania also effaced the fact that the locals in the film were Gypsies (Roma), who themselves suffer violent discrimination from the government and much of the Romanian population.

Shortly after *Borat*'s release, Romanian and foreign television crews and reporters stormed the village of Glod to investigate what had really happened. This "fool's crusade," as one journalist put it (Slotek, 2009), angered the humiliated villagers. Some Gypsies explained their participation in the film by pointing out that Americans intimidated them with bodyguards and expensive cars. "We endured it because we are poor and badly needed the money," they claimed (Pancevski & Ionescu, 2006). Most Romanians, however, ended up blaming the Gypsies for having tainted the country's image yet again. In *Evenimentul Zilei*, one of Romania's leading newspapers, Iulian Comanescu (2006) wrote, "How innocent can one be . . . to take part in that entire circus. To pretend that you just didn't know what you were doing is, given the circumstances, hypocritical." He concludes,

> There is no need to lament and ask ourselves why Romanians became Borat's virtual Kazakhstan. The answer is easy: because Nicolae Tudorache, a villager from Glod, agreed to wear a plastic penis as [a] hand prosthesis in the film. And he took four dollars for this. (Comanescu, 2006)

British journalist Simon Calder from *The Independent* was one of several journalists who traveled to Romania to discover Glod for themselves after *Borat*'s release. Notwithstanding his sensationalist account of the trip, which took him "[racing] down a steep-sided valley" past "roadside vendors selling strange-looking fungi," Calder (2007) suggested that the villagers of Glod were "sitting on a Glod mine and should capitalize on the film to draw people to a fascinating corner of the Balkans." He adds, "While nature reclaims the foolish excesses of state Marxism . . . Glod needs a visitor center," and recommends the following:

> A Borat Bar and Grill would be a winner (local delicacies include bear and boar), as would tours of the village in a car hauled by livestock,

as in the film. A Kazakh Hotel, done up as a bordello and featuring "the fourth-best prostitute in Kazakhstan" might be a tribute too far. But the memory of Vlad the Impaler, the 15th-century prince who dispatched his enemies so painfully, can legitimately be invoked to provide an extra dimension. This was his territory, and very beautiful it is, too. Tourists who are enticed here initially due to the film will discover a land where you can hike in splendid isolation for hours, go biking through virgin forest, or simply enjoy the tranquility of Boratland. Praise be to Glod.

When some of the residents of Glod filed a lawsuit against 20th Century Fox, claiming that they were duped into participating in what they thought was a documentary about poverty, the story made some international news. What most news stories failed to mention, however, was that the villagers had been persuaded by Edward Fagan, a controversial American reparations lawyer, "to teach Hollywood an expensive lesson" (Finn, 2006). Now disbarred from New York and New Jersey, Fagan's reputation is primarily linked to his lawsuits against Swiss banks on behalf of Holocaust survivors. His "negotiation process" with the Gypsy villagers and their trip to London are at the center of another documentary, also filmed in Glod. Dutch filmmaker Mercedes Stalenhoef's *Carmen Meets Borat* (2008) tracks what happened in the village before and after Borat/Baron Cohen's arrival. Initially told by Fagan that they were "the Gladiators" from Glod who would fight *Borat* and regain their dignity, some of the unwitting participants in *Borat* ended up being summarily dismissed at the 20th Century Fox reception desk in London. Dropped off by Fagan at the entrance of the building and not speaking a word in English, they found themselves yet again the object of ridicule in front of the cameras. Ironically, the poor villagers could not even receive visas to fly to America, so their much anticipated trip and the fantasies about what they would do with the potential millions from the case dissolved in disaster. Their case was dismissed in 2008 by U.S. District Judge Loretta A. Preska for lack of specific enough facts indicating that the villagers were misled. Meanwhile, *Borat* has become a reference point for a number of docu-fictional television shows that looked for and found in Romania the same cluster of poverty, medieval mysticism, and the irreparable, imposing shadow of communist dictatorship.

No Reservations

The Romanian episode of the Travel Channel's popular travel-food series *No Reservations*, which aired on February 25, 2008, became notorious among fans as the "worst episode ever." The host, Anthony Bourdain, is known for his disregard for political correctness, and this particular episode is punctuated throughout by his satirical grumbles in both voice-over and on-screen dialogues. The show opens with his companion-sidekick,

Russian Zamir, biting into a never-ending sausage, greeting locals as "comrades." Over the images of dark and foreboding mountains, Bourdain's voice-over introduces Romania "and its mythical region of Transylvania" as a "grey and distant place," which lies "deep in the heart of Eastern Europe." Standing in a Bucharest street, he adds, "There were some creepy communists here. I like that too, you know." His tasting tour includes two stops: One is Bucharest, where he and Zamir shake their heads at Ceaușescu's megalomaniac constructions and listen, bemused, to a local witness's account of the revolutionary events that led to the dictator's demise. The other one is rural Transylvania, introduced by wolf howls on the soundtrack and images of fog swirling around foreboding mountains. Once Bourdain and Zamir arrive there, they shake their heads at local efforts to turn Dracula into a tourist theme and drive the Dacia, "Romania's national car," described as "a strangely unbalanced structure on tiny wheels." The Dacia breaks down as scheduled, which justifies bringing out the ultimate icon of the premodern: a horse-drawn carriage. This provides appropriate transport to the final scene, a pig slaughter, performed by silent villagers in folk costumes, as Zamir sinks into drunken incoherence under Bourdain's satirical eyes.

Whereas Baron Cohen's parody at least partially targets uneducated Westerners who would believe gross Cold War stereotypes of Eastern Europe, Bourdain shows no sense of obligation to reflect on his own position of privilege and responsibility as the host of a globally syndicated television program reporting on Romania. As he repeatedly says, he is disgusted with local efforts to capitalize on the Western fascination with Dracula and Ceaușescu, which are, no doubt, at least partly staged for his own TV show, delivering the spectacle Americans want to see. He calls a theme restaurant in Bucharest an "insane museum of brick-a-bracks" and a "kitschy testament to imperialism." His only mission, he claims, is to find good local food which, his casual theory goes, should logically result from "years of nonconsensual sex with invading armies." "My quest for authentic food and culture has led me to this?" Bourdain asks with disdain when he is led by Zamir to the basement of the Transylvanian Dracula Hotel (near Bran Castle) on Halloween night, where a dress-up party is organized for tourists. Bourdain visibly suffers through the crowning of "Miss Transylvania" (originally from Nevada), and the subsequent arm-wrestling championship, in which Zamir pretends to lose to an American woman. Bourdain comments, "That's why you lost the Cold War." This arrogant dismissal of the former Eastern Bloc as goofy, weak, and feminized not only recasts the Cold War as an actual military event won by the United States, but also illuminates Zamir's real function in the episode. The only other participant with a speaking persona, Zamir, allegedly a guide and a "friend," is in fact a typical sidekick, harmless, jovial, round, and accented, whose job is to set up and then eagerly laugh at his tall, well-coiffed American master's sardonic jokes on cue. His role requires that he play the buffoon when necessary, using his former communist status to "go native" and perform what Bourdain presents as the comic absurdity of post-socialist Romania.

As soon as the show aired, Romanians also began to air their sense of betrayal and disappointment. Insulted fans, both in the country and living elsewhere in the world, filled online discussions with frustrated commentary on Bourdain's poor choices of places to visit and foods to try, the host's responsibility in providing a fair representation, and his choice of an ignorant and increasingly drunk Russian as a guide. The latter was seen by Romanians as an especially painful slap in the face: It ignored, or worse, cynically exploited, Cold War tensions with Russia, Romania's recent colonizer, and confirmed a monolithically gray view of the former Soviet Bloc where traditions, histories, and languages are irrelevant. For many Romanian viewers, the two narrators in this story presented an allegory of two former Cold War superpowers, one now subordinated to the other, teaming up for some good fun for old time's sake to bully the real losers.

While viewer comments abundantly pointed out the similarity between *Borat*'s and Bourdain's portrayals, they correctly deemed the latter even more damaging as a show whose mission is, precisely, to entice interest in lesser known places as destinations for tourists, consumers, and investors. The episode has acted as a powerful deterrent to Romania's self-branding as an attractive destination. Articles such as "The Star From the Travel Channel Crushed Us and We Paid the Bill" in the daily *Cotidianul*, tracked the fiasco caused by the show, reminding readers of the fact that Romanian authorities actually paid Bourdain and his team $20,000 to promote Romania (Vintilescu, 2008). To understand the scale of the damage done by *No Reservations*, it is enough to note that Bourdain's blog about Romania generated no fewer than 2,096 impassioned comments, while the average response to a show is around 100 postings. Profoundly insulted, many bloggers took Bourdain to task. One wrote:

> Of Romania's hour-long chance to prove to the world that we are NOT the gray and forgettable place on earth, you wasted 20 minutes by showing Nevada tourists embarrass themselves during a pretend Halloween party (not at all specific to our country). (Pop, 2008, p. 83)

An American identified as Joe, who had adopted a baby from Romania, described the trauma that his son, now 13, suffered after watching the show. "The damage you did to him is immeasurable," the aggrieved father lamented. Perhaps more than anything, Bourdain's description of Romanian cuisine as "primitive" struck a sensitive note with Romanians. "You are biased against Romania," another blogger reproached Bourdain, reminding him that in Asia he had no problem enjoying bugs, raw meat, and snake hearts.[2]

The outpouring of complaints provoked a response from Bourdain posted on his blog, "Tony's Travel Journal," on February 26, 2008. In this brief response, titled "Romania: What the Hell Happened?" Bourdain acknowledges that his "pal" Zamir may not have been the best choice to show him around Romania, but makes no apologies. "The fact is," he declares, "things WERE fucked up." Ultimately, he explains, he has no other obligation than to tell the truth as he sees it. "At the end of the day? That's what happened. That's what it felt like. Period. Frankly? I think it's a pretty funny show" (Bourdain, 2008).

Top Gear

BBC 2's most watched show, broadcast in over 100 countries, traveled to Romania in November 2009 to seek out "the best road in the world." Jeremy Clarkson and his two regular companions, Richard Hammond and James May, drove an Aston Martin DBS Volante, a Ferrari California, and a Lamborghini Gallardo Spyder down the Transfăgărăşan Highway, a dramatic road built by Nicolae Ceauşescu in the Carpathian Mountains. Their adventures in "Borat country," as they called Romania, included a stop in Bucharest's Revolutionary Square to marvel at Ceauşescu's megalomaniac construction, the People's Palace, and in a Gypsy village, where they were successfully stormed by curious Roma children, made fun of the Dacia, and got stuck on a narrow bridge in an unpaved, one-lane road. "Coming here in a car that cost £168,000 is a bit like turning up in the Sudan in a suit made entirely out of food," Clarkson commented light-heartedly.

At first, the presenters note a discrepancy between what they imagined about Romania, a country "full of oxen and people throwing stones at Gypsies," and the expensive cars they discover in the parking lot of a five-star hotel in Mamaia, a seaside resort. However, the recognition that the actual Romania may defy Westerners' usual assumptions soon gives way to a stubborn resolution to confirm stereotypes. Much like the characters Caldicott and Charters in Alfred Hitchcock's film *The Lady Vanishes* (1938), who adopt a superior attitude in their dismissal of Bandrika, an invented Eastern European country, the *Top Gear* presenters employ dark humor to deride their experiences in Romania and take pains to frame the country in a way that recycles their initial associations.

Jeremy Clarkson, who has gained a reputation for his political incorrectness and allegedly earns around £1 million a year as a *Top Gear* presenter, casts Romania in a bad light by packaging it as an insignificant, backward nation. Although at the end of the show he appears to be thrilled by the spectacular Transfăgărăşan Highway, Clarkson stages *Top Gear* Romania as an open invitation to laugh at the underdogs. If *No Reservations'* star Anthony Bourdain claims to genuinely seek out "authenticity," Clarkson neither fakes an interest in learning about Romanian culture nor is impressed with the country's natural resources. Whereas Borat acts as a linguistically and ideologically challenged yokel, ostensibly concerned with "cultural learnings" for "make benefit," Clarkson seeks to dismiss

Romania, fashioning himself as a "post-ironic" Brit who indulges in scandalous, over-the-top racist remarks. Unabashedly boasting his skepticism about Romania's potential to be interesting, he acts as a passive *anti-tourist* who just happens to run into trouble by chance.

When they receive the producer's envelope with the "challenge" to find Ceaușescu's highway, May, Clarkson, and Hammond can't be bothered to read the word "Transfăgărășan." As if Romanian were a joke language, they stutter and chuckle as they pass the note among each other: "Transf . . . Transf . . . Transfffff . . . what?" As he is driving through Bucharest, May opens a Romanian phrase book and starts reading aloud for amusement: "Buna Seara" ["Good Evening"]. "Let's buy a glass door and full double glazing." Slowing down, he addresses a boy walking in the street with: "Bunaaa searaaa. This time last year . . . I was in Scotland." At the People's Palace, a bemused Clarkson approaches a Romanian official waiting in his car: "These boxes are not the same size," he reads from his book in Romanian, laughing at the man's confused look. In another instance, May drives away exasperated when he cannot get English directions to the People's Palace from a man at a gas station. To add further insult and confirm their view of Romania as part of an undifferentiated tribal region, the trio confuses Romanian with Russian and Hungarian. When a Romanian man apologizes for not having seen their Dacia, into which he "accidently" backed his truck, May "translates" his words of excuse with a sneering and dismissive tone: "I think he's saying, in Hungarian or whatever that is, that it's my fault for parking the car."[3]

Top Gear's "fictional" voyage in Romania is like a sequel to British Orient Express narratives of the 1930s, strongly evocative of novels such as Ethel Lina White's *The Wheel Spins* (1936), on which *The Lady Vanishes* was based. First introduced in 1883, the Orient Express train was advertised in the 1920s as "the Magic Carpet of the East" and finally entered English literature in the 1930s, after the initial excitement associated with it slowly faded. Vesna Goldsworthy tracks a series of novels, including Graham Greene's *Stamboul Train* (1931), which established the conventions of the Orient Express story. The plot of these novels usually relies on unexpected snowstorms and subsequent delays, the Balkans becoming a sort of a "Bermuda Triangle" on a train's route.[4] In keeping with this view, *Top Gear* presents Romania as a territory off the map, where strange things may happen. The hosts inform us in voice-over that as they traveled further east, "the high-tech, modern Romania we knew ran out." May "gets lost" in his Lamborghini, as his GPS simply doesn't have the "points of interest" feature for Bucharest, Romania's capital. "The Italians don't acknowledge the existence of Romania!" he exclaims in a tone of bemused satisfaction. In the soundproof tunnels beneath the People's Palace, which today hosts the Romanian Parliament and Senate, Clarkson takes the opportunity to "bring a bit of science to the party" and runs a test otherwise impossible: Using a special measurement feature on his iPod, he is able to determine which car makes the loudest noise.

The Romanian people in *Top Gear*'s "mockumentary" come off as backward marionettes. At the People's Palace, Hammond embarrasses an English-speaking young Romanian man when he tells Clarkson, making a masturbatory gesture: "Jeremy, you are aware of the local customs, aren't you? When he stands to shake hands, you just . . . plop in. That's how it works, hahaha." Faced with a herd of cows blocking the road, the *Top Gear* team manages to get "really lost" when a "random" right turn brings them into a Gypsy village. The encounter with the poor villagers makes for another set of dismissive jokes, which are meant to confirm that Borat's country is actually real. "It is Gypsy country around here . . . I am told that they can be quite violent if they don't like the looks of you," Clarkson warns us. Once in the village, the *Top Gear* team dutifully reenacts Borat's narrative. Stuck in the narrow streets of the village, they register a place where humans and animals cohabitate, as poorly dressed children gather around the expensive cars while running past chickens, turkeys, and pigs. Recalling, once again, Miss Froy from *The Lady Vanishes*, who can only write her name on the train's window because it is soiled and greasy, the Roma children write their names on the cars' thick layer of accumulated dust, while Clarkson rolls his eyes.

The episode received mixed reactions in Romania. "Shocked and disappointed," the Romanian ambassador in London sent the BBC producers a request to remove the offensive remarks that linked his country with *Borat*. Some viewers, however, chose to overlook the show's condescending tone and speculated that the hype around Transfăgărăşan may turn out to be "the best advert for Romania seen on UK television at any time over the past 20 years" (Turp, 2009). This is exactly how Costin Giurgea, a young man who assisted the British team and the editor in chief of *Top Gear Romania*, defended the show. On his blog, hosted by the magazine, he argued that rather than damaging Romania's reputation, *Top Gear*'s episode about Transfăgărăşan was "the equivalent of country branding of massive proportions," or "the best thing that happened to Romanians since the Romans left Dacia" (Giurgea, 2009). In response to angry Romanians' comments about their sense of betrayal and humiliation, Giurgea blamed such viewers for failing to handle Clarkson's jokes. He claimed that those who are unable to grasp the essence of British humor suffer from a Romanian complex that can be best described as "one is not stupid enough until one brags about it." Using oversimplification and *non sequitur* arguments to praise a show for which he acted as the main liaison, Giurgea also noted that because *Top Gear* also mocked Americans, Romanians shouldn't feel offended or worried about the show's impact on their country's image. After all, as the saying goes, "There is no such thing as bad publicity" (Giurgea, 2009).

This line of thinking is reminiscent of place-branding expert Simon Anholt's reference to *Borat*'s influence on promoting tourism in Kazakhstan (Chilom, 2007). Yet, whereas *Borat* constructed the largely unknown

Kazakhstan, Clarkson reinforced long-held stereotypes about Romanians and the Roma. His serious warning that in Romania Gypsies can get violent "if they don't like the look of you" exploits potential tourists' fear for their safety in a country already associated with the dark and the mysterious. Indeed, as Spanish tourism consultant Eulogio Bordas comments, Romania's main problem is that tourists often associate the name with insecurity and consequently seek to avoid it (Constantin, 2010). As we discuss later, in 2010, the Romanian Ministry of Tourism hired Bordas' consulting company, THR, and a British market research consultancy, TNS, to create a new logo and slogan for Brand Romania. After TNS conducted quantitative research, billed at €400,000, to find out how foreign tourists perceived Romania, their study concluded that tourists were mostly exposed to negative news about the country. The new brand, developed by the THR-TNS team, attempts to reinvent Romania as "The Carpathian Garden." As Bordas commented, "Since the garden is perceived as a safe place, the symbol is meant to change the existing perception" (Constantin, 2010).

Whopper Virgins and Folgers Commercials

Perhaps the most widely circulating and thus most damaging examples of the "primitive Romania" brand are two commercials that first aired on major U.S. networks on December 8, 2008. In the first one, a wintry Victorian tableau of a poor village dwelling hidden among dark mountains, identified as "Romania," comes to life when an American Aid worker receives a package containing a precious jar of Folgers coffee. The locals gather around him, staring in amazement as he prepares his coffee in a makeshift cheesecloth coffee filter, anticipating their lives to be brightened by Folgers.[5] In the other ad, "Romanian" villagers, dressed in folk costumes, taste-test Burger King whoppers "for the first time." As Liviu Tamas, the mayor of Budesti, where the ad was filmed, explains, although he had refused to give the producers permission for their "experiment," they ignored him and proceeded to do a "casting" call for a "documentary" at a local restaurant, where they paid willing participants about $40 "just for tasting some food" (Muntean, 2008).

The portrayal of Romania as a forgotten land full of "Whopper virgins" is so blatant in these ads that it even inspired a *Saturday Night Live (SNL)* spoof on January 10, 2009. However, *SNL*'s "the making of the ad" skit, based on the Whopper virgins campaign's own online docu-mercial teasers, turned out to be yet another parody of local Romanians, rather than of Burger King's ethnocentric ad campaign, in which people in remote locations are subjected to the taste of civilization by being paid to try and compare a Whopper and a Big Mac. In the *SNL* skit, host Neil Patrick Harris acts as a Burger King spokesperson to introduce the Romanian taste test. The three villagers who participate are so backward that one is unable to hold a cheeseburger properly, another tries to run off with it "to feed his village for a whole month," and the third one puts it on his head while laughing maniacally.[6]

ROMANIAN SELF-BRANDING

The four snapshots in the previous section illustrate the powerful external political and media investment in freezing the legacy of Ceaușescu's mad communist reign, wrapped in a medieval layer of vampiric mysticism, as the core of Romania's identity. Next, we look at how the Romanian state has endeavored to withstand this pressure and reinvent itself in the aftermath of the Cold War by drawing on available historical discourses and national images that bypass the damning Draculescu legacy. We first show that, paradoxically, the Ceaușescu regime itself was far from provincial in its outlook and actively promoted a cosmopolitan, if not globalist, national image. Then, we examine how post-socialist national re-definitions and re-branding initiatives have attempted to reconcile this ambivalent cosmopolitanism with the Western expectation to adopt political trauma and fictional horror as the country's brand.

Duncan Light (2001a), a cultural geographer who has written extensively on tourism and Romania, claims that at least since the 18th century, there have been two competing representations of Romanian national identity:

> One—the "Western" position—seeks to champion "European" influences on Romania's development and to assert that Romania is part of the European mainstream; the second—or "Eastern" position—stresses the importance of native or indigenous Romanian values and is more hostile to "European" influences. (p. 1057)

Light explains that Romanian post-socialist administrations were reluctant to embrace political and economic reform until the mid-1990s and thus preferred the nativist, rather than the European, position. Some Romanian critics have questioned this duality of traditions altogether, considering it a simplistic interpretation of the way Romanians have traditionally positioned themselves within Europe.

A more nuanced point of view is offered by Alex Drace-Francis (2003) in an insightful article titled "Paradoxes of Occidentalism: On Travel Literature in Ceaușescu's Romania." Closely examining a series of published accounts of travel from Romania to Western Europe, Drace-Francis reminds us that Romanian communist authorities were far from advancing an anti-European attitude. Even during the 1980s, when the country entered a phase of extreme isolation from the rest of the world, the official accounts of the Western world emphasized lines of compatibility between Romanian and Western cultures. Romanian writers actively sought to present their national culture alongside the "great civilizations" and adopted various strategies to imbue Romanian cultural products with global significance. Travel writing, a genre extremely popular in communist Romania, received its legitimacy not only from the cultural elites but also from Ceauşescu, who made no fewer than 103 official foreign trips during his first 17 years in office (Drace-Francis, 2003, p. 75). Florea Ceauşescu, the dictator's younger brother, published a book in 1982, titled *Drumetind Prin Lume* [*Traveling Through the World*].

Drace-Francis concludes, "It was as if the Cold War did not exist in Romania and globalization had arrived early: an ideological position which sat well with Nicolae Ceauşescu's protestations of independence and claims to have surmounted the East-West divide" (2003, p. 77). It was precisely the constant reiteration of the fact that Romanians should "feel in Europe as if in a 'native land' without spiritual and cultural frontiers," as one nationalist writer close to Ceauşescu wrote in 1979, that aided the Romanian population's acceptance of the status quo of dictatorship (Drace-Francis, 2003, pp. 78–79). Within such a context, Light's claim that "Romania's first post-socialist president (Ion Iliescu) questioned whether Romania should embrace 'Western' values" (2001a, p. 1057) oversimplifies a much more complex reality. In fact, before Romania's accession to the EU in 2007, even extreme right-wing parties, such as Romania Mare (Greater Romania), were in favor of European integration (Drace-Francis, 2003, p. 80).

For critics such as Renata Salecl, Romanians continue to be stuck in the position of the "lamenting victim," blaming communism and its fall as the events responsible for the disarray in their lives (Salecl, 1999, p. 92). In a similar vein, while acknowledging Romania's efforts to re-brand itself as a tourist destination, Light (2001b) reproaches the country for its rejection of the Ceauşescu epoch. Focusing on three Bucharest institutions popular with foreign tourists (the People's Palace, the National History Museum, and the Military History Museum), Light identifies three strategies of institutional response to the communist heritage: "denial," "delay and prevarication," and "cautious and incremental engagement" (pp. 70–71). To him, these strategies ultimately reflect a profound ambivalence about how to engage with the communist period in order "to satisfy tourists" (p. 72). Light rightly points out that Romania's efforts to upgrade its brand are hampered by Western visitors' stubborn interest in the "old" Romania. Nevertheless, he laments that "there is little desire to exploit the commercial potential represented by the communist period" (p. 72). "Whether they like it or not," he contends, Romanians should exploit the country's "dark tourism." This, he speculates, would attest to the country's "maturity" as a post-communist democracy and would be "an important yardstick of its progress" (p. 73).

What such opinions do not consider is that in refusing to "tell the communist story" or to direct foreign tourists' gaze to the dark sides of the past, Romanians are trying to fight back the prejudiced attitudes with which the country is regularly approached. As Light (2001b) documents, travel guides such as *Rough Guide to Romania, The Lonely Planet Guide to Romania and Moldova, Let's Go Eastern Europe 1998,* or *Europe by Train 1998* primarily target "postmodern tourists," or "travelers" in search of dark experiences (pp. 61–64).[7]

Romania, "Land of Choice" and a "Carpathian Garden"

Contrary to accounts of Romanians as traumatized, passive, lamenting victims, recent debates around tourism branding and national identity in Romania reveal agonizing efforts to counter stereotypical representations. Here we evaluate state-supported efforts to improve the country's damaged image by creating an appealing tourism destination brand. Our goal is to make a case for a more subtle understanding of the particular complexity and dynamism involved in the projection of Romania's national image. Of course, nation branding encompasses the many ways in which a country is perceived by natives and foreigners, including its image, reputation, and identity, which are influenced by a range of economic, political, social, and cultural processes (Anholt, 2004). In other words, we are aware that tourism is "only the iceberg tip built upon the country's overall positioning" (Bivolaru, Andrei, & Purcăroiu, 2009, p. 110).

After the fall of communism, it took almost 10 years for Romanian tourism authorities to make a concerted effort to promote the country as a tourist destination. The first promotional campaign was launched around the total sun eclipse of August 11, 1999, and was called "The 1999 Eclipse." Using a budget of $1.5 million (Cosma, Negrusa, & Bota, 2007, p. 71), the campaign advertised the fact that the eclipse could be fully visible from various places in southern Romania. Only a small number of foreigners showed up for the event, however, dashing the hopes invested in promotional print materials presented at international fairs.

The second advertising campaign, four years later, produced a series of 60-second television commercials with the slogan "Romania—Simply Surprising," which aired between June and August 2004 on the Euronews, Eurosport, Discovery, CNN, and BBC networks. Although professionally produced, the commercials were criticized for their "infantile logo" and for having failed to distinguish Romania from other countries (Obae & Barbu, 2004). One of the more memorable ads from the series relies on the repetition of syntactic similarities for rhetorical effect. It posits that even though many tourist attractions in Romania may appear ordinary in their simplicity, this is just a matter of perspective. Thus, what may appear at first sight as a "simple sculpture" is in fact "a Brancusi masterpiece." Images of frescoes at the Voroneț Monastery featuring an intense shade of blue, known in Romania as "Voroneț blue," turn "a simple painting" into "a unique medieval monastery." What to outsiders appears as "a simple cross" is revealed to be part of the Merry Cemetery at Săpînța, where carved, colorful crosses caricature the imperfections of the deceased. In the same vein, the image of "a simple house" turns out to be the impressive Castle of Dracula, while "a simple landscape" is in fact an image representing "the Danube Delta, a living paradise."[8]

Whereas these campaigns primarily targeted foreigners, in 2006 a new spot was produced to advertise Romania for domestic tourists, with the strap line "A Trip is a Lesson of Life" (Cosma et al., 2007). It promoted the message that to read about one's country is not enough: One should have first-hand experiences. The main tourism promotion at the end of 2006 centered on the town of Sibiu, which was the European Capital of Culture in 2007.[9]

The release on May 1, 2009, of a musical-viral-tactical "tourism anthem" with the tag line "Come to Romania, the Land of Choice" began a new, aggressive branding project, spearheaded by Romanian Tourism Minister Elena Udrea. The "anthem" incited a heated debate about national identity. Harshly criticized on Romanian blogs and television discussions for its cheesiness and deceitful portrayal of the country as a glamorous destination, this initial promotional clip also generated a series of viral response videos that ironically foregrounded what the ad concealed about Romania. Videos named "The Truth About Romania" and "We Are the End of Choice" mocked Udrea's branding attempt, pointing to the dire situation of overpriced and underbooked seaside hotels.

Udrea's nation branding project made her one of the most controversial figures in the country and a frequent target of ridicule. Young, attractive and outspoken, she is often compared to Sarah Palin, especially given the blunders she has made during her public appearances. Accused of being the president's protégé, Udrea was also the subject of a parliamentary inquiry, which recommended opening a criminal investigation into the way she used public money to fund media campaigns. When she was appointed to be the cabinet minister responsible for regional development, in charge of administering the EU budget for the development of housing, infrastructure, and tourism, Udrea became the subject of international news. Newspapers such as *The Times Online*, *Welt Online*, or *7sur7* expressed serious concerns about how Udrea would handle the European aid budget given the serious allegations of poor management, incompetence, and shady transactions associated with her rich husband.

Rejecting all accusations as unfounded and politically motivated, Udrea continued the "Land of Choice" campaign with a new series of television commercials and postcards, which enlisted athletes Nadia Comăneci, Ilie Năstase, and Gheorghe Hagi as ambassadors of Brand Romania. Following a distribution recipe that had been used by countries such as Croatia and Bulgaria, Udrea released the new set of TV spots on Eurosport and CNN. One of these spots addressed potential tourists by challenging them to admit the surrealistic projections associated with Romania. It begins with the image of a happy bride in the company of four men dressed in suits. "This is Romania," Nadia Comăneci playfully comments, "the only country where a woman has the right to marry four men at the same time!" "Discover Romania, the country where people are riding zebras," urges Ilie Năstase. "Come to Romania and test the fish fruit!" Gheorghe Hagi beckons, leaving us with the image of a tree full of hanging fish while a voice-over says: "You know nothing about Romania, do you? It's time to come and discover it. Real Sites. Real Experiences. Real People."[10]

The new ads, however, were also received with skepticism by the Romanian press and public. While bloggers complained that the three famous Romanian sports stars were too old to make a strong impact on younger audiences in the West, journalists pointed out the fact that Udrea wasted too much money on badly planned campaigns that would ultimately prove futile.[11] Newly released statistics reveal that these ads were ineffective in attracting more tourists. Despite the €1.5 million budget of the "Land of Choice" campaign (Dumitrescu, 2010), the number of tourists who spent the night in Romanian hotels decreased by 21.9 % in 2009 (Ghira, 2010). Newspaper articles with headlines such as "Tourism in Free Fall" (Străuț, 2010), "Fewer Foreign Tourists in 2009" (Ghira, 2010), or "Romania, the European Country With the Lowest Number of Foreign Tourists" (Diaconu, 2010) reported a shrinking number of foreign visitors, even though Udrea had hoped for an increase of at least 10% ("Tourist-Promotion Video," 2009). Journalists were even more frustrated to report that the Ministry of Tourism spent an additional €45,000 to find out how the money Udrea had initially spent was wasted (Stan, 2009). The expensive study ordered by the minister showed that 48.2% of those interviewed had never even heard about the campaign, while only 33% of those who did hear about it had any hopes that it would be effective (INSOMAR, 2009).

Romania's latest tourist brand logo and slogan, "Explore the Carpathian Garden," were launched in July 2010 at the World Exhibit in Shanghai (Nahoi, 2010). The logo consists of the word "Romania" and a green leaf meant to symbolize nature, freshness, and growth.

Figure 8.1   Romania's tourism logo, introduced in 2010.

Soon after the new brand's release, however, the campaign triggered controversy as a blogger speculated that the leaf in the logo was taken from a clip-art image bank on the Internet and strongly resembled the leaf on England's ecological buses. The THR-TNS corporate team, responsible for the campaign, was accused of plagiarism and Udrea decided to freeze the payments until the issue was resolved (Constantin & Bunea, 2010). The "unlucky leaf" scandal, as it came to be known, prompted widespread criticism and made international news. The media bemoaned that even if the funds came from the European Union, the €900,000 used for the campaign was unwisely spent at a time of austerity. Some pointed out that the message "Explore the Carpathian Garden" not only fails to express anything about Romanian identity but also falsely promises unrealistic ecological tourism in the Carpathian Mountains (Arsenie, 2010). Others decried that the logo is merely a copy of something from abroad and fails to express the country's specificity. Writing for the daily Austrian newspaper *Wirtschaftsblatt*, marketing consultant Michael Brandtner commented that the image of the Carpathian Mountains is too blurry for an international tourist. At the end of his harsh critique of Romania's branding efforts, he suggests that a new slogan, such as "Explore Dracula's Land" may in fact create a clearer image about Romania in the tourists' minds (Drăghicescu, 2010).[12]

THE FUTURE: MONSTROUS MOLVANÎA?

Romania's struggle to "upgrade" its national destination brand offers ample lessons beyond the case's national specificities. Our larger purpose has been to amplify critical voices that caution against the myth of neoliberal market rationality that allegedly underscores nation branding experts' narratives of progress and democratization.[13] Romania's case is analyzed here to demystify the optimism, even celebration, with which nation branding tends to be embedded in marketing practices and related academic research.

The attraction of rationalism and progress held out to countries that follow the neoliberal mantra of the global marketplace helps cover up the mechanisms that sustain hierarchies among individual countries' access to positive self-representation. Simon Anholt, the high guru of place branding, claims that nation branding is an ethically neutral tool, which countries must use proactively to defend themselves against the trivializing tendency of international public opinion. It is vital for countries to ensure that public opinion is "as fair, as accurate and as positive as it possibly can be," he advises (Anholt, 2006, p. 2). The naïveté (or cynicism) is staggering. Aside from assuming that "accurate" and "positive" would not be in contradiction in most cases, one must ponder who decides and controls which representations are deemed "fair" or "accurate." Nation branding is most certainly not simply a tool, let alone an ethically neutral one. As an extension of branding, an inherently neoliberal, corporate practice, to the nation-state it only masquerades as devoid of ideology. According to Aihwa Ong, neoliberalism is not just an economic doctrine that seeks to limit the scope and activity of governing but also a new relationship between government and knowledge through which governing activities are recast as nonpolitical and nonideological problems that need technical solutions. It is a technology of government, which is a way of rationalizing governing and self-governing (Ong, 2006, p. 3).

Nation branding is described by its experts as not only an optimizing market force but also an ideologically neutralizing one, which purifies nationalism of its pesky and dangerous political content. Much like the docu-fictional media representations we analyzed, such a gesture necessitates erasing the violent history of Eastern Europe's colonial dependence on the West and Western Europe's continued interest in sustaining a two-tiered Europe where Eastern economies perpetually depend on Western investment. It conjures up a blank slate on which to re-draw nations as corporations engaged in friendly competition, rather than bloody war, channeling their citizens' love of brands instead of irrational hatred of others. For states not to "choose" the glorious opportunity to start over amounts to irrational and indefensible wallowing in traumas of the past. Anholt (2006) writes,

> I have always held that the market-based view of the world, on which the theory of place branding is largely predicated, is an inherently peaceful and humanistic model for the relationships between nations. It is based on competition, consumer choice and consumer power; and these concepts are intimately linked to the freedom and power of the individual. For this reason, it seems far more likely to result in lasting world peace than a statecraft based on territory, economic power, ideologies, politics or religion. (p. 2)

In much of the literature on place branding, which largely follows in Anholt's footsteps, the replacement of belligerent, territorial nationalism with peaceful brand loyalty tends to be celebrated as the triumph of individualism, consumerism, and free choice. Nations can be made over just like selves. A nation's brand profile, a marketable composite of already circulating images, places, traditions, and products, can be molded into a coherent country brand through strategic marketing campaigns, which, if done right, can and should also mobilize nationalism as an emotional resource tied to a corporate brand. The result is a cheery, post-national, and even post-political (see Aronczyk, 2007) patriotism, a win-win for states, citizens, and foreign investors. The European Union's own self-branding strategy, which new member states try to incorporate and emulate, works through metaphors of a freely chosen, flexible belonging, where the irrational and outdated sentiment of nationalism is transferred to the corporation in the free play of enterprising citizens. As Julie Aveline (2006) wistfully writes,

The EU diagram . . . becomes a form of free association, a portal, where the European citizen would see its civic right and moral references taking the form of wish lists, out of which could be drawn a networking of forums and communities of interests and belonging beyond the national frame. (p. 338)

This flexible notion of citizenship as an open and progressive database of identity choices is far from being universally accessible, however. In Ong's (1999) critical articulation, flexible citizenship refers to strategies by which individuals and states gather power and capital; it is propelled by the very neoliberal cultural logic of capitalist accumulation, travel, and displacement that induces subjects to respond fluidly and opportunistically to changing political-economic conditions (p. 6). In the case of small and disadvantaged post-socialist nations, nation branding is promoted, paradoxically, in the guise of a post-national order that magically relieves individuals of nationalism's ideological burden and converts its pleasures into a platform for consumer identification.

This thinking does not simply ignore nationalism's burden but actually exploits its appeal by erasing the violence at the heart of the banality of national pride. It compels but also authorizes nation-states to continue to suppress internal divisions and rally their citizens around the cause of the nation's economic recovery, visualized as a unifying brand. The post-national rhetoric of freely constructed individual and collective identities, in effect, perpetuates nationalism. It pits branded nations against one another in defensive competition, and it continues to preclude transnational affiliations and alliances among subnational constituencies. What Kaneva and Popescu (2011) call "national identity *lite*" in their analysis of Romanian and Bulgarian nation branding efforts is, in effect, a depoliticized, dehistoricized frame. Instead of rallying the population around an attractive brand, the new narratives have caused further internal division and deepened the crisis of post-socialist states by increasing citizens' suspicion about opportunistic governments who betray what is perceived as the true national cause and sell out the country.

But the contradictions of this logic readily present themselves when a nation's most lucrative prospect of a destination brand is the dual legacy of "Draculescu." For the Romanian state, let alone the actual citizens, constructing a "fair, accurate and positive" brand is hindered by Western investment in the dictator and the vampire, the last nostalgic reservoirs of East European Otherness. Although the state has followed rational marketing recipes and tried to reinvent itself as a desirable destination for rural tourism for foreign visitors, as we have shown, Romania has come to function as one of the last authentic destinations of dark tourism, where one's search for Otherness and quirkiness is still rewarded, unlike in Budapest or Prague, shinier places that have more confidently erased their communist past. In Romania, Ceaușescu's monstrous monument, the People's Palace, continues to be the most visited tourist site, despite post-socialist administrations' efforts to turn it into the seat of Parliament, the symbol of a democratic future (Light, 2001b). This persistent desire for inferior Otherness within Europe has also revived the Dracula myth, associated with the dark Carpathian Mountains at the edge of civilization, where civil unrest and instability are the very stuff of the people's and the place's soul, and where fictional horror is always ready to burst into real-life violence. Light (2001a) writes, "Romania's biggest attractions for Western tourists—Dracula and Ceauşescu—both confirm the country's Otherness" (p. 1066). Even though both the government and the people have been eager to forget the communist period and steer foreign fascination away from Dracula,

> they are able to have little influence on the situation, since both the promoters and consumers of this heritage are external to the country. This is yet another example of the way in which Romania finds itself powerless in the face of the forces of globalization. (Light, 2001b, p. 69)

Even the otherwise sympathetic Light (2001b) implies that Romanians should get over their stubborn reluctance, grow up, move into the market economy, and start to cash in on the money-earning potential of communism and mysticism (p. 71). This implication is fully borne out in marketing analyses such as this:

> As Anholt put it, image and progress go hand in hand, as a positive image is the consequence of progress, rather than vice-versa, and when the two of them are carefully managed in tandem, they help each other along and create an accelerated change. (Nicolescu, Păun, Popescu, & Drăghici, 2008, p. 62)

Even though Nicolescu et al. acknowledge that "branding initiatives become effective only beyond a certain level of competitive performance" (p. 63), they conclude that the way to do this is by making the Romanian business environment "more friendly" by reducing restrictions that foreign investors have to face (p. 66). Ultimately, they propose, Romania should capitalize on the positive images already existing abroad, those associated with Nadia Comăneci, Gigi Hagi, Constantin Brancusi, Eugen Ionesco, "the Romanian beautiful women," the People's Palace, and, yes, Dracula's Castle, "which should be used as Romanian symbols to promote Romania abroad" (p. 70).

Following this prescription, the most valuable resource for Brand Romania would be the hilarious Jetlag mock travel guide to "Molvanîa," a fictional East European country, "a land untouched by modern dentistry" (Cilauro, Gleisner, & Sitch, 2004). While the authors of this book compile a large number of negative clichés about Eastern Europe, the country's name rhymes most closely with that of Moldavia, a region whose largest part falls within modern-day Romania.[14] The best, or only, recipe for economic success seems to be for the state to market itself as a place of vampiric neo-liberalism, ready to incorporate its citizens and sell its embarrassments to visiting consumers eager to be horrified.

NOTES

1. For more on the 20th-century association of Dracula with Transylvania, following the success of Bram Stoker's novel, and on Romania's resistance to the vampire image, see Iordanova (2007) and Light (2007).
2. The bloggers' comments were posted on Bourdain's blog shortly after the show aired in February 2008 (Bourdain, 2008) and were last accessed in March 2008.
3. By blurring distinctions among Eastern European countries, *Top Gear* recycles a long tradition of writing and filmmaking that has presented the Balkans as an amalgam of undistinguishable countries. Take, for instance, Agatha Christie's character Boris Anchoukoff from *The Secret of Chimneys* (1925), a man with Slavic features and a harsh foreign accent, who prompts a shocked Englishman to comment after hearing him speak: "Pure bred Herzoslovakian, of course. Most uncivilized people. A race of brigands. Population, chiefly brigands. Hobby, assassinating kings and having revolutions" (quoted in Todorova, 1997, p. 122). Christie's invented country is set in Herzoslovakia, whose capital "Ekarest," blends in a portmeanteau word "East" and the Romanian capital of "Bucharest."
4. In *The Wheel Spins*, for instance, Iris travels "off the map," leaving behind her girlfriends to admire the marvelous natural scenery of the mountains. Soon, however, we learn that the mountains "overhung her like a concrete threat . . . As she cowered under the projecting cliffs, she felt that they were but to shake those towering brows, to crush her to powder beneath the avalanche of boulders. They dwarfed her to insignificance. They blotted out her individuality. They extinguished her spirit" (White, 1936/2002, p. 20).
5. The Folgers Christmas commercial can be viewed online at http://www.youtube.com/watch?v=teXC8QsfkxY (last accessed on December 12, 2010).
6. The *SNL* show on Whopper virgins can be viewed online at http://www.hulu.com/search?query=Whopper+Virgins+&st=0; its transcript can be found at http://snltranscripts.jt.org/08/08lwhopper.phtml (last accessed on December 12, 2010).
7. In her critique of Robert D. Kaplan's (1994) (in)famous travel book, *Balkan Ghosts: A Journey Through History*, Anca Rosu (2004) emphasizes that many Romanians anticipate the Western travelers' "projections of desire" to hear crude characterizations of their country (p. 152).
8. The spots can be viewed online at http://www.youtube.com/watch?v=wzcuBbztn-0&feature=related and http://www.youtube.com/watch?v=5GharErIGmM&feature=related (last accessed on December 12, 2010).
9. The commercial for Sibiu, European Cultural Capital for 2007, can be viewed online at http://www.youtube.com/watch?v=FpJ6SeDwxLc&feature=related (last accessed on December 12, 2010).
10. This ad can be viewed at http://www.youtube.com/watch?v=o8_JKZ9k_d8&feature=player_embedded (last accessed on December 12, 2010).
11. Udrea was reprimanded for having paid Ilie Năstase €10,000 to participate in a branding event for Romania in Paris by playing a demonstrative tennis

match. Investigations, brought to light by the daily *Cotidianul*, revealed that Năstase was playing the same match for the French Tennis Federation. As he had scheduled the event and was being paid by the French anyway, many deemed Udrea's actions as a waste of money (Gheorghiu, 2009).

12. Duncan Light (2007) explains how Romanians faced a dilemma of "identity versus economy" (p. 756) for a long time and only reluctantly tolerated the development of Dracula tourism. To be sure, whereas the Balkanist discourse from Bram Stoker's *Dracula* constructs the country as backward and full of superstitions, a sinister, marginal location, Romania wishes to present itself to the world as a modern, developed European country.

13. See, for example, Kaneva's (2007) analysis of Bulgaria's paradoxical self-branding efforts, which is generalizable across the post-socialist margins of the European Union.

14. It is important to make the distinction between the Republic of Moldova and the region of Moldavia in Romania. For the people in the region the stakes are high, because the Republic of Moldova is not part of the EU and is generally seen as much poorer than Romania.

REFERENCES

Anholt, S. (2004). Nation brands and the value of provenance. In N. Morgan, A. Pritchard, & R. Pride (Eds.), *Destination branding: Creating the unique destination proposition* (2nd ed., pp. 26–39). Burlington, MA: Butterworth-Heinemann.

Anholt, S. (2006). Is place branding a capitalist tool? *Place Branding and Public Diplomacy, 2*(1), 1–4.

Aronczyk, M. (2007). New and improved nations: Branding national identity. In C. Calhoun & R. Sennett (Eds.), *Practicing culture* (pp. 105–128). New York: Routledge.

Arsenie, D. (2010, August 5). "Explore the Carpathian garden"—România are un brand "amăgitor" ["Explore the Carpathian garden"—Romania has a deceptive brand]. *Evenimentul Zilei Online.* Retrieved August 06, 2010, from http://www.evz.ro/detalii/stiri/explore-the-carpathian-garden-romania-are-brand-amagitor-902465.html

Aveline, J. (2006). Branding Europe? Branding, design and post-national loyalties. *Place Branding and Public Diplomacy, 2*(4), 334–340.

Bivolaru, E., Andrei, R., & Purcăroiu, G. V. (2009). Branding Romania: A PESTEL framework based on a comparative analysis of two country brand indexes. *Management & Marketing, 4*(4), 101–112.

Borcila, A. (2003). Encounters with post-communist sites: Trajectories of inquiry (notes of a resident alien). *American Studies, 44*(1), 187–217.

Bourdain, A. (2008, February 26). Romania: What the hell happened?? *Anthony Bourdain Blog.* Retrieved January 10, 2010, from http://anthony-bourdain-blog.travelchannel.com/read/romania-what-the-hell-happened?fbid=xxDzmq8QRd7#comments

Calder, S. (2007, June 23). The man who pays his way: Why Romanians are sitting on a Glod mine. *The Independent.* Retrieved March 12, 2010, from http://www.independent.co.uk/travel/news-and-advice/the-man-who-pays-his-way-why-romanians-are-sitting-on-a-glod-mine-454235.html

Charles, L. (Director). (2006). *Borat: Cultural learnings of America for make benefit glorious nation of Kazakhstan.* [Motion picture]. Beverly Hills, CA: 20th Century Fox Home Entertainment.

Chilom, A. (2007, February 7). Branding România, o afacere în comă [Branding Romania, an affair in a coma]. *Capital.* Retrieved March 15, 2010, from http://www.capital.ro/articol/branding-rom-nia-o-afacere-n-com-x103-100911.html

Cilauro, S., Gleisner, T., & Sitch, R. (2004). *Molvanîa: A land untouched by modern dentistry.* Woodstock, NY: Overlook Press.

Comanescu, I. (2006, December 2). Romania, Kazahstan virtual [Romania, a virtual Kazakhstan]. *Evenimentul Zilei Online.* Retrieved January 30, 2010, from http://www.evz.ro/detalii/stiri/comanescu-romania-kazahstan-virtual-421434.html

Constantin, C. (2010, July 31). Preşedintele firmei THR, spaniolul Bordas: "Frunza este creaţia noastră" [President of firm THR, Spaniard Bordas: "The leaf is our creation"]. Retrieved December 12, 2010, from http://www.adevarul.ro/actualitate/eveniment/Spaniolul_Bordas-_-Frunza_este_creatia_noastra_0_307769801.html

Constantin, C., & Bunea, I. (2010, July 30). Elenei Udrea i-a căzut frunza la Shanghai [Elena Udrea's leaf fell in Shanghai]. *Adevarul.ro.* Retrieved August 2, 2010, from http://www.adevarul.ro/actualitate/eveniment/Elenei_Udrea_i-a_cazut_frunza_la_Shanghai_0_307169906.html

Cosma, A. C., Negrusa, L. A., & Bota, M. (2007). Romania branding process as a tourist destination. *International Journal of Business Research, 7*(5), 69–74.

Diaconu, S. (2010, February 22). România, tara europeană cu cei mai puţini turişti străini [Romania, the European country with the lowest number of foreign tourists]. *Evenimentul Zilei Online.* Retrieved March 12, 2010, from http://www.evz.ro/detalii/stiri/romania-tara-europeana-cu-cei-mai-putini-turisti-straini-887347.html

Drace-Francis, A. (2003). Paradoxes of Occidentalism: On travel literature in Ceauşescu's Romania. In A. Hammond (Ed.), *The Balkans and the West: Constructing the European Other, 1945–2003* (pp. 68–80). Burlington, VT: Ashgate.

Drăghicescu, I. (2010, August 4). Wirtschaftsblatt: "Noul logo touristic al României, o investiţie greşită" [Wirtschaftsblatt: "Romania's new tourism logo, a wrong investment"]. *Deutsche Welle Romania.* Retrieved August 05, 2010, from http://www.dw-world.de/dw/article/0,,5864583,00.html?maca=rum-newsletter_rum_themen_des_tages-4143-txt-nl

Dumitrescu, C. (2010, July 29). Minister Elena Udrea declares that Romania's new touristic logo respects copyright law. *Business Review.* Retrieved August 10, 2010, from http://business-review.ro/news/update-minister-elena-udrea-declares-that-romania-s-new-touristic-logo-respects-copyright-law/9686

Finn, N. (2006, November 20). Romanian village takes aim at *Borat. E! Online.* Retrieved March 12, 2010, from http://www.eonline.com/uberblog/b53803_Romanian_Village_Takes_Aim_at_Borat.html

Gheorghiu, L. (2009, August 25). Udrea a plătit 10.000 de euro ca să joace tennis cu Ilie Năstase [Udrea paid €10,000 to play tennis with Ilie Năstase]. *Cotidianul.* Retrieved March 12, 2010, from http://old.cotidianul.ro/udrea_a_platit_10_000_de_euro_ca_sa_joace_tenis_cu_ilie_nastase-96307.html

Ghira, A. (2010, February 22). Mai puţini turişti străini in 2009 [Fewer foreign tourists in 2009]. *Cotidianul.* Retrieved March 12, 2010, from http://old.cotidianul.ro/mai_putini_turisti_straini_in_2009-108612.html

Giurgea, C. (2009, November 23). Eterna si fascinanta Romanie, la *Top Gear* [Eternal and fascinating Romania, *Top Gear*]. *TopGear.ro.* Retrieved March 12, 2010, from http://www.topgear.ro/stiri/eterna-si-fascinanta-romanie-la-top-gear

Hitchcock, A. (Director). (1938). *The lady vanishes.* [Motion picture]. UK: Gainsborough Pictures.

INSOMAR. (2009). *Consumul de servicii turistice în România.* Raport de cercetare,VAL III, Noiembrie 2009 [The consumption of tourism services in

Romania. Research report, Quarter III, November 2009]. Retrieved December 13, 2010, from www.turism.gov.ro/ro/download/412

Iordanova, D. (2007). Cashing in on Dracula: Eastern Europe's hard sells. *Framework*, 48(1), 46–63.

Kaneva, N. (2007). Meet the "new" Europeans: EU accession and the branding of Bulgaria. *Advertising & Society Review*, 8(4). Retrieved December 10, 2010, from http://muse.jhu.edu/login?uri=/journals/asr/v008/8.4kaneva.html

Kaneva, N., & Popescu, D. (2011). National identity *lite*: Nation branding in postcommunist Romania and Bulgaria. *International Journal of Cultural Studies*, 14(2), 191–207.

Kaplan, R. D. (1994). *Balkan ghosts: A journey through history*. New York: St. Martin's Press.

Light, D. (2001a). "Facing the future": Tourism and identity-building in post-socialist Romania. *Political Geography*, 20(8), 1053–1074.

Light, D. (2001b). Tourism and Romania's communist past: Coming to terms with an unwanted heritage. In D. Light & D. Phinnemore (Eds.), *Post-communist Romania: Coming to terms with transition* (pp. 59–75). New York: Palgrave Macmillan.

Light, D. (2007). Dracula tourism in Romania: Cultural identity and the state. *Annals of Tourism Research*, 34(3), 746–765.

Morse, M. (1998). *Virtualities: Television, media art, and cyberculture*. Bloomington: Indiana University Press.

Muntean, M. (2008, December 5). Maramuresenii din reclama Burger King, acuzati ca s-au vandut pe un milion de lei [The people of Maramureş from the Burger King ad, accused that they sold themselves for 1 million Lei]. *eMaramureş.ro*. Retrieved March 10, 2010, from http://www.emaramures.ro/Stiri/18053/CRITICI-BURGER-KING-Maramuresenii-din-reclama-Burger-King-acuzati-ca-s-au-vandut-pe-un-milion-de-lei

Nahoi, O. (2010, July 29). Fiasco la lansarea brandului României de la Expo 2010 Shanghai: Imaginea României, promovată pe stil vechi [Fiasco of the release of Romanian brand at Expo 2010: Romanian image promoted in an old style]. *Adevarul.ro*. Retrieved December 13, 2010, from http://www.adevarul.ro/actualitate/Fiasco-Romanei-Expo-Beijing-Romaniei_0_307169755.html

Nicolescu, L., Păun, C., Popescu, I. A., & Drăghici, A. (2008). Romania trying to be a European brand. *Management & Marketing*, 3(1), 61–72.

Obae, P., & Barbu, P. (2004, September 2). Romania, "mereu surprinzatoare" cand isi liciteaza imaginea [Romania, "always surprising" when it tries to auction its image]. *Capital*, 36, 22–23.

Ong, A. (1999). *Flexible citizenship: The cultural logics of transnationality*. Durham, NC: Duke University Press.

Ong, A. (2006). *Neoliberalism as exception: Mutations in citizenship and sovereignty*. Durham, NC: Duke University Press.

Pancevski, B., & Ionescu, C. (2006, November 11). Borat film "tricked" poor village actors. *Mail Online*. Retrieved March 12, 2010, from http://www.dailymail.co.uk/news/article-415871/Borat-film-tricked-poor-village- actors.html

Pop, I. (2008). Romania: What the hell happened?? [Comment to blog post, p. 83]. *Anthony Bourdain Blog*. Retrieved December 12, 2010, from http://blog.travelchannel.com/anthony-bourdain/read/romania-what-the-hell-happened-2/#idc-cover

Rosu, A. (2004). Projections of desire. Robert D. Kaplan's *Balkan Ghosts* and the crisis of self-definition. In S. E. S. Forrester, M. J. Zaborowska, & E. Gapova (Eds.), *Over the wall/after the fall: Post-communist cultures through an East-West gaze* (pp. 146–157). Bloomington: Indiana University Press.

Salecl, R. (1999). The state as a work of art: The trauma of Ceauşescu's Disneyland. In N. Leach (Ed.), *Architecture and revolution: Contemporary perspectives on Central and Eastern Europe* (pp. 92–111). New York: Routledge.

Saunders, R. A. (2008). Buying into brand *Borat*: Kazakhstan's cautious embrace of its unwanted "son." *Slavic Review, 67*(1), 63–80.

Slotek, J. (2009, May 2). Mud in yer eye. *The Toronto Sun.* Retrieved December 12, 2010, from http://www.torontosun.com/entertainment/movies/2009/05/02/9321946-sun.html

Stalenhoef, M. (Director). (2008). *Carmen meets Borat.* [Motion picture]. Netherlands/Romania: Pieter Van Huystee/Sub-Cult-Ura.

Stan, E. (2009, October 21). Studiu de lux pentru Udrea [A luxury study for Udrea]. *Jurnalul.* Retrieved December 13, 2010, from http://www.jurnalul.ro/bani-afaceri/economia/studiu-de-lux-pentru-udrea-524622.html

Strǎuţ, D. (2009, July 6). Turismul, în cǎdere liberǎ [Tourism in free fall]. *Adevarul.ro.* Retrieved December 12, 2010, from http://www.adevarul.ro/actualitate/Turismul-cadere-in_0_74392587.html

Todorova, M. (1997). *Imagining the Balkans.* New York: Oxford University Press.

Tourist-promotion video presented in Paris. (2009, June 5). *Romanian Times.* Retrieved December 13, 2010, from http://romaniantimes.at/news/General_News/2009–06–05/1048/Tourist-promotion_video_presented_in_Paris-newentry

Turp, C. (2009, November 23). *Top Gear* in Romania: Do you know what good press is? *BucharestLife.net.* Retrieved January 10, 2010, from http://www.bucharestlife.net/2009/11/23/top-gear-romania-transfagarasan

Vintilescu, R. M. (2008, March 04). Vedeta de la Travel Channel ne-a zdrobit pe banii nostri [The star from the Travel Channel crushed us with our own money]. *Cotidianul.* Retrieved January 12, 2010, from http://www.cotidianul.ro/vedeta_de_la_travel_channel_ne_a_zdrobit_pe_banii_nostri-40506.html

White, L. E. (2002). *The wheel spins.* Rosetta Books. (Original work published 1936) Retrieved January 12, 2010, from http://www.rosettabooks.com/title.php?id=90

9 One Nation, One Brand?
Nation Branding and Identity Reconstruction in Post-Communist Hungary

László J. Kulcsár and Young-ok Yum

INTRODUCTION

Twenty years have passed since the onset of the post-communist transition, yet many former Eastern Bloc countries are still struggling with their emerging complex identities. In the aftermath of state socialism and its homogenizing political and cultural pressures, countries in Eastern Europe have had to redefine their national identities. This process has been influenced by two major forces. On the one hand, these countries rediscovered or reconstructed national and cultural traditions that, in turn, influenced societal discourses on national identity. In many cases, this resulted in efforts to construct national narratives around ideas of unity and uniformity, where most of the discourse was focused on who is (or can be) part of the nation. National identity was rearticulated against the perceived identities of internal and external "Others," such as minorities and historical adversaries. On the other hand, the forces of globalization, Westernization, and Europeanization also influenced the redefinition of national identities in Eastern Europe. These macro processes introduced such new concepts as diversity and multiculturalism into the discourses on national identity, resulting in additional conceptual complexity that was unfamiliar to many citizens in the region.

Nation branding was introduced to former communist nations within this context, and its premises (and promises) appeared timely and relevant to the region for a number of reasons. First, not only were Eastern Europeans struggling with their post-communist identities, but they had experienced certain difficulties with nationalism and identity formation throughout their modern histories. Second, many former communist countries were receiving a hefty amount of bad press in the West after the initial excitement around the fall of the Berlin Wall wore off. Although post-communist transformations were occurring in relatively peaceful ways in most of these countries, occasional violence and the resurfacing of authoritarian regimes in some of them created significant tensions. In addition, issues like corruption, crime, slow economic reforms, and ethnic strife were continually in the focus of Western observers. Against this backdrop and the harsh reality of market transition and growing inequalities among the population, it is understandable why Eastern Europeans were eager to find ways to offer positive and attractive images of themselves to the rest of the world. Nation branding offered them the ability to do exactly that. Moreover, it held out the promise of success in the global competition for capital and foreign investment, which the new market economies of Eastern Europe badly needed.

However, the various branding programs that sprung up in the region have not necessarily helped the process of reforming national identities, not least because of the inherent conflict between the totalizing logic of branding and the complexity of national identity formation. Adapted from the marketing and tourism industries' theories of destination branding, nation branding aims to (re)define and promote countries along a few well-defined core messages and concepts that are intended to capture a nation's desirable characteristics and image. At the same time, nation branding is distinct from destination (or place) branding because the image of the nation as a whole is at stake, as well as the heterogeneous places that are a part of it. Thus, nation branding has to be more than a tool for the promotion of various places within a country. As Jansen (2008) states, nation branding "selects, simplifies and deploys only those aspects of a nation's identity that enhance a nation's marketability" (p. 122). By contrast, national identities need to be "forged through representational practices that are historically and socially conditioned, multi-layered and dispersed" (p. 122) in order to garner support from the majority, if not all, of the constituents across a nation. In addition, national identity discourses often revolve around such themes as religious tolerance, sexual orientation, or anti-discrimination, which are well suited for heated political debate and which generate continuous tension instead of consensus. Many individuals may view these issues as matters of personal choice and within the realm of self-control, thus feeling they have the agency and prerogative to voice their preferences, derailing branding discourses that aim for simple, unified messages.

Several other factors also make nation branding in Eastern Europe a peculiar and problematic proposition. Nation branding discourses and practices in the region are nested in the conditions of unique post-communist political cultures, where governments generally have limited credibility and where nationalist sentiments are often used to mobilize apathetic electorates. Another issue concerns various failed governmental efforts to present nation branding as a possible way to develop a unified national identity, leading to tensions when post-communist governments created a centralized branding agency or hired multinational PR firms.

Our analysis in this chapter focuses on Hungary for two main reasons. First, Hungary was one of the more moderate communist states before 1990, primarily because of significant Western tourism and trade and experiences with market economy in the communist context. Because of this, Hungary was not unfamiliar with destination branding and was receptive to the ideas of nation branding as well. Second, Hungarians as a collective are hyper-conscious of their public image in the West—a tendency that may be attributed to Hungary's 20th-century history, especially the partition of the country after World War I. Hungarian politics have been quite sensitive to national identity issues, and this was also manifested in the controversies around the country's nation branding efforts. Nation branding in Hungary has changed according to the political climate and election results. It has tended to contrast cosmopolitan urbanites and corporate stakeholders with a traditionalist, rural, and conservative demographic, mirroring the fault lines that define Hungary's political space.

In this chapter, we provide a brief chronological review of specific controversies around nation branding in Hungary during the post-communist period. In addition, we offer a critical discussion of the different identity narratives that emerge in the context of various branding programs. The data for this study were collected using a mixed methods approach, including direct observations of relevant electronic and print sources by commercial travel agencies and the Hungarian government, as well as interviews with key informants involved in Hungary's branding programs. The main goal of our analysis is to address the question: To what extent can nation branding—a marketing and economic development tool—serve as a meaningful mechanism for the (re)definition, (re)negotiation, and (re)building of national identities in an inherently dialectical process that involves a multiplicity of stakeholders?

IDENTITY ISSUES IN EASTERN EUROPE

At the outset, it is important to provide some broad context for understanding the problems of national identity in Eastern Europe. National identity has been a contentious issue in this part of the world since the rise of modern nationalism in the 19th century. In the theoretical literature, nationalism is often divided into a Western and an Eastern variant. Western nationalism, exemplified by the cases of England, France, and later the United States, is typically seen as a progressive and constructive force (Greenfeld, 1992) and one that was instrumental to the emergence of modern democracy (Anderson, 1983) and civil values and norms (Kemp, 1999). By contrast, Eastern nationalism, using the 19th-century examples of Germany, Russia, and Eastern Europe, is considered to be collectivistic, ethnocentric, and emphasizing the romantic concept of *Volk* and shared culture, language, and territory (Brubaker, 1996; Harris, 2002). Whereas Western nationalism is presented as mostly inclusive of people who recognize the fundamental credos and norms of a given country, Eastern nationalism is seen as a particularistic, homogenizing force that excludes internal others (e.g., ethnic minorities) and is constructed against external historical adversaries and supranational entities (Berend, 2003). Although this is, admittedly, an overly simple summation, the point we want to make is that the version of nationalism that is assumed to prevail in Eastern Europe is generally considered to be more aggressive and exclusionary.

Communist control changed the dynamics of nationalist politics in the region. During the communist era, nationalism in Eastern Europe remained seemingly dormant due to the banner of internationalism. However, in reality nationalistic fervor was being fueled by both communist regimes, who used it to legitimize their rule, and by oppositional movements, who sought to mobilize the populace. Once communist regimes collapsed in 1989–1990, the full-force resurrection of nationalism was inevitable in Eastern Europe. Nationalism was particularly well suited to fill the void left in the political space by the discredited communist ideology. This was especially dramatic in nations that had recently regained their sovereignty after the dissolution of federal states. Nationalism was also often used as a cover argument by post-socialist elites seeking to divert the public's attention from other issues, such as economic failures or corruption. Many Eastern Europeans saw democracy as being muddled in corrupt party politics, economic liberalization as tangled in the accompanying recessions, and globalization as threatening national sovereignty and culture. In that context, the simplicity of nationalism was attractive to many who felt threatened and insecure during the post-socialist transformations.

The "marketplace of ideas" did not work very well in the region (Snyder, 2000) because conservatism, which has been the most popular alternative ideology to socialism, had not changed in Eastern Europe since 1945 (Schöpflin, 1993). Western conservatism evolved in reaction to social change and, by the late 1980s, had reached its clearest expression in Thatcherism in the United Kingdom. In this form, it incorporated both a traditional emphasis on religion and family values as well as a modern focus on free market and private enterprise. Contrary to this evolution, post-communist conservatism in Eastern Europe by and large had retained the outdated ideological and political characteristics of the interwar period and was closely linked to nationalism and anti-communism. At the same time, post-communist conservatism was not able to capture the major post-war identity discourses and fundamental changes in the social structure.

Existing divisions between Eastern and Western Europe were deepened during the Cold War. Western Europe became perceived as the repository of all positive cultural traits associated with being European, whereas the negative cultural and political characteristics were associated with Eastern Europe. Not surprisingly, once the Wall came down, most Eastern European countries were eager to show that they indeed belonged to the same club as their Western European counterparts. The question of identity construction aside, presenting themselves as "Western" or "European" was also important for facilitating a quick entry to the European Union (EU) and, in turn, gaining access to its substantial reconstruction funds. These ambitions were especially imperative in Hungary because the political elites, who were major actors in Hungary's nation branding discourse, considered the country to be ahead of most other post-communist countries in terms of its progress toward EU accession.

From the very beginning of the post-communist transformation process, Eastern European nations have struggled with a dual challenge regarding their identities. On the one hand, these countries had to reach back to their original, pre-communist identities to rediscover who they were as nations. On the other hand, the new national identities had to incorporate certain contemporary elements required of modern democratic states, including ethnic tolerance, multiculturalism, minority rights, and so forth. Many post-communist states were unaccustomed to such principles, and some post-communist governments found them to be politically inconvenient. The tension between these seemingly incongruent identities is not simply a theoretical issue for sociologists and political scientists but has also frequently emerged in everyday discourse in the region. With this complexity in mind, in the next section we turn our attention to the concepts of "national brand" versus "national identity" and discuss their significance for post-communist Eastern Europe and Hungary in particular.

NATIONAL BRANDS AND NATIONAL IDENTITIES

Unlike national identities, nation branding is a relatively new phenomenon in its focused and organized form. National identities can induce both pride and hatred, but until recently nation-states did not proactively seek to manage or commercialize their identities, or adopt the position of clients for branding and marketing consultants. With increasing global economic and cultural integration, nation-states have begun to take a more active role in redefining how they want to be regarded by others. For example, in addition to expressing national identity by using widely recognized anthems, coats of arms, flags, and other symbols, it has become increasingly common for governments to hire branding consultants to advise them on how to sell a desired national image to both domestic and global audiences. It is argued that traditional national symbols and artifacts often prove to be meaningless to global audiences, whose historical paths have hardly ever crossed and whose points of reference are significantly different from other nations. By contrast, the symbols and narratives of national brands are often designed with international audiences in mind and privilege their needs and interests.

In the context of Eastern Europe, this has meant that nation branding efforts aimed to appeal to Western audiences, including potential investors and tourists, and highlighted features deemed desirable by Westerners. In particular, nation branding strategists in post-communist Eastern Europe have assumed that Westerners look to the East for two types of stories. On the one hand, they expect exotic stories from the nostalgic past of quaint towns, natural beauty, and ancient heritage. On the other, they expect these pristine destinations to be furbished with bustling local markets, modern amenities, and infrastructure, as well as strong human capital. Case in point, the current slogan used on Gotohungary.com—the website of the Hungarian National Tourist Office (HNTO)—portrays Hungary as a travel destination full of "a love for life," exemplified by a combination of beautiful countryside, upscale spas, rich cultural heritage, trendy shopping districts, gastronomy, and wine.

Nation branding campaigns were seen as inevitable by post-communist states and political elites as they found themselves more and more in the role of *competitors for* rather than *regulators of* global flows of capital, trade, and human migration. Globalization inadvertently increased the importance of national image control at the global marketplace to highlight the idiosyncratic attributes among the countries in the region. These countries were compelled to push forward their national agendas by packaging their diverse local assets as part of national brands and to distinguish themselves from other former Eastern Bloc nations, although the differences exist largely in the semantics. For example, Estonia was labeled "a cool country with a warm heart," Slovenia was "the green piece of Europe," the Czech Republic claimed to be "in the heart of Europe," and Hungary was "the essence of Europe" (Hildreth, 2006).

An army of marketing and branding professionals was ready to sell their expertise in place branding, corporate PR, and product marketing to post-communist countries. However, what seemed to be a straightforward application of branding expertise to nations turned out to be a more challenging and ultimately less successful process, because the complexity of nation branding far exceeds that of smaller scale branding projects. Nation branding requires a serious consideration of the diverse backgrounds of the entire nation, consisting of divergent or conflicting narratives and identities that may be based on ethnicity, religion, education, and urban-rural locus of residence. Nation branding is far more politically contentious than destination or product branding, and the toolkit derived from the latter was inherently inadequate to address the deeply intertwined identities and emotions attached to these brands. Yet, the national governments, both as initiators and clients of branding programs, pushed for superficial and catchy campaigns, and made nation branding a top-down process, further contributing to the democratic deficit of the post-socialist transformation. Nation branding often became an executive exercise where political elites worked with business elites to construct investor-oriented and tourist-friendly images of the nation. For example, Brand Estonia appealed to multinational audiences by guaranteeing zero corporate income tax and near-zero import duties, as well as advanced information technology (enough to be nicknamed as wireless and paperless E-stonia) (Hildreth, 2002; Jansen, 2008, this volume).

In post-communist Eastern Europe, nation branding is close to public diplomacy or PR in that governments are heavily involved in or play a leading role in nation branding campaigns in order to exercise top-down control over national images in the international arena. In addition, governments in post-communist Eastern Europe often favor particular features among numerous local identities in search of short-term political gains. This illustrates that the indirect target of nation branding campaigns is frequently the domestic audience. In terms of nation branding, managing the ordinary citizens' perceptions of their country is as important as image control overseas. Government-run branding efforts in such cases can be perceived to be political propagandizing or maneuvering of public opinion, as will be shown by the Hungarian case. The government agencies handling nation branding, marketing, or PR are often repositories of people largely selected based on their alleged loyalty to the incumbent administration and/or their access to the country's influential individuals and groups.

Unethical, and thus counterproductive, practices undoubtedly not only adversely affect even the most professional nation branding projects but also cause domestic stakeholders to discredit the whole discourse on building cohesive national identities as propaganda. This, in turn, can make nation branding offensive to the national identity narratives of grassroots groups and/or unappealing to international audiences. Moreover, because nation branding tends to reduce the diverse definitions of a nation to a few trendy and catchy themes, some domestic constituents may feel left out and perceive the process as detrimental to the preservation of their authentic local identities. As a result, they may refuse to accept the legitimacy of the few select identities allegedly representative of the entire nation and collective consciousness. In Eastern Europe, this is further complicated when governments mix political legitimacy with promoting certain national visions and identities. Often resistance against a proposed national brand initiative is organized on a political basis, solely driven by the refusal to align with the ideology of the governing regime. In such cases, opposition to branding is detached from a professional discourse, although the close connections between politics and business in Eastern Europe make this separation somewhat murky.

Nation branding is an inherently Western endeavor with a rather simplistic ethnocentric view. Thus, even if the changing national identities of Eastern European countries were recognized by some Western nation branding gurus, the primary assumption was that Eastern European countries only needed to Westernize themselves. This implied an assumption that the already proven Western style of constructing brand messages would also work in the Eastern European setting.[1] To be fair, Eastern European countries and their populaces themselves assessed the situation in a very similar way. They had historically strived to brand themselves as Western and hence were receptive to Western-style branding practices that had shown their robustness in branding destinations, corporations, and products.[2]

Needless to say, both place images and national images are influenced by the products made in the place. In Hungary, these are mostly culinary products, explaining the dominance of gastronomy in various nation branding campaigns. Nation-states also employ certain actions for image control in the international stage, known as public diplomacy, which are an important factor in influencing how national brands are viewed by others. According to Szondi (2008), public diplomacy appears to provide more leverage for the state to act in the international arena and this is an important factor in Eastern Europe, where *etatism* (or statism) has traditionally been very strong. For corporations, action branding is an important PR tool because if they are perceived as good, socially responsible corporate citizens, this is beneficial to their business as well. Products and actions make nation branding appear similar to corporate branding; however, whereas corporations have a clear structure with roles and responsibilities in implementing such PR functions, democratic nations cannot control the behavior of all citizens, as well as those of the elected leaders and their representatives.

Reviewing nation branding in post-communist Eastern Europe, Szondi (2007) identified some of the challenges and functions of nation branding in the region. Szondi uses the term "country branding," avoiding the loaded term "nation," and argues that one of the explicit functions of country branding is redefining national identity in a way that allows post-communist countries to distance themselves from the communist past, change negative stereotypes, and legitimize themselves as reliable members of the new global system and the EU. Among the challenges Szondi lists, some are typical of the economic periphery (e.g., lack of resources and coordination, and unprofessional or untrustworthy messages), but others are more political in nature. Politicized messages, governmental self-promotion, and a lack of transparency and long-term vision are major problems in the nation branding campaigns of post-communist countries. In the next two sections we will use the Hungarian experience to illustrate the dynamic and arbitrary processes of nation branding and their relation to discourses on national identity.

FROM HOT DESTINATIONS TO GOVERNMENT PROPAGANDA (1990–2002)

During the second half of the communist era, the political regime in Hungary allowed the development of a communist "second economy" (Kornai, 1992). The second economy consisted of small enterprises, more or less regulated and tolerated by the communist party, which sought to divert public attention from the political oppression of the regime to the benefits of consumption. Small enterprises played a crucial role in the shortage economy, typical for planned economic systems, by providing both goods for consumption and opportunities to accumulate wealth, which in turn fed the hunger for consumption.

One of the most viable ways to participate in the second economy during the communist period was tourism. Because Hungary was more accessible to Western travelers than were most other Eastern Bloc countries, several destinations developed successful place brands. Lake Balaton, for example, was a popular meeting place for then West and East Germans, as both were allowed to travel to Hungary. Hortobágy, Hungary's first national park, offered a view of undisturbed grasslands with horse riding shows. The wine region of Tokaj in the north and the paprika-producing area around Kalocsa in the south were also popular destinations among Westerners, not to mention Budapest, which retained a lot of its pre-communist cityscape. The communist government encouraged this flow because it needed the hard currency Western tourists spent on their trips.

By the eve of the collapse of communism, this market experiment resulted in significant wealth accumulation for some and, even more importantly, created a certain image of Hungary, related to *open borders, hospitality, gastronomy,* and *tourism,* which subsequently contributed to the establishment of a Hungarian national brand. Some of the components of this brand were destination based, developed by the tourism industry (e.g., Lake Balaton), and some were product based, building on the traditions of Hungarian cuisine (e.g., Pick salami, Kalocsai paprika, and Tokaji wine). Once the borders opened, markets became reestablished, and foreign investments started to flow in, the branding of these already-familiar places and products became a standard practice corresponding to Western demands. The Hungarian National Tourist Office, a governmental organization, promoted destinations, while the product brands became individual market actors. In 1996, the Ministry of Agriculture and Rural Development established the Agricultural Marketing Center to promote high-quality Hungarian food products and help the domestic and foreign market penetration of less well-known product brands.

In the 1990s, only occasional campaigns departed from this destination- and product-driven approach and tried to market Hungary as a nation. These campaigns were mostly organized around global events. The first example was the 1992 Seville World Expo, where the traditional pavilion design of Imre Makovecz won international recognition (Rockwell, 1992). A particularly beneficial event would have been the Vienna-Budapest Expo. The idea for it originated in 1987, when the Austrian and Hungarian governments decided to build on the historical traditions of the dual Habsburg Monarchy to organize an exhibit in 1995 with the theme of bridges between East and West. When the Iron Curtain disappeared in 1990, this theme largely lost its relevance and the potential costs soon exceeded the perceived benefits (Greskovits, Borszéki, & Palócz, 1990). The expo was postponed to 1996 and eventually abandoned by Vienna. Budapest would have proceeded alone, but it soon became clear that the project was doomed due to high costs (stemming from corruption and land speculation) and ongoing political frictions. At that time, Budapest had liberal leaders while a conservative coalition ran the national government. The conservative parties with rural constituents strongly opposed the idea of the Budapest Expo, arguing that whereas the costs would be shared by all taxpayers, the benefits would mostly go to the liberal urbanites. The government withdrew support in 1994 and the project was cancelled (Eörsi, 2000).

In 2000, nation marketing became centralized when the government established the Country Image Center (CIC). The CIC was different from earlier branding efforts, because it connected the issue of national *identity* to branding at the government level and, at the same time, its intended audience was mainly the domestic populace. The CIC soon became a subject of professional and political controversy (Kürti, 2001). To understand how the CIC became a symbol of political propaganda and corruption, subsequently discrediting nation branding itself, first we need to address the politics of identity reconstruction in Hungary.

In the early 1990s, the identity building discourse had two distinctly different levels. On the one hand, academics discussed identity in the context of a potential "third way" of development.[3] The public discourse, on the other hand, was dominated by the identity vision of the first postcommunist government, a coalition of conservative parties. Fueled by state nationalism, a majority of the public supported the idea that Hungary's antebellum dominant geopolitical role in Eastern Europe should be reestablished. Western observers indirectly supported this public sentiment by putting Hungary (together with Poland and later the Czech Republic) ahead of other countries in the region in terms of accession to the European Union. This had profound internal consequences in Hungary, perpetuating etatist political dynamics and a democratic deficit in identity reconstruction.

Although the left came back to power between 1994 and 1998, the nationalist rhetoric did not disappear. During this time, as part of its preparations for EU accession, Hungary was urged to settle historic debates with its neighbors. These negotiations, especially the ones with Romania (see Kulcsár & Bradatan, 2007), provided ample opportunities for heated discussions on nationalism, European integration, and identity reconstruction. They were further fueled by the efforts of the conservative opposition to mobilize their electorate. In 1998, the conservatives eventually resurged; however, the new coalition was different from the 1990–1994 regime. It was led by the Fidesz, the born-again conservative party,[4] which turned the standard nationalistic rhetoric into more proactive policies, including the establishment of the CIC. This was partly a response to general public disappointment with the seemingly never-ending negotiations about EU membership, and a public discourse that questioned to what extent Europeanness could or should be part of Hungarian national identity.[5]

The year 2000 was designated as the Millennium Year, the 1000th anniversary of Hungary's statehood. Thus, the government saw a unique opportunity to launch a nation branding agency to promote Hungary to both domestic and foreign audiences. The first big international showcase for promoting the country was the Hanover 2000 World Expo. The Hungarian Pavilion emphasized the country's history and traditions. It was innovative in terms of its architecture (similarly to the 1992 Seville example), but somewhat less creative in branding Hungary beyond the usual destinations. It is noteworthy, however, that one exhibit focused on Hungarian innovations and talents, a recurring theme in Hungarian identity discourses.[6]

The 2000 Sydney Olympics provided another opportunity to market the country. During the Olympics, the CIC organized a three-day cultural event in Sydney promoting Hungarian cuisine, traditional crafts, and music (Kürti, 2001). This event drew criticism following allegations that the ministers and their entourage had misused public funds. Soon, the public started to see the CIC as a domestic propaganda machine outfitted with seemingly infinite resources and potentially in favor of the ruling party.

The single most important task for the CIC was to coordinate the domestic events for the Millennium Year, focusing on national identity, historical glories, and achievements since 1990. The CIC was also commissioned to highlight the government's new vision for the future—an improved standard of living, individual and collective affluence, all supposedly rooted in Hungary's rich cultural heritage and talent—exactly what people wanted to hear after ten exhausting years of transition. The CIC indeed organized various semi-academic conferences about the image of Hungary and circulated brochures and magazines in every household, promoting Hungarian culture (Kürti, 2001). However, the celebration was soon spoiled, for two reasons. One was that the CIC promoted a certain version of national identity, associated with the conservative-Christian ideology of the ruling coalition. Although it is not surprising that governments act on their ideological beliefs, the Fidesz elevated this practice to a new level because the party was still struggling to legitimize its relatively new conservative face. Thus, discourse on national identity seemed imperative for the political goals of the Fidesz. However, the public viewed the promotion of a particular ideology and national identity dictated by the government as the promotion of the government itself, not as an inclusive, bilateral dialogue.

The second reason for the CIC's failure was a lack of transparency in its operations, which led to a growing suspicion about high-level corruption and was even more upsetting to the public. It turned out that all CIC contracts had gone to a select group of businesses, close to the party elite of the Fidesz, often defeating more highly regarded corporations and media agencies. Contracts were classified so the public had very little information about how much public money was channeled to the "royal contractors" (Dusza, 2000), who were also producing most of the PR materials for Fidesz campaigns and party operations.

Another government organization working on country promotion, in addition to the CIC and the previously mentioned HNTO, was the Ministry of National Cultural Heritage. It was set up by the Fidesz government as an actor in cultural diplomacy and gained significant importance abroad using a network of Hungarian cultural institutes around the globe. It quickly found a connection to both Hungarian émigrés in the West, many of whom had left the country during the communist period and shared a conservative ideology, and ethnic Hungarians "near abroad," most of whom were understandably not satisfied with the successor countries' treatment of minorities.

The aggressive top-down, centralized approach to constructing a national identity was instrumental in the ousting of the Fidesz in 2002. Its importance for this study is that this approach discredited the idea of nation branding, or country image building, in the eyes of the broad Hungarian public. The CIC and the "royal contracts" later became subjects of a long and ultimately unsuccessful legal battle toward transparency and fiscal responsibility (Tanács, 2003). The lesson of the CIC was that government organizations charged with more than simple destination marketing were usually ill-suited for constructing a politically neutral national image, as far as internal audiences were concerned. The socialists, who returned to power after the 2002 election, were quick to disband the CIC and the Ministry of National Cultural Heritage and to discontinue any centralized, governmental nation branding efforts that were explicitly intertwined with a national identity discourse.

RISE AND FALL OF THE PANNON PUMA (2002–2010)[7]

After the 2002 election, the emphasis in Hungary's national promotion went back to destination and product branding. The socialist government was concerned that any discourse on broadly defined nation branding would probably lead to heated and volatile public discussions related to national identity, which would be politically disadvantageous. This political move changed the dynamics of nation branding. The Hungarian National Tourist Office was again designated as the most important government actor in nation branding, and tourism became the main vehicle for country marketing. A typical example was the 2004 campaign featuring Tony Curtis, who promoted Hungary in the United States.[8] One slogan of the campaign was "Some Like It Hot," linking Curtis's famous 1959 movie of the same name to the image of Hungary, a country with beautiful women. This was concurrent with a European campaign in the same year, featuring the Hungarian model Zsuzsa Laky, who had been Miss Europe in 2003.

While the HNTO's main task was to promote Hungarian destinations as well as Hungary itself as a destination, the campaigns occasionally tried to expand the country's image beyond tourism. Probably the most important of these efforts was the 2004–2005 "Talent for Entertaining" campaign (Hungarian National Tourist Office, 2005), which featured 11 notable Hungarians. Some of them were famous musicians, athletes, and gastronomy experts, but the campaign also included the less known chairman of the Hungarian Academy of Sciences and a pilot, promoting conference tourism and the Hungarian Airlines, respectively. The financial impact of this campaign is uncertain; however, it brought back the emphasis on Hungarian talent—a theme that had been previously explored in branding efforts.

One important actor in national product branding was the Hungaricum Club, founded in 1999 by four internationally known companies: Herend Porcelain Manufacturing Co., Pick Szeged Co., Tokaj Trading House, and Zwack Unicum (Honyi, 2000). Even with its elitist aura, this initiative performed specific functions in preparation for Hungary's 2004 EU accession. The product brands represented by the members of the Hungaricum Club were recognized in Hungary as part of the country's identity, and Hungarians were determined to protect them after EU accession, driven by a concern that foreign products under similar or identical names could be registered in the EU. The Hungaricum Club served as an authoritative claim for products that Hungarians felt should only be associated with Hungary.[9]

In 2006, Hungary faced another significant challenge in nation branding. Shortly after the national election was won by the incumbent socialists, Prime Minister Ferenc Gyurcsány had to admit publicly that he and his party had lied about the country's economic situation during the electoral campaign (HVG, 2006). What followed was a series of violent protest rallies against the government. Both the prime minister's deception and the subsequent violent reaction drew international media attention and caused Hungary to appear in political turmoil. To counter the unfavorable publicity, the Hungarian National Tourist Office increased its resources to implement extensive damage control measures and manage external perceptions. The 2006 incidents necessitated the use of public diplomacy and new online communication tools in shaping the country's image. These events also illustrate the gap in how outsiders and locals construct a country's image. In the eye of foreign tourists, a nation's image is simple and mostly concerned with particular destinations and personal experiences while in those places. An average foreign tourist probably would care less about whether the country's prime minister is a liar than about a postcard of a beautiful and pristine lake displayed on a travel website. However, for the local population, the country's image is much more complex and constructed via very different thought processes and experiences, with considerable emphasis on core cultural values and collective consciousness.

In recent years, governments in Hungary have often outsourced branding missions to multinational PR and advertising agencies, who promised to move beyond destination branding. One example for such action in Hungary was the "Image and Identity" Conference in 2006. It was organized by Demos, a Hungarian think tank with some connections to the government, and featured British company Saffron Brand Consultants, whose experts had advised Poland on nation branding (for more on the Polish case, see Surowiec, this volume). Saffron's presentation at the conference included a case study of the agency's work for Poland and emphasized the importance of inclusive and comprehensive core ideas as well as the need for extensive feedback from various stakeholder groups (Hildreth, 2006). It had little to say, however, about the political and organizational challenges of nation branding. Clearly, international firms see nation branding projects as business cases—an approach that has the benefit of distancing them from political contention but also has the disadvantage of missing an important part of the complexities of identity discourses. In other words, Saffron's presentation exemplifies a tendency of nation branding to depoliticize national identity.

The latest effort to refocus Hungary's nation branding efforts returned to the theme of putting the country's talent at the center stage of the marketing campaign. It consists of a short online video clip titled "Get Engaged," which was commissioned by the Budapest Business Region in 2009. This is a professionally produced video, listing Hungarian innovations while showing matching street scenes from Budapest and featuring a musical score with a combination of modern and traditional elements. The weakness of the narrative presented in the video is that it still gives the impression that Hungarian talent is connected mostly with Budapest. The capital city is indeed the center of the country, in terms of population, capital investment, research, and development. It is also the center of politics, traditionally run by left-liberal politicians even when most of the country votes for conservatives. Hence the message of the "Get Engaged" video is not necessarily reflective of Hungary's complex national identity, but rather places an emphasis on a national trait that appears unevenly distributed. Even so, spotlighting neutral elements, such as talents and achievements, may frame the reconstruction of national identity in a more progressive and constructive way in post-communist countries than destination and/or product branding alone.

Finally, another recent effort is noteworthy, as it offers an alternative to the top-down, government-initiated efforts to promote Hungary. The annual National Gallop, a combination of horse racing, cultural fair, and historical reenactments, was first organized in 2008 by various nongovernmental organizations and addressed both country promotion and identity discourse. It presented Hungary as a "nation of horsemen," an important identity component that most Hungarians would agree with. Although the National Gallop is not an official nation branding event, one of its goals is to promote an attractive image of Hungary for both foreign and domestic audiences. Moreover, although it takes place in Budapest, there is a large emphasis on promoting all Hungarian towns and villages. In fact, a lot of the program elements work in favor of rural Hungary, showcasing the traditions of the countryside. In that sense, the National Gallop combines the best of both worlds—garnering national and international media attention by holding the event in the capital of Hungary, while at the same time bridging the gap between urban and rural stakeholders. This appears to be a win-win approach—preserving the Hungarian identity (appreciating the traditional sport) and promoting a more general brand in a tasteful and appealing way.

The roller coaster of nation branding and its governmental control in Hungary are probably far from over. In the 2010 national elections, the Fidesz party defeated the discredited socialists, returning to power after eight years. Among the media promotion of the National Gallop in May 2010, there was a short newspaper article about the new government's intentions to resurrect the Country Image Center (Csuhaj, 2010). Hungary will take the rotating EU presidency in January 1, 2011, and the government probably wants to be in full control of the image of the country by that time. The question is whether the new branding machinery will narrowly focus on destinations, re-ignite the controversy about top-down construction of national identity, or possibly take over more successful, nongovernmental initiatives, such as the National Gallop.

One daunting challenge facing Hungary and other post-communist countries in their efforts to brand themselves is to find the middle ground between *destination marketing*, using the seemingly indistinguishable Eastern European landscapes, and the temptation for *top-down national identity branding* at the expense of local/individual identities. The Hungarian example shows that nation building through nation branding can become a charged political game, whereas destination marketing often lacks creativity and fails to engage the local populace. Neutral elements, such as the emphasis on talent, can frame the reconstruction of national identity in a more complex way, although with some caveats.

CONCLUSIONS

The context of nation branding in Eastern Europe is different from that of the West because of the heightened sensitivity about national identity in the region, as well as the unique political economy of nation branding. This study has revealed some commonalities and differences with respect to how the constituents preferred to present their nation to the rest of the global community. The Hungarian case also highlights some of the peculiar challenges of nation branding in Eastern Europe.

First, there is the conceptual challenge of integrating nation branding with the reconstruction of national identity. The Hungarian example shows two distinctly different, but equally unsuccessful, ways to address this challenge. Conservative governments focused on national identity, not developing a national brand *per se* but assuming that manifestations of a promoted version of national identity will serve the same purpose. Historical glory and cultural superiority were overemphasized because those are fundamental components of the political identity of conservative parties. Left-wing governments, on the other hand, largely dropped the idea of developing a unified national brand, mainly because the discourse was already contaminated with the ideological tropes of nationalism and there they had a disadvantage. Instead, they largely left assorted place branding projects to serve as a substitute for nation branding without much governmental direction. In the first approach, a particular vision was promoted that many Hungarians refused to buy, while in the second approach there was not much to buy to begin with. This highlights the significant limitations of nation branding as a contributor to national identity reconstruction.

Second, the political culture of etatism in Hungary (and in Eastern Europe more generally) increases the tendency of the state to be a central actor in the articulation of national identity and its connection to nation branding projects. In Hungary, the government determined the discourse on national identity, which often occurred along the lines of the political ideology of the ruling party. This tends to perpetuate political contention and raises questions about whether the government should, in fact, play a key role in nation branding efforts. The example of the National Gallop in Hungary indicates that nongovernmental actors can be successful in creating an image acceptable for most of the citizens, even across the traditional divide between urban and rural constituents. However, initiatives like the National Gallop can only be successful if the government does not have a strong nation branding project on its own to undermine them. For post-communist governments, it seems to be very difficult to resist the temptation of a top-down approach, which is deeply ingrained in Eastern European politics. However, an overly specific vision promoted by the government can be as useless as the adoption of overly generalized Western brand messages recommended by foreign experts.

Third, multinational experts, the assumed sources of creative and productive input, have been surprisingly inefficient in Eastern Europe. Projects in the region that are typically touted by Western consultants as examples of successful nation branding—such as Estonia's "A Nordic Country With a Twist" or Poland's "Creative Tension"—seem to convey better what Western experts think these countries should advertise than what the countries' publics really subscribe to. They suggest a "one-size-fits-all approach" as Jansen (2008, p. 135) puts it. International experts still tend to prescribe stereotypical and strongly promoted Western/global narratives. Today Eastern European countries are advised to show "creative coolness," just as they were advised to advertise idyllic, rural landscapes ten years ago.

Finally, there is a unique synergy between post-socialist governments and international experts in nation branding, which leads to a more speculative question about the usefulness of nation branding itself. The loudest promoters of nation branding are the nation branding experts themselves. These companies exploit the tendency of national governments in the region to buy into Western arguments about the need for countries to be trendy and image-conscious in order to succeed in a global competitive environment. The pressure on resource-poor countries, competing for foreign investments, is especially strong. Members of the political elites in Eastern Europe are usually not recruited from the business sphere or academia and thus are easily seduced by quasi-expertise and pseudo-scientific indicators, such as the Country Brand Index (a ranking published by brand consultant Simon Anholt). At the same time, political elites in Eastern Europe also find nation branding projects useful for promoting ideology, delivering positive messages, and diverting the public discourse at home from more risky topics, such as economic reforms or structural adjustments. Paradoxically, the only scenario when the international branding juggernaut is unsuccessful in penetrating the political elite is when the local political regime has its own preferred contractors for the job. But in either case, the process is top-down, driven by the political and business elites and thus raises the same question: Is nation branding in its current form necessary or at least useful for countries in the region?

The usefulness of nation branding could be interpreted in two spheres. One is economic development, investigating whether it leads to investment and economic growth. The assumption is that tourists are more likely to come if a country has a brand beyond the marketed destinations. For example, visitors are believed to be seduced by "the twist" in the Nordic country of Estonia. Similarly, investors are supposed to take their money to Poland because the country has "creative tension." In reality, however, business and travel decisions are more likely to be based on other factors, and evaluation of the relative contribution of national brands to development should be a future research agenda for social scientists.

The other sphere where the usefulness of nation branding could be questioned is in relation to the social construction of national identities. In its current form, nation branding is elite driven. Even if stakeholder input is collected from a variety of groups, national brands usually still squeeze complex identities into simple images and messages. Nation branding as a bottom-up process would probably be less efficient and more complicated, but as the example of the National Gallop in Hungary shows, initiatives not explicitly started as branding campaigns can be successful in conveying an attractive and unifying message. The National Gallop transformed a civic event (or civic space) into a nation branding event (or calculative space) without selling out its true cultural meaning. It re-conceptualized nation branding as a frame to construct a new identity that can bring people with diverse identities together.

If national brands should coincide with the overall consensus of national identities supported by the majority of the populace, nation branding should be more organic, participatory, and diverse. It should move from what it is today, a unified brand attempting to represent diverse societies and complex identities, to a more inclusive conceptual process built up from various pieces. Instead of being a self-serving, business enterprise or a politically motivated identity promotion, nation branding should be re-conceptualized to reflect how identities are constructed not by the elite but by the public. This is especially important in Eastern Europe, where nations still have a sizeable democratic deficit to overcome.

NOTES

1. In this sense, nation branding experts fell into the same trap as the transitologist school of political science in the 1990s (Bunce, 1995). Essentially borrowing the old modernization argument, transitologists had limited knowledge of the local context but infinite belief in the power of Western-style democratization and market transition.

2. A typical way to use the destination branding toolkit in Eastern Europe was to promote an authentic, traditional landscape. Because of the strong preference for urban development during the socialist era, the countryside in Eastern Europe could retain its traditional character, and soon country campaigns were filled with images of bucolic landscapes, old towns and castles, and people in traditional costumes. Some of these campaigns were professional, but only within the realm of destination branding (Hall, 2004).

3. The "third way" idea originated in the post-war writings of Hungarian writer and politician István Bibó. Over time, it has surfaced in many forms, including a communist version, called "democratic socialism." After 1990, it was both a geopolitical idea, a loosely defined neutral stand between the West and the East (the Swiss model), and a naive rejection of the neoliberal economic reforms. Its clearest post-1990 expression was the "Let's Invent Hungary" project started by Elemér Hankiss, a Hungarian intellectual, but it was largely confined within academic circles, partly because the general public never understood why Hungary had to be "re-invented."

4. The Fidesz ran and lost on a liberal platform in both 1990 and 1994. Promptly purging its liberal elements, the leadership redefined itself as a center-right party, successfully filling the void after the political discreditation of the conservative parties in the 1990–1994 government.

5. The most infamous example of this was the statement of Viktor Orbán, then prime minister and the president of the Fidesz, that "there is life outside the EU" (Új Szó, 2002). Orbán was understandably disappointed with the slow EU accession process (he wanted the accession to happen during his term). However, this statement was mostly directed at his radical followers in Hungary who opposed the liberal norms and values of the EU.

6. Hungary has an ambivalent relationship to its talented people and innovators. Hungary gave 14 Nobel Laureates to the world, and many known products originated from Hungarian innovators (the ballpoint pen, Rubik's cube, holography, vitamin C, etc.). At the same time, many of these achievements actually occurred to Hungarian innovators and scientists in emigration, showing that Hungary has a much better track record in producing talent than nurturing it. What further complicates the issue is that many of the inventors and talents were Jewish, which tends to fuel the occasional anti-Semitism of Hungarian politics. For example, when Imre Kertész received the 2002 Nobel Prize in Literature, there were voices who questioned his Hungarianness, partly because he lives in Germany and partly because he is Jewish.

7. The Pannon Puma became a pop culture reference after Janos Koka, then Minister of the Economy noted in 2005 that if Slovakia labels itself as the "Tiger of the Tatras" then Hungary is the Pannon Puma, both referencing the economic boom of the Asian Tigers. Koka's intention was to downplay the economic growth of Slovakia.

8. The parents of Tony Curtis were Hungarian immigrants. Curtis maintained ties to Hungary throughout his career and also spoke Hungarian, which made him a very good fit for this role.

9. Particularly infamous was the "palinka war" between Hungary and Romania about the use of the word *palinka* as a brand (HVG, 2004). *Palinka*

means brandy in Hungarian (and *palinca* is the same in Romanian), so the debate was on a one-letter difference which, of course, is significant in brand recognition. A similar debate occurred between Hungary and Slovakia when Slovak producers wanted to sell Tokaji wine, arguing that a small part of the Tokaj wine region is in fact in Slovakia (Kincs, 2005). Slovakia is only allowed to use the brand *Tokajsky* (the Slovak version of the same word) and is outproduced by Hungary 9 to 1 in volume. Both examples are more than simple brand wars though, addressing national identity and culture, reaching the national press and stirring up emotions.

REFERENCES

Anderson, B. (1983). *Imagined communities: Reflections on the origin and spread of nationalism.* London: Verso.

Berend, I. T. (2003). *History derailed: Central and Eastern Europe in the long nineteenth century.* Berkeley: University of California Press.

Brubaker, R. (1996). *Nationalism reframed: Nationhood and the national question in the New Europe.* Cambridge, UK: Cambridge University Press.

Bunce, V. (1995). Should transitologists be grounded? *Slavic Review, 54*(1), 111–127.

Csuhaj, I. (2010, May 5). A Fidesszel visszatér az Országimázs Központ [The Country Image Center will be back with the Fidesz]. *Nepszabadsag.* Retrieved August 25, 2010, from http://nol.hu/belfold/20100505-ujbol_lesz_orszagimazs-epites

Dusza, E. (2000, September 4). Továbbra sem tudni az ünnep költségeiről [Still no information about the costs of celebration]. *Magyar Hírlap.* Retrieved December 14, 2010, from http://www.magyarhirlap.hu/kronika/tovabbra_sem_tudni_az_unnep_koltsegeirol.html

Eörsi, J. (2000, May). Képtelen magyar expótörténet [Unreal history of the Hungarian Expo]. *Beszélő.* Retrieved December 14, 2010, from http://beszelo.c3.hu/00/05/11eorsi.htm

Greenfeld, L. (1992). *Nationalism: Five roads to modernity.* Cambridge, MA: Harvard University Press.

Greskovits, B., Borszéki, Z., & Palócz, E. (1990). *Hidak—de hová? Magyarország és a világkiállítás* [Bridges—but where do they lead? Hungary and the World Fair]. Budapest, Hungary: Heti Világgazdaság Kiadói Rt.

Hall, D. (2004). Branding and national identity: The case of Central and Eastern Europe. In N. Morgan, A. Nigel, A. Pritchard, & R. Pride (Eds.), *Destination branding: Creating a unique destination proposition* (pp. 87–106). Oxford, UK: Butterworth-Heinemann.

Harris, E. (2002). *Nationalism and democratisation: Politics of Slovakia and Slovenia.* Aldershot, UK: Ashgate.

Hildreth, J. (2002). The road from serfdom in Estonia. *The American Enterprise, 13*(8), 43.

Hildreth, J. (2006, October). *An introduction to robust nation branding (including a case study of Poland).* Presentation at "Image and Identity" Conference, Budapest, Hungary. Retrieved May 27, 2010, from http://www.slideshare.net/agocsadam/jeremy-hildreth-presentation-at-image-and-identity-conference-2006-hungary

Honyi, G. (2000, October 19). Megalakult a Hungaricum Club [Hungaricum Club founded]. *Napi Gazdaság.* Retrieved August 25, 2010, from http://www.napi.hu/default.asp?cCenter=article.asp&nID=41438

Hungarian National Tourist Office. (2005, May 5). *"Talent for entertaining": Az idei év legnagyobb turisztikai imázskampánya* ["Talent for entertaining": The

biggest tourist image campaign of this year] [Press release]. Retrieved August 25, 2010, from http://itthon.hu/sajtoszoba/2005-elso-felev/talent-for-entertaining
HVG. (2004, June 9). Kiújult a magyar-román pálinkaharc [The Hungarian-Romanian palinka war has restarted]. *HVG Hetilap.* Retrieved August 25, 2010, from http://hvg.hu/gazdasag/0000000000575F45
HVG. (2006, September 17). Gyurcsány: "Végighazudtuk az elmúlt másfél-két évet" [Gyurcsány: "We have lied over the past two years"]. *HVG Hetilap.* Retrieved August 25, 2010, from http://hvg.hu/itthon/20060919gyurcsany_beszed
Jansen, S. C. (2008). Designer nations: Neo-liberal nation branding—Brand Estonia. *Social Identities, 14*(1), 121–142.
Kemp, W. A. (1999). *Nationalism and communism in Eastern Europe and the Soviet Union: A basic contradiction?* New York: St. Martin's Press.
Kincs, A. N. (2005, January 5). Zavarok a hungarikumok körül [Trouble around the Hungaricums]. *HVG Hetilap.* Retrieved August 25, 2010, from http://hvg. hu/hvgfriss/2005.01/200501HVGFriss178
Kornai, J. (1992). *The socialist system: The political economy of communism.* Princeton, NJ: Princeton University Press.
Kulcsár, L., & Bradatan, C. (2007). Politics without frontiers: The impact of Hungarian domestic politics on the minority question in Romania. *Communist and Post-Communist Studies, 40*(3), 301–314.
Kürti, L. (2001). Országimázs Központ: Egy állami intézmény működése [Country Image Center: The operation of a governmental organization]. In S. Kurtán et al. (Eds.), *Magyarország Politikai Évkönyve* [The Political Yearbook of Hungary] (pp. 292–301). Budapest, Hungary: DKMKK Foundation.
Rockwell, J. (1992, May 7). The talk of Seville: In Expo architecture, mishmash means eclectic. *The New York Times.* Retrieved August 25, 2010, from http:// www.nytimes.com/1992/05/07/arts/the-talk-of-seville-in-expo-architecture-mishmash-means-eclectic.html
Schöpflin, G. (1993). *Politics in Eastern Europe, 1945–1992.* Cambridge, MA: Blackwell.
Snyder, J. (2000). *From voting to violence. Democratization and nationalist conflict.* New York: Norton.
Szondi, G. (2007). The role and challenges of country branding in transition countries: The Central and Eastern European experience. *Place Branding and Public Diplomacy, 3*(1), 8–20.
Szondi, G. (2008). *Public diplomacy and nation branding: Conceptual similarities and differences.* Discussion Papers in Public Diplomacy. Netherlands Institute of International Relations "Clingendael." Retrieved April 20, 2010, from http://www.clingendael.nl/publications/2008/20081022_pap_in_dip_ nation_branding.pdf
Tanács, I. (2003, July 9). Közpénz [Public money]. *Népszabadság.* Retrieved December 14, 2010, from http://nol.hu/archivum/archiv-117556
Új Szó. (2002, February 1). Orbán: van élet az EU-n kívül is [Orbán: There is life outside the Union]. *Új Szó.* Retrieved December 13, 2010, from http://ujszo. com/cimkek/regi-online-kiadas/2002/02/01/orban-van-elet-az-eu-n-kivul-is

10 The Musical (Re)branding of Serbia

Srbija: Sounds Global, Guča, and EXIT

Branislava (Brana) Mijatović

INTRODUCTION

Since the ousting of Slobodan Milošević from power in 2000, Serbia has made various efforts to transform the country's negative image, acquired during the political turmoil of the 1990s, into a positive one, imbued with hope, optimism, and opportunities. Although the idea of national re-branding was discussed in Serbian media from the start of the new millennium, constructing a new image posed a greater challenge for Serbia than for most other post-communist countries. In addition to the wars of the 1990s, Serbia's image was impacted by worldwide media coverage of the Hague trials, the assassination of the prime minister in 2003, Kosovo's independence and the related protests, and recent violence against foreigners at sports events.

In this context, the question of what kind of image Serbia should project to the world emerged dramatically in discourses and activities related to music, and this is the main focus of this chapter. A long-term music project, titled *Srbija: Sounds Global* (SSG), and two music festivals—Guča and EXIT—exemplify the processes of authoring national self-narratives through music. These projects succeeded in capturing the Serbian national imagination to a far greater extent than did state-sponsored nation branding initiatives. Further, they opened up new discussions about historically reproduced dichotomies of rural/traditional versus urban/modern identities in Serbian society.

My analysis is informed by the theoretical position that national identity is an "ongoing process, politically contested and historically unfinished" (Clifford, 1988, p. 9). From this starting point, I examine *Srbija: Sounds Global*, Guča, and EXIT in relation to the discourses of Serbian politicians, as well as Serbian and international nation branding experts, and describe the tensions that arise when politicians attempt to co-opt successful cultural practices for nation branding purposes. What emerges from this interplay of culture and politics is a complex interweaving of music practices and discourses with the politics of national identity that highlights the contradictions within the ideology of nation branding.

I use critical ethnographic methods and draw on qualitative field data collected between 2001 and 2010. During this period, I made multiple trips to Serbia and conducted numerous interviews with musicians, producers, and cultural workers. I also interviewed some of the main branding advisors to the Serbian government. My analysis also draws on media coverage and public discourses around the three musical projects and nation branding in general. In addition, I analyze the content and cover art of the first SSG compact disc. Throughout the chapter, I provide historical context as a way to situate my analysis of these diverse materials.

My main argument is that the musical re-branding of Serbia was, and continues to be, a complex process that both embodies and goes against typical nation branding strategies. On the one hand, SSG, Guča, and EXIT provide vivid, emotional, and positive messages and experiences—considered crucial ingredients for successful brands—to domestic and international audiences. All three projects exemplify successful music brands and have been, in turn, co-opted by politicians to present a positive image of Serbia. On the other hand, in contrast to nation branding strategies that advocate a unified brand message, these music projects testify to the multiple and fragmentary nature of individual and national identities. Thus, my goal is to examine how these music projects have served as a springboard for debates about a Serbian national brand and, in the process, opened up a space for renegotiating Serbian self-identity.

At the outset, it is important to note my own identity as a Serbian national (I lived in Serbia until 1995), which positions me as both an insider and an outsider to the culture. My personal experiences as a musician and scholar in Serbia and in the United States—someone who has witnessed, read, and written about music in different contexts—have necessarily influenced the stories I found compelling and the way I write about them in this chapter.

SERBIAN FOLK MUSIC: BRIEF HISTORICAL BACKGROUND

During the communist period (1945–1989), various top-down projects attempted to establish a "national" musical tradition and "elevate" folk music to a higher artistic level, similarly to other communist countries (see Buchanan, 2006).[1] At the same time, traditional rural music—that is, songs and dances performed as part of traditional village life and linked to seasonal work, weddings, fairs, and other communal customs—almost disappeared. The modernization of the 1950s and 1960s brought about changed work processes in the villages and extensive migration from villages to cities, resulting in the disappearance of occasions for performing a whole repertoire of songs. A new genre, called newly composed folk music, appeared in their place. This new genre, consisting of songs written in a folk manner but modernized and Westernized (with harmonies, arranging techniques, and instrumentation adopted from Western classical and pop music), "met the cultural needs of this transitional majority seeking to rid itself from the baggage of rural origin while psychologically unequipped to accept models of urban culture" (Rasmussen, 1999, p. 4). Because traditional rural music was never popularized through the mass media, its quiet disappearance was noted only by ethnomusicologists who attempted to document and archive it (see Golemović, 1994).

The political turmoil of the 1990s opened up a space for extreme nationalism and, with it, the resurrection of national myths and reexamination of past historical grievances, which found their way into song, mainly in the genre of newly composed folk music (Gordy, 1999; Hudson, 2007; Mijatović, 2003). Rock 'n' roll musicians, on the other hand, mainly opposed extreme nationalistic tendencies and resisted the Milošević regime (Gordy, 1999; Mijatović, 2003). These two broadly conceived genres—newly composed folk/turbo-folk and rock 'n' roll—stood for opposite political orientations and served as popular shorthand for the polarization of Serbian society of the 1990s. Eric Gordy (2005) writes that "what made the two forms fascinating in the 1990s were not their musical characteristics, but the fact that they were widely used as a way for ordinary people to understand the divisions in the society in which they lived" (p. 15). In public discourse, rock 'n' roll was identified with cosmopolitanism, anti-Milošević and anti-war sentiments, and distaste for extreme nationalist politics.[2] By contrast, newly composed folk and turbo-folk were identified with support for Milošević, the civil wars in Croatia and Bosnia, extreme nationalistic politics, and Serbian tradition in general.[3]

The newly composed folk genre played upon those elements from Serbian tradition that pertained to historical battles, military leaders, and stories of kingdoms past and misrepresented them as the core of Serbian tradition. By contrast, musicians interested in traditional rural music and its various fusions presented different aspects of Serbian tradition as important.[4] These included culturally and ethnically pluralistic views of Serbian history and proffered a narrative of Serbian identity as formed not in isolation, as the regime constantly emphasized through its megalomaniac and xenophobic discourse, but through cultural interaction with others. This perspective on tradition also emphasized Serbian identity as formed through hard work shared with neighbors, a communal spirit of celebration, love relationships, and shared customs and beliefs.[5]

By proposing a different understanding of tradition, traditional rural music performers opposed a range of regime-sponsored values and behaviors—from intolerance of different nationalities and ethnicities to the glorification of violence. In addition, they brought to light Serbian traditional cultural values that focused not on a fascination with death, as in the nationalistic misinterpretations of tradition, but on the celebration of life.[6] However, the voices and efforts of traditional music performers seemed to be isolated attempts at reclaiming Serbian tradition, until their vision was brought together by the project *Srbija: Sounds Global*.[7]

SRBIJA: SOUNDS GLOBAL

Srbija: Sounds Global (SSG) was initiated in 2000 by independent, Belgrade-based media company B92.[8] The project began as a music compilation compact disc (CD) released in November 2000, but soon grew into a popular brand and a slogan used by Serbian politicians throughout the decade that followed. Advertised locally as an effort to discover and reinterpret the rich tradition of ethno music in all its diversity, the first SSG compilation CD featured brass bands, singers performing village songs in traditional style, players of traditional Balkan instruments such as *duduk* and *tambura*, and virtuoso performers (violinists, clarinetists, accordionists) blending traditional and modern influences in original compositions.[9] The musicians' ethnicities encompassed Roma, Jewish, Hungarian, and Serbian, and the music included a variety of regional styles. Some performers were already famous, some were not; some were at the peak of their popularity, some were forgotten, some emerged as new stars. All, however, belonged to a broadly conceived musical category—traditional Serbian music—that had been, up to that point, quite unpopular among hip Serbian urbanites. The *Srbija: Sounds Global* project changed this perception dramatically. Not only did the first SSG CD become a bestseller, but its success attracted the kind of visibility that had been previously unimaginable for this genre. It spurred the appearance of new bands and created an interest among other domestic record companies and producers. Eventually, *Srbija: Sounds Global* became an umbrella brand, under which B92 released three more CDs (2002, 2004, 2008) and promoted numerous concerts and recordings featuring individual bands and performers associated with the original releases.

Originator of the idea and producer of the first SSG album was Bojan Djordjević, a lawyer, music producer, and organizer of Ring Ring, the first international festival of "world music" in Serbia (1996–2010). Djordjević was aware of the existence of disparate efforts to create a new appreciation and understanding of Serbian traditional music, but he was equally aware of the lack of opportunities and support for this genre. Recognizing that national record companies were not interested in traditional music, largely due to the fact that it had never been promoted through the media (Rosenbaum, 2004), Djordjević turned to a "rock/urban oriented alternative outlet" that had already proved successful in marketing the new and the unusual: radio and record label B92 (personal interview, December 29, 2006). His idea was to present "different forms of traditional and composed ethno music of Serbia, the richness of creative approaches and poetics, from documentary reinterpretation of the tradition, to innovative fusions of musical idioms cross-fertilized in these regions" ("Srbija Sounds Global: All Stars," n.d.). This compendium of traditional rural music and its fusions became associated with a new label—"Serbian world music"—which was commonly used to market this genre.[10]

Miloš Mitić, music producer at B92 who collaborated with Djordjević on all four SSG albums, stated, "We wanted to present a living tradition, not archival documents, and to include the complete tradition[al music] that exists in Serbia today" (personal interview, December 24, 2008). Discussing the music choices for the SSG compilations, Mitić stressed that the producers took into consideration the fact that Serbia was never a monolithic entity in either ethnic or cultural terms, and they wanted to include musicians of different ethnicities who played music of different styles. These thoughts are echoed in a description of "Serbian world music," written by Djordjević and Mitić for *CorD* magazine, an independent English-language monthly published in Belgrade:

> Serbian world music is an interplay between an oriental, Arabic heritage . . . European inflow, and, naturally, Serbia's native music . . . This *mélange* of different cultural inheritances and the large number of ethnic minorities living in Serbia are vital components of the country's rich musical tradition and the diversity of the "musical menu" in this genre. (Djordjević & Mitić, 2005, p. 64)

The four SSG compilation releases exemplify this variety of performers and compositions, from Serbian-Hungarian musicians, such as violinist and zither player Lajko Felix, to Serbian-Jewish band Shira Utfila, to several Serbian-Roma bands (Boban Marković, Earth-Wheel-Sky, Kal, Lelo Nika, Usti Opre All Stars, and Šaban Bajramović), to Serbian musicians from various regions. All of the CDs present three types of "living tradition": interpretations of traditional or composed songs using traditional vocal and instrumental techniques; novel interpretations of traditional instrumentals or songs; and innovative fusions of genres and styles.

The first SSG compilation did not have financial support from any government individual or organization and was promoted through TV and radio ads and an occasional interview (Mitić, personal interview, December 24, 2008). Djordjević and Mitić were surprised by the huge consumer interest and the overwhelmingly positive reviews in a variety of Serbian media.[11] This prompted B92 to capitalize further on SSG's popularity by announcing a second compilation CD and a concert series held in 2002 and 2003 under the title *Serbia Sounds Global: A Living Tradition* ("Concert Series," n.d.). In addition to the concerts, B92 promoted this music in a variety of other ways. In 2001, B92 organized and sponsored a concert as a part of a three-day international conference, "In Search of Truth and Responsibility—Towards a Democratic Future." The CD *Srbija: Sounds Global 2* was released in 2002 at a promotional concert during which the Yugoslav Ministry of National and Ethnic Minorities presented individual and corporate awards for contribution to tolerance in Yugoslavia. In addition, B92 produced and released individual albums by the artists featured on the SSG compilation CDs and, through their success, encouraged other labels to begin releasing albums of traditional music.

The sold-out concerts and rapid popularity of the SSG albums could be interpreted in two ways. First, they reflected a growing interest in the emerging world music genre related to Serbian traditional music. Second, there existed a genuine social and cultural need for musicians and audiences to distance themselves from the dominant musical genres of the 1990s. This latter sentiment was echoed in numerous interviews I conducted and in many published interviews with musicians interested in Serbian world music. As Djordjević stated, "Serbia is neither Milošević, nor the protests, nor the economic crisis, nor the bombing. [We wanted to show that] Serbia can also be this—good music; and world music is perhaps its most interesting genre" (personal interview, December 29, 2006).

The success of the cultural initiatives related to the SSG brand demonstrated that its impact was larger than B92's ability to bring to market a previously obscure music genre. More importantly, *Srbija: Sounds Global* had become associated with tolerance and had the potential to influence Serbia's overall image. As Serbian journalist Dragan Ambrozić (2003) wrote, SSG positioned Serbia "as an important destination on the world music map, giving it a recognizable brand and a door to a new cultural wealth hidden in vital reexamination of tradition."

Although both Djordjević and Mitić assured me that they did not start SSG with the idea to create a brand and that their efforts were led exclusively by their musical interests, their business backgrounds have inevitably influenced the evolution of the project. Given Djordjević's experience as a music producer, his role as distributor of the Putumayo World Music label for Serbia and Montenegro, and his awareness of the success of the *Buena Vista Social Club*, it seems that he followed his business instincts and this contributed to the success of SSG as a brand.

Numerous "how-to" books and articles on brand development emphasize that a successful brand needs to provide a unique, engaging, and intriguing message; it must clearly embody specific core values—qualities that need to be evident in every aspect of customers' interactions with the product. A brand also needs to have a statement, referred to as a "brand proposition," which should be "clearly understood, engaging, presented in the right context for relevancy, and offer a solution to the target audience's current wants and needs" (Bloise, n.d.). Most importantly, a brand's proposition needs to create "a positive emotional attachment to the brand which creates a response in its audience" (Bloise, n.d.).

In contrast to traditional concepts of brand awareness, which stress a brand's functionality, more recent notions of emotional branding emphasize the development of personal relationships between consumers and the brand, based on desire, cultural connection, and unique imagery (Gobe & Zyman, 2001). According to Elliott (1997), the symbolic meanings of products are oriented both outward, toward constructing the social world, and inward, toward constructing self-identity. If we apply this line of thinking to cultural products that reference the "global" and "local"—as SSG did—we could argue that the construction of the "social world" references the imagined international community and the construction of "self-identity" references the local (national) identity. Next, I examine how these constructions were utilized visually, verbally, and musically in the first SSG compilation CD.

The cover art of the first SSG CD (2000) featured glass jars filled with pickled vegetables juxtaposed with images of musical instruments, made to appear as if they were also packaged inside the jars. The jars do not have industrial covers, but are instead closed with a cloth tied with a rubber band. The jars are photographed on top of a crocheted lace doily, an example of old-fashioned handiwork. These images strongly reference the locality: both what is considered Serbian and what is considered "old-fashioned," "traditional," "of and from the village." All are also products, packaged (but homemade) goods. Thus, even before hearing the music, the visual elements provide potential customers with clues as to what they might expect to find on this recording. In spite of the connection with "the global" in the title, the music is not going to reflect widespread global trends (such as techno, electronica, rap, or rock genres), but, rather, would present something uniquely local, just as the visual elements indicate.

The title *Srbija: Sounds Global* adds to the intrigue of the brand message. First, it brings together two geographic/political/economic entities—Serbia and "the world"—which had been sharply opposed in the nationalistic discourses of the 1990s and closely aligned in the rock 'n' roll resistance movement.[12] In this way, the title alludes to the end of Serbia's cultural and political isolation and announces new hopes and new beginnings. The spelling used is also significant. Spelling the country's name using the local version (Srbija) instead of the internationally accepted one (Serbia) emphasizes a local voice and sends a message that, despite the English title, this is an album for Serbian listeners as well. The title implies not only that Serbia has something to offer to the world but that it is a part of that world as it participates in global trends through the world music genre.

In addition to being performed in spaces previously reserved for urban music genres (classical, jazz, and rock music), SSG was the first album of its kind to be produced by the ultimate urban label, B92. Merging the urban and rural in this manner represented a powerful shift from having the original locality as a marker of identity: rural music had become a symbol of urban identity.[13] This rural-meets-urban phenomenon reflects a positive emotional attachment to the brand on a large scale: a new cultural identity symbolic enough and ambiguous enough that it could engage both urban and rural populations in Serbia.[14] This also reflects the notion, expressed by marketing scholar Douglas Holt, that successful brands "target powerful ideological contradictions produced by society" (Lagace, 2002). In merging "urban" and "rural," SSG provided a sort of symbolic reconciliation of the ideological opposition of urban/cosmopolitan versus rural/nationalist orientations. In addition to being key to the success of SSG as a brand, this synthesis proved to be very appealing to Serbian politicians.

The phrase "Srbija sounds global" quickly became popular among politicians who co-opted it in their own efforts to associate Serbia with a more positive image. For example, at the conference of the European Ministers of Culture held in Croatia in October 2003, Serbian Minister of Culture Branislav Lečić discussed the various roles of cultural industries in the development of Serbian society. While he talked extensively about industries receiving governmental support, including cinema, publishing, and the music industry, the only two music projects he mentioned by name were *Srbija: Sounds Global* and *Aven Romalen*.[15] Lečić specifically emphasized the importance of the SSG concerts, stating that they "promoted the musical diversity of Serbia" and had "enormous success in breaking many prejudices and taboos" (Lečić, 2003). Similarly, Goran Svilanović, chairman of Working Table I of the Stability Pact for South Eastern Europe, stated at the Pact's 12th plenary session:

> There are so many heritages for which we can say with certainty that are a part of the regional identity, but it would be hard to determine where exactly they originated . . . Serbia sounds global, both at EXIT and in Guča, regardless of personal taste. (Svilanović, 2005)

However, the most prominent example of SSG's political co-optation— and one that made international news—came from an interaction in 2005 between Serbian President Boris Tadić and the popular U.S. band R.E.M. Not only did Tadić attend R.E.M.'s concert in Belgrade and request a favorite song, but he and the band's front man, Michael Stipe, exchanged gifts. Stipe presented Tadić with a copy of R.E.M.'s new CD and Tadić gave him a copy of a *Srbija: Sounds Global* CD, saying he hoped "the exotic sound might inspire new hits" (Associated Press, 2005). This intercultural exchange did not remain an isolated case. At the request of the Serbian government, SSG CDs have been distributed to all foreign embassies in Belgrade and used as gifts to visiting foreign dignitaries (personal interview with Bojan Djordjević, December 29, 2006).[16]

Arjun Appadurai (2002) contests the idea that "the local"—as the opposite of "the global"—is an "inert canvas" (p. 33) upon which globalization impresses various effects. He argues that locality is as much a process as globalization is and states that "any form of local social life requires agency, purpose, vision, design" (p. 33). The agency, purpose, vision, and design that Appadurai alludes to are exemplified in the project *Srbija: Sounds Global*. If we understand imagination as a social practice, a "collective tool for the transformation of the real" (p. 34), we can perceive how the locality is produced as much through the work of the imagination as through the work of material social construction. Functioning "as a kind of expansion of the horizon of the local" (p. 34), the global—in this case both the global expansion of branding and of the "world music" industry—created an opening for imagining a different, better, harmonious Serbia. Nevertheless, in reality this imagining does not necessarily result in a better and harmonious Serbia. Thus, we should be cautious not to mistake the ability of music to influence a nation's international image for a lack of political and cultural tensions within the nation. These underlying tensions reemerged in the discourses around the two music festivals—Guča and EXIT—which I discuss next.

GUČA AND EXIT: BRANDS IN CONFLICT

National identity, traditions, and their global representations continued to be debated within Serbia in relation to two music festivals—Guča and EXIT—with different program orientations. Functioning as brands long before they were co-opted by brand consultants and politicians, the festivals sparked numerous debates about their appropriateness for representing Serbia globally. Summarizing the symbolic positions of the two festivals in Serbian culture, Lukić-Krstanović (2008) states:

> During the times of crisis and transition in Serbia, the Dragačevo festival of trumpeters [Guča] and EXIT festival were incorporated into current politics and the creation of the whole corpus of values and lifestyles. In a way, they represented ambivalent sides of Serbia, one which glorifies the national-folklore tradition, and the other which remains on the positions of urban underground culture. Circulation between local and global has given these festivals the role of promoters, but also authenticators of an image of society in Serbia. (p. 139)

Thus, an analysis of Guča and EXIT can bring to light the complexity of nation branding and identity construction through music.

The full name of the music festival known as Guča is *Dragačevski Sabor Trubača* (Dragačevo Festival of Trumpeters). Held in the small town of Guča in central Serbia, the festival was founded in 1961 by a group of enthusiasts—writers, journalists, teachers, musicians—who wanted to preserve the tradition of trumpet (brass band) playing characteristic of this region (Timotijević, 2005). In addition to brass band performances and a trumpet competition, there were exhibitions of traditional songs and dances, costumes, handiwork, as well as traditional competitions in physical activities among men (e.g., shooting the wedding apple, or jousting).

While distinctly local in character, the festival was popularized extensively through the Yugoslav media since its inception, as well as by some foreign televisions (Italian RAI in 1965, Soviet Television in 1977, and

Japanese Hokkaido Broadcasting TV in 1979). However, only with the success of Goran Bregović's music for Emir Kusturica's films *Time of the Gypsies* (1988) and *Underground* (1995) did the Serbian brass band festival become popular worldwide. Music writer and journalist Garth Cartwright (2009) dubbed it "one of Europe's most popular and wildest festivals" and argued that it "captures the big, bold Balkan spirit perfectly."

Serbian politicians recognized the potential of the Guča festival for promoting Serbia due to its international appeal. In 2004, President Boris Tadić visited the festival, and the Ministry of Culture was its official sponsor. In 2006, Minister of Trade and Tourism Bojan Dimitrijević formally opened the festival and stated that it is "the biggest Serbian brand on international stage" ("Otvoren 46 Dragačevski Sabor," 2006). The same year, marketing agency PROFILE was hired to "elevate" the Guča festival to a "much higher level." The president of the agency, Milan Ristić (2006), stated:

> Our main goal and main task was, first of all, to establish a long-term basis for forming (repositioning) and leading this original, Serbian brand . . . The main elements of the concept are: Guča—the world capital of trumpet, folk (traditional) creativity, having fun, and freedom of emotions. (p. 9)

Acknowledging that Guča could play a part in improving the international image of Serbia, he added that the festival could communicate "the identity and values of Serbian people" (p. 10). Citing focus research conducted in five large Serbian cities, Ristić elaborated that

> Guča is an original, national (Serbian) brand, regardless of whether we talk with Guča fans or Guča detractors. For both of them, Guča is a picture of Serbia. The fans of trumpet see Serbia as relaxed, cheerful, open-hearted, hospitable, traditional, unspoiled [*neizvestacenu*], "real," simple, and positive. (p. 10)

The idea that the Guča brand could stand in for "Brand Serbia," provoked significant controversy, especially when it was rearticulated in a speech by then Prime Minister Vojislav Koštunica at the closing ceremony of the 46th festival in 2006. Elaborating on the relationship between Serbia, trumpet, and national identity, Koštunica stated:

> Guča represents in a best way what Serbia is today, its openness, belief in oneself, hospitality, party and music. [The] trumpet festival is a confirmation of our courage and joy, both in good and bad times . . . It speaks about who we are, what we are, [it relates] our urges. We express our joy and sadness with trumpet, we are born with sounds of trumpet, and also buried with sounds of trumpet. *Guča is [a] Serbian brand, it's a value that can represent Serbia in the world.* Those that

cannot understand and love Guča, cannot understand Serbia. (Cited in Bojić, 2006, emphasis mine)

This speech prompted a number of dramatic public reactions. For example, an article posted on B92's website quoted prominent Belgrade journalist Teofil Pančić and historian Branka Prpa, who sharply criticized the idea that Guča should stand in for Serbia. Pančić referred to the festival as "a parade of drunkenness and slush presented as an original Serbian identity," while Prpa commented that what was problematic in Koštunica's speech was the attempt to present the festival as "something essentially and authentically Serbian" ("Drunkenness and Slush," 2006). These criticisms were echoed in the blogosphere. A blogger who identified himself as Viktor posted the following:

> You don't have to love trumpet and Guča to understand Serbia. You don't even have to know what Guča is to love Serbia. Because Guča is far from [the] only thing that can represent Serbia, and that is exactly what the prime minister is clumsily trying to make out of it. ("Guča—Not the Only Serbian Brand," 2006)

These responses identify the most problematic aspect of the political efforts to co-opt the festival for the purposes of a unified national brand—namely, agreeing on a brand image that is both "authentic" and representative of the cultural variety of a country's "national essence." In the case of Serbia, attempts to narrow down the meaning of the national brand are particularly controversial given the country's history of conflict.

Similar challenges also emerged in the case of EXIT. The EXIT festival began in 2000 as a series of free concerts, film projections, parties, and theater shows organized by a group of students in Novi Sad as a form of protest and a countdown of the last days of Milošević's regime. The festival's website provides the following statement: "The last concert, on September 22, 2000, two days before the presidential election, with the message "*Gotov je*" ["He is finished"] in front of about 20,000 visitors, symbolically represented the EXIT from the decade-long madness" ("EXIT 00," n.d.).

Since then, EXIT has become an international festival that annually brings in 150,000 to 200,000 visitors, with music centered around British and U.S. performers,[17] but with offerings in numerous other genres, illustrated through the names of the various stages—Balkan Fusion Stage, Reggae Stage, Blues & Jazz, Electronic Culture Space, Metal Hammer, Latino, and so on. EXIT also continually provides a platform for nongovernmental organizations to campaign against drug abuse, ethnic intolerance, and human trafficking. Bojan Bošković, general manager of the festival and one of its founders, stated that one of EXIT's goals was to change the image of Serbia:

I want people to come here and discover a Serbia of young and friendly people, who are highly educated and not afraid of questioning their leaders . . . We are still trying to fight a lot of negative stereotypes in this part of the world . . . EXIT will keep up the fight—until the very end. (Quoted in Arun, 2006)

The Serbian government started supporting EXIT when it realized the international significance of the festival. In 2006, the Ministry of Finance signed a contract to sponsor the development of EXIT until 2010. Minister of Finance Mladjan Dinkić said at the signing: "EXIT is truly a Serbian brand and it needs to be an important element in the Serbian budget" ("Ministarstvo finansija," 2006).

EXIT achieved even greater international recognition in 2007 when it was named "Best European Festival"—an award given by Festival Awards UK, based on votes submitted by fans from around the world ("EGZIT dobio nagradu," 2007). The following year it was included in *The Guardian*'s annual guide to the most exciting destinations and events as "one of the most attractive festivals in Europe" (Madigan, 2008).

A study, conducted in 2006 to document the extent to which EXIT contributes to a positive image of Serbia internationally, showed that a majority of respondents reported they had come to the festival because of a friend's recommendation and they had experienced positive interactions between the locals and international visitors (Zakić, Ivkov-Džigurski, & Ćurčić, 2009). Specifically, the study revealed that "the interaction between foreign and domestic visitors resulted in better understanding of Serbian culture and hospitality, increased knowledge about the country, people, and their customs" (Zakić et al., 2009, p. 100). Additionally, the adjectives that foreign visitors used to describe the locals were *friendly, hospitable, nice, like to have fun,* and, *seem happy* (Zakić et al., 2009, p.100).

At the same time, EXIT has entered international political discourse as well. Olli Rehn, member of the European Commission Responsible for Enlargement, visited EXIT in 2006 together with Serbian President Boris Tadić, where they talked about lifting visa restrictions for Serbian citizens. Later that year, at an event organized by the European Policy Center and the King Baudouin Foundation in Brussels, Rehn (2006) stated:

I participated in the EXIT festival with people from the Western Balkans that you probably know . . . Created in 2000 as a symbol of exit of the dictatorship of Milošević and exit from the nationalist past, a great and very well organized festival, mainly by young people, and we had very good discussions there and the key issue for them is, apart from seeing the EU as a ticket to freedom and democracy, key issue was cheaper and easy access to visas because young people want to travel, to expand their perspectives. In the situation where 70 percent of Serbian students have not travelled abroad, we have to be concerned and we have to create conditions for the Europeanization of the next generation in Serbia and the other countries of the Western Balkans.

Rehn mentioned the festival again, and showed the plaque "Citizen of State of EXIT," at a press conference in Brussels in December 2009, when an official decision was announced to abolish visas for Serbian citizens at the end of the year. This gesture was a significant one—it showed that a particular representation of Serbia through the festival could potentially have far-reaching political consequences.

Besides the politicians' statements, the idea that Guča and EXIT are the best Serbian brands has been echoed in many other places, from online-forums to polls by dailies and professional branding magazines. In her study of EXIT and Guča as spectacles, Lukić-Krstanović (2008) states that the "circulation between local and global has given these festivals the role of promoters, but also authenticators of an image of society in Serbia" (p. 138). What has been debated, however, is the kind of image that is most appropriate to represent Serbia. Here is where the contestations of national identity representations come into place. On the one hand, Guča is presented as a bearer of rural, authentic, and national tradition, whereas EXIT is its opposite—an urban, multicultural, and cosmopolitan event. As one blogger, identified as Jasmina, stated, "Here in Serbia, nowadays, you can often hear the discussion about what 'the real face of Serbia' is like? Is it the EXIT festival or Guča? Is Serbia urban and modern like Belgrade, . . . or rural and traditional like the rest of the country?" (quoted in Bojić, 2006).[18]

In their analysis of the relationship between nationhood, national and cultural identity, and place branding, Skinner and Kubacki (2007) state that branding countries is problematic, because "a nation is itself difficult to define, and its brand values are so difficult to identify and therefore to communicate" (p. 312). Achieving a consensus on what the "essence" of the brand is or should be, and yet avoiding stereotyping has proven to be extremely difficult for most nations attempting to brand themselves. This is primarily because there is no "essence" of a nation, unless we are dealing with stereotypes. National identity, like any other form of identity, is not a fixed construct but exists within a dynamic environment, is changeable, and is changing in different contexts and at different times (p. 310).

Critical ethnography teaches us that identity is "mixed, relational, and inventive" (Clifford, 1988, p. 10). The two main positions on social (and national) identity—the essentialist and the constructivist—argue for "durable qualities, characteristics of a group that are thought to exist from time immemorial" on the one hand, and for "contingent, fragile, unstable, and changeable" identities, on the other (Rice, 2007, p. 24). Constructivist thought has greatly contributed to the deconstruction—if not the destruction—of "grand narratives," leading some political analysts to argue that country branding is a replacement for nationalism (van Ham, 2001). In reality, however, essentialist narratives of national identity are still prominent in Serbia and many other post-communist countries. However, there is an increasing awareness of the role politicians play in sustaining specific views of national identity. One blogger's comment illustrates this awareness:

> We need to condemn politicians who use those [music] festivals for propaganda purposes, as well as any other political utilization [of traditional and popular events] . . . all of these EXIT-Guča polemics are an indication of a distressful division of our people, as well as a reflection of an unexplainable need for that allotment. (Quoted in Bojić, 2006)

Serbian historian Branko Radun argues that reducing Serbian culture to EXIT and Guča is not realistic, because "there are many of those who belong to both, as well as those who don't identify with either of these two options" (Radun, 2007).[19] At the same time, government brand advisors insist that Serbia needs a unified brand image. In an interview for the daily newspaper *Blic*, Srba Jovanović, member of the Executive Council of the Public Relations Society of Serbia and vice president of consulting firm Hauska & Partner International Communications for Serbia, states that it is essential to define Serbian identity:

> It is necessary to find the most positive elements of identity—such as people's hospitality, excellent food, cosmopolitan atmosphere, educated youth, [and] their promotion, as well as the promotions of the events such as EXIT or Guča. (Cvejić & Čaluković, 2006)

Thus, the dichotomies between urban and rural, cosmopolitan and national, global and local, and their attendant positive and negative attributes in Serbian political and cultural discourse are generally ignored by politicians and branding experts as they look for unifying brand messages.

GOVERNMENT EFFORTS AT NATION BRANDING

The Serbian government has invested considerably in nation branding initiatives throughout the past decade. These include annual Brand Fairs featuring internationally renowned branding gurus, such as Simon Anholt, Wally Olins, and Mark Gobe; costly branding commercials on CNN; numerous smaller scale projects and events; and the creation of two local bodies for country brand development—the Council for Branding Serbia (composed of non-paid professionals from various fields) established in 2007, and the Group for National Brand of Serbia within the Ministry of Trade and Services. Without attempting to list all the initiatives and projects, this section will focus on the few controversial aspects of nation branding, including the inequalities existing between the various governmental agencies, controversial projects, and the contradictions inherent in the nation branding discourse.

My interviews with Milica Čuburilo, current member of the Council for Branding Serbia and former president of the Serbian Tourist Organization, and Ivan Tasovac, current president of the Council for Branding Serbia and director of the Belgrade Philharmonic, revealed the complexities of working on nation branding projects in terms of hierarchical power-wielding within governmental institutions. Both of them stated that the government viewed the Council for Branding Serbia as an afterthought and that there was no vision, no coordination between various governmental bodies, and no strategic plan of action. This is best illustrated by two examples of unsuccessful nation branding projects by the Serbian government. In 2006 the Ministry of International Economic Relations published an ad in *The Financial Times*, looking for an adviser in the strategic planning of a new image for Serbia. This created quite a controversy, in part because of the fact that due to certain requirements no Serbian agency could apply.

Another controversial example involves the Ministry of Trade and Tourism's promotional campaign, consisting of two video commercials, titled "The Sights and Sounds of Serbia." The spots were supposed to be played 507 times in the course of four months on CNN in 2007, at the cost of a half million Euros. The commercials, produced by CNN's production team from materials sent from Serbia, had glaring errors in visual and musical representation.[20] They were heavily criticized and ridiculed in Serbia (Bizinger, 2007; Čuburilo, personal interview, January 18, 2010). However, Strahinja Djuričanin, the newly appointed chairman of the Group for National Brand of Serbia within the Ministry of Trade and Services (formed at the end of 2007), argued that the government is taking the lessons learned through these sporadic efforts seriously and is in the process of developing a long-term strategic plan, which would be based on a comprehensive research of public opinion and foreign and domestic markets (personal interview, December 28, 2009).

Even when a positive impression is created—through successful, government-sponsored events—such as the Eurovision Song Contest in 2008, or the Summer Universiade in 2009—the effect is more a by-product of a short-term effort than a result of a vision and clearly set goals.[21] Similarly, the follow-up is generally nonexistent. However, politicians are quick to claim as a "true Serbian brand" and "the best thing to represent us to the world" anything that proves successful on its own, such as SSG, Guča, and EXIT.

Within the world of nation brand consulting itself, there is disagreement as to how to choose and position a nation's brand. Some hold that nation branding has to address the needs of different audiences in different ways, and thus include separate brands for trade and tourism ("Country Branding Consultant," 2009). Others assert that by doing so, brands work at cross-purposes:

You have the tourism board saying how wonderful the country looks and how welcoming the people are. You have the investment-promotion agency saying almost the opposite, that it's super modern and full of cars and roads and railways. And you have the cultural institute telling everybody how wonderful the film industry is. And you have the government occasionally doing public diplomacy, and perhaps occasionally attacking its neighbors. They're all giving off completely different messages about the country. (Anholt, quoted in Teslik, n.d.)

From the point of view of nation branding consultants, the fact that the Serbian government seems to have lacked both a unified vision and a clear strategy for promoting Serbia as a brand throughout the past decade is perceived as a failure. On the other hand, instituting a top-down unified message that should be presenting a new vision of a country's identity both internally and externally is too reminiscent of communist ideological projects. Furthermore, the notion that a unified vision, image, and a message that a country should use to represent itself to the world would "supplant nationalism" and contribute to pacification of Europe (van Ham, 2001), masks the political and economic inequalities of the global playing field. This discourse ignores the disadvantages of small emerging countries in terms of their financial resources as well as their unique historical and political contexts.

More specifically, Serbia is still dealing with the aftermath of the political situation of the 1990s, with political corruption, economic inequalities, and rebuilding of infrastructure destroyed during the preceding decade. While Strahinja Djuričanin expressed his optimism about the success of nation branding campaigns, which may take 10 or 20 years to (possibly) bring results, for the majority of Serbian citizens that might be too late. In light of reports that the disillusionment of young professionals in terms of their future in Serbia has reached a level comparable to the harshest years of the 1990s,[22] investing millions of Euros in long-term nation branding campaigns, which may or may not bring the desired results, might not garner the public support that nation brand consultants argue is crucial for the success of a national brand.

This is not to devalue the work of creative individuals and organizations that come up with various projects that are positively changing the image of Serbia on an international level, including the work of a number of nongovernmental organizations within the country as well as the Serbian Institute for Public Diplomacy in Brussels.[23] It is difficult, however, to assess a lasting effect or significance that all these processes will have on Serbia. On the one hand, they seem to be isolated events without too many unifying forces. On the other hand, their cumulative effect may be more beneficial than any unified and artificial top-down approach. Because their effect depends on the various mini-crises that influence the stability in the region, it is hard to determine whether any of these cultural events are able to not only change the picture of the Serbian past but also compete with the negative events and images of the present.

CONCLUSION

The mélange of discussions about national identity and nation branding in Serbia, while influenced by globalization discourses (where the very idea of branding is now taken for granted), have also attracted an unprecedented level of interest among ordinary citizens. Although the construction of national identities and brands is still very much controlled by elites, the number of different viewpoints shared and accessible through the media is greater than ever. The fact that many of these discussions in Serbia began as discussions about music, and continue to revolve around music, testifies to music's power to affect issues of representations, narrations, and mediations of national identity.

In addition, the analysis of music projects and festivals in this chapter reveals that, while the opposition between urban/cosmopolitan and rural/nationalistic narratives of identity is still important for some Serbs, there are also new narratives that attempt its, however imperfect, synthesis or transcendence. There is no consensus as to whether the turn to Serbian world music is led only by market demands or whether it is a part of the state's cultural policies. Some believe that Serbia today has no clearly defined and consistent cultural policy to speak of (Radun, 2007); others argue that the turn toward redefining Serbia through world music is an important but hidden part of cultural policy, a very useful tool for local politicians and institutions who promote the ideology of transformation (Nenić, 2006, p. 120). Through investigating musical sites of production of meaning, and the importance of history and tradition in that process, I hope to have illustrated the significance of music as a symbolic practice with a potentially powerful political influence.

Music's performativity and its participatory nature allow for strong emotional experiences that branding experts find crucial for any brand's success. Although governmental planning and building of a unified national image and brand have gathered momentum, the immediacy, longevity, and availability of music projects—such as *Srbija Sounds Global*, Guča, and EXIT—have already contributed to the processes of positive national transformation. This is not to suggest that these projects have put Serbian national identity debates to rest. I would argue, however, that the lack of resolution on that account is a positive development, because a total consensus about a picture-perfect national identity could only be achieved through top-down, repressive approaches. Thus, the importance of the music projects discussed here lies, in part, in their continued relevance for furthering discussions about identity in ways that state-sponsored nation branding projects do not. Music practices and discourses in response to SSG, Guča, and EXIT continue to open up spaces for problematizing ideological and hegemonic state narratives of identity in unprecedented ways, while at the same time attracting positive international attention. They serve as examples that the seductive discourse of nation branding has alternatives.

NOTES

1. Here I do not discuss government policies in relation to other musical genres, such as jazz and rock. For a discussion of this topic, see, for example, Žikić (1999) and Lučić-Todosić (2002).
2. There were some exceptions to this orientation in the rock genre (most vocally expressed by Bora Čorba, front man of the band Riblja Čorba), which has prompted some to argue that this polarization did not exist or was not important (Djurković, 2001, 2004).
3. The latter tendency was in spite of the fact that many newly composed folk songs were, unbeknownst to Serbian audiences, imports from Iran, Turkey, and Greece, with Serbian lyrics. It is not unusual for people to believe that a song "belongs" to them (to their nation), based on the fact that the lyrics reference something local, as was dramatically shown in Adela Peeva's 2003 documentary *Čija je ovo pesen?* [Whose is this song?] and researched by Buchanan (2008).
4. Examples of performers in these genres include Miloš Petrović with his project *History of Byzantium*, Dragomir Milenković Joga with band Hazari, Moba, Braća Teofilovići, Bora Dugić, Drina, Belo Platno, Ognjen i Prijatelji, Bilja Krstić and Bistrik, Sanja Ilić and Balkanika, Slobodan Trkulja and Balkanopolis, Svetlana Spajić, and others. Performers from other genres also included some "ethno" elements in their music. Examples include Jovan Maljoković and Vlada Maričić in jazz and Madam Piano in pop.
5. Importantly, these kinds of narratives of Serbian identity did not receive governmental support, which was reserved for a more dramatic form of Serbianness (see Hudson, 2007).
6. This sentiment was shared by a number of musicians I interviewed, including Braća Teofilovići (interviewed on November 5, 2001), Dragomir Milenković Joga from Hazari (interviewed on October 20, 2001), Bojan Djordjević (interviewed on December 29, 2006), and Jelena Jovanović from Moba (interviewed on January 6, 2010).
7. Two festivals—Ring Ring (1996) and Ethnomus Project (1997)—and the Serbian World Music Association (1997) were the first locally organized, bottom-up efforts to promote this music genre. However, they had limited success on a larger scale (Nenić, 2006).
8. B92 is comprised of a radio and TV station, music, film, and video production, and a publishing department. It began as a student radio station in 1989 and became famous for independent news reporting, alternative music broadcasts, and strong opposition to the Milošević regime (see also "B92 Company Profile," n.d.; Collin, 2001; Gordy, 1999).
9. For audio samples from the four SSG CDs see http://www.international-records.com/b92.html
10. For a discussion of the terminology of "ethno" versus "world" music, see Čolović (2006), Golemović (2004), and Marković (2004).
11. The album was reviewed in the leading liberal political weekly magazine *Vreme*, the reputable weekly news magazine *Nin*, the news dailies *Blic*, *Danas*, and *Politika*, in the weekly *Radio TV Revija*, and even in the Croatian biweekly "for cultural and social happenings" *Zarez*.

12. The term "the world" in Yugoslav cultural and political discourse, used in intellectual debates and in colloquial speech, indicates more than the geopolitical importance of the surroundings. During the 1990s, it was used by extreme nationalists as a symbol for all that was decadent, while it symbolized progress for those of cosmopolitan orientation. The phrase "we and the world" was transformed to the prison-speech lingo "inside and outside." The contrast of the "inside" and "outside" was not just geographical (where Serbia, with its borders effectively closed off by UN sanctions, was the "inside"), but cultural as well. While extreme nationalist discourses attempted to distance Serbia from "the world," student protesters in 1996–1997 emphasized Serbia's connectedness to the international community with a banner stating, "Belgrade is the world" (see Marović, 2006), later remembered and quoted as "Serbia is the world."

13. The rural/urban dichotomy can certainly be problematized further, especially in relation to newly composed folk and turbo-folk; however, this is beyond the scope of this chapter.

14. This is evidenced by the common presence of both types of audience members at concerts of these genres, which I have witnessed personally in the past decade.

15. *Aven Romalen* began in 2002 as a series of concerts representing Romani culture, presented by B92 in collaboration with the Serbian Ministry of Culture. It has since included a series of CDs by various Roma artists, presented both individually and in compilations such as *Romano Suno*.

16. The rediscovery of the "forgotten" Serbian heritage is a contested terrain in terms of topics and governmental support (see Hudson, 2007). In contrast to authors who emphasize institutional support for traditional culture without elaborating on the interests of individual actors (Hofman, 2007), I wish to emphasize the "bottom-up" efforts of musicians. My interviews with numerous performers confirm that their interest in traditional music predated institutional support and guided their work at a time when this music was far from popular.

17. Participants have included Prodigy, Franz Ferdinand, Arctic Monkeys, Basement Jaxx, Beastie Boys, Groove Armada, Robert Plant, Snoop Dog, Wu-Tang Clan, Gogol Bordello, Nightwish, Kraftwerk, Lily Allen, Grandmaster Flash, Korn, and others.

18. A recent illustration of this sentiment is an article by Serbian author Aleksandar Kocić, titled "Guča or Exit: Battle of Brands Serbian style" (Kocić, 2010).

19. For an extended discussion of this position, see also Simić (2007) and Hofman (2008).

20. The initial videos showed parts of Romania and used Kazakhstani music. The video with Kazakhstani music played for a month, before reporters from the newspaper *Blic* noticed this ("Dobra gledanost," 2007).

21. Interestingly, in contrast to earlier years, the winning song that brought Eurovision to Serbia was a typical, American-style pop ballad without any national, regional, or ethnic characteristics.

22. Recent research shows that two-thirds of Serbian students wish to leave the country upon graduation ("Dve trecine studenata napustilo bi Srbiju," 2010).

23. The Serbian Institute for Public Diplomacy in Brussels is a nonprofit organization focused on the relations between Serbia and the European Union, which has done a number of significant international campaigns and projects.

REFERENCES

Ambrozić, D. (2003, January 23). Novi standardi na srpskoj rok sceni: Iznenadjenja Novih Pokoljenja [New standards on Serbian rock scene: Surprises by new generations]. *Vreme, 629.* Retrieved September 12, 2010, from http://www.vreme.com/cms/view.php?id=331487

Appadurai, A. (2002). The right to participate in the work of the imagination. In J. Brouwer & A. Mulder (Eds.), *TransUrbanism* (pp. 33–46). Rotterdam, Netherlands: V2_Publishing/NAI.

Arun, N. (2006, July 6). Festival helps Serbia exit the past. *BBC NEWS: Europe.* Retrieved September 12, 2010, from http://news.bbc.co.uk/2/hi/europe/5153256.stm

Associated Press. (2005, January 21). *Serbian president says he's an R.E.M. fan.* Retrieved September 12, 2010, from http://new.accessnorthga.com/detail.php?n=153024&c=2

B92 Company Profile. (n.d.). Retrieved August 24, 2010, from http://www.b92.net/doc/aboutus.phtml

Bizinger, D. (2007, January 10). *Video spot Srbije na CNN-u* [Serbian video spot on CNN]. Retrieved September 17, 2010, from http://blog.b92.net/arhiva/node/3746.html

Bloise, J. (n.d.). *Successful brand development.* Retrieved August 30, 2010, from http://www.powerhomebiz.com/vol102/brand.htm

Bojić, L. (2006). Serbia: Guča and Exit Music Festivals. *Global Voices.* Retrieved September 15, 2010, from http://www.globalvoicesonline.org/2006/09/14/serbia-Guča-and-EXIT-music-festivals

Buchanan, D. A. (2006). *Performing democracy: Bulgarian music and musicians in transition.* Chicago: University of Chicago Press.

Buchanan, D. A. (2008). Oh, those Turks! Music, politics, and interculturality in the Balkans and beyond. In D. A. Buchanan (Ed.), *Balkan popular culture and the Ottoman Ecumene: Music, image, and regional political discourse* (pp. 3–56). Lanham, MD: Scarecrow Press.

Cartwright, G. (2009, May 23). Europe's wildest party. *The Guardian.* Retrieved September 12, 2010, from http://www.guardian.co.uk/travel/2009/may/23/guca-balkan-serbia-festival-party?page=2

Clifford, J. (1988). *The predicament of culture.* Cambridge, MA: Harvard University Press.

Collin, M. (2001). *This is Serbia calling: Rock 'n' roll radio and Belgrade's underground resistance.* London: Serpent's Tail.

Čolović, I. (2006). *Etno* [Ethno]. Belgrade, Serbia: Biblioteka XX Vek.

Concert series. Serbia sounds global: A living tradition. (n.d.). Retrieved August 30, 2010, from http://rexold.b92.net/zivatradicija/eng/index.html

Country branding consultant Jose Filipe Torres on branding Serbia. (2009). Retrieved September 17, 2010, from http://nation-branding.info/2009/03/18/country-branding-consultant-jose-filipe-torres-branding-serbia

Cvejić, M., & Čaluković, N. (2006, August 5). Kako svet da zavoli Srbiju [How to make the world fall in love with Serbia]. *Blic.* Retrieved December 4, 2010, from http://www.blic.rs/stara_arhiva/tema/116198/Kako-svet-da-zavoli-Srbiju

Djordjević, B., & Mitić, M. (2005, November). Language of music. *CoRD, 21,* 64–65.

Djurković, M. (2001). *Kulturna industrija i problem nacionalnog identiteta: Slučaj popularne muzike u Srbiji* [Cultural industry and the national identity problem: The case of popular music in Serbia]. Paper presented at Colloquium 292 organized by the Institute for Philosophy and Social Theory, Belgrade. Retrieved June 13, 2010, from http://147.91.230.48/ifdt/tribina/Predavanja/Trib292/prilozi/index.html#_ftnref10

Djurković, M. (2004). Ideological and political conflicts over popular music in Serbia. *Philosophy and Society, 2,* 271–279.

Dobra gledanost reklame na CNN [Good viewership for CNN ad]. (2007, March 13). *Blic.* Retrieved December 4, 2010, from http://www.blic.rs/stara_arhiva/drustvo/147698/Dobra-gledanost-reklame-na-CNN

"Drunkenness and Slush" in Guča. (2006, September 3). Retrieved September 17, 2010, from http://www.b92.net/eng/news/society-article.php?yyyy=2006&mm=09&dd=03&nav_category=126&nav_id=36470

Dve trecine studenata napustilo bi Srbiju [Two-thirds of students want to leave Serbia]. (2010, May 14). *Blic.* Retrieved September 18, 2010, from http://www.blic.rs/Vesti/Drustvo/189322/Dve-trecine-studenata-napustilo-bi-Srbiju

EGZIT dobio nagradu za najbolji evropski festival [EXIT received award as the best European festival] (2007, November 7). *Clubbing.rs.* Retrieved September 12, 2010, from http://www.clubbing.rs/exit-dobio-nagradu-za-najbolji-evropski-festival

Elliott, R. (1997). Existential consumption and irrational desire. *European Journal of Marketing, 31*(3/4), 285–296.

EXIT 00. (n.d.). *EXIT Festival History.* Retrieved June 15, 2010, from http://www.EXITfest.org/index.php?option=com_content&task=view&id=2560&Itemid=309

Gobe, M., & Zyman, S. (2001). *Emotional branding: The new paradigm for connecting brands to people.* New York: Allworth Press.

Golemović, D. (1994). Srpsko pevanje u proslosti i sadasnjosti/Djete, kako da pjevam, kad trijes' godina nijesam usta otvorila? [Serbian singing in the past and today: Child, how can I sing when I haven't opened my mouth in thirty years?]. *Glasnik EI SANU, 43,* 119–121.

Golemović, D. (2004). World music. *Novi Zvuk, 24,* 41–47.

Gordy, E. (1999). *The culture of power in Serbia: Nationalism and the destruction of alternatives.* University Park: Pennsylvania State University.

Gordy, E. (2005). Reflecting on *The Culture of Power,* ten years on. *Facta Universitatis: Series Philosophy, Sociology and Psychology, 4*(1), 11–19.

Guča—not the only Serbian brand. (2006, September 5). *Serbia Blog.* Retrieved September 12, 2010, from http://serbiablog.blogspot.com/2006/09/Guča-not-only-serbian-brand.html

Hofman, A. (2007). Tradicionalna kultura i dinamike oblikovanja nacionalnog identiteta u post-socijalističkoj Srbiji [Traditional culture and dynamic of forming national identity in post-socialist Serbia]. In L. Mitrović, D. Zaharijevski, & D. Gavrilović (Eds.), *Identiteti i Kultura Mira u Procesima Globalizacije i Regionalizacije Balkana* [Identities and the culture of peace in globalization and regionalization processes on the Balkans] (pp. 95–100). Niš, Serbia: Filozofski Fakultet—Centar za Sociološka Istraživanja.

Hofman, A. (2008).Urbano, civilizovano, evropski: EXIT festival u Novom Sadu [Urban, civilized, European: EXIT festival in Novi Sad]. Paper presented at the Conference of the Croatian Ethnological Society, *Instrumentiranje grada: Glasbe, gradovi, politike* [Orchestrating the city: Music, cities, politics], Zagreb, Croatia.

Hudson, R. (2007). Popular music, tradition and Serbian nationalism. In I. Biddle & V. Knights (Eds.), *Music, national identity and the politics of location: Between the global and the local* (pp. 161–178). Surrey, UK: Ashgate.

Kocić, A. (2010, April 1). Guča or EXIT—Battle of brands Serbian style. *Suite101.com.* Retrieved December 4, 2010, from http://www.suite101.com/content/guca-vs-exit-a220536

Lagace, M. (2002). Building "brandtopias"—how top brands tap into society: An interview with Douglas Holt. *Harvard Business School: Working Knowledge for Business Leaders.* Retrieved June 13, 2010, from http://hbswk.hbs.edu/item/2985.html

Lečić, B. (2003, October 20–22). *From conflict to reconciliation: Examples of good practice*. Speech delivered at the Conference of the European Ministers of Culture, Opatija, Croatia. Retrieved August 31, 2010, from http://www.coe.int/T/E/Com/Files/Ministerial-Conferences/2003-Culture/disc_Lecic.asp

Lučić-Todosić, I. (2002). *Od trokinga do tvista: Igranke u Beogradu 1945–1963*. [From trocking to twist: Dances in Belgrade 1945–1963]. Belgrade, Serbia: Etnološka Biblioteka.

Lukić-Krstanović, M. (2008). The festival order: Music stages of power and pleasure. *Issues in Ethnology and Anthropology, 3*(3), 129–143.

Madigan, C. (2008, January 1). 12 top trips for 2008. *The Guardian*. Retrieved September 12, 2010, from www.guardian.co.uk/travel/2008/jan/01/christmas-newyear.liverpool?page=all

Marković, M. (2004). World contra etno . . . protiv kao i obično. [World versus ethno . . . against, as usual]. *Novi Zvuk, 24*, 48–50.

Marović, I. (2006, November 20). *Desetogodišnjica!* [Ten-year anniversary!]. Retrieved September 12, 2010, from http://blog.b92.net/arhiva/node/2989.html

Mijatović, B. (2003). *Music and politics in Serbia (1989–2000)* (Doctoral dissertation, University of California, Los Angeles).

Ministarstvo finansija podrzava razvoj Exita [The Ministry of Finance supports the development of Exit]. (2006, November 9). Retrieved September 12, 2010, from http://www.mondo.rs/v2/tekst.php?vest=36173

Nenić, I. (2005). Politika turbo-folka [The politics of turbo-folk]. *Sveske Knjizevnost Umetnost Kultura, 77*, 89–99.

Nenić, I. (2006). Preko/unutar granica ideološkog: Popularna muzička kultura između alternativnih i zvaničnih modela organizacije [Over/within the borders of the ideological: Popular music culture between alternative and official organizational models]. *TkH, 11*, 115–121.

Otvoren 46 Dragačevski Sabor Trubača u Guči [46th Dragačevo Trumpet Festival begins in Guča]. (2006, August 31). *Naslovi.net*. Retrieved September 12, 2010, from http://www.naslovi.net/2006-08-31/danas/otvoren-46-dragacevski-sabor-trubaca-u-guci/203035

Radun, B. (2007). Kulturna "Pink" strategija [Cultural "Pink" strategy]. *Nova Srpska Politička Misao: Časopis za Politicku Teoriju i Drustvena Istrazivanja*. Retrieved September 17, 2010, from http://starisajt.nspm.rs/kulturnapolitika/2007_radun2t.htm

Rasmussen, L. V. (1999). *The newly-composed folk music of Yugoslavia (1945–1992)* (Doctoral dissertation, Wesleyan University). UMI Microform 9936237.

Rehn, O. (2006, October 11). Olli Rehn presents his new book "Europe's next frontiers." *SEETV*. Retrieved September 17, 2010, from http://www.seetv-exchanges.com/code/navigate.php?Id=254

Rice, T. (2007). Reflections on music and identity. *Ethnomusicology. Muzikologija/Musicology, Časopis Muzikološkog Instituta SANU, 7*, 17–37.

Ristić, M. (2006). Guča: Najjaci srpski brend [Guča: The strongest Serbian brand]. *Poslovna Politika, 35*(7/8), 9–11.

Rosenbaum, J. (2004, May 3). Interview with Bojan Djordjević. *Prague TV*. Retrieved September 17, 2010, from http://www.prague.tv/articles/zine/bojan-djordjevic

Simić, M. (2007). Exit to Europe: Popular music and political identity in contemporary Serbia. *Culture, 116/117*, 98–122.

Skinner, H., & Kubacki, K. (2007). Unravelling the complex relationship between nationhood, national and cultural identity, and place branding. *Place Branding and Public Diplomacy, 3*(4), 305–316.

Srbija Sounds Global: All Stars. (n.d.). *B92Music Katalog*. Retrieved August 29, 2010, from http://www.b92.net/music/catalogue/s/ssg_all_stars.htm

Svilanović, G. (2005). Statement at the 12th plenary session of the Stability Pact for South Eastern Europe, Strasbourg, France. Retrieved October 15, 2007, from http://www.danas.co.yu/20051129/dijalog1.html

Teslik, L. H. (n.d.). *Nation branding explained.* Retrieved September 18, 2010, from http://www.eastwestcoms.com/res_nb_explained.htm

Timotijević, M. (2005). *Karneval u Guči: Sabor Trubača 1961–2004* [Carnival in Guča: Festival of Trumpeters 1961–2004]. Čačak, Serbia: Legenda.

Van Ham, P. (2001). The rise of the brand state: The postmodern politics of image and reputation. *Foreign Affairs, 80*(5), 2–6.

Zakić, L., Ivkov-Džigurski, A., & Ćurčić, N. (2009). Interaction of foreign visitors of the EXIT music festival with domestic visitors and local population. *Geographia Panonica, 13*(3), 97–104.

Žikić, A. (1999). *Fatalni ringišpil: Hronika Beogradskog rokenrola, I deo: 1959–1979* [The fatal merry-go-round: Chronicle of Belgrade rock 'n' roll, part 1: 1959–1979]. Belgrade, Serbia: Geopoetika.

Contributors

Alice Bardan is an advanced Doctoral Candidate at the University of Southern California. She has studied English, French, and Cultural Studies at the Al. I. Cuza University of Iasi, Romania, and also holds a Visual Studies Degree Certificate from USC. Her research interests include contemporary European cinema, post-communist transformations, media globalization, and theories of gesture and affect. Alice has published in the journal *New Cinemas: Journal of Contemporary Film* (Intellect, 2007) and in the edited volume *Transnational Feminism in Film and Media* (Palgrave, 2007). Her recent work is forthcoming in two edited collections: *The Blackwell Companion to East European Cinemas* (Blackwell) and *Popular Television in Eastern and Southern Europe* (Routledge).

Anikó Imre is an Associate Professor of Critical Studies at the School of Cinematic Arts of the University of Southern California. She has published widely on media globalization, (post)socialism, and identities. She is the author of *Identity Games: Globalization and the Transformation of Post-Communist Media Cultures* (MIT Press, 2009); editor of *East European Cinemas* (Routledge, 2005), *The Blackwell Companion to East European Cinemas* (forthcoming); co-editor of *Transnational Feminism in Film and Media* (Palgrave, 2007), of *Popular Television in Eastern and Southern Europe* (Routledge, forthcoming), of a special issue of the *European Journal of Cultural Studies on Media Globalization and Post-Socialist Identities* (May 2009), and a special issue of *Feminist Media Studies* on *Transcultural Feminist Mediations* (December 2009). She co-edits the Palgrave book series Global Cinemas and is on the editorial board of the journal *Studies in East European Cinema*.

Sue Curry Jansen is Professor of Media and Communication at Muhlenberg College in Allentown, Pennsylvania. Her books include *Censorship: The Knot That Binds Power and Knowledge* (Oxford University Press, 1991) and *Critical Communication Theory: Power, Media,*

Gender, and Technology (Rowman & Littlefield, 2001). Recent publications have focused on neoliberalism and nation branding (*Social Identities: Journal of Race, Nation and Culture*, 2008), media and social justice (*Communication, Culture and Critique*, 2008), history of censorship (*The International Encyclopedia of Communication*, Blackwell, 2008) and critical reassessment of the history and implications of media research (*Communication and Critical/Cultural Studies*, 2009). She is currently co-editing a book titled *Media and Social Justice*.

Nadia Kaneva is an Assistant Professor in the Department of Media, Film, and Journalism Studies at the University of Denver. Her research draws on critical theories of culture and communication and explores the intersections of identities, power, and mediation in local and global contexts. Her work has been published in the *International Journal of Cultural Studies*, the *International Journal of Communication, Advertising & Society Review*, the *Journal of Communication Inquiry*, and in a number of edited volumes. She is also the co-editor, with Stewart Hoover, of *Fundamentalisms and the Media* (Continuum, 2009).

László Kulcsár is an Associate Professor of Sociology and Director of the Kansas Population Center at Kansas State University. He does research on population dynamics and social change in rural areas and participates in an NSF funded interdisciplinary research program, which ties population projections to system-level ecological and land use change and the transforming rural landscape in the Great Plains. He also studies the social and demographic transformation of Eastern Europe from a historical perspective, with a particular emphasis on the post-socialist period. His research has appeared in numerous scholarly journals and edited volumes.

Branislava (Brana) Mijatović is an Assistant Professor and Director of World Music Studies in the Department of Music at Christopher Newport University. Her research interests include the relationship between music, politics, and globalization. Her work has been published in academic journals, including *Ethnomusicology* and *Anthropology of East Europe Review*, as well as in a number of cultural critique magazines. She has presented her research at numerous national and international conferences.

Robert A. Saunders is an Assistant Professor in the Department of History, Economics & Politics at Farmingdale State College—SUNY. His research interests include post-totalitarian states, mass media, and minority nationalism. He is the author of *The Many Faces of Sacha*

Baron Cohen: Politics, Parody, and the Battle Over Borat (Lexington, 2008), of *Ethnopolitics in Cyberspace: The Internet, Minority Nationalism, and the Web of Identity* (Lexington, 2010), and co-author, with Vlad Strukov, of the *Historical Dictionary of the Russian Federation* (Scarecrow Press, 2010). His research has also appeared in numerous academic journals and edited volumes.

Gerald Sussman is Professor of Urban Studies, Politics, and Communications at Portland State University (Oregon), where he teaches graduate courses in international community development, political economy, political communication, and media studies. He is the author or chief editor of six books, including *Branding Democracy: U.S. Regime Change in Post-Soviet Eastern Europe* (Peter Lang, 2010), *Global Electioneering: Campaign Consulting, Communications, and Corporate Financing* (Rowman & Littlefield, 2005), *Communication, Technology and Politics in the Information Age* (Sage, 1997), and a forthcoming edited book, *The Propaganda Society: Promotional Culture and Politics in Global Context* (Peter Lang). Professor Sussman serves on a number of academic journal editorial boards as well as the Community Advisory Board of Portland, Oregon's public broadcasting station, KOPB.

Paweł Surowiec holds an M.A. in International Relations Studies from Wrocław University, Poland. He is a Lecturer and an advanced Ph.D. candidate at the Media School, Bournemouth University, UK. His dissertation explores crossovers between promotional culture, marketing ideologies, and national identities in post-Soviet Poland. His research is inspired by social theory approaches and analyzes propaganda's re-invention as public relations and public diplomacy and the way it colonizes new social spaces. He's particularly interested in the power relations within propaganda *praxis* in the context of political economy.

Zala Volčič is a Senior Lecturer and a Research Fellow at the Centre for Critical and Cultural Studies, University of Queensland–Brisbane, Australia. Her research focus is on the cultural consequences of nationalism, capitalism, and globalization, with a particular emphasis on international communication and media identities. Past publications include numerous journal articles and book chapters, a co-authored book (with Shuang Liu and Cindy Gallois) titled *Intercultural Communication* (Sage, 2010), and her single-authored book, *Serbian Spaces of Identity* (Hampton Press, 2011).

Young-ok Yum is an Associate Professor in the Department of Communication Studies, Theatre and Dance at Kansas State University. Her research interests are in the areas of intercultural communication, relational communication, and conflict management. Her publications have appeared in multiple academic journals, including *Human Communication Research*, *Journal of Intercultural Communication*, *Journal of Social Psychology*, and others. She has also authored a number of book chapters.

Index

A

Abkhazia, "I Love Abkhazia" campaign, 52
Absurdistan: A Novel (Shteyngart), 68–69
Ackerman, Peter, 37
Acxiom Corporation, 27, 44n3
Adam Mickiewicz Institute, 130, 131, 138
advertising, 3, 25–27, 114–116
Afghanistan, 58
AKPD Message and Media, 39
Albania, 50, 62–63
Alpion, Gëzim, 62–63
Anderson, Benedict, 32, 66, 79
Anholt, Simon, 11, 29–31, 61, 80, 81, 92–93, 177, 187, 226
  belligerent branding concept, 49
  on confusing country names, 58
  on ethics and nation branding, 184–185
  Nation Brand Index and, 134, 209
  nation branding term coined by, 29, 51
Appadurai, Arjun, 220–221
Armenia, 54, 55
  parody of, 68–69
Austin Powers films, 50
Aven Romalen, 220
Axelrod, David, 39
Azerbaijan, parody of, 68–69

B

B92 media company, 216–218, 223, 230n8
balkanization, 40
Balkans, 150, 152
  stereotypes of, 55–56, 62–63, 65, 169, 170–179
Baltic republics, 55. *See also* Estonia
Baltic Tiger, 82, 86

Barber, Benjamin, 34
Baron Cohen, Sacha, 58–61, 63, 66, 70, 169, 170
Barouh, Emmy, 102
Baruto (Kaido Hoovelson), 88
BBC, 64, 175, 177, 181
Beers, Charlotte, 32–33, 137–138
Belarus, 52, 54, 55
"belligerent branding," 49, 53–54, 68
Boozed Up Brits Abroad (TV series), 56–57
Borat: Cultural Learnings of America for Make Benefit Glorious Nation of Kazakhstan (film), 54, 58–61, 66, 169
  filmed in Romania, 170–172
  response of Kazakhstan to, 59–61, 170–171, 177
Bordas, Eulogio, 178
Boruc, Mirosław, 134
Bošković, Bojan, 223–224
Bourdain, Anthony, 172–175
Bourdieu, Pierre, 12, 15, 63, 99, 124, 125, 126, 130
  field theory of, 127–128
Brancusi, Constantin, 187
Brand America, 23, 25, 32–35
brand loyalty, 163, 185
branding, 27–32. *See also* nation branding
  global wealth derived from, 31
  as propaganda, 27–32, 35–36
  scope of applications, 10, 28
  of space, 28, 80
branding consultants. *See* consultants, marketing/branding
Brandtner, Michael, 184
Bregović, Goran, 222

Bringing Down a Dictator (film), 37
Britain. *See* United Kingdom (UK)
British Council, 103, 104, 105, 113
Brown, John, 34
Brubaker, Rogers, 124
Bulgaria, 15, 99–123
  branding consultants, 100, 103–107,
    110–111, 118
  branding costs/funding, 100,
    101–105, 107, 119
  branding initiatives, 104–110
    Branding Bulgaria, 104–107,
      113–114, 118
    comparison of, 104, 118
    Europalia Bulgaria, 102–103, 117,
      118
    Promotion Bulgaria, 104, 107–110,
      118
    public discussions/workshops,
      105–106, 107, 108, 118
  branding slogans, 99, 106, 108
  elites and power in, 100, 104,
    111–113, 119–120
  EU aspirations/accession, 101–102,
    116–117
  government institutions and agencies,
    100–104, 111
    Bulgarian Council for Economic
      Growth, 108
    Bulgarian Investment Agency
      (InvestBulgaria Agency), 101, 103
    Ministry of Foreign Affairs (MFA),
      101–102, 107
    Ministry of the Economy (ME),
      101, 107
    National Agency for Advertising
      and Information, 101
    information and telecommunication
      industry (ICT), 103
    Bulgarian ICT Cluster, 103
  logo, national, 99, 102, 108–109
  modernization, 113–115
  rose symbol, 108
  tourism promotion, 101, 106–107
Burawoy, Michael, 6
Burger King, 178–179
Burson-Marsteller, 34
Bush, George W., 25, 30, 32, 63
Byron, George Gordon (Lord Byron),
  55–56

C
"calculative space," 91, 126
capital, 10, 24, 119, 127, 198

"statist" capital (meta-capital), 127,
  128
capitalism, 9–10, 23–24, 28, 91, 169,
  186
  commodification of space, 28, 91
  digital capitalism, 23
  disaster capitalism, 25
  promotion/promotionalism and,
    24–27, 126, 163
  "transnational capitalist class," 126
Carmen Meets Borat (film), 172
Ceauşescu, Florea, 170
Ceauşescu, Nicolae, 168–169, 175,
  179, 180
  construction projects of, 169, 173,
    175, 186
  U.S. and European support for, 168
Central and Eastern European (CEE)
  branded state identities in, 40–42
  challenges for nation branding,
    54–55, 193–194, 197
  color revolutions in, 23, 35–40, 43
  definition of, 44n2
  differentiation of states from each
    other, 49, 54–55, 70, 198
  European Union and. *See* European
    Union
  identity issues in, 195–197. *See also*
    national identity
  names of countries, similarities in/
    confusion about, 55, 57–58, 152
  neoliberal reforms in, 29
  as "Other Europe," 55, 64, 70
  post-Soviet image and, 53–54
  "shock therapy" in, 8, 43, 84, 128
  sovereignty of nations in, 42–44
  stereotypes of. *See* stereotypes
  transition in, 6–7, 193–194, 195–197
  youth movements in, 35–40
Central Asian Republics (CARs), 55, 69
Chernobyl, 54, 66
Cilauro, Santo, 65, 68, 70
Clarkson, Jeremy, 175–178
Clinton, Bill, 39
Clinton, Hillary, 34
CNN, 3, 46, 151, 168, 181, 182, 226,
  227
Coca-Cola, 34, 37, 41, 81
Cold War, 8, 81, 168, 196
  stereotypes, 15, 53, 64–65, 69,
    169–170, 171, 173
colonization
  decolonization, 52
  self-colonization, 41–42

color revolutions, 23, 35–40, 43
  in Georgia (*Kmara*), 35, 37, 38
  logos of, 35, 37, 38
  in Serbia (*Otpor*), 35, 36–37, 38
  in Ukraine (*Pora*), 35, 38
Comăneci, Nadia, 182–183, 187
commercial nationalism, 148–149,
  158–163
commercialization, 148, 150, 157, 197.
  See also advertising; marketing
communism, 6, 115, 128–129, 179. *See
  also* post-communist Europe
  nationalism under, 196
  resistance and revolts under, 168
  transition from, 6–7, 193–194,
    195–197
competitive advantage, 30–31
competitive identity, 11, 130
competitiveness, 129–130, 140, 198
computer industry, in Estonia, 83, 88,
    90, 198. *See also* information
    and communication technolo-
    gies (ICTs)
Condee, Nancy, 65
conservatism, 196, 202–203, 207
constructivism, 128, 225–226
consultants, marketing/branding, 3, 10,
    15–16. *See also names of specific
    consultants and companies*
  in Bulgaria, 100, 103–107, 110–111,
    118
  in Estonia, 32, 79–80
  in Hungary, 201, 203–206
  in Poland, 131–139
  in Romania, 178, 184
  in Serbia, 36–37, 222, 226, 227
  in Slovenia, 155–157
consumerism, 23, 24–27, 42, 185
  nation branding and, 149, 158
Cool Britannia, 80
Cornelissen, Hans, 107
corporatization, 139, 200
  of government structures, 130
  in Poland, 133–134
  of public and foreign affairs, 124–125
corruption, 54, 193
cosmopolitanism, 179, 195, 215
costs of nation branding initiatives
  in Bulgaria, 101–102, 104, 107
  in Estonia, 85, 89
  in Poland, 138
  in Romania, 174, 178, 181, 183,
    184
  in Serbia, 227

in Slovenia, 151, 153, 155
  in U.S., 25–27, 34–35
country branding, 200. *See also* nation
    branding
Croatia, 3
Čuburilo, Milica, 227
culinary products, in Hungary, 199–
    200, 201, 205
cultural intermediaries, 127
Curtis, Tony, 204
cyber-attack, in Estonia, 83–84
Czech Republic, 29, 41, 198
Czechoslovakia, 49, 168

D

Daily Show, The (TV program), 63
data mining, 26–27
Davenport, Rory, 41
DDB Corporate Profiles, 131, 133, 136
Debord, Guy, 27, 28
democracy
  "democracy promotion" groups,
    35–36, 44n8
  nation branding and, 4, 11, 42–44
  nation branding as contrary to, 15,
    42, 91–92, 140
destination branding, 56, 80, 89–90,
    186–188. *See also* tourism
    promotion
dictators, 168
Dinnie, Keith, 4, 10, 52, 81
diplomacy (public diplomacy), 25, 51
  Middle East public diplomacy, U.S.,
    33–34, 160
  nation branding and, 4, 31, 80,
    198–199
  national advertising campaigns as,
    101–102
Ditchev, Ivaylo, 100
Djordjević, Bojan, 216, 218
Djuričanin, Strahinja, 227, 228
Drace-Francis, Alex, 179–180
Dracula, 70, 169, 172, 187
  historical basis for (Vlad Țepeș),
    169
  as tourism theme, 173, 184,
    187–188

E

Eagleton, Terry, 136
Eastern Bloc, 55, 65
Eastern Europe. *See* Central and East-
    ern European (CEE)
Eco, Umberto, 91–92

economy/economies, 11–12, 23, 126.
　　See also specific countries
　crises in, 8, 11, 43, 84
　free market, transition to, 6
　globalization and, 10, 30
　informational economy, 24–25
　Marxist theory and, 12, 43, 91
　nation branding and, 24–25, 29–31,
　　147
　restructuring of, 24, 82–83, 150
　"shock therapy," 8, 43, 84, 128
Eggspuehler, Cari, 33
"Electronik Supersonik" (song and
　　video), 50, 68
elites, 7, 8, 15, 39, 42, 49, 63, 126–
　　128, 196, 208–209
　in Bulgaria, 100, 104, 111–113,
　　119–120
　in Estonia, 82, 87
　in Hungary, 196–197, 198, 203
　in Kazakhstan, 60–61
　in Poland, 136, 138
　in Romania, 180
　in Serbia, 229
　in Slovenia, 151, 153, 155, 162
　transnational, 31, 126
Elliott, Richard, 218–219
Elwes, Anneke, 105, 106
Emor, 82
emotional branding, 218–219
entertainment industry, influence of, 60,
　　63, 70
Estonia, 15, 79–98
　admission to EU, 87
　as Baltic Tiger, 82, 86
　branding consultants, 32, 79–80
　branding costs, 85, 89
　branding initiatives
　　Brand Estonia, 81–90
　　EST–IT@2018, 87–90
　　Foresight Project 2018, 89
　　Industry Engines 2018, 89
　　My Estonia, 90–91
　　Service Economy 2018, 89
　　Welcome to Estonia (2002), 85–87
　branding slogans, 86, 89, 92, 198, 208
　computer industry in, 83, 88, 90, 198
　country name alternatives, 29, 57
　cyber-attack on, 83–84, 88
　e-government in, 86, 88, 90, 198
　economic crises and shock therapy,
　　84–85
　Eurovision Song Contest and, 85
　global markets, integration into, 80–81

institutions and agencies
　　Cooperative Cyber Defence Centre
　　　of Excellence, 88
　　Enterprise Estonia (EE), 82, 86, 88,
　　　89, 93–94
　　Estonian Tourist Board, 89
　logo, national, 85–86
　Singing Revolution, 83, 85
　Skype and, 88, 92
　social development/problems in,
　　86–87, 90
　Sumo wrestler from, 88
　tensions with Russia/Russian immi-
　　grants, 83–84, 87
　tourist industry, 86, 89
　website, official, 90
etatism, 200, 208
ethnicity, 13, 68–69, 83, 169, 195,
　　215–217, 220
Eurasia, 55
Euronews, 3, 181
Europalia Festival, 102–103
European Union (EU), 7, 40, 55
　European Commission Responsible
　　for Enlargement, 224
　European Policy Center, 224
　flexible citizenship idea, 186
　funding from, 100, 103, 105, 184
　membership aspirations, nation
　　branding and, 9, 41, 43, 129,
　　196–197, 202
　PHARE program, 105
　promotion/advertising to, 41–42, 80
　self-branding strategy, 185–186
Europeanization, 118, 128, 193, 225
　EU accession and, 196–197
Eurosport, 3, 181, 182
Eurotrip (film), 62
Eurovision Song Contest, 68, 227
　Estonia and, 85
　Molvanîa's fake entry, 50, 68
EXIT music festival, 223–226, 229–230
exoticism, 56, 66, 70, 168
Eyal, Gil, 136

F

Facebook, 25, 70, 90
Fagan, Edward, 172
Fairclough, Norman, 7, 117–118, 119
fictitious countries, 58, 64–69
　Molvanîa, 50, 65–68
Fidesz political party, 202–204, 207
field/field theory, 99, 100, 110, 127–
　　128, 130–131

films/movies. *See also* television
 Austin Powers films, 50
 Borat, 54, 58–61, 66, 170–172
 Bringing Down a Dictator, 37
 Carmen Meets Borat, 172
 Eurotrip, 62
 horror films, 61–62
 Hostel/Hostel: Part II, 61
 James Bond films, 53–54
 The Lady Vanishes, 175, 176, 177
 Some Like It Hot, 204
 The Terminal, 49, 54, 65
 Time of the Gypsies, 222
 Underground, 222
 Wag the Dog, 63
financial crises, 8, 11, 43, 84. *See also*
  economy/economies
Finland, 83
flexible citizenship, 186
Folgers, 178
folk music. *See* Serbia
food (cuisine), as branding aspect,
  199–200, 201, 205
foreign investment, attracting, 49, 79,
  150, 187, 194, 208
former Yugoslavia. *See* Yugoslavia,
  former
Foucault, Michel, 12
free market economy, 6, 40, 126. *See*
  also capitalism; globalization
Free to Choose (Friedman), 85
Freedom House, 35, 37, 38–39
Friedman, Milton, 85
funding. *See* costs of nation branding
  initiatives

G
generational differences, 105, 115–116,
  135–136
Georgia, 55
 Kmara movement in, 35, 37, 38
 parody of, 68–69
Gertner, David, 60
Gleisner, Tom, 65, 66
global information age, 51, 63–64, 69
global markets
 competitiveness and, 129–130, 140,
  198
 for ICTs, 103
 market fundamentalism and, 91
 nation branding and, 4, 193–194,
  198
 power and prestige related to, 81,
  119–120

globalization, 9–10, 81, 150, 162–163
 generational differences and, 115–116
 locality as equally important, 220, 229
 modernization and, 114, 115–116
Glod, Romania, 170–172
Gobe, Mark, 226
Goebbels, Joseph, 25
Gordy, Eric, 215
Greenberg Quinlan Rosner, 39
Greene, Graham, 176
Guča music festival, 221–223, 225–
  226, 229–230
Gypsies (Roma), 170–172, 175, 177,
  178, 217
Gyurcsány, Ferenc, 205

H
habitus, 127, 132
Hagi, Gheorghe (Gigi), 182, 183, 187
Hammond, Richard, 175, 176
Hanks, Tom, 65
Harris, Neil Patrick, 178
Harry Potter series, 62–63
Hauska & Partner International Com-
  munications, 226
Havel, Václav, 168
Hill & Knowlton, 29
Hitchcock, Alfred, 175
Holt, Douglas, 219–220
Hoovelson, Kaido (Baruto), 88
horror, 61–62, 168, 169, 187–188
Hostel films, 61
Hughes, Karen, 34
Hungary, 17, 193–212
 branding consultants, 201, 203–206
 branding initiatives, 200–207
  Expos and Olympics, 201–203
  government and, 204–209
  Image and Identity Conference,
   205–206
  Millennium Year (2000), 202–203
  Pannon Puma, 204–207, 210n7
  talent, emphasis on, 204–205, 206,
   210n6
  tourism/destination branding, 198,
   201, 204–205
 branding slogans, 198
 communist heritage, 168, 194–195,
  201
 conservatives in, 202–203, 207
 culinary products, 199–200, 201, 205
  Hungaricum Club, 205
 EU accession and, 196–197, 202, 205
 EU presidency (2011), 207

Fidesz political party, 202–204, 207
government institutions and agencies
   Agricultural Marketing Center, 201
   Country Image Center (CIC), 41,
      202–204, 207
   Hungarian National Tourist Office
      (HNTO), 198, 201, 204–205
   Ministry of Agriculture and Rural
      Development, 201
   Ministry of National Cultural
      Heritage, 203–204
Gyurcsány, Ferenc, 205
Kádár regime, 168
National Gallop, 206–207, 208, 209
national identity/image, 195,
   197–203, 206, 207
revolt in 1956, 168
second economy, 200–201
tourism/destination branding, 198,
   201, 204–205
website, official, 198

I
identity. *See* national identity
ideology. *See also* neoliberalism
   liberal democracies, transition to, 6
   marketing ideology, 125–128
   nation branding and, 4, 5, 9, 11,
      18–19, 124, 125–128, 209
   as post-ideological, 139, 149,
      185–186
Idrissov, Erlan, 60
Iliescu, Ion, 180
Ilves, Toomas Hendrik, 31, 87–88, 90
imagined communities, 66, 79, 163,
   219
Imago, 152
individualism, 136, 150, 185
industrialization, 8
information and communication technologies (ICTs), 51, 103, 198
   in Bulgaria, 103
   in Estonia, 83, 88, 90, 198
informational economy, 24–25, 42
Interbrand, 81, 82, 85–86, 150
international politics/diplomacy. *See*
   diplomacy (public diplomacy)
Internet. *See* websites, official
Ionesco, Eugen, 187
Iraq, 34
Ireland/Irish Republic, 58, 80, 137,
   148, 153, 157
IRI (International Republican Institute),
   35, 36, 44n8

J
James Bond films, 53–54
Jansa, Janez, 154, 163
Jansen, Sue Curry, 126, 148, 149, 194,
   208
Jetlag Travel Guide series, 65–66

K
Kaczyński, Lech and Jarosław, 138
Kallas, Siim, 86–87
Kaneva, Nadia, 41, 70, 186
Kazakhstan, 58–61
   Borat film and, 54, 58–61, 170–171,
      177
   James Bond films and, 53
   national image, 58–59, 61
Kennedy, Michael, 18
Khanna, Parag, 68
King Baudouin Foundation, 224
Klein, Naomi, 93
Kmara movement, 35, 37, 38
Kňažko, Milan, 61
Konečnik, Maja, 155, 158
Kosovo, 147–148
Koštunica, Vojislav, 37, 222–223
Kotkin, Stephen, 49, 53, 54
Kotler, Philip, 60
Kotler Marketing Group, 150
Kuneva, Meglena, 116–117
Kusturica, Emir, 222
Kwaśniewski, Aleksander, 135

L
Laar, Mart, 84, 87
Lady Vanishes, The (film), 175, 176, 177
Latvia, 55, 83
Lebedenko, Vladimir, 49
Lečić, Branislav, 220
Lefebvre, Henri, 28, 43
legitimation/legitimization
   of marketing practices, 125–128,
      129–130, 139
   nation branding and, 15–16, 112–
      113, 119–120, 139, 200
   of social order, 140
   transition and, 7
Light, Duncan, 179, 180–181, 187
Link Strategies, 39
Lipovetsky, Mark, 53, 65
Lippmann, Walter, 25
Lithuania, 55, 57–58, 83
logos
   Bulgaria, 99, 102, 108–109
   Estonia, 85–86

Kmara, 37, 38
Otpor, 37, 38
Poland, 131–132, 136
Romania, 178, 181, 183–184
Slovenia, 151, 154, 156
Lugar, Richard, 30
Lukács, Georg, 91, 137

M
Macedonia, 70
Makovecz, Imre, 201
Manafort, Paul, 40
manufacturing, decline in, 24, 25
market fundamentalism, 84, 91–92,
    126, 150, 185
marketing, 125–130, 139, 163
    nation branding as, 148, 160, 194.
        See also economy/economies;
        propaganda
marketing consultants. *See* consultants,
    marketing/branding
marketization, 5, 12, 16, 19, 113–116,
    117, 119, 129
Marovic, Ivan, 37
Marx, Karl, 43, 91
Marxism, 10, 12, 43, 91, 171
Matalin, Mary, 34
May, James, 175, 176
McCain, John, 40
media, 3, 36, 46, 60, 116–117. *See also*
    stereotypes
    globalization and, 10, 11, 15, 50, 69
    nation branding and, 4, 9,
        116–117
Mercedes Benz, 27
Middle East public diplomacy, 33–34,
    160
Mills, C. Wright, 13
Milošević, Slobodan, 35, 36, 37,
    213
    EXIT music festival and, 223
Mineva, Mila, 105, 106
Mission Impossible (TV series), 64
Mitić, Miloš, 217, 218
mockumentary, 170
Moldavia, 64, 187–188
Moldova, 54, 55, 181
Molvanîa, 50, 65–68, 187
movies. *See* films/movies
music. *See* Serbia
music festivals, 213, 216, 221–226,
    229–230
    EXIT, 223–226
    Guča, 221–223, 225–226

N
Nano, Fatos, 63
Năstase, Ilie, 182, 183
nation/nationhood, 10–11, 42–44, 50,
    124
    analyses of, 12–13
    definitions of, 32
    as imagined community, 32, 79, 162,
        163
    legitimating power of, 127
    nation-states, as relatively recent, 79
    new nations, 51, 52
Nation Brand Index, 29, 134, 209
nation branding. *See also* branding; *spe-
        cific countries*
    audiences for, 79–80, 197–199,
        227–228
    citizen participation/co-creation and,
        105–107, 155, 158–160
    critical studies of, 4–6, 11–14
    definitions of, 4–5, 29, 49, 113, 140n2
    depoliticization and, 31, 185–186, 206
    emergence of, 3, 40, 80
    homogenization of identities and,
        42–43
    ideology and, 5, 9, 125–128, 209
    legitimization and, 15–16, 112–113,
        119–120, 139, 200
    national identity and, 42–43, 93,
        149, 197–200
    national image and, 10–11, 50–52
    necessity of, 30–31, 52, 81, 92–93,
        137, 198
    questioned, 41, 94, 137–139,
        184–185
    political economic foundations of,
        23–48
    public opinion and, 11, 25–27, 112
    scope and range of, 10, 14, 29–31
    standardization of messages in,
        118–119, 194, 199, 208
    versus branding of products, 31, 158
nation branding slogans. *See* slogans
National Endowment for Democracy
        (NED), 35, 44n8
National Gallop (Hungary), 206–207,
        208, 209
national identity, 197–200. *See also*
        national image; nationalism;
        specific countries
    commercialization and, 149,
        158–163, 197
    communist heritage and, 115,
        128–129, 179, 193

depoliticization of, 16, 185–186, 206
marketing ideology and, 126, 148
nationalism and, 195–196
problems in CEE, 17, 18, 118–119,
    195–197
unified/simplified projections of, 140,
    194, 199
national image, 10–11, 32, 50–52. *See
    also* national identity
challenges for new countries, 52,
    54–55
elites and, 100, 111–112
globalization and, 63–64, 198
problems of, 52–58
public discussions on, 105–106
national logos. *See* logos
national reputation, 139–140
nationalism, 124, 161, 185–186
commercial nationalism, 148–149,
    158–163
constructivist theory of, 128
corpo-nationalism, 16, 124–144
in former Yugoslavia, 148
globalization and, 162–163
nation branding and, 11, 16–17,
    185–186
post-communism and, 5, 196
structuralist theory of, 124, 128
Western vs. Eastern variants,
    195–196
NATO, 39, 55, 59, 80, 84, 87, 88
NDI (National Democratic Institute),
    35, 44n8
negative branding, 17, 53–54, 62–63,
    170–179. *See also* stereotypes
neoliberalism, 12–13, 42, 125–128,
    162–163. *See also* capitalism
branding as tool of, 10, 28–29, 126,
    149
in Poland, 125–128, 136, 140
propaganda and, 24–25, 28–29
in Slovenia, 150, 162
transnational corporations and,
    31–32
Newly Independent States of Eurasia
    (NISE), 53, 54
NGOs. *See* nongovernmental
    organizations
9/11 terrorist attacks on U.S., 80, 160
No Logo (Klein), 93
No Reservations (TV program), 172–175
nongovernmental organizations
    (NGOs), 100, 103, 104
Nye, Joseph S., Jr., 51

O

Obama, Barack, 30, 39
objectification, 70
offshoring, 24, 25. *See also* outsourcing
Olins, Wally, 27–28, 80, 81, 92–93,
    150, 164n8, 226
consultant services in Poland, 132,
    133, 134, 135, 138
Omnicom, 82
Ong, Aihwa, 185, 186
Onion, The, 49–50, 54
Open Society Institute, 35, 100, 103,
    105
Orange Revolution, 39
Orbán, Viktor, 210n5
O'Reilly, Daragh, 10, 125
Orient Express, 176
orientalism, 56
Other Europe, 55, 57–58, 64, 70, 159,
    186–187
Other Europe, The (Walters), 55
Otherness, 186–187
Otpor movement, 35, 36–37, 38
*Our Dumb World: The Onion's Atlas
    of Planet Earth* (Dikkers),
    49–50, 54
outsourcing, 24, 25, 103
of nation branding, 32

P

Pakistan, 58
Palin, Sarah, 182
Pannon Puma, 204–207, 210n7
parody, 54, 58–63, 66–69, 170. *See
    also* stereotypes
responses to, 59–61, 70
participation, democratic, 155,
    159–160
Peegel, Erki, 82, 88
PHARE program, 105
Pissup Tours, 56–57
Poland, 16, 124–144
audit of perceptions, 135–136
branding consultants, 131–139
branding costs, 133, 138
branding initiatives, 128–139
    Academy of Brands, 133–134
    actors in, 125, 130–133, 141n7
    bottom-up approach, 132, 133
    Creative Tension, 136–137, 138, 208
    government stability/changes and,
        134, 135, 138
    "Poland: Europe is bigger" cam-
        paign, 131–132, 133

"Poland, the heart of Europe" campaign, 133–134
The Polska Year, 138
Program of National Marketing, 133
propaganda and, 128–129, 130
Public Relations 4 Poland, 132–133
resistance to, 134, 138–139, 140
The Session of the Century, 132
branding slogans, 133–134, 208
EU aspirations and accession, 129
generational differences in perceptions, 135–136
government, 129–131, 133
institutions and agencies
Adam Mickiewicz Institute, 130, 131, 138
Advertising for Poland Association, 132
Council of Poland's Promotion, 131
DDB Corporate Profiles, 131, 133, 136
Department of Promotion, 129, 130
Institute of Polish Affairs, 135
Institute of the Polish Brand, 126, 131, 134, 135, 138
Ministry of Cultural and National Heritage, 131
Ministry of Economics, 130, 131, 133, 134
Ministry of Foreign Affairs, 129, 130, 131, 132–133, 134
Polish Agency for Enterprise Development, 131
Polish Chamber of Commerce, 131, 133–134, 137, 140
Polish Investment and Information Agency, 130, 131, 134
Polish Tourism Organization, 130, 131, 132, 134, 138
legitimacy concepts/narrative, 125, 130, 139
logo, national, 131–132, 136
national identity, 31, 125, 135–137, 140
national reputation, 139–140
neoliberal ideology and, 124, 125–130, 136, 140
promotional culture and policy, 125, 129, 131, 140
Solidarity movement, 168
tourism promotion, 130, 132

political ideology. *See* ideology
politics. *See also* diplomacy (public diplomacy)
consumerism and, 162–163
depoliticization through nation branding, 31, 185–186, 206
Popovic, Srdja, 36
Pora movement, 35, 38
post-communist Europe, xi, 5, 18, 53–54
transition, 6–7, 193–194, 195–197
post-political, nation branding as, 139, 149, 185–186
post-socialist context, 149–150, 159, 162–163, 186, 193–194
post-Soviet image, 53–54, 193–194
Powell, Colin, 32, 33
power, 100, 127
global markets and, 81
shifts, nation branding and, 111–112, 119–120
PR professionals. *See* public relations professionals
Pristop, 155
privatization, 8, 40, 81, 93
professionals, 111, 127. *See also* consultants; elites
public relations professionals, 26, 29, 36–40
PROFILE, 222
promotion, 24–27, 42–44. *See also* consultants; propaganda
in Poland, 128–130, 133–139
promotional culture, 10, 124, 129, 140
propaganda, 23–48, 128–129, 199
corporatization and, 130
data mining and, 26–27
marketing ideology and, 125–128
nation branding as, 27–32, 92, 140, 199
neoliberal system and, 24–25, 28–29, 42
in Poland, 128–129, 130
public diplomacy and, 32–35
systemic propaganda, 25–27
in United States, 24–27, 32–35
public diplomacy. *See* diplomacy (public diplomacy)
Public Diplomacy and Public Affairs (PDPA), 32–34
public opinion, 112
nation branding and, 11
propaganda as means to influence, 25–27

public-private partnerships, 81, 126
public relations professionals, 26, 29,
    36–40. *See also* consultants

Q

Qorvis Communications, 41

R

Rehn, Olli, 224–225
R.E.M. (band), 220
reputation, 28, 29, 50–51, 54
revisionism, 126
revolutions, 168–169
    color revolutions, 23, 35–40, 43
    Orange Revolution, 39–40, 43
    Singing Revolution, 83, 85
Ring Ring music festival, 216
Roma (Gypsies), 170–172, 175, 177,
    178, 217
Romania, 17, 168–192
    athletes as ambassadors, 182–183,
        187
    branding consultants, 178, 184
    branding costs, 174, 178, 181, 183,
        184
    branding initiatives, 179–184
        "Carpathian Garden" campaign,
            178, 183–184
        eclipse campaign (1999), 181
        Elena Udrea and, 170, 182–184
        future of, 184–188
        green leaf logo, 183–184
        "Land of Choice" campaign,
            182–183
        "Romania—Simply Surprising"
            campaign, 181–182
        tourism promotion, 181–184,
            186–188
        Western representations and,
            170–179, 186–188
    branding slogans, 178, 181, 183, 184
    business environment, 187
    Ceaușescu, Nicolae, 168–169, 175,
        179, 180
        construction projects of, 169, 173,
            175, 186
    communist heritage, 168–170,
        179–180
    commercial potential of, 180,
        186–187
    Dacia (car), 173, 175
    Dracula story, 70, 169, 172, 187
        as tourism theme, 173, 184,
            187–188

globalization and, 180
Glod (village), 170–172
government institutions and agencies,
    178
Gypsies (Roma), 170–172, 175, 177,
    178
logo, national, 178, 181, 183–184
national image/identity, 179–180,
    182, 186–188
People's Palace, 176, 177, 180,
    186–187
revolution in 1989, 168–169
Romania Mare political party, 180
stereotypes, 168, 170–179
tourism and travel, 168, 170, 177,
    179–184
    "dark tourism," 168, 180–181,
        184, 186–188
    Dracula-themed, 173, 184, 187–188
Transfăgărășan Highway, 175–176, 177
Western media representations,
    170–179
    Borat, 170–172
    No Reservations, 172–175
    Romanian reactions to, 171–172,
        174, 177, 178
    Top Gear, 175–178
    Whopper virgins and Folgers com-
        mercials, 178–179
Roth, Eli, 61, 63
Rove, Karl, 34
Rowling, J. K., 50, 62–63, 70
Rupnik, Jacques, 5
Russia, 41, 53–54
    tensions with Estonia, 83–84

S

Saatchi & Saatchi, 147
Saffron Brand Consultants, 27, 133,
    135–139, 140, 205–206
Said, Edward, 56, 63
Saturday Night Live, 178–179
second economy, 200–201
Second World, 68
self-colonization, 41–42
self-exoticism, 56
selling of societies, 24–25. *See also*
    consumerism
Sennett, Richard, 92
Serbia, 17, 213–235
    B92 media company, 216–218, 223,
        230n8
    branding consultants, 36–37, 222,
        226, 227

branding costs, 227
branding initiatives, 214–229
  music, 214–226. *See also subentry for music, below*
  other than music, 226–229
  television, 226, 227
Democratic Opposition of Serbia (DOS), 36–37
Eurovision Song Contest, 227
EXIT festival, 223–226, 229–230
government institutions and agencies
  Council for Branding Serbia, 226, 227
  Executive Council of the Public Relations Society of Serbia, 226
  Group for National Brand of Serbia, 226, 227
  Ministry of Finance, 224
  Ministry of International Economic Relations, 227
  Ministry of National and Ethnic Minorities, 217
  Ministry of Trade and Services, 226
  Ministry of Trade and Tourism, 222, 227
  Serbian Institute for Public Diplomacy, 228
  Serbian Tourist Organization, 227
Guča festival, 221–223, 225–226, 229–230
Milošević and, 35, 36, 37, 213, 215
  EXIT festival and, 223
music
  ethnic diversity and, 216, 217, 220
  folk vs. urban, 215, 225, 226, 229
  fusions, 216
  newly composed folk/turbo-folk, 214–215
  politicians' co-optation of, 220, 226
  rock 'n' roll, 215, 216, 219
  Srbija: Sounds Global (SSG), 213, 216–221, 229–230
  tolerance promoted through, 217, 218, 220–221
  traditional Balkan instruments, 216
  traditional rural, 214–215, 216, 218
  world music, 17, 216–218, 219, 221, 229
music festivals, 213, 216, 221–226
  EXIT, 223–226, 229–230
  Guča, 221–223, 225–226, 229–230

national identity, 214, 221, 222–226
nationalism and, 215
Otpor movement, 35, 36–37, 38
"Shared Values" Initiative (SVI), 33, 80
Shevardnadze, Eduard, 35
shock therapy (economic), 8, 43, 84, 128
Shteyngart, Gary, 68–69
Shuleva, Lydia, 107
Silverstein, Ken, 69
Simpsons, The (TV cartoon series), 62
Singapore, 92
Sitch, Rob, 65
Skype, 88, 92
slogans, nation branding, 3, 4
  Bulgaria, 99, 106, 108
  Estonia, 86, 89, 92, 198, 208
  Hungary, 198
  Poland, 133–134, 208
  Romania, 178, 181, 183, 184
  Slovenia, 151, 154–155, 156, 157, 198
Slovakia, 61–62, 63
Slovenia, 16–17, 147–167
  branding consultants, 155–157
  branding costs, 151, 153, 155
  branding initiatives, 150–158, 154
    citizen participation/co-creation in, 155, 158–160
    early initiatives, 150–153
    environmentally-friendly initiatives, 31, 157, 158–159
    green slogans/focus, 151, 155, 156–157, 158–159, 198
    "I feel *Slove*nia," 153–158
  branding slogans, 151, 154–155, 156, 157
  elites in, 151, 153, 155, 162
  EU accession, 151
  EU presidency, 153
  government, 150
  government institutions and agencies
    Ministry of the Economy, 153, 155
    Ministry of Tourism, 150–151
    Slovenian Tourist Board, 150–151, 157
  internalizing ("living") the brand, 160–162
  logo, national, 151, 154, 156
  national identity, 147, 153, 158–159
  national image, 151–158
  nationalism and, 148, 161
    commercial nationalism, 148–149, 161–163

neoliberalism and, 150
stereotypes, 158–159
tourism, 150–151
website, official, 152
Yugoslav context, 147, 148, 152
Smith, Adam, 91
Smith, Anthony, 32
social power, 12–14
social space, 126–127
social theory, 5, 124, 127, 136, 139.
    See also Bourdieu, Pierre
socialism
    economic theory and, 84, 91, 196
    economic transformation after,
        150
    heritage of, 169, 193
    nation branding and, 115, 148, 160
    post-socialist context, 149–150, 159,
        162–163, 186, 193–194
sociological imagination, 13–14, 15
Some Like It Hot (film), 204
Soros, George, 35, 84
Soviet Union (USSR), breakup of, 52,
    81
space
    branding of, 28, 80
    "calculative space," 91, 126
    social space, 126–127
Spain, 80, 137
Srbija: Sounds Global (SSG). *See*
    Serbia
Stamboul Train (Greene), 176
"Stans" (country names ending in stan),
    55, 58–59
    parody of (*Absurdistan*), 68–69
state, 127. *See also* nation/nationhood
    neoliberal statism, 128–130
state propaganda, 159
statism (etatism), 200, 208
stereotypes, 50, 54, 57–70, 93,
    170–179. *See also specific*
    countries
    backward/primitive, 54, 56, 169,
        178–179
    barbarism, 56
    Central Asian, 59
    Cold War, 15, 53, 64–65, 69,
        169–170, 171, 173
    corruption, 54
    danger, 56, 61–62
    exoticism, 56, 66, 70, 159,
        197–198
    in horror films, 61–62, 168, 169,
        187–188

in James Bond films, 53–54
of post-Soviet countries, 53–54,
    193–194
of Russia/USSR, 53–54
sexualization, 53, 56, 57
the unknown, 56, 57–58, 61–62
villains, 50
xenophobia, 54
Stewart, Jon, 63
Stipe, Michael, 220
Stoker, Bram, 56, 66, 169
structuralist theory, 124, 128
Sumo wrestler (Baruto), 88
Szelényi, Iván, 136
Szondi, György, 29, 30, 200
Sztompka, Piotr, 127

T
Tadić, Boris, 220, 222
Tasovac, Ivan, 227
technology, information, 23, 90, 198.
    See also information and
    communication technologies
    (ICTs)
Tee Time in Berzerkistan: A Doonse-
    bury Book (Trudeau), 69
television
    BBC, 64, 175, 177, 181
    Boozed Up Brits Abroad, 56–57
    CNN, 3, 46, 151, 168, 181, 182,
        226, 227
    Da Ali G Show, 59, 170
    The Daily Show, 63
    Euronews, 3, 181
    Eurosport, 3, 181, 182
    Mission Impossible, 64
    No Reservations, 172–175
    Saturday Night Live, 178–179
    The Simpsons, 62
    Top Gear, 175–178
Ţepeş, Vlad, 169
Terminal, The (film), 49, 54, 65
Thatcherism, 196
Theory of Moral Sentiments (Smith),
    91
think tanks, 126, 205
THR, 178, 184
Time of the Gypsies (film), 222
TNS, 178, 184
Todorova, Maria, 56, 69
Top Gear (TV program), 175–178
tourism promotion, 209
    in Bulgaria, 101, 106–107
    in Estonia, 86, 89

in Hungary, 198, 201, 204–205
in Kazakhstan, 59–60, 61, 170–171
in Poland, 130, 132
in Romania, 168, 170, 179–181, 186–188
in Slovenia, 150–151, 155, 156–157
Trading Identities (Olins), 80
Transfăgărăşan Highway, 175–176, 177
transition, post-communist, 6–7, 193–194, 195–197
transnational capitalist class, 126
transnational corporations (TNCs), 31–32, 42
Transylvania, 56, 70, 169, 173
travel. *See* tourism promotion
Tronti, Mario, 28
Trudeau, G. B., 69, 70
Turkmeniscam: How Washington Lobbyists Fought to Flack for a Stalinist Dictatorship (Silverstein), 69
Turkmenistan, 54
Tutwiler, Margaret, 33–34
Twitter, 25
Tymoshenko, Yulia, 39

U
Udrea, Elena, 170, 182–184
UK. *See* United Kingdom
Ukraine, 54–55
 Eurovision and, 68
 Orange Revolution in, 39–40, 43
 Pora movement in, 35, 38
 Znayu movement in, 38–39
UN (United Nations), 80
Underground (film), 222
United Kingdom (UK)
 British Council, 103, 104, 105, 113
 Cool Britannia, 80
 Thatcherism, 196
United States
 advertising expenditures and focus, 25–27, 34–35
 anti-Americanism, campaign to combat, 25, 29, 32–35
 Brand America, 23, 25, 32–35
 Middle East public diplomacy, 33–34, 160
 9/11 terrorist attacks, 80, 160
 offshoring by, 24, 25

 propaganda of, 24–27, 29, 35, 36
 public diplomacy, 32–35
 service economy, 24, 25, 26
 "Shared Values" Initiative (SVI), 33, 80
 support for color revolutions in CEE, 35–40
 ur-fascist, 92
USAID, 35, 37, 100, 103
USSR, 52, 81

V
vampires. *See* Dracula
van Ham, Peter, 11, 51, 148
Verdery, Katherine, 6, 10
vested interests in nation branding, 14, 19, 42, 124
Vienna-Budapest Expo, 201–202
Vitkova, Ekaterina, 107, 109
Vladcik, Zladko ("Zlad"), 50, 66

W
Wacquant, Loïc, 126, 130
Wag the Dog (film), 63
Wałęsa, Lech, 168
"Washington consensus," 81
Wealth of Nations (Smith), 91
Weber, Max, 91, 118
websites, official
 Estonia, 90
 Hungary, 198
 Slovenia, 152
Wernick, Andrew, 10
West/Western
 East/West binary, 7–9
 economic model of, 126
 imitation of, 8
 stereotypes of CEE countries, 55–56
 as superior or ideal, 8, 41, 43, 58, 199
 vested interest in nation branding, 14, 19
The Wheel Spins (White), 176
White, Ethel Lina, 176
Whopper virgins, 178–179
WikiLeaks, 11
Wikipedia, 11
Wolff, Larry, 57
world music, 17, 216–218, 219, 221, 229
WTO (World Trade Organization), 80

X

xenophobia, 54

Y

Yanukovych, Viktor, 35, 39–40
Yeltsin, Boris, 53
"Young Europeans" campaign (Irish
    Republic), 80, 148

youth movements, 35–40
Yugoslavia, former, 49, 52, 147–148,
    152, 217. *See also* Serbia
Yushchencko, Viktor, 39, 43

Z

Znayu movement, 38–39
Znepolski, Ivaylo, 6